STUDY GUIDE TO ACCOMPANY
ROBERT S. FELDMAN

UNDERSTANDING PSYCHOLOGY

THIRD EDITION

MARK GARRISON
Kentucky State University

McGraw-Hill, Inc.
New York St. Louis San Francisco Auckland Bogotá
Caracas Lisbon London Madrid Mexico Milan
Montreal New Delhi Paris San Juan
Singapore Sydney Tokyo Toronto

ISBN 0-07-020786-0

The editors were Christopher Rogers and David Dunham,
and the production supervisor was Friederich W. Schulte.
Semline, Inc., was printer and binder.

TABLE OF CONTENTS

PREFACE

This *Student Study Guide* has been prepared with several very important student concerns in mind. First, students need a comprehensive guide to supplement Robert Feldman's *Understanding Psychology*, taking advantage of the many features in the book that support effective study habits. Second, students need practice and drill work that focus on the full content of each chapter and present practice questions that are similar to those provided in the instructor's *Test File*. In order to provide a study guide that responds to both of these concerns, the chapter summaries have been organized using the key terms and concepts in the text, and the student learning objectives have page references to the text. In addition, the definitions in the text of the key terms were used to develop the key term drills found throughout the study guide.

You will also find two practice essay questions for each chapter. These questions are intended to provide you opportunities to practice writing and critical analysis skills. In the answer key at the back of the *Study Guide*, a list of points that should be covered in your answer to each question has been provided. These questions are meant to be difficult and to require you to draw on both conceptual and factual knowledge. Some require that you apply concepts to situations, and others may require that you compare several ideas.

The introduction explains the organization of the *Study Guide* and offers tips on how to use the features of the *Study Guide* to improve your study skills and make your time spent with the text more effective.

Acknowledgments

Developing this *Student Study Guide* has proved to be a challenging and quite exciting project. I wish to thank the editors at McGraw-Hill, Chris Rogers and Naomi Sofer. I am especially indebted to Robert Feldman, for without a high-quality text, a student study guide would be meaningless. His contribution to the introduction is one of many examples of his concern for students. I also appreciate the confidence that Chris and Bob have shown in my work. Finally, I must thank Diane Garrison, whose patience and willingness to help typeset several parts of the *Study Guide* have made the project go far more smoothly than it would have otherwise. She has contributed greatly to its quality.

Mark Garrison
Kentucky State University
Frankfort, Kentucky

INTRODUCTION

USING
UNDERSTANDING PSYCHOLOGY:
Strategies for Effective Study

Understanding Psychology has been written with the reader in mind, and it therefore includes a number of unique features that will help you to maximize your learning of the concepts, theories, facts, and other kinds of information that make up the field of psychology. The *Student Study Guide* was designed to help you take full advantage of the features in the textbook, and the steps recommended for the text have been incorporated into this *Study Guide.* By using the *Guide,* you will not only get the most out of *Understanding Psychology,* but you will also develop habits that will help you to study other texts more effectively and to think critically about material you are learning.

To take full advantage of *Understanding Psychology,* follow these steps:

■ Familiarize yourself with the logic of the book's structure. Begin by reading the Table of Contents. It provides an overview of the topics that will be covered and gives a sense of the way the various topics are interrelated. Next, review the Preface, which describes the book's major features. Note how each chapter is divided into three or four self-contained units; these provide logical starting and stopping points for reading and studying. Also note the major highlights of each chapter: a chapter-opening outline, a Prologue, a Looking Ahead section that includes chapter objectives, Recaps and Reviews of key information following each of the major units, and—at the end of every chapter—a Looking Back section and a list of key terms and concepts. Because every chapter is structured in the same way, you are provided with a set of familiar landmarks as you chart your way through new material, allowing you to organize the chapter's content more readily. This study guide is designed to lead you through each of these steps.

■ Use a study strategy. Although we are expected to study and ultimately to learn a wide array of material throughout our schooling, we are rarely taught any systematic strategies that permit us to study more effectively. Yet, just as we wouldn't expect a physician to learn human anatomy by trial and error, it is the unusual student who is able to stumble upon a truly effective studying strategy.

Psychologists, however, have devised several excellent (and proven) techniques for improving study skills, two of which are described here. By employing one of these two procedures—known by the initials "SQ3R" and "MURDER"—you can increase your ability to learn and retain information and to think critically, not just in psychology classes but in all academic subjects.

The SQ3R method includes a series of five steps, having the initials S-Q-R-R-R. The first step is to *survey* the material by reading the chapter outlines, chapter headings, figure captions, recaps, and Looking Ahead and Looking Back sections, providing yourself with an overview of the major points of the chapter. The next step—the "Q" in SQ3R—is to *question.* Formulate questions—either aloud or in writing—prior to actually reading a section of the material. For instance, if you had first surveyed this section of the book, you might jot down in the margin, "What do 'SQ3R' and 'MURDER' stand for?" The reviews that end each section of the chapter are also a good source of questions. But it is important not to rely on them entirely; making up your own questions is critical. *Understanding Psychology* has wide margins in which you can write out your own questions. Such questioning helps you to focus in on the key points of the chapter, while putting you in an inquisitive frame of mind as well.

It is now time for the next, and most crucial, step: to *read* the material. Read carefully and, even more importantly, actively and critically. For instance, while you are reading, answer the questions you have asked yourself. You may find yourself coming up with new questions as you read along; that's fine, since it shows you are reading inquisitively and paying attention to the material. Critically evaluate material by considering the implications of what you are reading, thinking about possible exceptions and contradictions, and examining the assumptions that lie behind the assertions made by the author.

The next step—the second "R"—is the most unusual. This "R" stands for *recite*, in which you look up from the book and describe and explain to yourself, or to a friend, the material you have just read and answer the questions you have posed earlier. Do it aloud; this is one time when talking to yourself is nothing to be embarrassed about. The recitation process helps you to identify clearly your degree of understanding of the material you have just read. Moreover, psychological research has shown that communicating material to others (even imaginary others, if you are reciting aloud to yourself and not a friend) aids you in learning it in a different—and deeper—way than material which you do not intend to communicate. Hence, your recitation of the material is a crucial link in the studying process.

The final "R" refers to *review*. As we will discuss in Chapter 8, reviewing is a prerequisite to learning and remembering fully the material you have studied. Look over the information; reread the Recaps and Looking Back summaries; answer in-text review questions; and use this *Student Study Guide*. Reviewing should be an active process, in which you consider how different pieces of information fit together and develop a sense of the overall picture.

An alternative approach to studying—although not altogether dissimilar to SQ3R—is provided by the MURDER system. Despite the unpleasant connotations of its title, the MURDER system is a useful study strategy.

In MURDER, the first step is to establish an appropriate **M**ood for studying by setting goals for a study session and choosing a time and place in which you will not be distracted. Next comes reading for **U**nderstanding, in which careful attention is paid to the meaning of the material being studied. **R**ecall is an immediate attempt to recall the material from memory, without referring to the text. **D**igesting the material comes next; you should correct any recall errors, and attempt to organize and store newly learned material in memory.

You should work next on **E**xpanding (analyzing and evaluating) new material, and try to apply it to situations that go beyond the applications discussed in the text. By incorporating what you have learned into a larger information network in memory, you will be able to recall it more easily in the future. Finally, the last step is **R**eview. Just as with the SQ3R system, MURDER suggests that systematic review of material is a necessary condition for successful studying.

Both the SQ3R and MURDER systems provide a proven means of increasing your study effectiveness. It is not necessary, though, to feel tied to a particular strategy; you might want to combine other elements into your own study system. For example, learning tips and strategies for critical thinking will be presented throughout *Understanding Psychology*, such as in Chapter 8 when the use of mnemonics (memory techniques for organizing material to help its recall) are discussed. If these tactics help you to master successfully new material, stick with them.

■ Use the *Study Guide*. The *Study Guide* is designed for use of the SQ3R system. In addition to guidelines providing a systematic way of using the features of the text, the major sections of the *Study Guide* chapters include a check box to the right of the page that will help remind you of the type of activity that the section involves. It is a good idea to check each box as you complete the section:

Survey: ☐
Question: ☐
Read: ☐
Recite: ☐
Review: ☐

■ Study at the best time and in the right place. The last aspect of studying that warrants mention is that *when* and *where* you study are in some ways as important as *how* you study. One of the truisms of the psychological literature is that we learn things better, and are able to recall them longer, when we study material in small chunks over several study sessions, rather than massing our study into one lengthy period. This implies that all-night studying just prior to a test is going to be less effective—and a lot more tiring—than employing a series of steady, regular study sessions.

In addition to carefully timing your studying, you should seek out a special location to study. It doesn't really matter where it is, as long as it has minimal distractions and is a place that you use *only* for studying. Identifying a special "territory" allows you to get in the right mood for study as soon as you begin.

A final comment
By using the proven study strategies presented above, as well as by making use of the pedagogical tools integrated in the text, you will maximize your understanding of the material in *Understanding Psychology* and you will master techniques that will help you learn and think critically in all your academic endeavors. More importantly, you will optimize your understanding of the field of psychology. It is worth the effort: the excitement, challenge, and promise that psychology holds for you is immense.

Robert Feldman

Mark Garrison

1

INTRODUCTION TO PSYCHOLOGY

DETAILED OUTLINE

This detailed outline contains all the headings in Chapter 1: Introduction to Psychology. If you are using the SQ3R method, then an examination of the outline is the best way to begin your survey of the chapter.

The Informed Consumer of Psychology Distinguishing legitimate psychology from pseudo-psychology
● **Recap and Review III**

Looking Back
Key Terms and Concepts

► Now that you have surveyed the chapter, read **Looking Ahead**, pages 2-4.   *Question:* ☐
Focus on the questions on page 4.   *Read:* ☐
Note that in this chapter, the introductory remarks continue into the
heading **The Study of Behavior and Mental Proceses** and the basic format
of the book is described in this section which ends with the questions on page 4.

┌───┐
│ **CONCEPTS AND LEARNING OBJECTIVES** │   *Survey:* ☐
└───┘

These are the concepts and the learning objectives for Chapter 1. Read them carefully as part of your
preliminary survey of the chapter.

Concept 1: Psychology is a diversified scientific approach to the understanding of human and animal
behavior. Psychologists explore ways of understanding behavior and mental processes as they are
manifested in biology, sensation, perception, language, thought, memory, feelings, and many other
processes.

1. Define psychology and explain what makes it a science. (pp. 2-4)

2. Name and describe the different branches of psychology. (pp. 4-10)

3. Distinguish the major fields of psychology: biopsychology, experimental psychology,
   developmental psychology, personality, and others identified in the text. (pp. 4-10)

4. Give examples of the work and workers that illustrate the goals of each field. (pp. 4-11)

Concept 2: Psychology dates its beginning with the foundation of a research laboratory in 1879 by
Wilhelm Wundt. The major historical models have been structuralism, functionalism, and gestalt
psychology. The five contemporary conceptual models are biological, psychodynamic, cognitive,
behavioral, and humanistic.

5. Discuss the early beginnings of the science of psychology and the approaches taken by early
   psychologists. (pp. 11-15)

6. Define what is meant by the term **model**, and name each of the five models of psychology.
   (pp. 15-18)

7. Identify at least one distinguishing feature of each of the five models. (pp. 15-18)

8. Be prepared to distinguish how each model may investigate a particular topic. (pp. 15-19)

Concept 3: Five issues serve as the common link that brings diverse psychological specialties together. They are: Nature versus nurture; conscious versus unconscious control of behavior; observable behavior versus internal mental processes; freedom of choice versus determinism; and individual differences versus universal principles.

9. List the key issues for psychology and be able to identify statements that represent each issue. (pp. 19-22)

10. Be familiar with ways of distinguishing rigorous psychological approaches from popularizations. (pp. 22-24)

CHAPTER SUMMARY

There are several ways you can use this summary as part of your systematic study plan. You may read each concept summary and then read the corresponding pages in the text, or you may read the entire summary and then read the entire chapter in the text. As you finish each section, complete the **Recap and Review** questions that are supplied in the text.

CONCEPT 1: Prologue and Looking Ahead
    The Study of Behavior and Mental Processes:
        The Common Link among Psychologists
    Psychologists at Work

Survey: ☐
Read: ☐

Pages 2-11

Psychology is defined as the study of behavior and mental processes. Psychologists investigate scientifically what people do as well as their thoughts, feelings, perceptions, reasoning processes, memories, and the biological foundations of these processes. Psychology relies upon scientific method to discover ways of explaining, predicting, modifying, and improving behavior. The study of behavior and mental processes involves examining animal as well as human subjects to find the general laws that govern the behavior of all organisms.

Contrary to the mistaken view held by many people that psychology is interested only in abnormal behavior, psychologists examine a wide array of behaviors and mental processes. The specialty areas are described in the order in which they appear through the text.

Biopsychology explores the relationship between fundamental biological processes and behavior. The study is focused on the brain and the nervous system, and both diseases and healthy functions are examined for their contribution to the understanding of behavior.

Experimental psychology is both a specialty and a task undertaken by most psychologists. The scientific work of psychology requires experimental methods to be applied wherever possible. **Cognitive psychology** is a specialty within experimental psychology that focuses on higher mental functions like thought, language, memory, problem solving, reasoning, and decision making, among other processes.

Developmental psychology examines how a person changes and grows throughout life, and **personality psychology** seeks to explain how a person's behavior is consistent through time and why different people respond differently to the same situation.

Several types of psychologists study ways of improving health and assessing and treating mental illness. **Health psychology** explores the relationship between physical and mental health and, especially, the role of stress in health. **Clinical psychology** is primarily involved with the assessment, diagnosis, and treatment of abnormal behavior. **Counseling psychology** focuses on the problems of adjustment to challenges that everyone faces in life. **Educational psychology** examines how educational processes occur, with close examination, for instance, of the student-teacher interaction. **School psychology** is devoted to the assessment and remedy of problems encountered in education, including both learning disabilities and emotional problems.

Social psychology studies the way people's thoughts, feelings, and actions are affected by others. Social psychologists may examine the problem of aggression or the nature of friendship. **Industrial-organizational psychology** applies psychological principles to the workplace and studies topics like job satisfaction and productivity. **Consumer psychology** applies psychological principles to consumer behavior in order to test advertising strategies and to improve products. To determine similarities and differences between groups, **cross-cultural psychology** examines topics common to a number of psychological specialties in different cultural and ethnic settings.

Emerging areas of psychology include: **environmental psychology**, the study of how physical environments influence behavior; **forensic psychology**, the study of law and psychology; and **program evaluation**, the application of psychologically based assessment principles to large programs. Finally, the area of space travel and future life in space has given rise to an area called **space psychology**.

About two-thirds of all psychologists are males, but recent trends show a move toward a more equal distribution. Only about two percent are black and another two percent are Hispanic, though the percentage for minorities currently in graduate school is higher. Though psychologists are mostly employed in academic settings, they can be found in almost every setting relating to health care and human service.

Concept 2: A Science Evolves: The Past and the Future

Survey: ☐
Read: ☐

Pages 11-19

Trephining (drilling holes in the skull to let evil spirits escape), Hippocrates' theory of humors, Gall's "science" of phrenology (the association of bumps on the head with traits), and Descartes' concept of animal spirits reflect the psychology of past times. The era of scientific psychology is usually dated from the establishment by Wilhelm Wundt of an experimental psychology laboratory in 1879. Today psychology is based on a number of systems of interrelated ideas and concepts called conceptual **models**.

The model associated with Wundt's laboratory is called **structuralism**. Structuralism utilized a technique called **introspection** to examine the basic elements of thought, consciousness, and emotions. Introspection required the subject to report how a stimulus was experienced. A model called **functionalism** replaced structuralism, and instead of focusing on the structure of mental elements, it focused on how the mind works and how people adapt to environments. William James was the leading functionalist in the early 1900s, and one of the leading educators, John Dewey, took a functionalist approach in his development of school psychology. **Gestalt psychology** was another reaction to struturalism that developed in the early 1900s. The gestalt approach is to view phenomena in terms of the whole experience rather than the individual elements, and they are identified with the maxim "the whole is greater than the sum of the parts."

Two early female contributors to the field of psychology were Leta Stetter Hollingsworth, known for the term "gifted" and for an early focus on women's issues, and June Etta Downey, who studied personality traits in the 1920s.

The field of psychology is now dominated by five major conceptual models. The **biological model** is focused on the study of the relationship between biological processes and behavior. The **psycho-dynamic model** views behavior as motivated by inner and unconscious forces over which the individual can exert little control. The psychodynamic perspective, developed by Sigmund Freud in the early 1900s, has been a major influence in twentieth-century thinking and continues to have an influence in the treatment of mental disorders. The **cognitive model** has evolved the structuralists' concern with trying to understand the mind into a study of how we internally represent the outside world and how this representation influences behavior. The **behavioral model** began as a reaction to the failure of other early perspectives to base the science of psychology on observable phenomena. John B. Watson developed behaviorism as a study of how environmental forces influence behavior. The newest model, the **humanistic model**, rejects the deterministic views of the other models and instead focuses on the unique ability of humans to seek higher levels of maturity and fulfillment and to express **free will**. All the major models have active practitioners and continuing research programs. The *Psychology at Work* box uses the example of the AIDS epidemic to illustrate the many ways these models can approach a specific problem.

CONCEPT 3: The Links Between Psychology's Branches and Models

Survey: ☐
Read: ☐

Pages 19-24

Few psychologists identify exclusively with one model. However, not every branch can utilize any model equally well. Biopsychology is far more focused on the biological model than on others. Social psychologists are more likely to find the cognitive model to be more useful than the biological model.

Major issues and questions form a common ground for psychology. The question of nature versus nurture places models that focus on the environmental influences on behavior against the perspectives that focus on inheritable traits. The model to which a psychologist subscribes determines the view taken concerning this issue. The question of whether behavior is determined by conscious or unconscious forces also separates psychological models. The psychodynamic model interprets behavior as influenced by unconscious forces whereas the cognitive model may attribute abnormal behavior to faulty (conscious) reasoning. The issue of observable behavior versus internal mental processes places the behavioral model against the cognitive model. The very controversial question of free choice versus **determinism** raises such issues as whether abnormal behavior is a result of intentional choice. Finally, interests in individual differences conflict with the desire to find universal principles. These five key issues should not be viewed in an either-or manner, but instead they should be understood as creating a continuum along which psychologists would place themselves.

In the future, psychology is likely to become more specialized, new models will probably arise, treatment for psychological problems will become more accessible, and psychology's influence over public issues will continue to grow.

The informed consumer of psychology must be able to distinguish the popular conceptions of psychology from rigorous, research-supported claims. To be fully informed, one must know the source of information and advice, realize that complex problems are rarely solved cheaply or quickly, and recognize that there are few universal cures for anything and that even qualified, professional advice is not definitive.

► Now that you have surveyed, questioned, and read the chapter and completed the **Recap and Review** questions, review **Looking Back**, page 25.

Review: ☐

► For additional practice through recitation and review, test your knowledge of the chapter material by answering the questions in the *Key Word Drill*, the *Practice Questions*, and the *Essay Questions*.

KEY WORD DRILL

Recite: ☐

The following **Fill in the Blank** and **Matching Questions** test key words from the text. Check your answers with the Answer Key in the back of the *Study Guide*.

FILL IN THE BLANK

1. _____ the scientific study of behavior and mental processes.

2. _____ _____ studies how people's thoughts, feelings, and actions are affected by others.

3. _____ psychology is the branch of psychology that considers the relationship between people and their physical environment.

4. The assessment of large-scale programs to determine whether they are effective in meeting their goals is called _____ _____.

5. _____ are systems of interrelated ideas and concepts used to explain phenomena.

6. The early approach to psychology, _____, focused on the fundamental elements that form the foundation of thinking, consciousness, emotions, and other kinds of mental states and activities.

7. A procedure used by structuralists to study the structure of the mind, _____ required subjects to describe in detail what they were experiencing when they were exposed to a stimulus.

8. Another early approach to psychology, _____ concentrated on what the mind does—the functions of mental activity—and the role of behavior in allowing people to adapt to their environments.

9. _____ psychology is an approach to psychology that focuses on the organization of perception and thinking in a "whole" sense, rather than on the individual elements of perception.

10. The human ability to make decisions about one's life is called _____ _____ while the view suggesting that people's behavior is shaped primarily by factors outside their control is called _____.

MATCHING QUESTIONS

_____ 11. biopsychology

_____ 12. experimental psychology

_____ 13. cognitive psychology

_____ 14. developmental psychology

_____ 15. personality psychology

a. The branch of psychology that studies the processes of sensing, perceiving, learning, and thinking about the world.

b. The branch of psychology that studies consistency and change in a person's behavior over time as well as the individual traits that differentiate the behavior of one person from another when each confronts the same situation.

c. The branch of psychology that specializes in the biological basis of behavior.

d. The branch of psychology that studies how people grow and change throughout the course of their lives.

e. The branch of psychology that focuses on the study of higher mental processes, including thinking, language, memory, problem solving, knowing, reasoning, judging, and decision making.

_____ 16. health psychology

_____ 17. clinical psychology

_____ 18. counseling psychology

_____ 19. educational psychology

_____ 20. school psychology

a. The branch of psychology that explores the relationship of psychological factors and physical ailments or disease.

b. The branch of psychology devoted to assessing children in elementary and secondary schools who have academic or emotional problems and to developing solutions to such problems.

c. The branch of psychology that focuses on educational, social, and career adjustment problems.

d. The branch of psychology that deals with the study, diagnosis, and treatment of abnormal behavior.

e. The branch of psychology that considers how the educational process affects students.

_____ 21. industrial-organizational psychology

_____ 22. consumer psychology

_____ 23. cross-cultural psychology

_____ 24. forensic psychology

a. The branch of psychology that investigates the similarities and differences in psychological functioning in various cultures and ethnic groups.

b. The branch of psychology that focuses on legal issues, such as deciding what criteria indicate that a person is legally insane and whether larger or smaller juries make fairer decisions.

c. The branch of psychology that considers our buying habits and the effects of advertising on buyer behavior.

d. The branch of psychology that studies the psychology of the workplace, considering productivity, job satisfaction, and decision making.

_____ 25. biological model

_____ 26. psychodynamic model

_____ 27. cognitive model

_____ 28. behavioral model

_____ 29. humanistic model

a. The psychological model that suggests that observable behavior should be the focus of study.

b. The psychological model that views behavior from the perspective of biological functioning.

c. The psychological model based on the belief that behavior is motivated by inner forces over which the individual has little control.

d. The psychological model that suggests that people are in control of their lives.

e. The psychological model that focuses on how people know, understand, and think about the world.

_____ 30. Sigmund Freud

_____ 31. Hippocrates

_____ 32. Franz Josef Gall

_____ 33. Wilhelm Wundt

_____ 34. William James

_____ 35. Leta Stetter Hollingsworth

a. The first laboratory

b. Giftedness

c. The four temperaments

d. Psychoanalysis

e. Phrenology

f. Functionalism

| PRACTICE QUESTIONS | *Recite and Review:* ☐ |

Test your knowledge of the chapter material by answering these true-false and multiple choice questions. Check your answers with the Answer Key in the back of the *Study Guide*.

TRUE-FALSE QUESTIONS

T   F   1.   A counseling psychologist would be likely to work with someone who is suicidal.

T   F   2.   Clinical psychology focuses for the most part on educational, social, and career adjustment problems.

T   F   3.   Because the psychologists involved in space research are predominately psychoanalysts, the primary area of research interest is sexual behavior.

T   F   4.   The formal discipline of psychology has been in existence for approximately 200 years.

T   F   5.   Structuralism was the first major approach in psychology.

T   F   6.   According to the text, a model is a system of interrelated ideas and concepts used to explain phenomena.

T   F   7.   If a gestalt psychologist were working today, she might be interested in how we experience stereophonic sound.

T   F   8.   Cognitive psychology is based on the belief that behavior is motivated by inner forces over which the individual has little control.

T   F   9.   Psychologists consider one of their contributions to the AIDS crisis to be that of promoting safer sexual behavior.

T   F   10.   In addition to being a medical problem, AIDS is considered to be a behavioral disease.

MULTIPLE CHOICE QUESTIONS

1.   What kind of psychologist would have a special interest in studying the aspects of the Oakland fire that people are most likely to recall?
    a.   social psychologist
    b.   consumer psychologist
    c.   educational psychologist
    d.   cognitive psychologist

2. A motorist's car stalls on the highway on a cold, windy, and snowy night. Which type of psychologist would be most interested in whether other motorists offered assistance?
   a. a social psychologist
   b. an environmental psychologist
   c. a clinical psychologist
   d. an industrial-organizational psychologist

3. Which of the following techniques distinguishes the kind of inquiry used by scientists from that used by professionals in nonscientific areas like literature, art, and philosophy?
   a. intuitive thought
   b. scientific methods
   c. common sense
   d. construction of new theoretical models

4. According to the text, the definition of psychology must include:
   a. human consciousness and memory.
   b. mental, behavioral, and biological processes.
   c. studying why people think the way they do.
   d. understanding how people will behave in a wide range of circumstances.

5. Biopsychology is the branch of psychology that specializes in:
   a. the biological basis of behavior.
   b. how people grow and change both physically and socially throughout their lives.
   c. how people's thoughts, feelings, and actions are affected by others.
   d. the study, diagnosis, and treatment of abnormal behavior.

6. The relationship of experimental psychology and cognitive psychology might best be described as:
   a. only experimental psychology conducts experiments.
   b. cognitive psychology is not interested in studying learning.
   c. cognitive psychology is a specialty area of experimental psychology.
   d. experimental psychology is a specialty of cognitive psychology.

7. Psychologists often work with several major theoretical models. Which model below does **not** belong among the rest?
   a. cognitive
   b. psychodynamic
   c. therapeutic
   d. behavioral

8. Professor Greenland has identified a trait he calls persistence, and he has begun to conduct research on the consistency of this trait in various situations. Dr. Greenland is most likely:
   a. a social psychologist.
   b. a cross-cultural psychologist.
   c. an educational psychologist.
   d. a personality psychologist.

9. Health psychology is the branch of psychology that explores:
   a. educational, social, and career adjustment problems.
   b. the relationship between psychological factors and physical ailments.
   c. the diagnosis and treatment of abnormal behavior.
   d. the processes of perceiving, learning, and thinking about the world.

10. Which of the following health-oriented psychologists is involved primarily in administering tests and utilizing evaluative instruments for the assessment of abnormal behavior?
    a. counseling psychologist
    b. health psychologist
    c. personality psychologist
    d. clinical psychologist

11. According to the text, the major distinction between educational and school psychology is that:
    a. educational psychology is devoted to improving the education of students who have special needs, and school psychology is devoted to increasing achievement in all students.
    b. school psychology is devoted to improving the schooling of students who have special needs, and educational psychology is devoted to better understanding of the entire educational system.
    c. school psychology attempts to examine the entire educational process, and educational psychology looks at individual students.
    d. educational psychology attempts to examine the entire educational process, and school psychology is devoted to assessing and correcting academic and school-related problems of students.

12. The ways in which people respond to advertisements is an area of study for:
    a. consumer psychologists.
    b. industrial psychologists.
    c. clinical psychologists.
    d. social psychologists.

13. Questions such as how we are influenced by others and why we form relationships with each other are studied by:
    a. counseling psychologists.
    b. social psychologists.
    c. clinical psychologists.
    d. health psychologists.

14. A forensic psychologist would be particularly interested in:
    a. the nature of stress.
    b. the study of perception.
    c. human relationships.
    d. legal issues.

15. The effectiveness of government programs such as Head Start and Medicaid would be the focus of psychologists interested in:
    a. experimentation.
    b. evaluation.
    c. forensics.
    d. cognition.

16. Of the following, an environmental psychologist would be most likely to study:
    a. the impact of smoking on health.
    b. experimental ethics.
    c. the effects of crowding on behavior.
    d. program effectiveness.

17. An architect interested in designing an inner-city apartment building that would not be prone to vandalism might consult with:
    a. a clinical psychologist.
    b. a school psychologist.
    c. a forensic psychologist.
    d. an environmental psychologist.

18. According to the discussion in the text, the problem that psychology faces of losing its diversity as a discipline can best be corrected by:
    a. social psychologists becoming more active trainers of psychologists.
    b. more studies in cultural psychology based on demonstrating the importance of diversity.
    c. increasing the ethnic sensitivity of counseling and clinical psychologists.
    d. increasing the number of minorities in the profession.

19. Most psychologists work in:
    a. hospitals.
    b. public schools.
    c. industry.
    d. universities.

20. Today's scientists believe that the purpose of trephining was to:
    a. enable one person to read another's mind.
    b. allow evil spirits to escape.
    c. increase telekinetic powers.
    d. heal the patient of mental illness.

21. Who established the first psychology laboratory, and when?
    a. William James, 1875
    b. Sigmund Freud, 1899
    c. June Etta Downey, 1884
    d. Wilhelm Wundt, 1879

22. Wilhelm Wundt trained people to describe carefully, in their own words, what they experienced upon being exposed to various stimuli. This procedure for studying the mind is called:
    a. cognition.
    b. mind expansion.
    c. perception.
    d. introspection.

23. Functionalism shifted the focus of study in psychology from elements to:
    a. cognitions.
    b. processes.
    c. biological underpinnings.
    d. observable behaviors.

24. Which pair of individuals have been associated with functionalism?
    a. Leta Stetter Hollingsworth and June Etta Downey
    b. Sigmund Freud and Wilhelm Wundt
    c. William James and John Dewey
    d. Wilhelm Wundt and William James

25. "The whole is greater than the sum of the parts" is a postulate of:
    a. structuralism.
    b. functionalism.
    c. gestalt psychology.
    d. behaviorism.

26. Gestalt psychology was developed:
    a. around 1850.
    b. in 1879.
    c. during the early 1900s.
    d. in the 1950s.

27. Leta Stetter Hollingsworth is known for her contribution of:
    a. the concept of a kindergarten.
    b. the concept of gifted.
    c. the idea that males and females were psychologically different.
    d. the study of personality traits.

28. June Etta Downey is known for her work in:
    a. personality traits.
    b. establishing the first psychology laboratory in 1884.
    c. the concept of the kindergarten.
    d. the psychoanalysis of women.

29. The influence of inherited characteristics on behavior would be studied with the:
    a. cognitive model.
    b. psychodynamic model.
    c. behavioral model.
    d. biological model.

30. John B. Watson was the first American psychologist to follow the:
    a. behavioral model.
    b. humanistic model.
    c. cognitive model.
    d. psychodynamic model.

31. Which of the following sources of evidence would be the least acceptable to behaviorists like John B. Watson?
    a. evidence gathered using introspective
    b. evidence from intelligence tests
    c. evidence regarding emotional growth and development
    d. evidence from perception and sensation experiments

32. The _____ model of psychology places the greatest emphasis on the environment.
    a. biological
    b. psychodynamic
    c. behavioral
    d. humanistic

33. According to the psychodynamic approach, dreams and slips of the tongue:
    a. represent a distortion of what a person is really feeling.
    b. come from subconscious activity.
    c. become more prevalent as a person grows older.
    d. can be controlled consciously with a little effort.

34. A psychodynamic psychologist would be most interested in:
    a. the learning process.
    b. our perceptions of the world around us.
    c. dreams.
    d. the functioning of the brain.

35. Sigmund Freud believed that behavior is motivated by:
    a. subconscious inner forces.
    b. a desire to achieve personal fulfillment.
    c. the natural tendency to organize data through perception.
    d. inherited characteristics.

36. Which of the following types of psychologist would most likely be involved in the study of the physiological aspects of AIDS?
    a. clinical psychologist
    b. biopsychologist
    c. health psychologist
    d. social psychologist

37. The humanistic model places an emphasis on:
    a. observable behavior.
    b. inner forces.
    c. free will.
    d. understanding concepts.

38. More than the others listed below, _____ psychologists frequently employ many, and sometimes all, of the major models of psychology.
    a. experimental
    b. social
    c. clinical
    d. industrial

39. Which of the following types of psychologists would be most interested in the "unconscious" side of the conscious versus unconscious determinants of behavior issue?
    a. a behavioral experimental psychologist
    b. a humanistic psychologist
    c. a psychodynamic clinical psychologist
    d. a structuralist

40. According to the text, as the field progresses, models of psychology are likely to become:
    a. broader than at present.
    b. merged to form new ones.
    c. narrower than at present.
    d. discarded altogether.

41. Often drug manufacturers claim that a new drug is safe and present studies to support their claims that they themselves paid to have done. Which of the following is this most like?
    a. self-help experts who claim that their system is best
    b. the self-help program that will solve major problems with a very low cost
    c. the expectation that there exists a universal cure for each major problem
    d. the view that the creators of an idea know best since they were expert enough to have the original idea

| ESSAY QUESTIONS |

Essay Question 1.1: *Conceptual Models*

Describe the conceptual model that best fits your current understanding of why people behave the way that they do. Be sure to explain why you selected this particular model. Which models do you reject? Why?

Essay Question 1.2: *Key Issues*

Select two of the key issues for psychology and describe how the resolution of these issues one way or the other would change the way you view yourself and others, your goals, and your immediate responsibility for your own success.

_____

_____

_____

_____

_____

_____

_____

_____

_____

_____

_____

_____

_____

_____

_____

_____

_____

_____

_____

_____

2

PSYCHOLOGICAL RESEARCH

| DETAILED OUTLINE | *Survey:* ☐ |

This detailed outline contains all the headings in Chapter 2: Psychological Research. If you are using the SQ3R method, then an examination of the outline is the best way to begin your survey of the chapter.

Prologue: Erica Morris
Looking Ahead

Posing Questions: The Scientific Method
    Developing theories: Specifying broad explanations
    Hypotheses: Crafting testable predictions
● **Recap and Review I**

Finding Answers: Psychological Research
    Archival research
    Naturalistic observation
    Survey research
    The case study
    Correlational research
    Experimental research
        The final step: Random assignment of subjects to treatments
        Choosing the appropriate subjects
        Were Latané and Darley right?
● **Recap and Review II**

Research Issues
    The ethics of research
    Should animals be used in research?
    Threats to experiments: Experimenter and subject expectations
    The significance of research
The Cutting Edge Integrating Research Using Meta-analysis
The Informed Consumer of Psychology Critical Thinking about Research
● **Recap and Review III**

Looking Back
Key Terms and Concepts

➤ Now that you have surveyed the chapter, read **Looking Ahead**, pages 30-31. *Question:* ☐
  Focus on the questions on page 31. *Read:* ☐

CONCEPTS AND LEARNING OBJECTIVES   *Survey:* ☐

These are the concepts and the learning objects for Chapter 2. Read them carefully as part of your preliminary survey of the chapter.

Concept 1: The scientific method is crucial to the way psychologists study phenomena of interest to psychology. The scientific method allows for careful, organized, and meaningful research, and using the method, psychologists develop formal theories and testable hypothesis.

1. Describe the three steps of the scientific method. (pp. 30-32)

2. Define theory and its role in scientific inquiry and describe how hypotheses are formed. (pp. 32-34)

Concept 2: Psychologists employ a variety of research methods to investigate the relationships between factors, to predict phenomena, and to establish cause-and-effect relationships. These research techniques include archival methods, naturalistic observation, case study, survey, correlational methods, and experiments.

3. Define research and distinguish archival, naturalistic observation, survey, and case study research methods. (pp. 34-37)

4. Describe how correlational research shows the relationship between two variables. (pp. 37-39)

5. Define the key elements common to all experiments, including independent and dependent variables, the random selection of participants, and a hypothesis that links the variables. (pp. 39-44)

6. Discuss the importance of replicating experiments and testing the limits of theories for proving the existence of a causal relationship between variables. (pp. 44-45)

Concept 3: When conducting research, psychologists must remain aware of a number of factors that may influence the outcome or affect the subjects in the study. The ability to evaluate and make critical judgments about research findings is an important one for our society.

7. Describe the ethical concerns involved with the use of deceptive techniques as well as the welfare of human and animal subjects. (pp. 45-47)

8. Identify the possible sources of bias that may undermine the conclusions drawn from an experiment. (pp. 47-48)

9. Discuss the importance of statistical techniques used to establish that the outcome of an experiment was significant. (pp. 48-50)

10. Apply knowledge of scientific methods to evaluate how well research supports particular findings. (pp. 50-51)

CHAPTER SUMMARY

There are several ways you can use this summary as part of your systematic study plan. You may read each concept summary and then read the corresponding pages in the text, or you may read the entire summary and then read the entire chapter in the text. As you finish each section, complete the **Recap and Review** questions that are supplied in the text.

CONCEPT 1: Prologue and Looking Ahead
Posing Questions: The Scientific Method

Survey: ☐
Read: ☐

Pages 30-34

The famous cases of Erica Morris and Kitty Genovese illustrate the complex task of conducting research in order to explain phenomena that otherwise appear inexplicable. Research into the question of why bystanders fail to help—and under what conditions they are more likely to offer help—is used throughout the chapter to illustrate research methods.

A major aim of research in psychology is to discover which of our assumptions about human behavior is correct. First, questions that interest psychologists must be set into the proper framework so that a systematic inquiry may be conducted to find the answer to the question. Psychologists use an approach called the **scientific method** to conduct their inquiry. The scientific method has three main steps: (1) identifying questions of interest; (2) formulating an explanation; and (3) carrying out research designed to lend support or refute the explanation.

Theories are broad explanations and predictions about phenomena that interest the scientist. Because psychological theories grow out of the diverse major conceptual models (presented in Chapter 1), they vary in breadth and detail. Psychologists' theories differ from our informal theories by being formal and focused. Latané and Darley proposed a theory of **diffusion of responsibility** to account for why bystanders and onlookers did not help either Erica Morris or Kitty Genovese.

After formulating a theory, the next step for Latané and Darley was to devise a way of testing the theory. They began by stating a **hypothesis**, a prediction stated in a way that allows it to be tested. Latané and Darley's hypothesis was: The more people who witness an emergency, the less likely it is that help will be given to a victim. Formal theories and hypotheses allow psychologists to organize separate bits of information and to move beyond the facts and make deductions about phenomena not yet encountered.

CONCEPT 2: Finding Answers: Psychological Research

Survey: ☐
Read: ☐

Pages 34-45

Research refers to systematic inquiry aimed at the discovery of new knowledge. It is a central ingredient of the scientific method. Research is the means of actually testing hypotheses and theories. In order to research a hypothesis, the hypothesis must be stated in a manner that is testable. **Operationalization** refers to the translation of a hypothesis into specific, testable procedures that can be observed and measured. If we examine scientific methods closely, we can then make more critically informed and reasoned judgments about everyday situations.

Archival research requires examining existing records and collecting data regarding the phenomena of interest to the researcher. Latané and Darley would have begun by examining newspaper clippings and other records to find examples of situations like those they were studying. The problem with the archival record is that it may be incomplete, collected in the wrong form, or collected haphazardly.

Naturalistic observation involves the researcher observing naturally occurring behavior without intervening in the situation. Unfortunately, the phenomena of interest may be infrequent. Furthermore, when people know they are being watched, they may act differently.

In **survey research**, participants are chosen from a larger population and asked a series of questions about behavior, thoughts, or attitudes. Techniques are sophisticated enough now that small samples can be drawn from large populations to make predictions about how the entire population will behave. For instance, the sampling technique is used to predict how the population will vote in a presidential election. The potential problems are that some people may not remember how they felt or acted at a particular time, or they may give answers they believe that the researcher wants to hear. Recently people have been asked to participate so much that they are beginning to refuse to participate. The result is that opinions and attitudes that are measured reflect only those of the people who were willing to respond.

When the phenomena of interest is uncommon, psychologists may use a **case study**, an in-depth examination of an individual or small group of people. The application of insight gained through a case study must be done carefully because the individuals studied may not be representative of a larger group.

Correlation research examines the relationship between two factors and the degree to which they are associated, or "correlated." The correlation is measured by a mathematical score ranging from $+1.0$ to -1.0. A positive correlation says that when one factor *increases*, the other correlated factor also *increases*. A negative correlation says that as one factor *increases*, the other negatively correlated factor *decreases*. When little or no relationship exists between two factors, the correlation is close to 0. Correlation can show that two factors are related and that the presence of one predicts another, but it cannot prove that one causes the other. Correlation research cannot rule out alternative causes when examining the relationship between two factors.

Experiments must be conducted in order to establish cause-and-effect relationships. A formal **experiment** examines the relationship of two or more factors in a setting that is deliberately manipulated to produce a change in one factor and then to observe how the change affects other factors. This **experimental manipulation** allows psychologists to detect the relationship between these factors. These factors, called **variables**, can be behaviors, events, or other characteristics that can change or vary in some way. The first step in developing an experiment is to operationalize a hypothesis (as did Latané and Darley). At least two groups of subjects must be observed. One group receives the **treatment**, the manipulated variable, and is called the **treatment group**. The other group is called the **control group** and is not exposed to the manipulated variable. Latané and Darley created a bogus emergency and then varied the number of bystanders present, in effect creating several different treatment groups. The variable that is manipulated is the **independent variable**—the condition that distinguishes the treatment groups—and in this example was the number of people present. The **dependent variable** is the variable that is measured to reveal the effect of the manipulation. In this example, the dependent variable was how long it took the **subject** to offer help.

In order to be assured that some characteristics of the subject do not influence the outcome of an experiment, a procedure called **random assignment to condition** must be used to assign subjects to treatment or control groups. The objective of random assignment is to make each group comparable.

A problem with psychology experiments is that often the subjects are college students. The advantage of using college students is their availability, and the major disadvantage is that they may not be representative of the population—they tend to be middle-class, white, and hold better informed attitudes.

Latané and Darley utilized a trained **confederate**, who feigns an epileptic seizure, to create the bogus emergency. The results of their experiment suggested that the size of the audience did indeed influence the time it took for subjects to offer help. To be sure, they had to analyze their results according to statistical procedures to prove that it was unlikely that their results were caused by chance. Also, to be certain of their results, other psychologists must try to repeat the experiment under the same or similar circumstances and test other variations of the hypothesis. The process is called **replication**.

CONCEPT 3: Research Issues

Survey: ☐
Read: ☐

Pages 45-51

Issues other than the quality of research are of concern to psychologists. The ethics of certain research practices come into question when there exists a possibility of harm to a subject. The use of deception—like that of the Latané and Darley experiment—and similar tactics has led to the need to assure subjects and the scientific community that no harm will come to the subjects. Guidelines have been developed for the treatment of human and animal subjects, and most proposed research is now reviewed by a panel to assure that guidelines are being met. The concept of **informed consent** has become a key ethical principle. Prior to participating in an experiment, subjects must sign a form indicating that they have been told of the basic outlines of the study and what their participation will involve.

The ethical guidelines call for assurance that animals in experiments do not suffer as a consequence of being subjects in the experiment. Not only is physical discomfort avoided, but psychological discomfort is avoided as well. The need for using animals in experiments has become a controversial topic. The advantages of using animals include the fact that they have a shorter life span, that their behavior may be less complex than human behavior, and finally, that circumstances can be manipulated that could not be manipulated with humans.

Another problem that researchers face is **experimental bias**, the factors that distort the experimenter's understanding of the relationship between the independent and dependent variables. **Experimenter expectations** occur when the experimenter unintentionally conveys cues about how the subjects should behave in the experiment. **Subject expectations** are the subject's expectations about the intended goal of the experiment. The subject's guesses about the hypothesis can influence behavior and thus the outcomes. One approach is to disguise the true purpose of the experiment. Another is to use a **placebo** with the control group so that the subjects remain unaware of whether or not they are being exposed to the experimental condition. The **double-blind procedure** guards against these two biases by informing neither the experimenter nor the subject about which treatment group the subject is in.

Psychologists utilize statistical procedures to determine if the results of a research study are significant. A **significant outcome** means that the results of the experiment were not likely to be a result of chance. It does not imply that the outcome has real-life significance. **Meta-analysis** is a technique that allows researchers to use statistical procedures on the data that has been reported by other researchers, thereby combining the results of several research reports.

An informed consumer of psychology must be able to evaluate research by examining the methods used to reach conclusions. Basic questions that an individual may ask include questions concerning whether the research is based in clearly specified theory, how the hypothesis was developed and tested, how well the study was conducted—including the specific methods used—and what the assumptions were of the researchers. If the sponsor of the research would benefit from one conclusion or another is also significant in an evaluation of research.

▶ Now that you have surveyed, questioned, and read the chapter and completed

the **Recap and Review** questions, review **Looking Back**, page 52.   *Review:* ☐

➤ For additional practice through recitation and review, test your knowledge of the chapter material by answering the questions in the *Key Word Drill*, the *Practice Questions*, and the *Essay Questions*.

KEY WORD DRILL

Recite: ☐

The following **Fill in the Blank** and **Matching Questions** test key words from the text. Check your answers with the Answer Key in the back of the *Study Guide*.

FILL IN THE BLANK

1. In order to verify the results of the original experiment, the experiment must undergo

   _____.

2. Prior to an experiment, the procedures of the study, the conditions and risks of participation are

   explained to the subject, who then must sign a form that indicates _____

   _____.

3. _____ _____ could lead an experimenter to an erroneous conclusion about the effect of the independent variable on the dependent variable.

4. _____ _____ are an experimenter's unintentional message to a subject about results expected from the experiment.

5. Subject _____ reflect the subject's interpretation of what behaviors or responses are expected in an experiment.

6. The _____ is a biologically ineffective pill used in an experiment to keep subjects, and sometimes experimenters, from knowing whether or not the subjects have received a behavior-altering drug.

7. In _____-_____ _____ both the experimenter and the subject are kept from knowing which subjects received a drug, making any observed behavior variations more reliable.

8. Whenever the results from an experiment are said to confirm a hypothesis in a the statistically

   meaningful way, the experiment is considered to have a _____

   _____.

9. _____-_____ is often used to compare and summarize the quatified outcomes of different studies.

10. The first step of the _____ _____ is to pose questions about phenomena of interest.

MATCHING QUESTIONS

_____ 11. scientific method

_____ 12. theories

_____ 13. hypothesis

_____ 14. research

_____ 15. operationalization

_____ 16. subject

_____ 17. random assignment to condition

_____ 18. confederate

a. A participant in an experiment who has been instructed to behave in ways that will affect the responses of other subjects.

b. Systematic inquiry aimed at discovering new knowledge.

c. The assignment of subjects to given groups on a chance basis alone.

d. A prediction stated in a way that allows it to be tested.

e. A participant in research.

f. The process of translating a hypothesis into specific testable procedures that can be measured and observed.

g. The process of appropriately framing and properly answering questions, used by practitioners of psychology and those engaged in other scientific disciplines, to come to an understanding about the world.

h. Broad explanations and predictions concerning phenomena of interest.

_____ 19. experimental manipulation

_____ 20. variable

_____ 21. treatment

_____ 22. treatment group

_____ 23. control group

_____ 24. independent variable

_____ 25. dependent variable

a. The variable that is manipulated in an experiment.

b. The experimental group receiving the treatment, or manipulation.

c. A behavior or event that can be changed.

d. The change deliberately produced in an experiment to affect responses or behaviors in other factors to determine causal relationships between variables.

e. The manipulation implemented by the experimenter to influence results in a segment of the experimental population.

f. The variable that is measured and is expected to change as a result of experimenter manipulation.

g. The experimental group receiving no treatment.

_____ 26. archival research

_____ 27. naturalistic observation

_____ 28. survey research

_____ 29. case study

_____ 30. correlational research

_____ 31. experiment

a. A study carried out to investigate the relationship between two or more factors by deliberately producing a change in one factor and observing the effect that change has upon other factors.

b. Observation without intervention, in which the investigator records information about a naturally occurring situation and does not intervene in the situation.

c. The examination of existing records for the purpose of confirming a hypothesis.

d. An in-depth interview of an individual in order to understand that individual better and to make inferences about people in general.

e. Research to determine whether there is a relationship between two sets of factors, such as certain behaviors and responses.

f. Sampling a group of people by assessing their behavior, thoughts, or attitudes, then generalizing the findings to a larger population.

PRACTICE QUESTIONS

Recite and Review: ☐

Test your knowledge of the chapter material by answering these **True-False** and **Multiple Choice Questions**. Check your answers with the Answer Key in the back of the *Study Guide*.

TRUE-FALSE QUESTIONS

T   F   1. According to the text, a hypothesis is a broad explanation and prediction concerning phenomena of interest to a researcher.

T   F   2. One of the drawbacks of naturalistic observation is that people may act differently if they know they are being watched.

T   F   3. With the exception of the experiment, all research methods are limited by the inability to demonstrate that a cause-and-effect relationship exists.

T   F   4. It has been determined that people who drive red cars also get more speeding tickets. This is an example of a cause-and-effect relationship.

T   F   5. When Carter came into the mental-health clinic, he was given a series of tests and asked many questions regarding his past. This procedure is called experimental research.

T   F   6.   A concern with the use of college students as subjects in psychological research is that they may not be representative of other groups.

T   F   7.   The primary purpose of replication in psychological experiments is to be sure that the treatment group did not in any way change, thus upsetting the controls.

T   F   8.   In humans, the best way to investigate the effects of a severe brain injury on learning is through an experiment.

T   F   9.   A medical researcher is experimenting with a new medication to help mentally ill patients. Some patients are in the experimental group and some are in the control group. Neither the researcher nor the patients know which patients are in each group. This procedure is called a double blind.

T   F   10.   Psychologists use special statistical procedures to ensure that their research findings are not the result of chance.

MULTIPLE CHOICE QUESTIONS

1. In the example of Kitty Genovese, how many bystanders probably heard her call for help?
   a. 38
   b. 2
   c. 1
   d. 107

2. According to the text, identifying questions of interest is one of the steps of:
   a. survey research.
   b. case study methods.
   c. scientific method.
   d. experimental design.

3. According to the text, formulating an explanation is one of the steps of:
   a. naturalistic explanation.
   b. experimenter bias.
   c. ethics review panel.
   d. scientific method.

4. Carrying out research designed to lend support to or to refute an explanation of a phenomenon is a main step in:
   a. scientific method.
   b. developing theories.
   c. naturalistic observation.
   d. statistical analysis of significance.

5. Which of the following is not one of the steps of the scientific method as described in the text?
   a. carry out research.
   b. identify questions of interest.
   c. graph results.
   d. formulate an explanation.

6. A hypothesis is:
   a. a broad explanation of phenomena of interest.
   b. the step of identifying phenomena of interest.
   c. observation that occurs without intervention by the observer.
   d. a prediction stated in such a way that it can be tested.

7. Which of the following would most likely come first in the course of conducting research?
    a. hypothesis
    b. determining significance
    c. analyzing the correlation
    d. collecting data

8. Hypotheses are to predictions as:
    a. explanations are to theories.
    b. theories are to explanations.
    c. explanations are to operationalizations.
    d. operationalizations are to explanations.

9. Operationalization requires that:
    a. data always be useful.
    b. procedures are followed exactly.
    c. variables are correctly manipulated.
    d. predictions be made testable.

10. Which of the following would provide the **least** useful operationalization of the emotion "love"?
    a. the self-reports of children who consider themselves in love
    b. the change in heart rate when two people are together
    c. the number of letters written by lovers to each other
    d. the length of time a couple has been together

11. The process by which a predictive statement is translated into particular experimental procedures is called:
    a. operationalization.
    b. hypothesis formation.
    c. intuitive thought.
    d. basic research.

12. Which of the following requires that the researcher not intervene into the situation?
    a. naturalistic observation.
    b. case study.
    c. correlational research.
    d. survey research.

13. To learn more about circumstances that lead up to suicides, Carroll Becker begins to study existing records on such incidents. Dr. Becker is doing:
    a. case research.
    b. archival research.
    c. survey research.
    d. situational research.

14. By examining school records, a school psychologist found that 10 percent of the students in the district were diagnosed as having a learning disability. This type of research is:
    a. correlational.
    b. observational.
    c. experimental.
    d. archival.

15. Calling up large numbers of people to gather information concerning their attitudes toward television is a form of:
    a. case study research.
    b. survey research.
    c. experimental research.
    d. archival research.

16. The technique of conducting an in-depth interview of an individual in order to understand better that individual and make inferences about people in general is called a:
    a. focused study.
    b. generalization study.
    c. case study.
    d. projection study.

17. Freud based his theory of psychoanalysis on in-depth examinations of the patients he was treating for psychological problems. This method of research relies on the use of:
    a. case studies.
    b. correlational data.
    c. dependent variables.
    d. naturalistic observation.

18. A prospective executive may undergo intensive interviews and extensive psychological testing. The executive may also have to provide references from previous and current occupational and personal sources. This process is most similar to:
    a. a survey.
    b. an experimental study.
    c. naturalistic observation.
    d. a case study.

19. Which of the following research methods most frequently incorporates the other methods listed?
    a. correlational methods
    b. survey methods
    c. case study
    d. archival methods

20. When the strength of a relationship is represented by a mathematical score ranging from +1.0 to −1.0, we are dealing with a:
    a. dependent variable.
    b. manipulation.
    c. correlation.
    d. treatment.

21. Which of the following statements is **not** true?
    a. A correlation of 1.0 means that there is a strong positive relationship between two factors.
    b. A correlation of 0.0 means that there is no systematic relationship between two factors.
    c. Correlations tell us that there is a relationship between two factors.
    d. Correlations tell us that one factor is caused by another.

22. A researcher finds a positive correlation between a student's Scholastic Aptitude Test (SAT) score and the income of the student's parents. This correlational finding means:
    a. larger incomes cause better SAT scores.
    b. parents with larger incomes can provide experiences which boost SAT scores.
    c. income and SAT scores are somewhat related, so one can be roughly predicted from the other.
    d. the SAT gives an advantage to upper-middle-class students.

23. Cause-and-effect relationships may be established through:
    a. case studies.
    b. surveys.
    c. experimentation.
    d. correlation studies.

24. A variable is:
    a. the experimental group receiving no treatment.
    b. the experimental group receiving treatment.
    c. a behavior or event that can be changed.
    d. a participant in research.

25. In an experiment with two groups, the group that receives no treatment serves as:
    a. a control.
    b. a case.
    c. an independent variable.
    d. a measured variable.

26. In order for proper assignment of subjects to the conditions in an experiment, the assignment must be by:
    a. someone who does not know the subjects.
    b. chance.
    c. someone who does know the subjects.
    d. factors relevant to the experiment.

27. The event that is measured and is expected to change as a result of the experiment is called the:
    a. dependent variable.
    b. independent variable.
    c. control variable.
    d. confounding variable.

28. The variable that is manipulated by the experimenter is called the:
    a. dependent variable.
    b. independent variable.
    c. control variable.
    d. confounding variable.

29. Professor Taylor has been studying the effects of light on the tolerance of stress in monkeys for several years. Each experiment varies the conditions slightly, but usually only one factor is altered each time. Dr. Taylor is most likely trying to:
    a. develop a new statistical test.
    b. operationalize her hypothesis.
    c. formulate a new hypothesis.
    d. test the limits of her theory.

30. The document signed by the subject in an experiment that affirms that the subject knows generally what is to happen is called:
    a. "in loco parentis."
    b. subject expectations.
    c. informed consent.
    d. experimenter expectations.

31. Informed consent can be dispensed with if a subject:
    a. is assigned to the control group.
    b. has spent time in a mental institution.
    c. is merely given a placebo.
    d. is part of a purely observational study in a public location.

32. Whether a behavioral scientist uses human or animal subjects in an experiment, there are _____ which the scientist must satisfy in order not to violate the rights of the participants.
    a. moral obligations
    b. religious principles
    c. professional standards
    d. ethical guidelines

33. A subject's interpretation of what behaviors or responses are expected in an experiment is called:
    a. the placebo effect.
    b. experimenter expectations.
    c. subject expectations.
    d. treatment condition.

34. Deception—disguising the true nature of a study—is sometimes used in experiments in order to:
    a. eliminate subject expectations.
    b. confuse the subject.
    c. eliminate experimenter expectations.
    d. confuse the experimenter.

35. A pill without any significant chemical properties that is used in an experiment is called a(n):
    a. control.
    b. placebo.
    c. dependent variable.
    d. independent variable.

36. The double-blind procedure is used to:
    a. keep the confederate from influencing other subjects.
    b. eliminate dependent variables.
    c. control the placebo effect.
    d. eliminate subject and experimenter expectations.

37. Once the data from an experiment has been recorded and summarized, the next step is to determine:
    a. whether the results can be replicated.
    b. if all the data are correct.
    c. if the hypothesis has been confirmed.
    d. whether the results are better than chance events.

38. Dr. Graves has analyzed the death rates reported in several hundred studies of suicides. He has compared the statistical results from each study and been able to create a summary analysis. To complete his analysis, he most likely has used:
    a. significant outcomes.
    b. meta-analysis.
    c. correlational research.
    d. experimental techniques.

39. To say that an experiment has a significant outcome is to suggest that:
    a. its results are very important.
    b. it is unlikely that the results were because of chance.
    c. the experiment has importance, but not necessarily to anyone but the experimenter.
    d. all the variables showed an interaction with one another.

40. In terms of judging the quality of the research itself, the reason one would want to know the basic assumptions behind a particular research study would be to:
    a. determine how the results can be applied.
    b. assess the adequacy of the methods for testing the assumptions.
    c. judge the researcher's ability.
    d. plan an experiment of one's own.

| ESSAY QUESTIONS | *Recite and Review:* ☐ |

Essay Question 2.1: *Designing Experiments*

Select one of the ten statements on pages 31-32 and design an experiment to test the statement. Remember, your design must include a testable hypothesis, independent and dependent variables, and a method of establishing control. What problems will your research encounter?

_____

_____

_____

_____

_____

_____

_____

_____

_____

_____

_____

_____

_____

_____

_____

_____

_____

_____

_____

_____

Essay Question 2.2: *Deceptive Practices*

Imagine yourself in the Latané and Darley experiment as one of the subjects who delays responding because of the diffusion of responsibility (you thought there were others around to help). After the experiment, you discover that your behavior has been deceptively manipulated and that the epileptic seizure was staged. What are your reactions to this deception? What are the ethical constraints on the researchers? Can you suggest alternatives to this kind of research? Is it justified?

_____

_____

_____

_____

_____

_____

_____

_____

_____

_____

_____

_____

_____

_____

_____

_____

_____

_____

ACTIVITIES AND PROJECTS

1. Using naturalistic observation, select a person or group to observe what you see. You might observe students immediately before taking an examination, someone on a bus or train, or a child. When you record your observations, make sure you write down behaviors—only what can be seen. Do not make any inferences about what the behaviors might mean or what the person might be feeling. Recording behaviors appropriately, without making inferences, takes practice.

2. Go to the library and select an article from a psychology journal in which an experiment is described. What is the format of the article? What is the investigator trying to discover? What are the independent and dependent variables? What are the treatment and control groups? What are the results and implications?

3

THE BIOLOGY UNDERLYING BEHAVIOR

| **DETAILED OUTLINE** | *Survey:* ☐ |

This detailed outline contains all the headings in Chapter 3: The Biology Underlying Behavior. If you are using the SQ3R method, then an examination of the outline is the best way to begin your survey of the chapter.

Prologue: Andrea Fyie
Looking Ahead

Neurons: The Elements of Behavior
The structure of the neuron
Firing the neuron
● **Recap and Review I**

Where Neuron Meets Neuron: Bridging the Gap
Varieties of neurotransmitters

The Nervous System
Neuronal architecture
Central and peripheral nervous systems
Activating the autonomic nervous system
● **Recap and Review II**

The Brain
Studying the structure and functions of the brain
The central core: Our old brain
The Cutting Edge Are Men's and Women's Brains Different?
The limbic system: Beyond the central core
● **Recap and Review III**
The cerebral cortex: Up the evolutionary ladder
The motor area of the brain
The sensory area of the brain
The association area of the brain
The specialization of the hemispheres: Two brains or one?
Psychology at Work The Commercial Value of the Brain
The split brain: Exploring the two hemispheres
Brain modules: The architecture of the brain, revisited

The Endocrine System: Of Chemicals and Glands
The Informed Consumer of Psychology Learning to Control Your Heart—and Brain—through
   Biofeedback
● **Recap and Review IV**

Looking Back
Key Terms and Concepts

➤ Now that you have surveyed the chapter, read **Looking Ahead**, pages 56-58.   ***Question:*** ☐
   Focus on the questions on pages 57 and 58.   ***Read:*** ☐

CONCEPTS AND LEARNING OBJECTIVES

Survey: ☐

These are the concepts and the learning objects for Chapter 3. Read them carefully as part of your
preliminary survey of the chapter.

Concept 1: The biology of the organism affects its behavior. The brain, and its basic building blocks,
   the neurons, are the biological components that have the greatest influence on behavior.

1. Understand the importance placed on the biology that underlies behavior and identify reasons
    why psychologists study these biological underpinnings—especially the brain and the nervous
    system. (pp. 56-58)

2. Describe the structure of the neuron and its parts. (pp. 58-61)

3. Describe the action potential and the resting potential of the neuron and how the neuron
    communicates its electrochemical message from initial stimulation to transmission across the
    synapse. (pp. 61-62)

Concept 2: Neurotransmitters are critical to various functions because they are the means by which the
   neural message is communicated from one neuron to another. The major division of the nervous
   system include the central and peripheral division, the autonomic and somatic division, and the
   sympathetic and parasympathetic divisions.

4. Name key neurotransmitters and their functions and describe their known or suspected roles
    in behavior as well as in illnesses like Alzheimer's and Parkinson's diseases. (pp. 63-68)

5. Describe the major divisions of the nervous system, including the central and the peripheral,
    the parasympathetic and sympathetic, the autonomic and motor divisions. (pp. 68-71)

Concept 3: The central core and the limbic system control and monitor basic life functions as well as
   self-preservation needs.

6. Name the techniques used to map and study the brain and describe some of the anatomical
    differences between the brain in males and females that have been discovered using these
    techniques. (pp. 73-75)

7. Name the components of the central core and the limbic system and describe the functions of their individual parts. (pp. 75-79)

Concept 4: The higher functions are associated with the cerebral cortex. The role of the endocrine system is to communicate hormones that control growth and behavior through the bloodstream.

8. Name the major areas of the cerebral hemispheres, especially the lobes and the cortex areas, and describe the roles of each area in behavior. (pp. 79-85)

9. Discuss the issues involved with brain specialization, brain lateralization, and the split-brain operation, and what has been learned about the two hemispheres from the procedure. (pp. 85-90)

10. Name the major hormones and describe the function of the endocrine system. (pp. 90-91)

11. Describe how biofeedback can be used to control some of the basic biological processes. (pp. 91-92)

CHAPTER SUMMARY

There are several ways you can use this summary as part of your systematic study plan. You may read each concept summary and then read the corresponding pages in the text, or you may read the entire summary and then read the entire chapter in the text. As you finish each section, complete the **Recap and Review** questions that are supplied in the text.

CONCEPT 1: Prologue and Looking Ahead
Neurons: The Elements of Behavior

Survey: ☐
Read: ☐

Pages 56-63

Advanced brain scanning techniques, like positron emission tomography, can now give extremely detailed and accurate pictures of the brain to aid the diagnosis of disease. This and other techniques have been applied to the study of the brain and the **nervous system**, and as a result, psychologists' understanding of the brain has increased dramatically in the past few years. **Neuroscientists** examine the biological underpinnings of behavior, and **biopsychologists** explore the ways the biological structures and functions of the body affect behavior.

Specialized cells called **neurons** are the basic component of the nervous system. There are between 100 billion and 200 billion neurons in the body. Every neuron has a nucleus, a cell body, and special structures for communicating with other neurons. **Dendrites** are the receiving structures and **axons** are the sending structures. At the ends of the axons are **terminal buttons** that serve to connect with other neurons. The message is communicated in one direction from the dendrites, through the cell body, and down the axon to the terminal buttons. A fatty substance known as the myelin sheath surrounds the axons of most neurons and serves as an insulator for the electrical signal being transmitted down the axon. It also speeds the signal. In multiple sclerosis, the myelin sheath disintegrates, causing short circuits where electrical messages are communicated to nearby axons of other neurons. Certain substances necessary for the maintenance of the cell body travel up the axon to the cell body in a reverse flow. Amyotrophic lateral sclerosis, or Lou Gehrig's disease, is a failure of the neuron to work in this reverse direction.

Epilepsy is thought to result when dendrites in certain areas of the brain "leak" information that is supposed to travel to the cell body.

The neuron communicates its message by "firing," which refers to its changing from a **resting state** to an **action potential**. Neurons express the action potential in an all-or-nothing fashion, that is, firing only when a certain level of stimulation is reached. The stimulation involves a reversal of the electrical charge inside the neuron from -70 millivolts to a positive charge. This reversal flows very rapidly through the neuron, and the neuron quickly returns to its resting state. Just after the action potential has passed, the neuron is in an **absolute refractory period**. During this period, the neuron cannot fire again. A **relative refractory period** follows, during which the neuron can fire if a very strong stimulus is present. The thickness of the myelin sheath and the diameter of the axon determine the speed of the action potential, with action potentials traveling down thicker axons much more rapidly. A neuron can fire as many as 1000 times per second if the stimulus is very strong. However, the communicated message is a matter of how frequently or infrequently the neuron fires, not the intensity of the action potential, since the action potential is always the same strength.

CONCEPT 2: Where Neuron Meets Neuron: Bridging the Gap
The Nervous System

Survey: ☐
Read: ☐

Pages 63-73

The message of a neuron is communicated to the receiving neuron by the release of a **neurotransmitter** across the **synapse**. The synapse is the small space between the terminal button of one neuron and the dendrite of the next. Neurotransmitters can either excite or inhibit the receiving neuron. The exciting neurotransmitter is called an **excitatory message** and the inhibiting neurotransmitter is called an **inhibitory message**. A neuron must summarize the excitatory and inhibitory messages it receives in order to fire. Once the neurotransmitters are released, they lock into special sites on the receiving neurons. They must then be reabsorbed through **reuptake** into the sending neuron or deactivated by enzymes.

About fifty neurotransmitters have been found. Neurotransmitters can be either exciting or inhibiting depending on where in the brain they are released. A common neurotransmitter is **acetylcholine (ACh)**, which produces contractions of skeletal muscles. **Alzheimer's disease** has been associated with the restricted production of ACh in areas of the brain. **Gamma-amino butyric acid (GABA)** is one of the major inhibiting neurotransmitters. The poison strychnine apparently causes death by restricting the flow of GABA across the synapse so that neurons fire without inhibition, leading to convulsions. Drugs like Valium increase the activity of GABA. **Dopamine (DA)** has both an inhibitory and an excitatory effect, depending on location. A loss of the ability to produce dopamine has been found in Parkinson's disease patients. Some researchers believe that overproduction of dopamine may be responsible for schizophrenia and other disturbances. **Endorphins** are the body's natural morphine, and they interact with sites called **opiate receptors**. Endorphins reduce pain and produce a state of euphoria. This state is often called runner's high when experienced by joggers. Placebos and acupuncture may be effective because they cause endorphins to be released.

Neurons are linked into **neural networks** which allow the brain to modify information as it travels to and from the brain. Computational neuroscience is devoted to understanding these neural networks. Several circuit patterns have been identified. **Linear circuits** transmit information from one neuron to another. **Multiple-source/convergent circuits** transmit information from many neurons to one neuron. **Single-source/divergent circuits** transmit information from one neuron to many neurons. The total number of connections estimated in the brain is about 1 quadrillion.

The nervous system is divided into the **central nervous system**—composed of the brain and the spinal cord—and the **peripheral nervous system**. The spinal cord is a bundle of nerves that descend from the brain. The main purpose of the spinal cord is as a pathway for communication between the brain and the body. Some involuntary behaviors, called **reflexes**, involve messages that do not travel to the brain but instead stay entirely within the spinal cord. **Sensory (afferent) neurons** bring information from the periphery to the brain. **Motor (efferent) neurons** carry messages to the muscles and glands of the body. **Interneurons**, a third type of neuron, connects the sensory and the motor neurons, carrying messages between them. The spinal cord is the major carrier of sensory and motor information. Its importance is evident in injuries that result in **paraplegia**, a condition in which the sufferer cannot move the bottom half of his or her body. While basic reflexes may stay intact, the paraplegic cannot voluntarily control muscles nor can sensations be experienced. The **peripheral nervous system** branches out from the spinal cord. It is divided into the **somatic division**, which controls muscle movement, and the **autonomic division**, which controls basic body functions like heartbeat, breathing, glands, and lungs.

The role of the autonomic nervous system is to activate the body through the **sympathetic division** and then to modulate and calm the body through the **parasympathetic division**. The sympathetic division prepares the organism for stressful situations, and the parasympathetic division returns the body to help the body recover after the emergency has ended.

CONCEPT 3: The Brain

Survey: ☐
Read: ☐

Pages 73-80

The brain weighs about three pounds and is composed of billions of neurons. Some knowledge of the structure and function of the brain has been gained by studying the results of injuries to the brain, and today, much additional knowledge is being added by using **brain scans**, techniques that picture the brain without having to perform an autopsy. The **electroencephalogram (EEG)** records the electrical activity of the brain by using electrodes placed outside the skull. **Computerized axial tomography (CAT)** utilizes computer imaging to construct an image that is made by combining thousands of separate x-rays taken from different angles. **Magnetic resonance imaging (MRI)** uses powerful magnets to create a picture of the brain. **Positron emission tomography (PET) scan** records the location of radioactive isotopes in the brain during brain activity, thus allowing a picture of the activity.

Because it evolved very early, the **central core** of the brain is referred to as the old brain. It is composed of the **medulla**, which controls functions like breathing and heartbeat, the **pons**, which transmits information helping to coordinate muscle activity on the right and left halves of the body, and the **cerebellum**, which coordinates muscle activity. The reticular formation is a group of nerve cells that serve to alert other parts of the brain to activity. The central core also includes the **thalamus**, which transmits sensory information, and the **hypothalamus**, which maintains **homeostasis** of the body's environment. The hypothalamus also plays a role in basic survival behaviors like eating, drinking, sexual behavior, aggression, and child-rearing behavior. The **Cutting Edge** discusses the physical differences between male and female brains. The major difference that has been discovered is that the connecting fibers between the two hemispheres, called the **corpus callosum**, have different shapes in men and women.

The **limbic system** is a set of interrelated structures that includes pleasure centers, structures that control eating, aggression, reproduction, and self-preservation. Intense pleasure is felt through the limbic system, and rats with electrodes implanted in their limbic systems will often stimulate their pleasure centers rather than eat. The limbic system also plays important roles in learning and memory.

CONCEPT 4: The Brain (continued)

The cerebral cortex: Up the evolutionary ladder

The Endocrine System: Of Chemicals and Glands

Survey: ☐
Read: ☐

Pages 80-93

The **cerebral cortex** is identified with the functions that allow us to think and remember. A cortex is a covering, and the cerebral cortex is deeply folded in order to increase the surface area of the covering. The cortex is divided into four main sections, or **lobes**. They are the **frontal lobes**, the **parietal lobes**, the **temporal lobes**, and the **occipital lobes**. The cortex and its lobes have been divided into three major areas, the motor area, the sensory area, and the association area.

The **motor area** of the brain is responsible for the control and direction of voluntary muscle movements. There are three areas devoted to the **sensory area**, that of touch, called the **somatosensory area**, that of sight, and that of hearing. The **association area** takes most of the cortex and is devoted to mental processes like language, thinking, memory, and speech. The condition called **apraxia** when a person cannot integrate activities rationally or logically. An **aphasia** occurs when a person has difficulty with verbal expression. **Broca's aphasia** refers to difficulty with the production of speech. Wernicke's aphasia refers to brain damage that involves the loss of the ability to understand the speech of others.

The two halves of the brain are called **hemispheres**. The left hemisphere controls the right side of the body, and the right hemisphere controls the left side. Since each hemisphere appears to have functions that it controls, it is said that the brain is lateralized. The left hemisphere concentrates on verbally based skills, like thought and reason. The right half deals with spatial understanding and pattern recognition. This **lateralization** appears to vary greatly with individuals, and there may be general differences between the brains of males and females, as males appear to have language more lateralized. The two halves of the brain are, however, quite interdependent on each other.

Roger Sperry pioneered the study of the surgical separation of the two hemispheres for cases of severe epilepsy. Those who have had the procedure are called **split-brain patients**.

Brain modules refers to a current way of understanding how the brain works. Brain modules are units of the brain that carry out specific tasks. These modules incorporate components of different brain areas and parts and specialize in the tasks. They also appear to operate relatively independently of each other.

The **endocrine system** is a chemical communication network that delivers hormones into the bloodstream which, in turn, influence growth and behavior. Sometimes called the "master gland," the **pituitary gland** is the major gland of the endocrine system. The hypothalamus regulates the pituitary gland.

The informed consumer of psychology discusses the use of **biofeedback** to control a variety of body functions. It has been successfully applied to the control of headaches, blood pressure, and other medical and physical problems.

➤ Now that you have surveyed, questioned, and read the chapter and completed the **Recap and Review** questions, review **Looking Back**, pages 93-94.

Review: ☐

➤ For additional practice through recitation and review, test your knowledge of the chapter material by answering the questions in the *Key Word Drill*, the *Practice Questions*, and the *Essay Questions*.

| **KEY WORD DRILL** |

Recite: ☐

The following **Fill in the Blank** and **Matching Questions** test key words from the text. Check your answers with the Answer Key in the back of the *Study Guide*.

FILL IN THE BLANK

1. The psychologists and researchers who study the nervous system are called _____, while the psychologists who study the ways biological structures and body functions affect behavior are known as _____.

2. _____ _____ _____ follows the triggering of a neuron, and during this period, the neuron cannot fire again, no matter how much stimulation it receives.

3. _____ _____ is an electric nerve impulse that travels through a neuron when it is set off by a "trigger," changing the cell's charge from negative to positive.

4. The type of neuron called _____ _____ acts to reduce the experience of pain.

5. _____ usually results from an injury to the spinal cord and refers to the inability to voluntarily move any muscles in the lower half of the body.

6. An organism tries to maintain an internal biological balance or steady state through the process called _____.

7. The _____ _____ _____ scan produces a powerful magnetic field in order to provide a detailed, computer-generated image of brain structure or any other biological structure.

8. The _____ records the electrical signals being transmitted inside the brain.

9. When one hemisphere of the brain controls a specific function, the function is considered _____.

10. The term _____ _____ refers to the separate units of the brain that carry out specific tasks.

MATCHING QUESTIONS

_____ 11. neurons

_____ 12. dendrites

_____ 13. axon

_____ 14. terminal buttons

_____ 15. myelin sheath

a. Specialized cells that are the basic elements of the nervous system that carry messages.

b. Small branches at the end of an axon that relay messages to other cells.

c. A long extension from the end of a neuron that carries messages to other cells through the neuron.

d. An axon's protective coating, made of fat and protein.

e. Clusters of fibers at one end of a neuron that receive messages from other neurons.

_____ 16. neurotransmitter

_____ 17. excitatory message

_____ 18. inhibitory message

_____ 19. neural networks

_____ 20. linear circuits

_____ 21. multiple-source/convergent circuits

_____ 22. single-source/divergent circuits

a. A chemical secretion that makes it more likely that a receiving neuron will fire and an action potential will travel down its axons.

b. A hierarchical network of neurons in which information from several neurons is channeled into a single neuron.

c. A network of neurons in which a single neuron transmits messages to a potentially vast number of recipients.

d. A chemical secretion that prevents a receiving neuron from firing.

e. A chemical that carries the message from one neuron to another when secreted as the result of a nerve impulse.

f. Groups of organized communication links between cells.

g. Neurons joined in a single line, receiving and transmitting messages only to the next neuronal link.

_____ 23. peripheral nervous system

_____ 24. somatic division

_____ 25. autonomic division

_____ 26. sympathetic division

_____ 27. parasympathetic division

a. The part of the autonomic division of the peripheral nervous system that calms the body, bringing functions back to normal after an emergency has passed.

b. All parts of the nervous system *except* the brain and the spinal cord (includes somatic and autonomic divisions).

c. The part of the nervous system that controls involuntary movement (the actions of the heart, glands, lungs, and other organs).

d. The part of the autonomic division of the peripheral nervous system that prepares the body to respond in stressful emergency situations.

e. The part of the nervous system that controls voluntary movements of the skeletal muscles.

_____ 28. central core

_____ 29. medulla

_____ 30. pons

_____ 31. cerebellum

_____ 32. reticular formation

_____ 33. thalamus

_____ 34. hypothalamus

_____ 35. corpus callosum

a. The part of the brain that joins the halves of the cerebellum, transmitting motor information to coordinate muscles and integrate movement between the right and left sides of the body.

b. A bundle of fibers that connects one half of the brain to the other.

c. The part of the brain's central core that transmits messages from the sense organs to the cerebral cortex and from the cerebral cortex to the cerebellum and medulla.

d. The part of the central core of the brain that controls many important body functions, such as breathing and heartbeat.

e. The part of the brain that controls bodily balance.

f. The "old brain," which controls such basic functions as eating and sleeping and is common to all vertebrates.

g. A group of nerve cells in the brain that arouses the body to prepare it for appropriate action and screens out background stimuli.

h. Located below the thalamus of the brain, its major function is to maintain homeostasis.

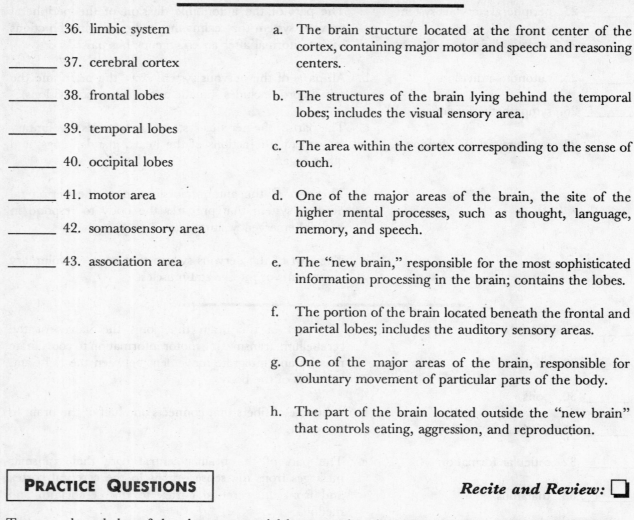

_____ 36. limbic system

_____ 37. cerebral cortex

_____ 38. frontal lobes

_____ 39. temporal lobes

_____ 40. occipital lobes

_____ 41. motor area

_____ 42. somatosensory area

_____ 43. association area

a. The brain structure located at the front center of the cortex, containing major motor and speech and reasoning centers.

b. The structures of the brain lying behind the temporal lobes; includes the visual sensory area.

c. The area within the cortex corresponding to the sense of touch.

d. One of the major areas of the brain, the site of the higher mental processes, such as thought, language, memory, and speech.

e. The "new brain," responsible for the most sophisticated information processing in the brain; contains the lobes.

f. The portion of the brain located beneath the frontal and parietal lobes; includes the auditory sensory areas.

g. One of the major areas of the brain, responsible for voluntary movement of particular parts of the body.

h. The part of the brain located outside the "new brain" that controls eating, aggression, and reproduction.

| **PRACTICE QUESTIONS** | *Recite and Review:* ❑ |

Test your knowledge of the chapter material by answering these **True-False** and **Multiple Choice Questions**. Check your answers with the Answer Key in the back of the *Study Guide*.

TRUE-FALSE QUESTIONS

T   F   1.   The all-or-nothing law states that neurons are either firing or in a resting state, but nothing in between.

T   F   2.   Generally speaking, the autonomic nervous system operates without conscious effort of the individual.

T   F   3.   Sexual arousal is mainly controlled by the parasympathetic nervous system.

T   F   4.   Research has failed to show differences in the functional organization of the brain between human males and human females.

T   F   5.   The two cerebral hemispheres work interdependently to produce the full range and richness of human thought.

T   F   6.   Broca's aphasia is a language disorder in which the afflicted individual has difficulty comprehending what others say.

T   F   7.   The motor area of the cerebral cortex is responsible for planning and coordinating a sequence of behavior, such as putting a suitcase in the trunk of a car.

T   F   8.   The chemical messengers of the endocrine system are called hormones.

T   F   9.   As electroencephalogram records brain activity over time, electrical impulses are emitted and recorded on paper.

T   F   10.   The diameter of an neuron influences how quickly an impulse travels from the dendrites to the axon.

T   F   11.   Parkinson's disease is caused by decreased production of dopamine in the adrenal glands.

T   F   12.   A neuroscientist might investigate how personality is influenced by muscle and bone changes associated with aging.

MULTIPLE CHOICE QUESTIONS

1. Which of the following specializes in investigating the role of the central nervous system in behavior?
   a. neurologists
   b. biopsychologists
   c. physiologists
   d. zoologists

2. Dendrites, cell body, axon, and terminal buttons are parts of the:
   a. neurotransmitter.
   b. spinal cord.
   c. muscle spindle.
   d. neuron.

3. Neurons communicate with each other through specialized structures known as:
   a. glial cells.
   b. myelin sheaths.
   c. somas.
   d. dendrites and axons.

4. The myelin sheath surrounds:
   a. a dendrite.
   b. an axon.
   c. a cell body.
   d. a terminal button.

5. In multiple sclerosis, the _____ deteriorates, exposing parts of the _____. The result is a short circuit between the nervous system and muscle, which leads to difficulties with walking, vision, and with general muscle coordination.
   a. cell body; nucleus
   b. dendrite; terminal button
   c. terminal button; nucleus
   d. myelin sheath; axon

6. Epilepsy is associated with all of the following **except**:
    a. misfiring electrical discharges from the dendrites.
    b. seizures and convulsions.
    c. a leak of information to nearby neurons.
    d. reverse flow.

7. Which of the following determines the rate at which a neuron can fire?
    a. presence of ions
    b. reverse flow mechanism
    c. resting state
    d. refractory period

8. The gap between neurons is called the:
    a. terminal button.
    b. cell body.
    c. synapse.
    d. refractory period.

9. The purpose of reverse flow of some substances from the axon to the cell body is to:
    a. release neurotransmitters.
    b. clear metabolites from the cell.
    c. bring nourishment to the cell.
    d. regenerate an action potential after firing.

10. Immediately after firing, the neuron cannot fire again. This is called the:
    a. action potential.
    b. all-or-nothing law.
    c. relative refractory period.
    d. absolute refractory period.

11. Neural impulses travel:
    a. electrically between and within each neuron.
    b. chemically between and within each neuron.
    c. electrically between neurons and chemically within each neuron.
    d. chemically between neurons and electrically within each neuron.

12. A chemical that is released from the terminal button upon the arrival of an action potential is called:
    a. a neurotransmitter.
    b. an enzyme.
    c. a synapse.
    d. a stimulator.

13. In most cases, after neurotransmitters have sent their message to the receiving neuron, they are:
    a. deactivated by enzymes.
    b. reabsorbed by the terminal buttons.
    c. absorbed into the body and filtered through the kidneys.
    d. absorbed into the receiving neuron.

14. A deficiency of acetylcholine is associated with:
    a. depression.
    b. Alzheimer's disease.
    c. Parkinson's disease.
    d. Huntington's chorea.

15. Morphine and other opiates are most like which of the following neurotransmitters?
    a. acetylcholine
    b. dopamine
    c. endorphins
    d. norepinephrine

16. According to the text, the main function of the endorphins is:
    a. contraction of muscle tissue.
    b. reduction of pain in the body.
    c. smooth and coordinated motor movements.
    d. alertness and emotional expression.

17. The portion of the nervous system that is particularly important for reflexive behavior is the:
    a. brain.
    b. spinal cord.
    c. sensory nerve.
    d. motor nerve.

18. Afferent is to _____ as efferent is to _____.
    a. sensory; association
    b. sensory; motor
    c. motor; association
    d. motor; sensory

19. Reflexes:
    a. are learned from infancy.
    b. involve the peripheral nervous system.
    c. involve both the peripheral and central nervous systems.
    d. do not involve the brain at all.

20. Which of the following, taken together, constitute the peripheral nervous system?
    a. somatic nervous system and autonomic nervous system
    b. brain and spinal cord
    c. sympathetic nervous system and brain
    d. spinal cord and parasympathetic nervous system

21. The autonomic nervous system controls:
    a. habitual, automatic movements such as applying the brakes of an automobile.
    b. the functions of the spinal cord.
    c. the body's response to an emergency or crisis.
    d. most of the spinal reflexes.

22. Sympathetic division is to parasympathetic division as:
    a. fight is to flight.
    b. central is to peripheral.
    c. arousing is to calming.
    d. helpful is to hurtful.

23. Which of the following is not likely to happen during activation of the sympathetic division of the nervous system?
    a. increase in digestion
    b. increase in heart rate
    c. increase in sweating
    d. increase in pupil sizes

24. The technique that measures the activity of the brain by sensing a radioactive tracer in the person being studied is:
    a. positron emission tomography (PET) scan.
    b. the electroencephalogram (EEG).
    c. nuclear magnetic resonance (NMR) scan.
    d. computerized axial tomography (CAT) scan.

25. Which of the following structures is **not** part of the "central core" of the old brain?
    a. medulla
    c. hypothalamus
    b. pituitary
    d. reticular formation

26. The word most closely associated with the function of the limbic system is:
    a. thinking.
    c. emergency.
    b. survival.
    d. emotion.

27. According to the text, which of the following may be the most critical structure for maintaining homeostasis, a steady internal state of the body?
    a. hippocampus
    c. hypothalamus
    b. cerebral cortex
    d. cerebellum

28. Which of the following structures is **not** directly involved in the control of motor function?
    a. cerebellum
    c. pons
    b. medulla
    d. spinal cord

29. Which of the following controls important bodily functions such as heartbeat and breathing?
    a. medulla
    c. thalamus
    b. cerebellum
    d. hypothalamus

30. Damage to or lesions in which of the following brain structures would be most likely to cause dramatic changes in emotionality and behavior?
    a. pons
    c. cerebellum
    b. medulla
    d. limbic system

31. The capacities to think and remember probably best distinguish humans from other animals. These qualities are most closely associated with the function of the:
    a. cerebral cortex.
    c. cerebellum.
    b. medulla.
    d. limbic system.

32. _____ in the cerebral cortex create(s) the most sophisticated integration of neural information by providing for much greater surface area and complex interconnections among neurons.
    a. Convolutions
    c. Lateralization
    b. Mapping
    d. Hemispheric dominance

33. Which of the following is true of both the sensory and motor areas of the cortex?
    a. They both contain pleasure centers.
    b. More cortical tissue is devoted to the most important structures.
    c. Electrical stimulation produces involuntary movement.
    d. Destruction of any one area affects all the senses.

34. The diagram with parts of the "little man" on the surface of the motor cortex of a cerebral hemisphere shows that:
    a. body structures requiring fine motor movements are controlled by large amounts of neural tissue.
    b. major motor functions are controlled by the right hemisphere.
    c. large body parts on the diagram (e.g., fingers on a hand) receive little motor input.
    d. certain areas of the body are more responsive to touch, temperature, and other stimulation.

35. The area of the brain associated with thinking, language, memory, and speech is called the:
    a. sensory area.
    c. motor area.
    b. somatosensory area.
    d. association area.

36. Which area has the largest portion of the cortex?
    a. motor area
    c. sensory area
    b. somatosensory area
    d. association area

37. Phineas Gage was a shrewd, energetic business executive who persistently carried out all his plans of operation. The dramatic changes in him following his accident suggest which area of his cerebral cortex was injured?
    a. neuromuscular
    c. sensory-somatosensory
    b. association
    d. motor

38. When a person is unable to carry out purposeful, sequential behaviors, the condition is known as:
    a. dyslexia.
    c. apraxia.
    b. aphasia.
    d. paraplegia.

39. Which of the following is characterized by difficulty understanding the speech of others and producing coherent speech?
    a. Wernicke's aphasia
    c. Broca's aphasia
    b. Lou Gehrig's disease
    d. Phineas Gage's disease

40. Left hemisphere is to _____ function as right hemisphere is to _____ function.
    a. sequential; successive
    c. successive; sequential
    b. sequential; global
    d. global; sequential

41. Wernicke's aphasia is to _____ as Broca's aphasia is to _____.
    a. spasticity; flaccidity
    b. motor cortex; sensory cortex
    c. overeating; irregular gait
    d. difficulty in comprehending words; searching for the correct word.

42. Appreciation of music, art, and dance, and understanding of spatial relationships are more likely to be processed in the:
    a. right side of the brain.
    c. occipital lobes.
    b. left side of the brain.
    d. temporal lobe.

43. According to the text, in right-handed people, which of the following is usually responsible for logical thought processes and reasoning?
    a. occipital lobes
    b. temporal lobes
    c. left hemisphere
    d. right hemisphere

44. Damage to which of the following areas is most likely to cause people to have difficulty with pattern recognition tasks and spatial memory?
    a. frontal lobe
    b. left hemisphere
    c. right hemisphere
    d. temporal lobe

45. Which statement about the cerebral hemispheres does **not** apply to most right-handed people?
    a. The left hemisphere processes information sequentially.
    b. The right hemisphere processes information globally.
    c. The right hemisphere is associated with language and reasoning.
    d. Women display less hemispheric dominance than men, particularly with skills such as language.

46. One primary difference in the organization of male and female brains is that:
    a. logical abilities are on the opposite sides in males and females.
    b. language abilities are more evenly divided between the two hemispheres in females.
    c. the right hemisphere is almost always dominant in females.
    d. spatial abilities are on the opposite sides in males and females.

47. A split-brain patient has had:
    a. a stroke.
    b. the nerves between the hemispheres cut.
    c. damage to one of the hemispheres.
    d. epilepsy.

48. Which part of the brain is most closely linked to the function of the endocrine system?
    a. hypothalamus
    b. pons
    c. limbic system
    d. cerebellum

49. Which response listed below is **least** likely to be treated with biofeedback?
    a. impotence
    b. headaches
    c. high blood pressure
    d. problems with maintaining optimal skin temperature

50. Which of the following is primarily intended to be a procedure by which we can come to control our internal physiological processes?
    a. biofeedback
    b. hypnosis
    c. electrical stimulation
    d. hypothalamic regulation

| ESSAY QUESTIONS | *Recite and Review:* ☐ |

Essay Question 3.1: *The Benefits of Knowledge about the Brain*

Describe the specific benefits of our knowledge of brain function and the effect of injury on the brain. What are the possible consequences of research in neurotransmitters, biofeedback, and even sex differences in the brain?

_____

_____

_____

_____

_____

_____

_____

_____

_____

_____

_____

_____

_____

_____

_____

_____

_____

Essay Question 3.2: *Ethics and Brain Research*

Several recent developments raise important questions for ethical consideration. What are the problems that arise when surgery separates the two hemispheres? What are the potential dangers of transplanting tissue into the brain? Discuss these ethical and moral issues. Are there other issues?

_____

_____

_____

_____

_____

_____

_____

_____

_____

_____

_____

_____

_____

_____

_____

_____

_____

_____

ACTIVITIES AND PROJECTS

1. Fill in the labels that are missing from the following diagram of a neuron.

← Incoming messages

← Outgoing messages

2. Fill in the labels that are missing from the diagram of the brain.

3.   Fill in the labels that are missing from this flowchart describing the parts of the nervous system.

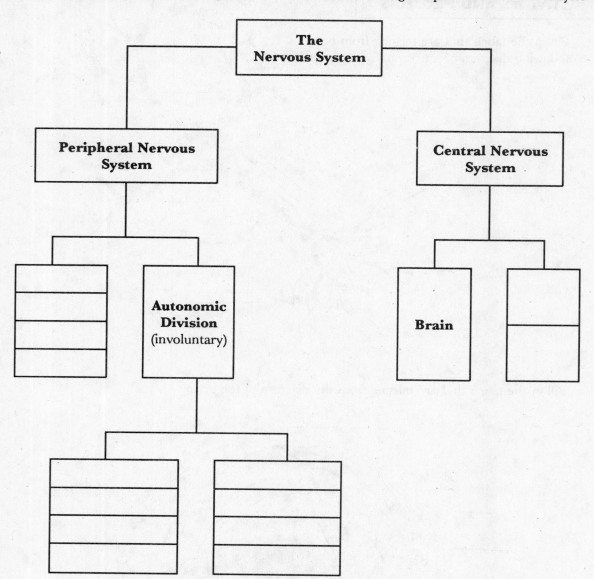

4

SENSATION

DETAILED OUTLINE

Survey: ☐

This detailed outline contains all the headings in Chapter 4: Sensation. If you are using the SQ3R method, then an examination of the outline is the best way to begin your survey of the chapter.

Prologue: Pete Townshend
Looking Ahead

Sensing the World Around Us
    Absolute thresholds
    Signal detection theory
    Just noticeable differences
    Sensory adaptation
● **Recap and Review I**

The Five + Senses
    Vision: The eyes have it
        Illuminating the structure of the eye
        Sending the message from the eye to the brain
        Processing the visual message
        Adaptation: From light to dark
        Color vision and color blindness: The 7-million color spectrum
● **Recap and Review II**
    The sense of sound and balance
        The ear: The site of sound
        The physical aspects of sound
Psychology at Work Improving the Senses with Technology
        Balance: The ups and downs of life
    Smell, taste, and the skin senses
        Smell and taste
The Cutting Edge Discovering the Origins of Food Preferences
        The skin senses: Touch, pressure, temperature, and pain
        Fighting pain
The Informed Consumer of Psychology Self-examination: The Protective Touch
● **Recap and Review III**

Looking Back
Key Terms and Concepts

➤ Now that you have surveyed the chapter, read **Looking Ahead**, pages 98–99. **Question:** ☐
Focus on the questions on page 99. **Read:** ☐

CONCEPTS AND LEARNING OBJECTIVES

Survey: ☐

These are the concepts and the learning objects for Chapter 4. Read them carefully as part of your preliminary survey of the chapter.

Concept 1: Sensation is the means by which information from the world around us is conveyed to the brain. The study of sensation requires examining the nature of physical stimuli and its relationship to the kinds of sensory responses they can evoke.

1. Define sensation and physical stimulus. (pp. 98-100)

2. Distinguish the concept of absolute threshold from the role of signal detection theory of stimuli. (pp. 100-102)

3. Describe the concept of just noticeable differences, Weber's law, and sensory adaptation. (pp. 102-104)

Concept 2: Vision is the most studied of the five plus senses, and the details of the transfer of a light image from its entrance into the eye, through its transformation into a neural message, to its destination in the visual cortex illustrates the complexity of sensation.

4. Describe the structural components of the eye, the retina, and the optic nerve, and explain how visual light is initially processed. (pp. 105-109)

5. Discuss how the image is conveyed from the eye to the brain and the role of feature detection in processing visual information, and describe how we adapt to different light levels. (pp. 109-112)

6. Distinguish the two theories of color vision, and discuss how they describe complementary processes. (pp. 112-115)

Concept 3: The ear is responsible for detecting sound, body position, and movement. Smell and taste are detected through chemical contact. The skin senses include touch, pressure, temperature, and pain.

7. Describe the structure of the ear and the role of each part in detecting sound. (pp. 117-122)

8. Describe how the semicircular canals detect motion and produce the sense of balance. (p. 122)

9. Describe the mechanisms that produce the senses of smell and taste. (pp. 122-127)

10. Describe the skin senses of touch, pressure, and temperature and discuss the gate-control theory of pain. (pp. 127-131)

CHAPTER SUMMARY

There are several ways you can use this summary as part of your systematic study plan. You may read each concept summary and then read the corresponding pages in the text, or you may read the entire summary and then read the entire chapter in the text. As you finish each section, complete the **Recap and Review** questions that are supplied in the text.

CONCEPT 1: Prologue and Looking Ahead
Sensing the World Around Us

Survey: ☐
Read: ☐

Pages 98-104

The loss of hearing experienced by Pete Townshend illustrates how valuable our senses are to us. His illness, called tinnitus, is the result of frequent exposure to loud sound—in his case, loud music. To a musician, this kind of loss is devastating.

We detect the world around us through our senses. A **stimulus** is any physical energy that can be detected by a sense organ. A **sensation** is the activity of the sense organ when it detects a stimulus. Stimuli vary in type and intensity. **Intensity** refers to the physical strength of the stimulus. Psychophysics studies the relationship between the strength of a stimulus and the nature of the sensory response it creates.

Absolute threshold refers to the smallest amount of energy, the smallest intensity, needed to detect a stimulus. The absolute threshold for sight is illustrated by a candle burning at 30 miles on a dark night; for hearing, the ticking of a watch 20 feet away in a quiet room; for taste, one teaspoon of sugar in two gallons of water; for smell, one drop of perfume in three rooms; and for touch, a bee's wing falling one centimeter onto a cheek. **Noise** refers to the background stimulation for any of the senses.

The ability to detect a stimulus is influenced not only by the stimulus but also by conditions like expectations and experience. **Signal detection theory** attempts to explain the role of psychological factors in detecting stimuli. Two miscalculations are made: one, that a stimuli is present when it is not, and the other, that the stimuli is not present when it actually is. Signal detection theory has great practical importance, ranging from helping people who must distinguish various items on radar screens to improving how witnesses identify suspects in a police lineup.

The smallest noticeable difference between two stimuli is called the **difference threshold**, or the **just noticeable difference**. The amount of stimulus required for the just noticeable difference depends upon the level of the initial stimulus. **Weber's law** states that the just noticeable difference is a constant proportion for each sense. Weber's law is not very accurate at extreme high or low intensities.

After prolonged exposure to a sensory stimulus, the capacity of the sensory organ adjusts to the stimulus in a process called **adaptation**. The receptor cells are most responsive to changes in stimuli, because constant stimulation produces adaptation. Context also affects judgments about sensory stimuli. People's reactions to sensory stimuli do not always accurately represent the physical stimuli that cause it.

CONCEPT 2: **The Five + Senses**

Vision: The Eyes Have It

Survey: ☐
Read: ☐

Pages 105-117

Most psychological research has focused on vision and hearing. The stimulus that produces vision is **light**. Light is the electromagnetic radiation that our visual apparatus is capable of detecting. The range of visible light is called the **visual spectrum**.

Light enters the eye through the **cornea**, a transparent, protective window. It then passes through the **pupil**, the opening in the **iris**. The iris is the pigmented muscle that opens and closes the pupil depending on how much light is in the environment. The narrower the pupil is, the greater is the focal distance for the eye. After the pupil the light passes through the **lens**, which then bends and focuses the light on the back of the eye by changing its thickness, a process called **accommodation**. The light then strikes the **retina**, a thin layer of nerve cells at the back of the eyeball. The retina is composed of light-sensitive cells called rods, which are long and cylindrical, and cones, which are shorter and conical in shape. The greatest concentration of cones is in the **fovea**, an area that is extremely sensitive. Cones are responsible for color vision, and rods are insensitive to color and play a role in **peripheral vision**, the ability to see objects to our side, and in night vision.

Rods contain **rhodopsin**, a complex substance that changes chemically when struck by light. This chemical change sets off a reaction. The response is then transmitted to two other kinds of cells, first to the **bipolar cells** and then to **ganglion cells**. The ganglion cells organize and summarize the information and then convey it to the **optic nerve**. Where the optic nerve goes from the retina back through the eyeball there are no rods or cones, which results in the blind spot. The optic nerves from both eyes meet behind the eyes at the **optic chiasm** where each optic nerve splits. Nerve impulses from the right half of each eye go to the right side of the brain, and nerve impulses from the left half of each eye go to the left half of the brain. The disease called **glaucoma** is a restriction of the nerve impulses across the optic nerve. The restriction is caused by buildup of fluid in the eye, and as the pressure increases, the vision become more restricted, resulting in **tunnel vision**.

The visual message is processed from the beginning by ganglion cells, and continues to the visual cortex, where many neurons are highly specialized. Their roles are specialized to detect certain visual features, and the process is called **feature detection**.

When a person goes into a dark room from a well-lit space, **light adaptation** is experienced. Light adaptation is the temporary insensitivity to light dimmer than that to which the eye has most recently been exposed. After time, the person becomes accustomed to the dark and experiences **dark adaptation**, the adjustment to low levels of light. The changes that make this adjustment are chemical changes in the rods and cones.

A person with normal color vision can distinguish about seven million different colors. Color vision involves two processes. The first of these processes is called the **trichromatic theory of color vision**. The trichromatic theory says that there are three types of cones: one sensitive to blue-violet colors, another sensitive to green, and another sensitive to red-yellow. This theory does not explain how two colors mix to make gray, and it does not explain afterimages. **Opponent-process theory** explains afterimages as the result of the opposing color of linked pairs of cones continuing to compensate for the stimulation of the first color. Apparently, the trichromatic process is at work at the level of the retina, and the opponent processes are at work at the retina level and at later stages in the processing of visual information. The processing of visual information takes place in all parts of the visual system.

CONCEPT 3:   The Five + Senses (continued)
The Sense of Sound and Balance

Survey: ☐
Read: ☐

Pages 117-132

The **outer ear** collects sounds and guides them to the internal portions of the ear. **Sound** is the movement of air that results from the vibration of objects. Sounds are funneled into the **auditory canal** toward the **eardrum**. Sound waves hit the eardrum, which in turn transmits its vibrations into the **middle ear**. The middle ear contains three small bones, the **hammer**, the **anvil**, and the **stirrup**. These three bones transmit the vibrations to the **oval window**. Each step of the way amplifies the sound waves that reach the ear. The **inner ear** contains the organs for transmitting the sound waves into nerve impulses as well as the organs for balance and position. The **cochlea** is a coiled tube that contains the **basilar membrane**. The basilar membrane is covered with **hair cells** that vibrate. Sound may also enter the cochlea through the bones that surround the ear.

Sound is characterized by **frequency**, or the number of waves per second, and **pitch** is our experience of this number as high or low. **Intensity** may be thought of as the size of the waves—how strong it is. Intensity is measured in **decibels**. The **place theory of hearing** is based on the fact that parts of the basilar membrane are sensitive to different pitches. The **frequency theory of hearing** suggests that the entire basilar membrane vibrates in response to any sound, and the nerves send signals that are more frequent for higher pitches and less frequent for lower pitches. Both of these theories appear to have merit. The auditory cortex appears to be like a map of frequencies, with cells that respond to similar frequencies close to each other.

The inner ear is also responsible for the sense of balance. The disturbance of the sense of balance is called **vertigo**. The structures responsible for balance are the **semicircular canals**, three tubes filled with fluid that moves around in the tubes when the head moves. The fluid affects **otoliths**, small motion-sensitive crystals in the semicircular canals.

We are able to detect about 10,000 different smells, and women have a better sense of smell than do men. Some animals can communicate using odor. **Pheromones** are chemicals that can produce a reaction in members of a species. These chemicals have a role in sexual activity and identification. Odor is detected by molecules of a substance coming into contact with the **olfactory cells** in the nasal passages. Each olfactory cell responds to a narrow band of odors. Taste is detected by **taste buds** on the tongue. Taste buds detect sweet, sour, salty or bitter flavors. The experience of taste also includes the odor and appearance of food.

The **skin senses** include touch, pressure, temperature, and pain. Receptor cells for each of these senses are distributed all over the body, though each sense is distributed in varying concentrations. The major theory of pain is called the **gate-control theory of pain**. This theory states that nerve receptors send messages to the brain areas related to pain, and whenever they are activated, a "gate" to the brain is opened and pain is experienced. The gate can be shut by overwhelming the nerve pathways with non-painful messages. It can also be closed by the brain producing messages to reduce or eliminate the experience of pain. **Acupuncture** may be explained by the first option in which the needles shut off the messages going to the brain. Endorphins may also close the gate.

A number of methods for dealing with pain have been developed. They include drug therapy, hypnosis, biofeedback, relaxation techniques, surgery (cutting the nerve fiber that carries the pain message), nerve and brain stimulation (using **transcutaneous electrical nerve stimulation**, or **TENS**), and psychological counseling.

▶ Now that you have surveyed, questioned, and read the chapter and completed

the **Recap and Review** questions, review **Looking Back**, page 132–133.   *Review:* ☐

➤ For additional practice through recitation and review, test your knowledge of the chapter material by answering the questions in the **Key Word Drill**, the **Practice Questions**, and the **Essay Questions**.

KEY WORD DRILL	*Recite:* ☐

The following **Fill in the Blank** and **Matching Questions** test key words from the text. Check your answers with the Answer Key in the back of the *Study Guide*.

FILL IN THE BLANK

1. A _____ can be any source of physical energy that produces a response in a sense organ.

2. _____ studies the relationship between the physical nature of stimuli and a person's sensory responses to them.

3. _____ _____ theory acknowledges that observers may miscalculate in one of two ways, ether by reporting that a physical stimulus is present when it is not or by failing to report when it is, and the theory uses data about these miscalculations to address the role of psychological factors in our ability to identify stimuli.

4. The range of wavelengths to which humans are sensitive is known as _____

   _____.

5. The ability of the lens to vary its shape in order to focus incoming images on the retina is called

   _____ and _____ refers to an adjustment in sensory capacity following prolonged exposure to stimuli.

6. _____ _____ is the ability to see objects outside the eyes' main center of focus.

7. The _____ theory of color vision suggests that the retina has three kinds of cones, each responding to a specific range of wavelengths, perception of color being influenced by the relative strength with which each is activated.

8. The _____-_____ theory of color vision suggests that receptor cells are linked in pairs, working in opposition to each other.

9. At least 1000 separate _____ _____ have been identified so far, and each of these responds to a very small band of different odors.

10. The _____ theory of hearing states that different frequencies are responded

    to by different areas of the basilar membrane; and the _____ theory of hearing suggests that the entire basilar membrane acts like a microphone, vibrating in response to sound.

MATCHING QUESTIONS

_____ 11. sensation

_____ 12. intensity

_____ 13. absolute threshold

_____ 14. noise

_____ 15. difference threshold

a. The strength of a stimulus.

b. The smallest detectable difference between two stimuli.

c. The process of responding to a stimulus.

d. The smallest amount of physical intensity by which a stimulus can be detected.

e. Background stimulation that interferes with the perception of other stimuli.

_____ 16. pupil

_____ 17. cornea

_____ 18. iris

_____ 19. lens

_____ 20. retina

_____ 21. fovea

_____ 22. rhodopsin

a. The colored part of the eye.

b. The part of the eye that converts the electromagnetic energy of light into useful information for the brain.

c. A complex reddish-purple substance that changes when energized by light, causing a chemical reaction.

d. A dark hole in the center of the eye's iris which changes size as the amount of incoming light changes.

e. A very sensitive region of the retina that aids in focusing.

f. A transparent, protective window into the eyeball.

g. The part of the eye located behind the pupil that bends rays of light to focus them on the retina.

_____ 23. rods

_____ 24. bipolar cells

_____ 25. bipolar cells

_____ 26. ganglion cells

_____ 27. optic nerve

a. Light-sensitive receptors that are responsible for sharp focus and color perception, particularly in bright light.

b. Nerve cells that collect and summarize information from rods and carry it to the brain.

c. Nerve cells leading to the brain that are triggered by nerve cells in the eye.

d. Light-sensitive receptors that perform well in poor light but are largely insensitive to color and small details.

e. A bundle of ganglion axons in the back of the eyeball that carry visual information to the brain.

_____ 28. outer ear

_____ 29. auditory canal

_____ 30. eardrum

_____ 31. middle ear

_____ 32. hammer

_____ 33. anvil

_____ 34. stirrup

_____ 35. oval window

a. A small bone in the middle ear that transfers vibrations to the oval window.

b. The visible part of the ear that acts as a collector to bring sounds into the internal portions of the ear.

c. A tiny chamber containing three bones—the hammer, the anvil, and the stirrup—which transmit vibrations to the oval window.

d. The part of the ear that vibrates when sound waves hit it.

e. A thin membrane between the middle ear and the inner ear that transmits vibrations while increasing their strength.

f. A tubelike passage in the ear through which sound moves to the eardrum.

g. A tiny bone in the middle ear that transfers vibrations to the anvil.

h. A minute bone in the middle ear that transfers vibrations to the stirrup.

_____ 36. cochlea

_____ 37. basilar membrane

_____ 38. hair cells

_____ 39. frequency

_____ 40. pitch

_____ 41. decibel

_____ 42. otoliths

a. A measure of sound loudness or intensity.

b. The number of wave crests occurring each second in any particular sound.

c. A structure dividing the cochlea into an upper and a lower chamber.

d. A coiled tube filled with fluid that receives sound via the oval window or through bone conduction.

e. Crystals in the semicircular canals that sense body acceleration.

f. The characteristic that makes sound "high" or "low."

g. Tiny cells that, when bent by vibrations entering the cochlea, transmit neural messages to the brain.

_____ 43. glaucoma

_____ 44. feature detection

_____ 45. light adaptation

_____ 46. dark adaptation

_____ 47. afterimage

a. The activation of neurons in the cortex by visual stimuli of specific shapes or patterns.

b. A heightened sensitivity to light resulting from being in low-level light.

c. The eye's temporary insensitivity to light dimmer than that to which it has most recently been exposed.

d. A dysfunction of the eye in which fluid pressure builds up and causes a decline in visual acuity.

e. The image appearing when the eyes shift from a particular image to a blank area.

PRACTICE QUESTIONS

Recite and Review: ❑

Test your knowledge of the chapter material by answering these **True-False** and **Multiple Choice Questions.** Check your answers with the Answer Key in the back of the _Study Guide._

TRUE-FALSE QUESTIONS

T   F   1. The study of the relationship between the physical nature of stimuli and a person's sensory responses to them is called psychophysics.

T   F   2. Noise is defined as sounds above 10,000 cycles per second that is over 50 decibels.

T   F   3. A candle flame can be seen 45 miles away on a dark, clear night.

T   F   4. The structure which converts electromagnetic radiation into neural impulses is called the cornea.

T   F   5. When viewing a constellation of stars at night, you will see it most clearly if you focus directly at it.

T   F   6. Glaucoma, a disorder that may result in loss of vision, is most common in adults between 20 and 35 years of age.

T   F   7. When people walk from a darkened room into bright sunlight, until light adaptation occurs they will experience the sunlight as annoyingly bright.

T   F   8. The outer ear contains no neural receptors that communicate vibrations to the brain.

T   F   9. The basilar membrane divides the cochlea into two sections.

T   F   10. According to the text, pheromones play a significant role in human sexual responses.

MULTIPLE CHOICE QUESTIONS

1. _____ is to pinprick as _____ is to sharp pain.
   a. Threshold; just noticeable difference
   b. Stimulus; sensation
   c. Difference threshold; context
   d. Sensory adaptation; short-duration stimulation

2. The physical energy that activates a sense organ is called a:
   a. sensation.   c. transmitter.
   b. stimulus.   d. threshold.

3. The study of the relationship between the physical nature of stimuli and a person's sensory responses to them is called:
   a. introspection.   c. psychophysics.
   b. operationalization.   d. perception.

4. Psychophysicists define absolute threshold as the:
   a. minimum amount of change in stimulation which is detectable.
   b. range of stimulation to which each sensory channel is sensitive.
   c. maximum intensity which is detectable to the senses.
   d. minimum magnitude of stimulus which is detectable.

5. An absolute threshold:
   a. is similar for a given sense (e.g., vision) in humans and in various animals.
   b. demonstrates that the amount of energy required to stimulate the eye, ear, skin, and other receptors is very similar.
   c. is the minimum physical energy required to produce a response to sensory stimulation in a sense receptor.
   d. is the degree of change required in sensory stimulation in order for the stimulus to be detected as different.

6. Your text defines noise as:
   a. background stimulation that interferes with other stimuli.
   b. sounds that the individual finds distasteful.
   c. stimuli that interfere with healthy bodily functioning.
   d. the relative amount of auditory stimulation in urban versus rural areas.

7. An antiaircraft operator watching a radar scope may fail to identify the blips signaling the presence of an aircraft because they occur so infrequently. This suggests that:
   a. expectations about the frequency of events influence detection.
   b. detection of a stimulus depends only upon sensory factors.
   c. radar operators are highly atypical in their sensitivity to stimulation.
   d. past exposure is relatively unimportant in stimulus detection.

8. The objective of signal detection theory in psychophysics is to:
   a. determine absolute thresholds.
   b. explain the role of psychological factors.
   c. explain magnitude estimation.
   d. determine the nature of the stimulus.

9. When you first visit a farm you notice noxious odors. After only one week you no longer notice them. This example illustrates the value of:
   a. sensory adaptation.
   b. the just noticeable difference.
   c. Weber's law.
   d. signal detection theory.

10. Sensory adaptation is the same as:
    a. getting used to a stimulus.
    b. first being aware of a stimulus.
    c. noticing a slight increase in a stimulus.
    d. sensing a stimulus that is not there.

11. Sam rented an apartment just across the street from the fire station. At first, he woke up every time the siren went off at night. After a few weeks, however, Sam failed to notice the siren and slept right through it. This example illustrates:
    a. signal detection theory.
    b. Weber's law.
    c. a just noticeable difference.
    d. absolute thresholds.

12. The text compares the structure of the human eye to the structure of:
    a. a light funnel.
    b. a camera.
    c. an antenna.
    d. a computer.

13. As the available light diminishes, the pupil:
    a. gets larger.
    b. gets smaller.
    c. remains the same.
    d. changes according to the wavelength of the light.

14. The function of the pupil is to:
    a. protect the rest of the eye.
    b. bring objects into focus.
    c. regulate the amount of light entering the eye.
    d. filter the color of incoming light.

15. The process that causes incoming images to be focused in the eye is called:
    a. accommodation.
    b. constriction.
    c. adaptation.
    d. contraction.

16. Which statement about the rods and the cones of the retina is accurate?
    a. The rods are concentrated in the fovea of the retina; the cones are in the periphery.
    b. The rods are the receptors for dim illumination; the cones are for high illumination levels.
    c. The rods are responsible for the first 0-10 minutes of the dark adaptation curve; the cones are responsible for the remaining 11-40 minutes.
    d. Cones are found in larger numbers on the retina than are rods.

17. The function of the retina is to:
    a. turn the image of the object upside down.
    b. redistribute the light energy in the image.
    c. convert the light energy into neural impulses.
    d. control the size of the pupil.

18. Which of the following are found primarily in the fovea of the retina?
    a. ganglion cells
    b. rods
    c. bipolar cells
    d. cones

19. The visual receptors most useful for night vision are called:
    a. buds.
    b. cones.
    c. ossicles.
    d. rods.

20. What portion of the eye is blind at night?
    a. the muscles
    b. the fovea
    c. the rods
    d. the cornea

21. Which type of receptor is used in peripheral vision?
    a. cone
    b. rod
    c. fovea
    d. rhodopsin

22. The blind spot is located:
    a. at the center of the iris.
    b. in the fovea.
    c. at the opening for the optic nerve.
    d. at the corner of the lens.

23. One of the most frequent causes of blindness is:
    a. an underproduction of rhodopsin.
    b. a restriction of impulses across the optic nerve.
    c. tunnel vision.
    d. an inability of the pupil to expand.

24. Glaucoma may lead to blindness through:
    a. deterioration of the cones.
    b. deterioration of the rods.
    c. buildup of the myelin sheaths around the optic nerve.
    d. buildup of pressure within the eye.

25. Feature detection is best described as the process by which specialized neurons in the cortex:
    a. identify fine details in a larger pattern.
    b. see things clearly that are far away.
    c. discriminate one face from another.
    d. recognize particular shapes or patterns.

26. The most complex processing of visual information takes place in the highly specialized cells of the:
    a. retina.
    b. optic chiasm.
    c. cortex.
    d. optic tract.

27. Dark adaptation refers to the fact that:
    a. our eyes are less sensitive to a dim stimulus when we look directly at it rather than slightly to the side of it.
    b. the color of objects changes at dusk as light intensity decreases.
    c. the eyes become many times more sensitive after being exposed to darkness.
    d. some people have great difficulty seeing things under low levels of illumination.

28. The trichromatic theory is based on the assumption that:
    a. there are three different kinds of cones in the retina.
    b. each cone can respond to only three different colors.
    c. the retina is divided into three areas which have different densities of rods versus cones.
    d. light passes through three tiny filters as it is detected in the cone.

29. According to the text, afterimages can best be explained by the:
    a. opponent-process theory of color vision.
    b. trichromatic theory of color vision.
    c. place theory of color vision.
    d. receptive-field theory of color vision.

30. The primary function of the hammer, anvil, and stirrup in the middle ear is to:
    a. protect the inner ear from infection.
    b. suppress interference from the visual system.
    c. transmit vibrations to the oval window.
    d. conduct sound toward the eardrum.

31. People hear the sound of their own voice differently from the way others hear it primarily because of:
    a. bone conduction.
    b. tympanic vibrations.
    c. low-frequency vibrations.
    d. gradual hearing loss associated with age.

32. Suppose you could hear nothing but your own voice. Of the following, which might your physician suspect as the source of the problem?
    a. the cochlea.
    b. the basilar membrane.
    c. the auditory cortex.
    d. the middle ear.

33. A neural message is sent to the brain through the auditory nerve when the:
    a. hair cells on the basilar membrane are bent.
    b. oval window is activated by the ossicle.
    c. eardrum is stimulated.
    d. auditory cortex is activated by the eardrum.

34. On a piano keyboard, the keys for the lower-frequency sounds are on the left side; the keys for the higher-frequency sounds are on the right. If you first pressed a key on the left side of the keyboard, and then a key on the right side, you might expect that:
    a. pitch would depend on how hard the keys were struck.
    b. the pitch would be lower for the first key that was played.
    c. the pitch would be lower for the second key that was played.
    d. the pitch would be identical for each.

35. Intensity is to _____ as frequency is to _____.
    a. resonance; loudness
    b. loudness; pitch
    c. acoustic nerve; auditory canal
    d. external ear; consonance

36. Which of the following would refer to the number of wave crests that occur in a second when a tuning fork is struck?
    a. pitch
    b. intensity
    c. decibel level
    d. frequency

37. Loudness is to _____ as frequency is to _____.
    a. decibels; cycles per second
    b. millimicrometers; loudness
    c. cycles per second; wavelength
    d. cochlea; auditory nerve

38. The _____ theory of hearing states that different sound frequencies stimulate different areas of the basilar membrane.
    a. place
    b. opponent-process
    c. frequency
    d. volley

39. Which sensory structure below is **not** associated with the function that follows it?
    a. otoliths; balance
    b. eardrum; hearing
    c. anvil; taste
    d. rod; vision

40. Which of the following is most responsible for space sickness?
    a. the cochlea
    b. the muscle spindle
    c. the middle ear
    d. the otoliths

41. Which statement about smell is **not** correct?
    a. Some animals have lower olfactory thresholds than humans.
    b. People over 60 years of age do not sense odors as well as younger people.
    c. The olfactory sensitivities do not differ between men and women.
    d. A small number of people have no olfactory sensitivity at all.

42. According to the text, which factor does **not** influence the sense of smell in humans?
    a. illness
    b. smoking
    c. age
    d. weight

43. Chemical molecules that promote communication between members of a species are called:
    a. pheromones.
    b. neurotransmitters.
    c. hormones.
    d. odorants.

44. The receptors in the nose are called:
    a. pheromones.
    b. olfactory cells.
    c. rhodopsin.
    d. opponent processes.

45. The sense of taste and the sense of smell are alike in that they both:
    a. have four basic qualities of sensation.
    b. depend on chemical molecules as stimuli.
    c. use the same area of the cortex.
    d. utilize opponent processes.

46. Which statement about the taste buds is accurate?
    a. Each receptor is able to respond to many basic tastes and to send the information to the brain.
    b. Over twelve types of receptors for different basic flavors have been described.
    c. Taste receptors on the tongue, the sides and roof of the mouth, and the top part of the throat send complex information about taste to the brain, where it is interpreted.
    d. Receptors for the four basic flavors are located on different areas of the tongue.

47. Which alternative below is **not** one of the four basic tastes?
    a. sweet
    b. tangy
    c. sour
    d. salty

48. Which of the following theories holds that certain nerve receptors lead to specific areas of the brain that sense pain?
    a. endorphin
    b. opiate
    c. opponent process
    d. gate control

49. The gate control theory relates to the sensation of:
    a. pain.
    b. taste.
    c. smell.
    d. ticklishness.

50. The most common treatment for reducing pain is:
    a. surgery.
    b. biofeedback.
    c. drug therapy.
    d. relaxation.

51. Which statement about pain relief is **not** accurate?
    a. Stimulation by low-voltage electrical current applied to certain areas of the body can relieve pain.
    b. Techniques which teach people how to relax their bodies are sometimes helpful in reducing pain.
    c. Biofeedback can relieve pain if the painful impulses sent to the brain can be electronically amplified and displayed so the person experiencing the pain can be trained to control them.
    d. Medications for pain may bring some relief.

| ESSAY QUESTIONS | *Recite and Review:* ☐ |

Essay Question 4.1: *Understanding Color Vision*

Compare the two theories of color vision. Describe the experience one who is color blind would have. Is it simply like watching a black and white movie, or is there more to it? What would be the problems encountered by the color-blind?

_____

_____

_____

_____

_____

_____

_____

_____

_____

_____

_____

_____

_____

_____

_____

_____

_____

Essay Question 4.2: *The Problem of Extra Senses*

Consider what it would be like if our senses were not within their present limits. What visual problems might we face? What would we hear if our hearing had a different range? What if we were more sensitive to smell? What about the other senses?

_____

_____

_____

_____

_____

_____

_____

_____

_____

_____

_____

_____

_____

_____

_____

_____

_____

ACTIVITIES AND PROJECTS

1. Fill in the labels that are missing from this diagram of the eye.

2. Fill in the labels that are missing from this diagram of the ear.

Inner Ear

Semicircular canals
(contain otolith)

5

PERCEPTION

| DETAILED OUTLINE | *Survey:* ☐ |

This detailed outline contains all the headings in Chapter 5: Perception. If you are using the SQ3R method, then an examination of the outline is the best way to begin your survey of the chapter.

Prologue: Flight 901
Looking Ahead

Perceptual Organization: Our View of the World
 The gestalt laws of organization
  Figure and ground: Half full or half empty?
  The whole is greater than its parts: Where one plus one equals more than two
 Feature analysis: Focusing on the parts of the whole
The Cutting Edge Perceiving the Spoken Word
 Top-down and bottom-up processing
● **Recap and Review I**

 Perceptual constancy
 Depth perception: Translating 2-D to 3-D
 Motion perception: As the world turns
 Selective attention: Sorting out the world
Psychology at Work Subliminal Messages: Undercover Perception?
● **Recap and Review II**

Perception in Everyday Life
 Visual illusions: Misperceptions of the eye
The Informed Consumer of Psychology Discovering and Treating Dyslexia
● **Recap and Review III**

Looking Back
Key Terms and Concepts

➤ Now that you have surveyed the chapter, read **Looking Ahead**, pages 136–137. *Question:* ☐
Focus on the questions on page 137. *Read:* ☐

CONCEPTS AND LEARNING OBJECTIVES

These are the concepts and the learning objects for Chapter 5. Read them carefully as part of your preliminary survey of the chapter.

Concept 1: Perception is the means of organizing and giving meaning to sensory information. The gestalt approach begins with perceptual organization founded on basic laws of organization. Feature analysis identifies the components of sensory information and combines them into complex perception.

1. Define perception and distinguish it from sensation. (pp. 136-137)

2. Distinguish the gestalt approach from feature analysis. (pp. 137-141)

3. Distinguish top-down and bottom-up processing. (pp. 141-143)

Concept 2: The characteristics of perception include perceptual constancy, the ability to perceive depth even though the retinal image is two-dimensional, and the selective nature of attention.

4. Describe the types of perceptual constancy and how it affects perception, and contrast constructive and ecological theories of perceptual constancy. (pp. 144-146)

5. Describe how depth perception is achieved through binocular disparity and monocular clues. (pp. 146-149)

6. Describe how motion is perceived. (p. 149)

7. Discuss the role of selective attention in perception and the possibility of perception occurring beyond our awareness through subliminal perception. (pp. 149-153)

Concept 3: Visual illusions are misperceptions that arise as a result of the nature of some physical stimuli. Like an illusion, dyslexia reverses many features of written letters, creating a reading disability.

8. Describe and illustrate the major illusions, especially the Müller-Lyer and the Poggendorf illusions. (pp. 153-158)

9. Describe the symptoms, effects, and treatments of dyslexia. (pp. 158-159)

CHAPTER SUMMARY

There are several ways you can use this summary as part of your systematic study plan. You may read each concept summary and then read the corresponding pages in the text, or you may read the entire summary and then read the entire chapter in the text. As you finish each section, complete the **Recap and Review** questions that are supplied in the text.

CONCEPT 1:   **Prologue and Looking Ahead**   *Survey:* ☐
                 Perceptual Organization: Our View of the World   *Read:* ☐

Pages 136-144

The fate of Flight 901 illustrates that visual illusions can lead to extremely serious misjudgments. Human perceptual errors play a central role in many airline fatalities. Errors in perception occur because **perception** is an *interpretation* of sensory information. The difference between perception and sensation is that sensation involves the organism's first encounter with physical stimuli, and perception is the process of interpreting, analyzing, and integrating sensations.

Through perception we try to simplify complex stimuli in the environment. This tendency toward simplicity and organization into meaningful wholes follows basic principles called the **gestalt laws of organization**. **Gestalt** refers to a "pattern." Basic patterns identified by the gestalt psychologists are: (1) *closure*, groupings tend to be in complete or enclosed figures; (2) *proximity*, elements close together tend to be grouped together; (3) *similarity*, elements that are similar tend to be grouped together; and (4) *simplicity*, the tendency to organize patterns in a basic, straightforward manner.

The distinction between **figure** and **ground** is crucial to perceptual organization. The tendency is to form an object in contrast to its ground, or background. This is illustrated by the two faces versus a single vase. Because we must actively organize this figure, we cannot see both the faces and the vase at the same time. The gestalt psychologists argued that perception goes beyond combining individual elements and that when we organize the elements, we actively make the result more than the parts.

In contrast to the gestalt view that we perceive by putting elements into an organized whole, the recent approach called **feature analysis** suggests that we perceive first the individual components and then formulate an understanding of the overall picture. Specific neurons respond to highly specific components of stimuli, suggesting that each stimuli is composed of a series of component features. In this view, our perception involves matching new stimuli to components in memory. Biederman has identified thirty-six fundamental components, called **geons**, that form the basic components of complex objects. The three steps of feature analysis are: (1) identify component features; (2) combine the features; and (3) compare the combined features to existing memories.

Perception proceeds in two ways, though top-down or through bottom-up processing. In **top-down processing** perception is controlled by higher-level knowledge, experience, expectations, and motivation. Top-down processing helps sort through ambiguous stimuli or missing elements. Context is critical for filling in missing information. Isolated stimuli illustrate how context is important for top-down processing. **Bottom-up processing** consists of recognizing and processing information about individual components. If we cannot recognize individual components, recognizing the complete picture would be very difficult. Both processes are at work simultaneously in perception.

CONCEPT 2:   **Perceptual Organization: Our View of the World (cont.)**   *Survey:* ☐
                 Perceptual Constancy   *Read:* ☐

Pages 144-153

One phenomenon that contributes to our perception of the world is that of **perceptual constancy**, the tendency for objects to be perceived as unvarying and consistent even as we see them from different views and distances. The rising moon is one example of how perceptual constancy works. The moon illusion is explained as resulting from the intervening cues of landscape and horizon which give it context. When it rises, there are no context cues. Perceptual constancies occur with size, shape, and color. Perceptual constancy depends upon experience, as cross-cultural studies have illustrated. Two theories have been offered to account for perceptual constancy. The **constructive theory** states that prior experience and expectations are used to make judgments about location of objects that have a known size. We then infer location because of our prior experience of size. Ecological theory states that relationships between different objects provide clues about size and location. The appearance of the surface textures of distant objects will be different, thus allowing a direct judgment about location.

The ability to view the world in three dimensions is very important to our ability to get around in it. This ability is called **depth perception**. Depth perception is primarily a result of our having two eyes. The main aspect of having two eyes is that the two slightly different positions of the eyes give rise to minute differences in the visual representation in the brain, a phenomenon called **binocular disparity**. Discrepancy between the two images from the retinas gives clues to the distance of the object or the distance between two objects. The larger the disparity, the larger the distance. Two ears develop the same kind of disparity that helps us locate the sources of sounds. Other cues for visual depth perception can be seen with only one eye, and so they are called **monocular cues**. **Motion parallax** is a monocular cue in which the position of distant objects moves on the retina slower than does the position of closer objects when the head moves. **Relative size** depends on the distant object having a smaller retinal image. **Linear perspective** is the phenomenon where railroad tracks appear to join together.

Motion perception judges the movement of objects relevant to stable objects. However, our perception compensates for head and eye movements. When objects move too fast for the eye to follow, we tend to anticipate the direction and speed of movement.

Selective attention refers to the process by which we choose which stimulus we will focus upon. We attend to the bright, large, loud, novel, or contrasting stimulus. Meaning and interest also attract our attention to stimuli. The **Stroop task** illustrates a situation during which our attention can be divided between two kinds of stimuli. The task requires the subject to attend to both the color and the meaning of a word, and the word "red" may be colored blue or green (see Figure 5-10). Selective attention in the auditory system is tested using **dichotic listening** procedure in which a person hears a different message in each ear. The person is asked to repeat, called **shadowing**, the message that is coming to one ear. The individual is then asked about the message heard in the other ear. People are able to recall whether the voice was male or female and whether their name was mentioned. The importance of the message in the shadowed ear is also important, and if the message shifts to the other ear, the listener will switch ears also. **Subliminal perception** is the process of perceiving messages without our awareness of their being presented. Research has shown that the subliminal message does not lead to attitude or behavior change. Selective attention can have negative consequences if people fail to attend to important information that then leads to accidents. Research has developed principles for designing instruments to prevent errors. They include minimizing the number of sources of information, simplifying the display, and keeping the sources close together.

SECTION 3: Perception in Everyday Life

Survey: ☐
Read: ☐

Pages 153-160

The importance of our knowledge about perception has been evident since the time of the ancient Greeks. The Parthenon in Athens is built with an intentional illusion to give the building a greater appearance of straightness and stability. **Visual illusions** are physical stimuli that produce errors in perception. The **Poggendorf illusion** and the **Müller-Lyer illusion** are two of the more well-known illusions. Explanations of the Müller-Lyer illusion focus on the apparatus of the eye and the interpretations made by the brain. The eye-based explanation suggests that the eyes are more active where the arrow tips point inward, giving the illusion of greater length. The brain-base explanation suggests that we interpret the lines with the inward arrows as being interior spaces and the outward pointing lines as close exterior spaces. In comparison the inside corner then seems larger. Cultural differences play an important role also. We have difficulty drawing the "devil's tuning fork" because it is contradictory to our expectations. However, for individuals for whom the picture has no meaning, it is easy to draw by simply copying the lines.

The suspected cause of **dyslexia** is a brain malfunction related to vision. Dyslexics tend to reverse letters, have difficulty distinguishing left from right, make unusual spelling errors, and appear more clumsy than their peers. Treatment techniques include sounding out words, repetitive practice with making the sound of a letter, writing it, and viewing it. Self-esteem and self-confidence are also very important.

➤ Now that you have surveyed, questioned, and read the chapter and completed

the **Recap and Review** questions, review **Looking Back**, pages 160–161.   *Review:* ☐

➤ For additional practice through recitation and review, test your knowledge of the chapter material by answering the questions in the *Key Word Drill*, the *Practice Questions*, and the *Essay Questions*.

| **KEY WORD DRILL** | *Recite:* ☐ |

The following **Fill in the Blank** and **Matching Questions** test key words from the text. Check your answers with the Answer Key in the back of the *Study Guide*.

FILL IN THE BLANK

1. _____ is the sorting out, interpretation, analysis, and integration of sensations from our sensory organs.

2. A series of principles, the _____ _____ of organization describe how we organize pieces of information into meaningful wholes.

3. In _____ _____ perception of a shape, pattern, object, or scene occurs by responding to the individual elements that make it up.

4. Psychologists describe perception guided by knowledge, experience, expectations, and motivations as

   _____-_____ processing; and recognition and processing of information about the individual components of a stimulus is considered

   _____-_____ processing.

5. _____ theory suggests that prior experience and expectations about the size of an object are used to make inferences about its location.

6. _____ theory suggests that the relationship between objects in a scene give clues about the objects' sizes.

7. The perception of messages about which a person has no awareness is called

_____ _____.

8. With the _____ illusion, a line passes diagonally through two parallel lines.

9. In the _____-_____ illusion, two lines of the same length appear to be of different lengths because of the direction of the arrows at the ends of each line; the line with arrows pointing out appears shorter than the line with arrows pointing in.

10. _____ is a disability with a perceptual basis that can result in the reversal of letters during reading and writing, confusion between left and right, and difficulties in spelling.

MATCHING QUESTIONS

_____ 11. gestalts

_____ 12. closure

_____ 13. proximity

_____ 14. similarity

_____ 15. simplicity

_____ 16. figure/ground

_____ 17. geons

a. The tendency to group together those elements that are similar in appearance.

b. The thirty-six fundamental component elements that when combined can produce more than 150 million objects.

c. Patterns studied by the gestalt psychologists.

d. The tendency to perceive a pattern in the most basic, straightforward, organized manner possible—the overriding gestalt principle.

e. The tendency to group together those elements that are close together.

f. Figure refers to the object being perceived, whereas ground refers to the background or spaces within the object.

g. The tendency to group according to enclosed or complete figures rather than open or incomplete ones.

_____ 18. perceptual constancy

_____ 19. depth perception

_____ 20. binocular disparity

_____ 21. monocular cues

_____ 22. motion parallax

_____ 23. relative size

a. The ability to view the world in three dimensions and to perceive distance.

b. The change in position of the image of an object on the retina as the head moves, providing a monocular cue to distance.

c. The phenomenon by which, if two objects are the same size, the one that makes a smaller image on the retina is perceived to be farther away, a monocular cue.

d. The phenomenon by which physical objects are perceived as unvarying despite changes in their appearance or the physical environment.

e. Signals that allow us to perceive distance and depth with just one eye.

f. The difference between the images that reach the retina of each eye; this disparity allows the brain to estimate distance.

_____ 24. linear perspective

_____ 25. selective attention

_____ 26. Stroop task

_____ 27. dichotic listening

_____ 28. shadowing

_____ 29. visual illusion

a. A physical stimulus that consistently produces errors in perception (often called an optical illusion).

b. A procedure in which an individual wears earphones through which different messages are sent to each ear at the same time.

c. The perceptual process of choosing a stimulus to focus attention upon.

d. A technique used during dichotic listening in which a subject is asked to repeat one of the messages aloud as it comes into one ear.

e. An exercise requiring the division of our attention between two competing stimuli—the meaning of words and the colors in which they are written.

f. The phenomenon by which distant objects appear to be closer together than nearer objects, a monocular cue.

| **PRACTICE QUESTIONS** |

Recite and Review: ❏

Test your knowledge of the chapter material by answering these **True-False** and **Multiple Choice Questions**. Check your answers with the Answer Key in the back of the *Study Guide*.

TRUE-FALSE QUESTIONS

T   F   1. Perception is generally considered to involve simpler and more fundamental processes than sensation.

T   F   2. Perception is an ongoing process through which we attempt to create a meaningful situation from our sensory input.

T   F   3. Learning and experience play an important role in perception.

T   F   4. The fact that you perceive the color of your favorite shirt as being the same regardless of the lighting conditions is due to color constancy.

T   F   5. Ecological theory and constructive theory are sometimes used to explain figure/ground phenomena.

T   F   6. A person who has been blind in one eye most of her life probably should not fly an airplane, since she lacks depth perception.

T   F   7. According to the theory of selective attention, if you are considering buying a certain model of car, you are more likely to notice a car of this model when it passes on the road.

T   F   8. Visual illusions can occur because of cultural factors.

T   F   9. Dyslexics are generally less intelligent than nondyslexics and therefore have to work harder.

T   F   10. There is no known treatment to improve the language skills of dyslexic youngsters.

T   F   11. According to research presented in the text, many of the limitations of dyslexia can be overcome by training.

MULTIPLE CHOICE QUESTIONS

1. Perception differs from sensation in that:
   a. perception is less dependent upon prior learning and experience.
   b. perception considers only information from the receptors, without the need for higher mental processing while sensation requires higher mental processing.
   c. perception is less dependent upon the organism's developmental history.
   d. perception involves interpretation, analysis, and integration of sensory information while sensation provides sensory information.

2. According to your text, one of the principal functions served by perception is to:
    a. stabilize figure/ground relationships.
    b. simplify the complexity of environmental stimuli.
    c. code stimuli into neural messages.
    d. transfer sensations directly into memory.

3. In the study of perception, "gestalts" refers to:
    a. patterns.
    b. colors.
    c. monochromatic stimuli.
    d. auditory stimuli.

4. The gestalt laws of organization are best described as:
    a. patterns of perceiving determined by specific functions of neural receptors.
    b. principles that describe how people perceive.
    c. an explanation for how neural networks in the sensory system operate.
    d. explanations of how people determine the quality of a work of art.

5. The early psychologists who contributed most to our understanding of perception were the:
    a. gestalt psychologists.
    b. behaviorists.
    c. psychoanalysts.
    d. functionalists.

6. One of the basic processes we use to reduce the world of stimuli into something understandable is:
    a. simplification.
    b. edification.
    c. reduction.
    d. complication.

7. Closure refers to:
    a. the basic element.
    b. filling in gaps.
    c. constancy.
    d. grouping together like elements.

8. Look at these letters: *ppp ppp ppp ppp*. You see four groups, each containing three *p*'s, rather than a single row of twelve *p*'s because of the gestalt principle known as:
    a. similarity.
    b. proximity.
    c. closure.
    d. constancy.

9. When you look at 000 XXX 000 XXX you tend to see groups of 0's and X's. This tendency best illustrates the gestalt laws of:
    a. closure and proximity.
    b. simplicity and similarity.
    c. perspective and simplicity.
    d. similarity and proximity.

10. The fact that a number of instruments all blend together to form a symphony orchestra demonstrates:
    a. a figure/ground relationship.
    b. the law of similarity.
    c. that the whole is more than the sum of its parts.
    d. the law of perceptual constancy.

11. An interesting reversible figure/ground stimulus for perceptual demonstrations:
    a. has a predominant ground.
    b. has a predominant figure.
    c. always gives the same dramatic visual image, no matter how it is viewed.
    d. has a figure and a ground that can alternate when viewed in certain ways.

12. A shopper sorts a large pile of grocery coupons into similar groupings, such as dairy items, vegetables, and fruits. This activity illustrates the gestalt principle of:
    a. figure/group.   c. proximity.
    b. closure.   d. similarity.

13. Which principle of perceptual organization is used when we group items together that look alike or have the same form?
    a. proximity   c. figure/ground
    b. similarity   d. closure

14. According to which gestalt principle do we perceive a pattern in the most basic, straightforward manner?
    a. closure   c. similarity
    b. proximity   d. simplicity

15. Perception that is guided by higher-level knowledge, experience, expectations, and motivations is called:
    a. top-down processing.   c. perceptual constancy.
    b. bottom-up processing. d. feature analysis.

16. Top-down processing depends on all of the following except:
    a. expectation.   c. motivation.
    b. experience.   d. relative size.

17. Making sense of a verbal message by first understanding each word and then piecing them together is:
    a. top-down processing.   c. selective attention.
    b. bottom-up processing. d. perceptual constancy.

18. Top-down processing allows you to:
    a. perceive depth with one eye.
    b. fill in the gaps.
    c. perceive motion.
    d. concentrate on individual elements of a stimulus.

19. As you look at a car, you can see only the last part of the make, reading "mobile." You determine that the car is probably an Oldsmobile. This illustrates:
    a. top-down processing.   c. selective attention.
    b. bottom-up processing. d. feature analysis.

20. Objects are perceived as unvarying despite changes in their appearance or the surrounding environment because of:
    a. similarity.
    b. simplicity.
    c. closure.
    d. constancy.

21. We can judge the size of a large rock by viewing a person standing in front of it. This illustrates:
    a. feature analysis.
    b. ecological theory.
    c. the gestalt laws of organization.
    d. constructive theory.

22. Which of the following suggests that the relationships among different objects in a scene give us clues about their sizes?
    a. perceptual constancy
    b. ecological theory
    c. the gestalt laws of organization
    d. constructive theory

23. The idea that perceptual constancy is brought about by direct perception of all the stimuli in a scene is the basis of:
    a. constructive theory.
    b. the overriding gestalt principle of simplicity.
    c. ecological theory.
    d. the law of proximity.

24. Binocular disparity refers to the fact that:
    a. the world looks different with prescription glasses than without.
    b. objects appear closer when they are larger.
    c. the visual image on the retina of each eye is slightly different.
    d. objects progressing into the distance, such as railroad tracks, appear to converge.

25. The brain estimates the distance to an object by comparing the different images that it gets from the right and left retinas using:
    a. the gestalt principle of figure/ground.
    b. binocular disparity.
    c. monocular cues.
    d. motion parallax.

26. Which one of the following statements concerning depth perception is true?
    a. It is not always necessary to use two eyes to perceive depth.
    b. Distant objects appear smaller because of linear perspective.
    c. The greater the discrepancy between two retinal images, the more difficult it is to reconcile depth.
    d. If two objects are the same size, the one that projects the smaller image on the retina is closer.

27. The text describes all of the following as monocular cues for depth perception **except**:
    a. perceptual constancy.
    b. relative size.
    c. motion parallax.
    d. linear perspective.

28. Railroad tracks appear to come closer together as they move away from the observer as a result of:
    a. linear perspective.
    c. binocular disparity.
    b. figure/ground.
    d. motion parallax.

29. Suppose that you happened upon two buffalo grazing in an open field. Although both had horns, one buffalo looked substantially larger than the other. You would assume, on the basis of relative size, that:
    a. the smaller one was a baby.
    b. the larger one was farther away.
    c. they were both at the same distance.
    d. the smaller one was farther away.

30. Suppose that you happened upon two buffalo grazing in an open field, and one looked substantially larger than the other. Now suppose that the image of the smaller buffalo began to expand. You would probably assume that:
    a. it was growing.
    c. it was moving away from you.
    b. it was running toward you.
    d. it was turning sideways.

31. According to the text, which of the following processes is most important in order for major-league baseball players to be able to hit the ball when it reaches the plate?
    a. tracking
    c. anticipation
    b. focusing
    d. eye coordination

32. Selective attention refers to:
    a. choosing which stimulus to monitor.
    b. listening to two messages at once.
    c. repeating aloud a message that is heard in only one ear.
    d. determining whether an enlarging retinal images means the object is getting closer or growing in size.

33. Dichotic listening and shadowing are procedures for studying:
    a. binocular disparity.
    c. motion parallax.
    b. selective attention.
    d. linear perspective.

34. Which factor is **least** likely to increase the audience's attention to TV advertising for a product?
    a. a printed description at the bottom of the TV screen stating the advertisement's message
    b. the meaningfulness of the advertisement's message
    c. running the advertisement at times of the day when its message is most relevant
    d. bright contrast and higher volume

35. The reason small children who have very little interest in television will stop what they are doing and watch a commercial illustrates how we are especially attentive to all of the features of a commercial **except**:
    a. loudness.
    b. novelty.
    c. contrast with the video images that precede it.
    d. content.

36. Which kind of stimulus is **least** likely to attract or hold a person's attention?
    a. novel
    b. large
    c. loud
    d. continuous

37. As a part of a listening task, a subject is fitted with earphones and hears a different message played simultaneously in each ear. The subject is asked to repeat aloud one of the two messages while it is being played into the subject's ear. This technique is called:
    a. selective attention.
    b. perceptual screening.
    c. dichotic listening.
    d. shadowing.

38. Jeff is interested in learning to speak Russian, so he purchases some tapes that he is supposed to play while he is asleep. The concept that supports the notion of being able to learn in this manner is called _____. According to the text, will his tapes work?
    a. selective attention; yes
    b. selective attention; no
    c. subliminal perception; yes
    d. subliminal perception; no

39. The Parthenon in Athens looks as if it:
    a. is leaning backward from the viewer.
    b. is completely upright with its columns formed of straight lines.
    c. has bulges in the middle of the columns.
    d. is ready to fall over.

40. Architects and engineers sometimes use perceptual devices to cause certain behaviors to occur. Which alternative is **not** mentioned in your text as an application for such objectives?
    a. getting people to slow down before a toll booth by painting perpendicular lines on the highway
    b. encouraging people to interact at social functions by using colors and shapes associated with kindness and affection in childhood relationships.
    c. using lines and angles to make tall buildings look perfectly vertical when, in fact, they slant inward
    d. using different colors in the seating section of a stadium so that it always looks full.

41. Of the following alternatives, visual illusions are most likely due to:
    a. errors in interpretation of sensations.
    b. distorted retinal images.
    c. distortions of visual memory.
    d. architectural errors.

42. According to the text, which alternative below is **not** an important factor that influences illusions?
    a. amount of formal education
    b. cultural experiences
    c. structural characteristics of the eye
    d. interpretive errors of the brain

43. _____ is a reading disability with a perceptual basis.
    a. Dysphonia
    b. Dysgraphia
    c. Dyslexia
    d. Dystonia

44. According to one theory, dyslexia is related to:
    a. chemical abuse in pregnant mothers.
    b. an inability to metabolize certain amino acids.
    c. major pathways from the eyes to the brain being out of sync.
    d. abnormal changes in brain chemistry during the first six months of life.

| ESSAY QUESTIONS | *Recite and Review:* ☐ |

Essay Question 5.1: *The Importance of Perceptual Constancy*

Describe the advantages of perceptual constancy and illustrate examples of each form of constancy. What would perception be like if we did not have principles like perceptual constancy?

_____

_____

_____

_____

_____

_____

_____

_____

_____

_____

_____

_____

_____

_____

_____

_____

_____

_____

Essay Question 5.2: *Gestalt versus Feature Analysis*

What are the basic differences between the gestalt organizational principles and the feature analysis approach to perception? Are there some phenomena that one or the other explains better? Are there phenomena that would be difficult for one to explain?

_____

_____

_____

_____

_____

_____

_____

_____

_____

_____

_____

_____

_____

_____

_____

_____

_____

_____

_____

ACTIVITIES AND PROJECTS

1. Look at the Necker cube below. Stare at it until it reverses. What makes this illusion work?

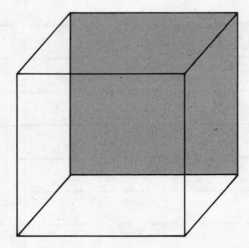

2. Look at the following figure. It is an ambiguous figure. What do you see? How long did it take to see both images? (You may wish to time yourself and others to see how long it takes to see both images.)

6

STATES OF CONSCIOUSNESS

DETAILED OUTLINE   *Survey:* ☐

This detailed outline contains all the headings in Chapter 6: States of Consciousness. If you are using the SQ3R method, then an examination of the outline is the best way to begin your survey of the chapter.

Prologue: Ryan Shafer
Looking Ahead

Sleep and Dreams
    The cycles of sleep
        REM sleep: The paradox of sleep
    Is sleep necessary?
    Circadian rhythms: Life cycles
  The Cutting Edge Illuminating Circadian Rhythms
    The function and meaning of dreaming
    Daydreams: Dreams without sleep
    Sleep disturbances: Slumbering problems
  The Informed Consumer of Psychology Sleeping Better
  ● **Recap and Review I**

Hypnosis and Meditation: Altered States of Consciousness
    Hypnosis
    A different state of consciousness?
    Meditation: Regulating your own state of consciousness
  ● **Recap and Review II**

Drug Use: The Highs and Lows of Consciousness
    Stimulants: Drug highs
        Cocaine
        Amphetamines
    Depressants: Drug lows
        Barbiturates
  Psychology at Work The Sound of Intoxication
    Narcotics: Relieving pain and anxiety
    Hallucinogens: Psychedelic drugs
  The Informed Consumer of Psychology Identifying Drug and Alcohol Problems
  ● **Recap and Review III**

Looking Back
Key Terms and Concepts

➤ Now that you have surveyed the chapter, read **Looking Ahead**, pages 164–166.   *Question:* ☐
Focus on the questions on page 166.   *Read:* ☐

CONCEPTS AND LEARNING OBJECTIVES   *Survey:* ☐

These are the concepts and the learning objects for Chapter 6. Read them carefully as part of your preliminary survey of the chapter.

Concept 1: Consciousness is a person's awareness of sensations, thoughts, and feelings that are being experienced at any given moment. Other than full alertness, sleep is one of the most important states of consciousness that we experience.

1. Define consciousness and altered states of consciousness. (pp. 164-166)

2. List and define the cycles of sleep and discuss the roles of circadian rhythms in our lives. (pp. 166-172)

3. Distinguish the various theories concerning the function of and meaning of dreaming and daydreaming. (pp. 172-177)

4. Describe the sleep disturbances identified in the text and discuss ways of improving sleep. (pp. 177-179)

Concept 2: Hypnosis and meditation are two altered states of consciousness that are achieved without the aid of any drugs or other substances. They are two important, and sometimes controversial areas of research into altered states of consciousness.

5. Describe hypnosis, the controversy regarding whether it is an altered state, and the therapeutic values it has. (pp. 180-183)

6. Describe how meditation works and the changes that occur during meditation. (pp. 183-184)

Concept 3: Psychoactive drugs represent a major social problem. Psychologists study addiction, the consequences of drug abuse, and how to help people overcome drug dependency. Some psychoactive drugs, like caffeine and alcohol, have socially accepted uses.

7. Describe the characteristics, addictive properties, and psychological reactions to stimulants and depressants. (pp. 185-193)

8. Describe the characteristics, addictive properties, and psychological reactions to narcotics and hallucinogens. (pp. 193-195)

9. Discuss the symptoms of drug abuse. (pp. 195-196)

> ## CHAPTER SUMMARY

There are several ways you can use this summary as part of your systematic study plan. You may read each concept summary and then read the corresponding pages in the text, or you may read the entire summary and then read the entire chapter in the text. As you finish each section, complete the **Recap and Review** questions that are supplied in the text.

CONCEPT 1: Prologue and Looking Ahead
               Sleep and Dreams

Survey: ☐
Read: ☐

Pages 164-180

The story of Ryan Shafer illustrates the tragic consequences of extreme drug abuse. Drug use is one of many ways to alter the experience we call consciousness. **Consciousness** is defined as our awareness of the sensations, thoughts, and feelings being experienced at any given moment. Consciousness can range from the perceptions during wakefulness to dreams. The variation in how we experience stimuli can be wide as well, and consciousness varies from active to passive states. Because of its personal nature, the use of introspection made early psychological approaches appear unscientific. Today the study of consciousness depends on several approaches that have measurable, scientific bases, like the use of electrical recording, studying the effects of drugs, and other approaches. **Altered states of consciousness** refers to conscious states that differ from a normal waking state. Altered states of consciousness share common characteristics. Thinking may be disturbed, the sense of time becomes distorted, perceptions may be changed, we may lose our sense of self-control, and we may not be able to understand rationally the experience when we are in an altered state of consciousness.

The example of Donald Dorff's sleep-walking condition illustrates the range of sleep experiences. Much of our knowledge of sleep itself comes from the use of the **electroencephalogram** (**EEG**) to record brain activity throughout the cycles of sleep. The amplitude and frequency of the wavelike patterns formed by the EEG during sleep show regular and systematic patterns of sleep. These patterns identify four stages of sleep. The first stage, called **stage 1 sleep**, is the stage of transition to sleep, and the brain waves are rapid, low-voltage waves. **Stage 2 sleep** is characterized by slower, more regular waves and by occasional sharply pointed waves called spindles. **Stage 3 sleep** brain waves become even slower with higher peaks and lower valleys. **Stage 4 sleep** has even slower wave patterns. Stage 4 is experienced soon after falling to sleep, and through the night sleep becomes lighter and is characterized by more dreams.

The period of sleep associated with most of our dreaming is identified by the rapid back and forth movement of the eyes called **rapid eye movement**, or **REM, sleep**. REM sleep, which occupies about twenty percent of the total sleep time, is also called paradoxical sleep because the body is in a state of paralysis even as the eyes are moving about rapidly. People who are deprived of REM sleep by being awakened whenever it begins to occur experience a rebound effect that is marked by a significant increase in the amount of REM sleep during subsequent sleep.

Sleep requirements vary from person to person and over time, individual sleep patterns change. Some people need very little sleep, others need much more. People deprived of sleep over long periods of time, up to 200 hours in some experiments, do not experience any long-term effects, but they do experience weariness, loss of concentration, decline in creativity, irritability, and tremors while they remain awake in the studies.

Circadian rhythms refers to the daily rhythms of the body, including the sleep and waking cycle, as well as the cycles of sleepiness throughout the day. People who work on night shifts experience difficulty in changing their basic rhythms. Sleep researchers have found that exposure to bright lights helps reset the circadian rhythms, and this technique was used to prepare a space shuttle crew for night shift on the *Columbia*.

Nightmares are unusually frightening dreams. They appear to occur frequently, perhaps about 24 times a year on average. **Night terrors** are even more frightening than nightmares, and the emotion can be so intense that the dreamer awakens screaming. Most dreams, however, involve daily, mundane events. Freud believed that dreams were a guide into the unconscious and that they expressed **unconscious wish fulfillment**. The true meaning of these wishes was disguised, and Freud used the label of **latent content of dreams**, because the meanings were too threatening. Freud called the story line of the dream the **manifest content of dreams**. Freud sought to uncover the latent content by interpreting the symbols of the dream. Many psychologists reject this theory of dreams, instead preferring to interpret the content in terms of its more obvious references to everyday concerns. Another theory of dreams is called the **reverse learning theory**. This theory suggests that dreams flush away unnecessary information accumulated through the day. Dreams then have little meaning. Another theory is the **dreams-for-survival theory** which suggests that dreams involve a reconsideration and reprocessing of critical information from the day. Dreams in this theory have meaning as they represent important concerns drawn from daily experiences. Currently, the most influential theory is the **activation-synthesis theory** which claims that dreams are by-products of biological processes. These processes are random firings related to changes in neurotransmitter production. Because these activities activate memories that have importance, what begins randomly becomes meaningful.

Another form of dreaming is **daydreams**—fantasies produced while awake. Daydreams are under the control of individuals, and thus their content is relevant to current concerns and immediate events. Evidence suggests that people may daydream for about 10 percent of the time. There is little relationship between daydreaming and psychological disturbances.

The most common sleep disturbance is **insomnia**, the experience of difficulty in falling asleep. As many as one-quarter of the people in the United States experience insomnia. Affecting about 20 million people, **sleep apnea** is another sleep disturbance. In sleep apnea, a person has difficulty breathing and sleeping at the same time. In extreme cases a person may awaken as many as 500 times a night. **Sudden infant death syndrome**, a syndrome in which apparently healthy infants die in their sleep, may be related to sleep apnea. Finally, **narcolepsy**, an uncontrollable urge to fall asleep, afflicts many people. In narcolepsy, the sleeper falls directly into REM sleep. Sleepwalking and sleeptalking are two usually harmless disturbances.

The *Informed Consumer of Psychology* section recommends tips for dealing with insomnia. These include exercising before bed, choosing a regular bedtime, using bed for sleep and not for watching TV or studying, avoiding caffeine drinks after lunch, drinking a glass of warm milk, avoiding sleeping pills, and if all fails, trying not to go to sleep. Research suggests that people with insomnia may actually sleep more than they think, but may also be aware of events around them even when they are asleep, thus having the impression of being awake.

CONCEPT 2: Hypnosis and Meditation: Altered States of Consciousness

Survey: ☐
Read: ☐

Pages 180-184

Hypnosis is a state of heightened susceptibility to the suggestion of others. When people are hypnotized, they will not perform antisocial behaviors, they will not carry out self-destructive acts, they will not reveal hidden truths about themselves, and they are capable of lying. Between 5 and 20 percent of the population cannot be hypnotized at all, and about 15 percent are highly susceptible. Hilgard has argued that hypnosis does represent a state of consciousness that is significantly different from other states. The increased suggestibility, greater ability to recall and construct images, increased memories from childhood, lack of initiative, and ability to accept suggestions that contradict reality suggest that hypnotic states are different from other states. Some researchers have established that some people do pretend to be hypnotized. Moreover, adults do not have special ability to recall childhood events while hypnotized. Hypnotism has been used successfully to control pain, to end tobacco addiction, in psychotherapy, for law enforcement, and in professional sports.

Meditation is another altered state. Meditation is a learned technique for refocusing attention that brings about the altered state. Transcendental meditation (TM), brought to the United States by the Maharishi Mahesh Yogi, is perhaps the best-known form of meditation. TM uses a **mantra**, a sound, word, or syllable, that is said over and over. In other forms, the meditator focuses on a picture, flame, or body part. In all forms the key is to concentrate intensely. Following meditation, people are relaxed, they may have new insights, and in the long term, they may have improved health. The physiological changes that accompany meditation are similar to relaxation: heart rate declines, oxygen intake declines, and brain-wave patterns change. The simple procedures of sitting in a quiet room, breathing deeply and rhythmically, and repeating a word will achieve the same effects as trained meditation techniques.

CONCEPT 3: Drug Use: The Highs and Lows of Consciousness

Survey: ☐
Read: ☐

Pages 185-196

Psychoactive drugs are drugs that affect consciousness by influencing a person's emotions, perceptions, and behavior. Drug use among high school students has declined, as today about half of the seniors have used an illegal drug in their lives, where the figure has been as much as 20 to 25 percent higher in the past. The most dangerous drugs are those that are addictive. **Addictive drugs** produce psychological or biological dependence in the user, and the withdrawal of the drug leads to cravings for it. The reasons for taking drugs range from seeking altered spiritual states, to taking them simply for the experience, to escaping the pressures of life, to the thrill of doing something illegal.

Drugs that affect the central nervous system by increasing its activity and by increasing heart rate, blood pressure, and muscle tension are called **stimulants**. The stimulant **caffeine** is found in coffee, soft drinks, and chocolate. Caffeine increases attentiveness and decreases reaction time. Too much caffeine leads to nervousness and insomnia. Stopping caffeine can cause headaches and depression. **Nicotine** is the stimulant found in tobacco products. **Cocaine** and its derivative crack are illegal stimulants. Cocaine produces feelings of well-being, confidence, and alertness when taken in small quantities. (See Table 6-3 in the text for a listing of illegal drugs and their effects.) Cocaine blocks the reuptake of excess dopamine, which in turn produces pleasurable sensations. Cocaine abuse makes the abusers crave the drug and go on binges of use. The withdrawal from cocaine has three stages: first a "crash"; then a withdrawal marked by boredom and lack of motivation, and although cravings decrease, the users are highly sensitive to cues related to cocaine; and then a third stage in which the cravings are further reduced and moods are more normal.

Amphetamines are a group of very strong stimulants that bring about a sense of energy and alertness, talkativeness, confidence, and a mood "high." The amphetamine, Benzedrine, is commonly known as speed, and excessive amounts of the drug can lead to overstimulation of the central nervous system, convulsions, and death.

Drugs that slow the central nervous system are called **depressants**. Feelings of **intoxication** come from taking small doses. **Alcohol** is the most common depressant. The average person drinks about 200 alcoholic drinks a year (based on liquor sales). People's reactions to alcohol vary widely. The relaxation, feelings of happiness, and loss of inhibitions make people perceive the effects of alcohol as increasing sociability and well-being (the opposite of depression). **Alcoholics** are people who abuse alcohol, rely upon it, and continue to use it when they have serious problems. Alcoholism requires some people to drink just to be able to function normally. In some cases, alcoholics have sporadic binges and drink excessive quantities. The reasons for the tolerance to alcohol that leads to alcoholism are not clear, though there is evidence that there may be genetic factors. Environmental stressors are thought to play a role as well.

Barbiturates are a form of depressant drug used to induce sleep and reduce stress. They are addictive and can be deadly when combined with alcohol. Quaalude is an illegal drug similar to barbiturates.

Narcotics increase relaxation and relieve pain and anxiety. **Morphine** and **heroin** are two powerful narcotics. Morphine is used to reduce pain, but heroin is illegal. Heroin effects include an initial rush followed by a sense of well-being. When the sense of well-being ends, the heroin user feels anxiety and the desire to use the drug again. With each use, more heroin is needed to have any effect. A successful treatment for heroin addiction is the use of **methadone**, a drug that satisfies the cravings but does not produce the high. Methadone is biologically addicting.

Drugs that produce hallucinations are called **hallucinogens**. The most common hallucinogen is **marijuana**, and its active ingredient is tetrahydrocannabinol. The effects of marijuana include euphoria and well-being, and sensory experiences can be more intense. There is no scientific evidence for marijuana being addictive, and the short-term effects appear to be minor. However, the long-term effects of heavy use include temporary decreases in the male sex hormone, decreased activity of the immune system, and damage to the lungs.

Vivid hallucinations are produced by **lysergic acid diethylamide**, or **LSD**. Perceptions of colors, sounds, and shapes are altered, time perception is distorted, or the user may have a terrifying experience. After use, people can also experience flashbacks during which they hallucinate. **Phencyclidine**, or **PCP**, is similar to LSD, but can be more dangerous with side effects that include paranoid and destructive behavior.

The text lists a number of signs that could indicate drug abuse problems. Individuals with these symptoms should be encouraged to seek professional help.

➤ Now that you have surveyed, questioned, and read the chapter and completed
   the **Recap and Review** questions, review **Looking Back**, page 196–198.   *Review:* ☐

➤ For additional practice through recitation and review, test your knowledge of the chapter material by answering the questions in the *Key Word Drill*, the *Practice Questions*, and the *Essay Questions*.

| **KEY WORD DRILL** | *Recite:* ☐ |

The following **Fill in the Blank** and **Matching Questions** test key words from the text. Check your answers with the Answer Key in the back of the *Study Guide*.

FILL IN THE BLANK

1. The term _____ refers to a person's awareness of the sensations, thoughts, and feelings that he or she is experiencing at a given moment.

2. Experiences of sensations or thought that differ from a normal waking consciousness are said to be

   _____ _____ of _____.

3. The biological processes that occur repeatedly and on approximately a twenty-four-hour cycle are

   _____ _____.

4. Sigmund Freud proposed that dreams result from _____ _____

   _____, in other words, that dreams represent unconscious wishes that a dreamer wants to fulfill.

5. _____ is the state of heightened susceptibility to the suggestions of others.

6. Virtually every religion has some form of _____, a learned technique for refocusing attention that brings about an altered state of consciousness, and many forms use a

   _____, a sound, word, or syllable repeated over and over to take one into the altered state.

7. Drugs that influence a person's emotions, perceptions, and behavior are called

   _____ drugs.

8. Psychologists have named drugs that produce a physical or psychological dependence in the user

   _____ drugs.

9. Drugs that affect the central nervous system, causing increased heart rate, blood pressure, and muscle

   tension are called _____; and drugs that slow down the nervous system are

   called _____.

10. _____ refers to the class of drugs that increase relaxation and relieve pain and anxiety.

MATCHING QUESTIONS

_____ 11. stage 1 sleep

_____ 12. stage 2 sleep

_____ 13. stage 3 sleep

_____ 14. stage 4 sleep

_____ 15. rapid eye movement (REM) sleep

a. The deepest stage of sleep, during which we are least responsive to outside stimulation.

b. Sleep characterized by increased heart rate, blood pressure, and breathing rate, erections; and the experience of dreaming.

c. A sleep deeper than that of stage 1, characterized by sleep spindles.

d. The state of transition between wakefulness and sleep, characterized by relatively rapid, low-voltage brain waves.

e. A sleep characterized by slow brain waves, with greater peaks and valleys in the wave pattern.

_____ 16. latent content of dreams

_____ 17. manifest content of dreams

_____ 18. reverse learning theory

_____ 19. dreams-for-survival theory

_____ 20. activation-synthesis theory

a. According to Freud, the "disguised" meanings of dreams, hidden by more obvious subjects.

b. Hobson's view that dreams are a result of random electrical energy stimulating memories lodged in various portions of the brain, which the brain then weaves into a logical story line.

c. The view that dreams have no meaning in themselves, but instead function to rid us of unnecessary information that we have accumulated during the day.

d. The proposal that dreams permit information critical for our daily survival to be reconsidered and reprocessed during sleep.

e. According to Freud, the overt story line of dreams.

_____ 21. rebound effect

_____ 22. nightmares

_____ 23. night terrors

_____ 24. daydreams

_____ 25. insomnia

_____ 26. sleep apnea

_____ 27. sudden infant death syndrome

_____ 28. narcolepsy

a. An inability to get to sleep or stay asleep.

b. A disorder in which seemingly healthy infants die in their sleep.

c. Unusually frightening dreams.

d. An uncontrollable need to sleep for short periods during the day.

e. An increase in REM sleep after one has been deprived of it.

f. Profoundly frightening nightmares which wake up the dreamer.

g. Fantasies people construct while awake.

h. A sleep disorder characterized by difficulty in breathing and sleeping simultaneously.

_____ 29. caffeine

_____ 30. nicotine

_____ 31. cocaine

_____ 32. amphetamines

_____ 33. alcohol

_____ 34. intoxication

a. An addictive stimulant present in cigarettes.

b. Strong stimulants that cause a temporary feeling of confidence and alertness but may increase anxiety and appetite loss and, taken over a period of time, suspiciousness and feelings of persecution.

c. An addictive stimulant that, when taken in small doses, initially creates feelings of confidence, alertness, and well-being, but eventually causes mental and physical deterioration.

d. The most common depressant, which in small doses causes release of tension and feelings of happiness, but in larger amounts can cause emotional and physical instability, memory impairment, and stupor.

e. An addictive stimulant found most abundantly in coffee, tea, soda, and chocolate.

f. A state of drunkenness.

_____ 35. barbiturates

_____ 36. morphine

_____ 37. heroin

_____ 38. methadone

_____ 39. hallucinogen

_____ 40. marijuana

_____ 41. lysergic acid diethylamide (LSD)

_____ 42. phencyclidine (PCP)

a. A powerful depressant, usually injected, that gives an initial rush of good feeling but leads eventually to anxiety and depression; extremely addictive.

b. Addictive depressants used to induce sleep and reduce stress, the abuse of which, especially when combined with alcohol, can be deadly.

c. A powerful hallucinogen that alters brain-cell activity and can cause paranoid and destructive behavior.

d. A chemical used to detoxify heroin addicts.

e. One of the most powerful hallucinogens, affecting the operation of neurotransmitters in the brain and causing brain cell activity to be altered.

f. A drug that is capable of producing changes in the perceptual process, or hallucinations.

g. A common hallucinogen, usually smoked.

h. Derived from the poppy flower, a powerful depressant that reduces pain and induces sleep.

PRACTICE QUESTIONS

Recite and Review: ☐

Test your knowledge of the chapter material by answering these **True-False** and **Multiple Choice Questions**. Check your answers with the Answer Key in the back of the *Study Guide*.

TRUE-FALSE QUESTIONS

T   F   1.   The body and brain are active, rather than dormant, during the night.

T   F   2.   Stage 4 sleep is characterized by rapid brain waves with high peaks and valleys.

T   F   3.   Dreams are not experienced by everyone during a night's sleep.

T   F   4.   If a person is deprived of rapid eye movement (REM) sleep, normal mental functioning becomes impaired.

T   F   5.   Sleep deprivation has lasting effects on the performance of cognitive tasks.

T	F	6.	Experiments with the neurotransmitter acetylcholine caused sleepers to enter rapid eye movement (REM) sleep quickly and to report dream activity similar to that occurring during normal sleep.
T	F	7.	Daydreaming is a common sign of psychological disturbance.
T	F	8.	A psychological addiction is characterized by a person believing that he or she needs a substance in order to deal with the stress of the day.
T	F	9.	Although most people perceive alcohol as a stimulant, its actual effects are those of a depressant.
T	F	10.	Tetrahydrocannabinol is the active ingredient in marijuana.

MULTIPLE CHOICE QUESTIONS

1. Most psychologists today agree that the study of consciousness is:
   a. better left to philosophers.
   b. improper for scientific study.
   c. not highly personal.
   d. a legitimate area of study for psychologists.

2. Which of the following is **not** characteristic of altered states of consciousness?
   a. undisturbed thought processes
   b. disturbed sense of time
   c. changed perception of the world
   d. loss of self-control

3. Sleep involves four different stages. What is the basis for differentiating these stages of sleep?
   a. They are defined according to the electrical properties recorded by an electroencephalogram (EEG) attached to the sleeper.
   b. They are defined by the amount of time elapsed from the onset of sleep.
   c. They are based on the mental experiences described when sleepers are awakened and asked what they are thinking.
   d. They are characterized by patterns of overt body movements recorded with a videocamera that is positioned over the sleeper.

4. During the course of a night's sleep, we tend to _____ as morning approaches.
   a. sleep less deeply
   b. dream less
   c. be less responsive to outside stimulation
   d. sleepwalk more often

5. Which stage represents the transition from wakefulness to sleep?
   a. stage 1
   b. stage 2
   c. stage 3
   d. rapid eye movement (REM)

6. Stage 1 sleep is characterized by:
   a. slow, low-voltage brain waves.
   b. rapid, low-voltage brain waves.
   c. slow, high-voltage brain waves.
   d. rapid, high-voltage brain waves.

7. As we progress through the stages of sleep toward deepest sleep, within a single sleep cycle the EEG pattern gets:
   a. faster and more regular.
   c. slower and lower in amplitude.
   b. faster and more irregular.
   d. slower and more regular.

8. Which sleep stage is characterized by electrical signals with the slowest frequency, by waveforms that are very regular, and by a sleeper who is very unresponsive to external stimuli?
   a. rapid eye movement (REM)
   c. stage 3
   b. stage 2
   d. stage 4

9. Which of the following stages of sleep is characterized by irregular breathing, increased blood pressure, and increased respiration?
   a. stage 1
   c. rapid eye movement (REM)
   b. stage 2
   d. non-rapid eye movement (NREM)

10. REM sleep is referred to as paradoxical because:
    a. brain activity is low but eye movement is high.
    b. brain activity is low, but muscle activity is high.
    c. eye movement becomes rapid and brain activity is high.
    d. the brain is very active, but body muscles are paralyzed.

11. The major muscles of the body act as if they are paralyzed during:
    a. stage 1 sleep.
    c. stage 4 sleep.
    b. stage 3 sleep.
    d. rapid eye movement (REM).

12. The increase in REM sleep during periods after a person has been deprived of it is called:
    a. paradoxical sleep.
    c. latent dreaming.
    b. the rebound effect.
    d. somnambulism.

13. A friend comes to you concerned about his health after having stayed up for thirty-six hours straight studying without sleep. The most valid thing you could tell him is that:
    a. if he is going to stay up for so long, he should see a doctor regularly.
    b. if he continues to stay up for so long, he will probably get sick.
    c. there will most likely be rather severe long-term consequences of not sleeping for that amount of time.
    d. research has demonstrated that lack of sleep will affect his ability to study.

14. The effects of sleep deprivation:
    a. are long-term and debilitating.
    b. are not known at the present time.
    c. are short-term, with no enduring effects.
    d. show how important sleep is to survival.

15. According to Freud, dreams:
    a. are reflections of day-to-day activities.
    b. are reflections of conscious activity.
    c. are reflections of unconscious wish fulfillment.
    d. are remnants of our evolutionary heritage.

16. Freud referred to the story line of a dream as its:
    a. libidinal content.
    b. unconscious content.
    c. manifest content.
    d. latent content.

17. Freud called the disguised meaning of dreams the:
    a. latent content.
    b. sexual fantasy.
    c. manifest content.
    d. image fantasy.

18. Sharon dreams that Jim climbs a stairway and meets her at the top. According to Freudian dream symbols described in the text, this would probably suggest:
    a. that Sharon would like to start a friendship with Jim.
    b. that Sharon is really afraid to talk to Jim, though she would like to start a friendship.
    c. that Jim and Sharon probably work together in a building where there are stairs.
    d. that Sharon is dreaming of sexual intercourse with Jim.

19. If you had a dream about carrying grapefruits down a long tunnel, Freud would interpret the grapefruit as a dream symbol suggesting a wish to:
    a. take a trip to the tropics.
    b. caress a woman's body.
    c. caress a man's genitals.
    d. return to the womb.

20. When injected into people, drugs similar to which of the following are most likely to induce rapid eye movement (REM) stage of sleep and active dreaming?
    a. noradrenalin
    b. acetylcholine
    c. tryptophan
    d. serotonin

21. While in calculus class, Rob fantasized about sailing to Tahiti. He was experiencing a:
    a. nervous breakdown.
    b. daydream.
    c. diurnal emission.
    d. mantra.

22. Which of the following does **not** describe a common characteristic of daydreams?
    a. fantastic and creative
    b. mundane, ordinary topics
    c. a part of normal consciousness
    d. a predomination of sexual imagery

23. According to studies, the average person daydreams about:
    a. 10 percent of the time.
    b. 20 percent of the time.
    c. 30 percent of the time.
    d. 40 percent of the time.

24. People pass directly from a conscious, wakeful state to REM sleep if they suffer from:
    a. narcolepsy
    b. insomnia
    c. somnambulism
    d. rapid eye movement (REM) showers

25. Insomnia is a condition in which a person:
    a. uncontrollably falls asleep.
    b. sleeps more than twelve hours per night on a routine basis.
    c. has difficulty sleeping.
    d. exhibits abnormal brain wave patterns during rapid eye movement (REM) sleep.

26. The uncontrollable need to sleep for short periods that can happen at any time during the day is called:
    a. narcolepsy.
    b. sleep apnea.
    c. hypersomnia.
    d. insomnia.

27. Having difficulty sleeping and breathing simultaneously is called:
    a. narcolepsy.
    b. sleep apnea.
    c. hypersomnia.
    d. insomnia.

28. According to research discussed in the text, which of the following may account for sudden infant death syndrome?
    a. narcolepsy
    b. sleep apnea
    c. somnambulism
    d. insomnia

29. Which of the following statements about sleep difficulties is **not** correct?
    a. Insomnia is the most common sleep disorder.
    b. Sleep apnea sometimes causes people to have inadequate oxygen in their blood while they sleep.
    c. Narcolepsy is an uncontrollable need to sleep for short periods during the day.
    d. Sudden infant death syndrome kills infants who have unusually irregular sleep patterns.

30. Which of the following statements about sleepwalking is **not** true?
    a. Sleepwalkers should not be awakened.
    b. Sleepwalking occurs in stage 4 sleep.
    c. Sleepwalkers are somewhat aware of their surroundings.
    d. Sleepwalking occurs most frequently in children.

31. Generalizing from the text, all of the following are typical suggestions for overcoming insomnia **except**:
    a. Choose regular bedtimes.
    b. Don't try to go to sleep.
    c. Avoid drinks with caffeine.
    d. Watch TV in bed.

32. Which of the following is true regarding a person under hypnosis?
    a. The person can be induced to perform antisocial behaviors.
    b. The person cannot be hypnotized against his or her will.
    c. The person can commit self-destructive acts.
    d. The person's ability to draw on memories decreases.

33. The procedure, introduced in the United States by Maharishi Mahesh Yogi, in which a person focuses on a mantra to reach a different state of consciousness is called:
    a. transactional analysis.
    b. Zen Buddhism.
    c. exorcism.
    d. transcendental meditation.

34. During transcendental meditation, a person repeats a(n) _____ over and over again.
    a. mantra
    b. allegory
    c. banta
    d. analogy

35. In what way is meditation and hypnosis similar?
    a. They are both accompanied by changes in brain activity.
    b. They both result in a decrease in blood pressure.
    c. They are both based on Eastern religious practices.
    d. They both result in total relaxation.

36. _____ drugs are considered most dangerous to physical and mental well-being.
    a. Sleep-inducing
    b. Over-the-counter
    c. Birth-control
    d. Addictive

37. A psychoactive drug:
    a. affects a person's behavior only if he or she is receptive to "mind expanding" experiences.
    b. influences thoughts and perceptions and is usually physically addictive.
    c. affects a person's emotions, perceptions, and behavior.
    d. acts primarily on biological functions such as heart rate and intestinal mobility.

38. Which of the following statements about addiction to drugs is **not** true?
    a. Addiction may be biologically based.
    b. Addictions are primarily caused by an inherited biological liability.
    c. All people, with few exceptions, have used one or more "addictive" drugs in their lifetime.
    d. Addictions may be psychological.

39. Caffeine, nicotine, cocaine, and amphetamines are considered:
    a. anesthetic agents.
    b. central nervous system stimulants.
    c. anti-anxiety drugs.
    d. hallucinogens.

40. The most common central nervous system depressant is:
    a. phenobarbital.
    b. alcohol.
    c. Valium.
    d. Quaalude.

41. Which alternative below does **not** belong with the others?
    a. coffee
    b. alcohol
    c. nicotine
    d. amphetamines

42. Nembutal, Seconal, and phenobarbital are all depressants and forms of:
    a. opiates.
    b. barbiturates.
    c. hallucinogens.
    d. hypnotics.

43. The most common hallucinogen in use in the United States is:
    a. PCP.
    b. LSD.
    c. cocaine.
    d. marijuana.

44. Which of the following is a hallucinogen?
    a. heroin
    b. cocaine
    c. marijuana
    d. morphine

45. Which of the following appears to be nonaddictive with minimal withdrawal symptoms?
    a. alcohol
    b. nicotine
    c. marijuana
    d. morphine

| **ESSAY QUESTIONS** | *Recite and Review:* ☐ |

Essay Question 6.1: *Hypnotism*

Discuss the competing theories of hypnotism. Is it a real phenomenon? Do you consider it to be an altered state? Defend your answer.

_____

_____

_____

_____

_____

_____

_____

_____

_____

_____

_____

_____

_____

_____

_____

_____

_____

Essay Question 6.2: *Decriminalizing Psychoactive Drugs*

Debates regarding the legalization of drugs, especially marijuana, seem to come and go. If that debate were to arise today, what should psychology contribute? What are your feelings? Should some drugs be legalized or given through prescription? Defend your answer.

_____

_____

_____

_____

_____

_____

_____

_____

_____

_____

_____

_____

_____

_____

_____

_____

_____

ACTIVITIES AND PROJECTS

1.   Prepare a dream journal. Some people are able to record their dreams in the morning when they awaken, others will place a notepad and pencil next to their bed at night and record their dreams throughout the night by waking and writing a few notes immediately after the dream occurs. To use this second method, before you fall asleep you should give yourself the suggestion to awaken after each dream (you may wish to include in your suggestion that you will be able to record your dream and fall back to sleep without any problem). After about one week of keeping a journal, you should examine it for any patterns or recurrent themes (recurrent dreams will be very noticeable without keeping a journal). If other students in the class are doing this activity, you may wish to share a few of your dreams and discuss their possible meanings or other source.

2.   Go to a local drug store or to the section of the campus bookstore that has cold remedies, sleep aids, and other over-the-counter medications. Record the active ingredients and the name of the product. Then go with the list to any medical reference and find the description of the active ingredient. This drug should also be classified according to what type of psychoactive drug it is. Is it a depressant or a stimulant? Is it related to a narcotic or hallucinogen? Is it classed as antianxiety or antidepressant? (Check Chapter 18 for a description of these two drug classes.)

3.   Your library should have a relaxation tape that you can check out. If not, ask your psychology instructor or someone in the campus counseling center. After locating a tape, find a quiet spot where you will not be disturbed and you can play the tape. Before playing the tape, take a pulse rate and count the number of breaths you take in a minute. Now play the tape. After the tape is over, wait a few moments and take your pulse and breathing rates again. How do you feel? In what way is this like meditation? In what way is it different?

CHAPTER

7

LEARNING

Cognitive Approaches to Learning
Rule-learning in animals
Observational learning: Learning through copying
Learned helplessness: Accepting the unacceptable
The unresolved controversy of cognitive learning theory

The Informed Consumer of Psychology Behavior Analysis and Behavior Modification
● **Recap and Review IV**

Looking Back
Key Terms and Concepts

➤ Now that you have surveyed the chapter, read **Looking Ahead**, pages 202–203.   ***Question:*** ☐
Focus on the questions on page 203.   ***Read:*** ☐

| **CONCEPTS AND LEARNING OBJECTIVES** | ***Survey:*** ☐ |

These are the concepts and the learning objects for Chapter 7. Read them carefully as part of your preliminary survey of the chapter.

Concept 1: Learning is the relatively permanent change in behavior that results from experience. Classical conditioning, the learning theory pioneered by Ivan Pavlov, understands learning to be the substitution of a new stimulus for a preexisting stimulus in a stimulus-response association.

1. Define learning and describe the basic concepts and application of classical conditioning. (pp. 202-207)

2. Define and describe the major principles of classical conditioning, including extinction, spontaneous recovery, stimulus generalization, stimulus discrimination, and higher-order conditioning. (pp. 207-210)

3. Identify the challenges that have been made to the traditional views of classical conditioning. (pp. 210-212)

Concept 2: Operant conditioning, developed by B. F. Skinner, utilizes the consequences of behavior to shape behavior. Reinforcement is the principle that accounts for the increase of particular behaviors.

4. Describe the basic procedures of operant conditioning. (pp. 213-215)

5. Define positive and negative reinforcement, types of reinforcers, and punishment. (pp. 215-219)

Concept 3: Most reinforcement of behavior follows schedules that provide partial reinforcement, which often leads to greater resistance to extinction. Operant conditioning has a number of applications, including computerized programmed instruction.

6. Outline the schedules of reinforcement and define the operant view of generalization and discrimination, superstitious behavior, and shaping. (pp. 220-225)

7. Describe applications of operant conditioning, especially programmed instruction. (pp. 225-226)

8. Discuss the distinction between classical and operant conditioning and the limits to conditioning like biological constraints. (pp. 226-229)

Concept 4: Cognitive approaches to learning focus on the role of cognitive processes, especially observation, in the learning of new behaviors.

9. Describe the cognitive learning aspects of latent learning, rule-learning behavior and observational learning. (pp. 229-233)

10. Describe Seligman's concept of learned helplessness. (pp. 234-235)

11. Outline the methods of behavior modification discussed in the text. (pp. 235-237)

CHAPTER SUMMARY

There are several ways you can use this summary as part of your systematic study plan. You may read each concept summary and then read the corresponding pages in the text, or you may read the entire summary and then read the entire chapter in the text. As you finish each section, complete the **Recap and Review** questions that are supplied in the text.

CONCEPT 1: Prologue and Looking Ahead
           Classical Conditioning

Survey: ☐
Read: ☐

Pages 202-213

The Prologue illustrates how effectively learning principles can be applied to animal behavior by describing the behavior of Bo, Brad Gabrielson's dog. Bo was able to go and find a neighbor to help Brad back into his wheelchair, and though it appears incredible, this was a result of Bo's training.

    Learning is distinguished from **maturation** on the basis of whether the resulting change in behavior is a consequence of the environment (learning) or of growth (maturation). Short-term changes in performance, the key measure of learning, can also result from fatigue, tension, and other factors that are not reflections of learning. According to some, learning can only be inferred indirectly from performance, and performance does not always indicate learning.

    Ivan Pavlov's studies concerning the physiology of digestive processes led him to discover the basic principles of **classical conditioning**. In classical conditioning, an organism learns to respond to a stimulus that did not bring about the response earlier. An original study involved Pavlov's training a dog to salivate when a tuning fork was sounded. In this process, the tuning fork's sound is considered the

neutral stimulus because it does not bring about the response of interest. The meat powder, which does cause salivation, is called the **unconditioned stimulus (UCS)**. The salivation, when it occurs due to the presence of the meat powder (UCS), is called the **unconditioned response (UCR)**. The conditioning process requires repeated pairing of the UCS and the neutral stimulus. After training is complete, the neutral stimulus—now called the **conditioned stimulus (CS)**—will now bring about the UCR, now called the **conditioned response (CR)**. Pavlov noted that the neutral stimulus had to precede the UCS by no more than several seconds for the conditioning to be the most effective.

One of the more famous applications of classical conditioning techniques to humans is the case of the 11-month-old infant, Albert. Albert was taught a fear of a white rat, to which he had shown no fear initially, by striking a bar behind him whenever he approached the rat. Whenever we associate one stimulus with another and then behave differently as a result of the association, we are experiencing classical conditioning.

The process of ending the association of the UCS and the CS is called **extinction**, which occurs when a previously learned response decreases and disappears. If the tuning fork is repeatedly sounded without the meat powder being presented, the dog will eventually stop salivating. Extinction is the basis for the treatment principle called **systematic desensitization**, which is used to treat phobias. Systematic desensitization requires the repeated presentation of the frightening stimulus (a CS) without the presentation of the occurrence of the negative consequences.

When a CS has been extinguished, and a period of time has passed without the presentation of the CS, a phenomenon called **spontaneous recovery** can occur. The CS is presented and the previously extinguished response recurs, though it is usually weaker than in the original training and can be extinguished again more easily.

Stimulus generalization occurs when a conditioned response occurs in the presence of a stimulus that is similar to the original conditioned stimulus. In the case of baby Albert, the fear response was generalized to white furry things, including a white Santa Claus mask. The generalized response is not usually as intense as the original, though the more the new stimulus resembles the original, the more similar the response will be. **Stimulus discrimination** occurs when an organism learns to differentiate (discriminate) one stimulus from another and responds only to one stimulus and not the others.

When a conditioned stimulus has been established and is then repeatedly paired with another neutral stimulus until the conditioned response becomes conditioned to the new stimulus, then **higher-order conditioning** has occurred. Some investigators have used the concept of higher-order conditioning to explain how people develop and maintain prejudices against members of racial and ethnic groups.

Many of the fundamental assumptions of classical conditioning have been challenged. The cognitive learning theorists argue that the learner develops an expectancy concerning which UCSs are matched to CSs. Leon Kamin's study of **blocking**, a process in which the learning of one CS-UCS connection blocks the learning of another response to a second stimulus, is an example. If the first CS causes sufficient expectations regarding the response, the animal is likely to ignore a second stimulus. The notion that learners *ignore* a stimulus suggests the presence of cognitive processes. Another challenge has been to question the length of the interval between the neutral stimulus and the unconditioned stimulus. Garcia found that nausea caused by radiation, a state that occurred hours after exposure, could be associated with water drunk that has unusual characteristics or with water drunk in a particular place. Garcia's findings that the association could be made with delays as long as eight hours is a direct challenge to the idea that the pairing must be made within several seconds to be effective.

CONCEPT 2: Operant Conditioning

Survey: ☐
Read: ☐

Pages 213-220

Operant conditioning is learning in which the response is strengthened or weakened according to whether it has positive or negative consequences. The term "operant" suggests that the organism operates on the environment in a deliberate manner to gain a desired result.

Edward L. Thorndike found that a cat would learn to escape from a cage by performing specific actions in order to open a door that allows it access to food, a positive consequence of the behavior. Thorndike formulated the **law of effect**, stating that responses with satisfying results would be repeated, those with less satisfying results would be less likely to be repeated.

B. F. Skinner took Thorndike's law of effect and suggested that chance behaviors that lead to desirable consequences are then repeated. Pigeons will accidentally peck a key that releases food pellets, and then begin to peck until satisfied, learning the contingency between the pecking and the food.

The food released by the pecking is called a **reinforcer**, which is any stimulus that increases the probability that a preceding behavior will be repeated. A **primary reinforcer** satisfies a biological need without regard to prior experience. A **secondary reinforcer** is a stimulus that reinforces because of its association with a primary reinforcer.

Operant conditioning has been used to train animals to help in rescue missions. Dolphins can locate and tag divers in the Navy's Marine Mammal Program, and pigeons have been trained to locate missing sailors in the ocean by pecking a series of keys when they sight the orange color of the life jacket.

Reinforcers are also distinguished as positive or negative. **Positive reinforcers** bring about an increase in the preceding response. **Negative reinforcers** lead to an increase in a desired response when they are *removed*. Negative reinforcement requires that an individual take an action to remove an undesirable condition. Negative reinforcement is used in **escape conditioning**, where an organism learns to escape from an aversive situation, and in **avoidance conditioning**, where the organism learns to act to avoid the aversive situation. **Punishment** refers to the use of an **aversive stimulus**, by adding it to the environment, in order to *decrease* the probability that a behavior will be repeated. Punishment includes the removal of something positive, such as the loss of a privilege.

The effectiveness of punishment depends greatly on how it is used. The use of punishment is usually an opportunity for reinforcing an alternate, preferred behavior. Also, in rare cases, such as autism, quick and intense physical punishment may be used to prevent or end self-destructive behavior. The disadvantages of punishment make its use questionable. It must be delivered shortly after the behavior or it will be ineffective. Physical punishment may convey the idea that physical aggression is an appropriate behavior. Punishment does not convey information about alternative behaviors.

CONCEPT 3: Operant Conditioning (Continued)

Survey: ☐
Read: ☐

Pages 220-229

The frequency and timing of reinforcement depends upon the use of **schedules of reinforcement**. With continuous reinforcement, the behavior is reinforced every time it occurs. **Partial reinforcement** describes the technique of using reinforcement some of the time but not for every response. Partial reinforcement schedules maintain behavior longer than continuous reinforcement before extinction occurs.

A **cumulative recorder** automatically records the number of responses and the amount of time between responses. It also records the number of times a reinforcement is given (see Figure 7-5).

A **fixed-ratio schedule** delivers a reinforcement after a certain number of responses. A **variable-ratio schedule** delivers reinforcement on the basis of a varying number of responses. The number of responses often remains close to an average. The fixed- and variable-ratio schedules depend upon a *number* of responses, and the fixed- and variable-interval schedules depend upon an *amount of time*. **Fixed-interval schedules** deliver reinforcements to the first behavior occurring after a set interval, or period, of time. **Variable-interval schedules** deliver reinforcement after a varying interval of time. Fixed intervals are like weekly paychecks, variable intervals are like pop quizzes.

Discrimination and generalization are achieved in operant conditioning through **stimulus control training**. In stimulus control training, a behavior is reinforced only in the presence of specific stimuli. The specific stimulus is called a **discriminative stimulus**, a stimulus that signals the likelihood of a particular behavior being reinforced. Stimulus generalization occurs when an organism responds in situations similar to the original and expects reinforcement in the new situation just as the original was reinforced.

Superstitious behavior refers to a behavior that involves the repetition of elaborate rituals. Learning theory accounts for superstitious behavior as behavior that occurs prior to a reinforcement but is coincidental to the behavior that leads to the reinforcement. Also, these behaviors are strengthened because they are only partially reinforced.

When a complex behavior is desired, a trainer may shape the desired behavior by rewarding closer and closer approximations of the behavior. Initially, any similar behaviors are reinforced, and gradually the reinforcement is restricted to ever closer approximations. Many complex human and animal skills are acquired through shaping.

The most common application of shaping in human learning is in the use of programmed instruction, now mostly relying on computers, though developed sixty years ago. In **programmed instruction**, correct responses to questions are immediately reinforced and errors are used to direct the user to review previous material. The use of computers has allowed the development of sophisticated programs that can be highly individualized and can move quickly between kinds of information and activities. Critics of programmed instruction feel that it may distract from real laboratory work and that students are limited by the program's ability to answer specific questions. In contrast, computers are now beginning to learn the way humans learn, and the computer is being used to imitate human neural networks.

Classical and operant conditioning can be distinguished on several grounds even though it is important to remember that they have similarities, like the processes of generalization and discrimination. Most of our behavior is probably learned through a mixture of both processes. The key distinction between them, however, is that in classical conditioning, the unconditioned stimulus precedes the response and the response is elicited by the unconditioned stimulus. In operant conditioning, the response is emitted prior to the reinforcement and is therefore intentionally done.

Sometimes learning is constrained by behaviors that are biologically innate, or inborn. Not all behaviors can be taught to all animals equally well because of these **biological constraints**. Pigs might root a disk around their cages and raccoons might hoard and then clean similar disks.

CONCEPT 4: Cognitive Approaches to Learning
      The Informed Consumer of Psychology **Behavior Analysis
      and Behavior Modification**

Survey: ☐
Read: ☐

Pages 229-237

The approach that views learning in terms of thought processes is called **cognitive learning theory**. This approach does not deny the importance of classical and operant conditioning. They include the consideration of unseen mental processes as well. **Latent learning** is behavior that is learned but not demonstrated until reinforcement is provided for demonstrating the behavior. Latent learning occurs when rats are allowed to wander about a maze without any reward at the end, but once they learn that a reinforcement is available, they will quickly find their way through the maze even though they had not been reinforced for doing so in the past. The wandering around apparently leads them to develop a **cognitive map** of the maze. Humans apparently develop cognitive maps of their surroundings based on landmarks.

Experiments with pigeons have led cognitive learning psychologists to conclude that pigeons can learn to respond according to rules, such as whether or not a tree is present in a picture, and the rule can be made of several components, such as the presence of leaves or branches or a particular size. Animals can also learn elaborate sequences of numbers. This evidence suggests that animals act upon a thoughtful, internal representation of the world.

Albert Bandura has proposed that observational learning accounts for a large portion of learning in humans. **Observational learning** is learning that occurs by observing the behavior of another person, called the **model**. The classic experiment involved children observing a model strike a Bobo doll, and then later those who had seen the behavior were more prone to act aggressively. Four processes are necessary for observational learning: (1) paying attention to critical features; (2) remembering the behavior; (3) reproducing the action; and (4) being motivated to repeat the behavior. We also observe the kinds of reinforcement that the model receives for the behavior.

Martin Seligman has proposed that **learned helplessness**, the learned belief that no control can be exerted over the environment, can be used to understand why people give up or fail to try to eliminate an aversive stimulus. After repeated exposure to stimuli over which animals and humans have no control, they will fail to try later, even when they do have control. Learned helplessness has been used to explain why battered children will not seek relief when they have the opportunity and also to explain depression.

One view of the difference between cognitive theory—that depends on internal factors—and classical and operant conditioning—that depends on external factors, is to argue that neither of these approaches is sufficient to account for behavior but instead must be taken as complementary approaches.

Behavior modification refers to the formalized use of basic principles of learning theory to change behavior by eliminating undesirable behaviors and encouraging desirable ones. Behavior modification can be used to train mentally retarded individuals, to help people lose weight or quit smoking, and to teach people to behave safely. The steps of a typical behavior program include: (1) identifying goals and target behaviors; (2) designing a data recording system and recording preliminary data; (3) selecting a behavior change strategy; (4) implementing the program; (5) keeping careful records after the program has been implemented; and (6) evaluating and altering the ongoing program.

► Now that you have surveyed, questioned, and read the chapter and completed the **Recap and Review** questions, review **Looking Back**, page 238-239.

Review: ☐

► For additional practice through recitation and review, test your knowledge of the chapter material by answering the questions in the ***Key Word Drill***, the ***Practice Questions***, and the ***Essay Questions***.

| **KEY WORD DRILL** |

Recite: ☐

The following **Fill in the Blank** and **Matching Questions** test key words from the text. Check your answers with the Answer Key in the back of the *Study Guide*.

FILL IN THE BLANK

1. When a relatively permanent change in behavior is brought about by experience,

   _____ is said to have occurred.

2. In contrast to learning, _____ is the unfolding of biologically predetermined patterns of behavior due to aging.

3. When the association of one conditioned stimulus with an unconditioned stimulus obstructs the

   learning of a response to a second stimulus, conditioning has been _____.

4. Edward Thorndike proposed the _____ _____
   that says that responses that satisfy are more likely to be repeated, whereas those that don't satisfy are less likely to be repeated.

5. When learning is based on the coincidental association between the idea, object, or behavior and subsequent reinforcement, the mistaken belief that particular ideas, objects, or behavior will cause

   certain events to occur is called _____ _____.

6. _____ is the process of teaching a complex behavior by rewarding closer and closer approximations of the desired behavior.

7. The development of learning by using _____ _____
   requires building gradually on basic knowledge, with review and reinforcement when appropriate.

8. _____ _____ are built-in limitations in an organism's ability to learn particular behaviors.

9. A _____ _____ is a mental representation of spatial locations and directions.

10. _____ _____ occurs when a belief that one has no control of the environment is learned.

MATCHING QUESTIONS

_____ 11. classical conditioning

_____ 12. operant conditioning

_____ 13. escape conditioning

_____ 14. avoidance conditioning

_____ 15. cognitive learning theory

_____ 16. latent learning

_____ 17. observational learning

a. The study of the thought processes that underlie learning.

b. Learning that involves the imitation of a model.

c. A previously neutral stimulus comes to elicit a response through its association with a stimulus that naturally brings about the response.

d. A new behavior is acquired but not readily demonstrated until reinforcement is provided.

e. A voluntary response is strengthened or weakened, depending on its positive or negative consequences.

f. A response to a signal of an impending unpleasant event in a way that permits its evasion.

g. A response which brings about an end to an aversive situation.

_____ 18. neutral stimulus

_____ 19. unconditioned stimulus (UCS)

_____ 20. unconditioned response (UCR)

_____ 21. conditioned stimulus (CS)

_____ 22. conditioned response (CR)

a. A stimulus that brings about a response without having been learned.

b. A stimulus that, before conditioning, has no effect on the desired response.

c. A once-neutral stimulus that has been paired with an unconditioned stimulus to bring about a response formerly caused only by the unconditioned stimulus.

d. A response that, after conditioning, follows a previously neutral stimulus (e.g., salivation at the sound of a tuning fork).

e. A response that is natural and needs no training (e.g., salivation at the smell of food).

_____ 23. extinction

_____ 24. systematic desensitization

_____ 25. spontaneous recovery

_____ 26. stimulus generalization

_____ 27. stimulus discrimination

_____ 28. higher-order conditioning

a. The weakening and eventual disappearance of a conditioned response.

b. The reappearance of a previously extinguished response after a period of time during which the conditioned stimulus has been absent.

c. Occurs when an already conditioned stimulus is paired with a neutral stimulus until the neutral stimulus evokes the same response as the conditioned stimulus.

d. Response to a stimulus that is similar to but different from a conditioned stimulus; the more similar the two stimuli, the more likely generalization is to occur.

e. The process by which an organism learns to differentiate among stimuli, restricting its response to one in particular.

f. A form of therapy in which fears are minimized through gradual exposure to the source of fear.

_____ 29. primary reinforcer

_____ 30. secondary reinforcer

_____ 31. positive reinforcer

_____ 32. negative reinforcer

_____ 33. punishment

_____ 34. aversive stimuli

a. An unpleasant or painful stimulus that is added to the environment after a certain behavior occurs, decreasing the likelihood that the behavior will occur again.

b. Unpleasant or painful stimuli.

c. A reward that satisfies a biological need (e.g., hunger or thirst) and works naturally.

d. A stimulus added to the environment that brings about an increase in the response that preceded it.

e. A stimulus that becomes reinforcing by its association with a primary reinforcer (e.g., money, which allows us to obtain food, a primary reinforcer).

f. A stimulus whose removal is reinforcing, leading to a greater probability that the response bringing about this removal will occur again.

_____ 35. continuous reinforcement schedule

_____ 36. partial reinforcement schedule

_____ 37. cumulative recorder

_____ 38. fixed-ratio schedule

_____ 39. variable-ratio schedule

_____ 40. fixed-interval schedule

_____ 41. variable-interval schedule

a. Reinforcement occurs after a varying number of responses rather than after a fixed number.

b. Reinforcing of a behavior every time it occurs.

c. A device that records and graphs the pattern of responses.

d. Reinforcement is given at various times, usually causing a behavior to be maintained more consistently.

e. Reinforcing of a behavior some, but not all, of the time.

f. Reinforcement is given at established time intervals.

g. Reinforcement is given only after a certain number of responses is made.

_____ 42. reinforcer

_____ 43. schedules of reinforcement

_____ 44. stimulus control training

_____ 45. discriminative stimulus

_____ 46. model

_____ 47. behavior modification

a. A formalized technique for promoting the frequency of desirable behaviors and decreasing the incidence of unwanted ones.

b. A person serving as an example to an observer; the observer may imitate that person's behavior.

c. Any stimulus that increases the probability that a preceding behavior will be repeated.

d. A stimulus to which an organism learns to respond as part of stimulus control training.

e. The frequency and timing of reinforcement following desired behavior.

f. Training in which an organism is reinforced in the presence of a certain specific stimulus, but not in its absence.

PRACTICE QUESTIONS

Recite and Review: ☐

Test your knowledge of the chapter material by answering these **True-False** and **Multiple Choice Questions**. Check your answers with the Answer Key in the back of the *Study Guide*.

TRUE-FALSE QUESTIONS

T   F   1.   Learning cannot be observed directly; it must be inferred.

T   F   2.   Something that naturally causes a response without previous learning is called a conditioned stimulus.

T   F   3.   When a response recurs after extinction, spontaneous recovery has taken place.

T   F   4.   Watson's experiments with Baby Albert involved conditioning trials with a white rat. Yet Baby Albert also became fearful of other white, furry objects. This is an example of stimulus discrimination.

T   F   5.   In his experiments with rats that avoided water in the radiation chamber, Garcia showed that conditioning will not occur if there is a long delay between the presentation of the conditioned stimulus and the unconditioned stimulus.

T   F   6.   Sue wrote an exceptional term paper for psychology class; when her instructor graded it, he wrote many comments of praise on it. This behavioral sequence illustrates operant conditioning.

T   F   7.   Running away from a situation which you find noxious illustrates negative reinforcement.

T   F   8.   Punishing a child for misbehavior illustrates negative reinforcement.

T   F   9.   Behavior acquired under a continuous reinforcement schedule is learned faster and is maintained longer than behavior learned under a partial reinforcement schedule.

T   F   10.   Behaviors learned on a partial reinforcement schedule are more resistant to extinction than those learned on a continuous reinforcement schedule.

MULTIPLE CHOICE QUESTIONS

1.   Your text describes the story of Brad Gabrielson and Bo, his helper. The story illustrates:
   a.   the complete devotion of the dog at all costs.
   b.   another handicapped person with lesser liabilities.
   c.   a person who was highly trained to care for Gabrielson's handicap because of participation in a special experimental government training program.
   d.   how specially trained animals can improve the lives of handicapped individuals.

2.   All performance improvements that result from simply getting older are considered:
   a.   maturation.   c.   modeling.
   b.   learning.   d.   imitation.

3. Learning is best defined as:
    a. a change in behavior brought about by growth and maturity of the nervous system.
    b. a measurable change in behavior brought about by conditions such as drugs, sleep, and fatigue.
    c. a behavioral response that occurs each time a critical stimulus is presented.
    d. a relatively permanent change in behavior brought about by experience.

4. The changes in behavior brought about by learning:
    a. are hard to measure.   c. must be measured indirectly.
    b. are easily extinguished.   d. are generally maturational.

5. In classical conditioning, the stimulus that comes to elicit a response that it would not previously have elicited is called the:
    a. classical stimulus.   c. conditioned stimulus.
    b. unconditioned stimulus.   d. discriminative stimulus.

6. Through conditioning, a dog learns to salivate at the sound of a bell because the bell signals that food is coming. In subsequent learning trials, a buzzer is sounded just prior to the bell. Soon the dog salivates at the sound of the buzzer. In this case, the bell acts as the:
    a. unconditioned stimulus.   c. unconditioned response.
    b. conditioned stimulus.   d. conditioned response.

7. In classical conditioning, the unconditioned stimulus automatically produces the:
    a. unconditioned response.   c. conditioned stimulus.
    b. neutral stimulus.   d. generalized response.

8. In preparing food for her daughter, Joanna uses a juicer. Soon the baby knows that the sound of the juicer signals that food is on the way. In this case, the food acts as:
    a. an unconditioned stimulus.   c. an unconditioned response.
    b. a conditioned stimulus.   d. a conditioned response.

9. In preparing food for his young son, Ron uses a blender. Soon the baby knows that the sound of the blender signals that food is on the way. In this case, the blender acts as:
    a. an unconditioned stimulus.   c. an unconditioned response.
    b. a conditioned stimulus.   d. a conditioned response.

10. The primary result of classical conditioning is that:
    a. the conditioned stimulus produces a conditioned response, signifying that learning has occurred.
    b. voluntary responses become associated with the unconditioned stimulus.
    c. the unconditioned response is elicited by the conditioned stimulus whenever it is presented.
    d. it has been demonstrated in a variety of animal species.

11. The child who stands fearfully in line while waiting to be inoculated is exhibiting:
    a. an unconditioned response.   c. systematic desensitization.
    b. an innate, involuntary response. d. a conditioned response.

12. Prior to the conditioning trials in which Watson planned to condition fear of a rat in Baby Albert, the rat—which Albert was known not to fear—would have been considered:
    a. an unconditioned stimulus.   c. a discriminative stimulus.
    b. an adaptive stimulus.   d. a neutral stimulus.

13. Which of the following takes place after conditioning, when the conditioned stimulus is presented repeatedly without being paired with the unconditioned stimulus?
    a. learning
    b. perception
    c. systematic desensitization
    d. extinction

14. Systematic desensitization is achieved by:
    a. no longer allowing the conditioned stimulus and the unconditioned stimulus to be paired in real-life situations.
    b. constructing a hierarchy of situations that produce fear and then gradually pairing less stressful situations with strategies to relax.
    c. identifying the situations that produce fear in order to modify or eliminate them.
    d. gaining exposure to the most fearful situations so that the unpleasant reactions can be extinguished quickly.

15. Systematic desensitization is most closely associated with:
    a. operant conditioning.
    b. token economy.
    c. spontaneous recovery.
    d. extinction.

16. A previously conditioned response becomes weaker and eventually disappears through:
    a. operant conditioning.
    b. token economy.
    c. spontaneous recovery.
    d. extinction.

17. A classically conditioned response can be extinguished by:
    a. adding another conditioned stimulus to the pairing.
    b. no longer presenting the unconditioned stimulus after the conditioned response.
    c. using stimulus substitution.
    d. reintroducing the unconditioned stimulus.

18. Victor participates in aversive conditioning in order to stop smoking. Now he dislikes cigarettes and has also linked his dislike to the store where he used to buy them. This reaction illustrates:
    a. operant conditioning.
    b. stimulus discrimination.
    c. higher-order conditioning.
    d. systematic desensitization.

19. You can distinguish a certain make of automobiles by the design of the grillwork. This ability is an example of:
    a. stimulus discrimination.
    b. higher-order conditioning.
    c. spontaneous recovery.
    d. instrumental conditioning.

20. The U.S. Customs Service uses dogs at airports and docks to stop illegal drug shipments. Typically, the dogs are trained to sniff out a specific drug, such as cocaine, and to ignore all other drugs. The ability of the dogs to respond only to the specific drug they were trained to detect is an example of:
    a. stimulus discrimination.
    b. response generalization.
    c. partial reinforcement.
    d. spontaneous recovery.

21. Pavlov's assumption that stimuli and responses were linked in a mechanistic, unthinking way has been challenged by:
    a. cognitive learning theorists.
    b. the animal trainers, the Brelands.
    c. Edward Thorndike's law of effect.
    d. operant conditioning.

22. Garcia's behavioral investigations of rats which were treated with doses of radiation illustrate that:
    a. rats obey slightly different principles of classical conditioning than humans do.
    b. some research findings involving classical conditioning do not appear to obey Pavlov's conditioning principles.
    c. classical conditioning is a very robust form of learning, since it is not weakened even by large doses of medication.
    d. changes in classical conditioning are highly sensitive indicators of radiation effects.

23. Operant conditioning is to _____ as classical conditioning is to _____.
    a. voluntary response; involuntary response.
    b. observational learning; cognitive map
    c. volitional behavior; free will.
    d. negative reinforcer; positive reinforcer.

24. Brushing your teeth is an example of behavior that is learned through:
    a. cognitive learning.
    b. spatial conditioning.
    c. maturation.
    d. operant conditioning.

25. Which alternative below is **not** an example of operant conditioning?
    a. A cat pushes against a lever to open a door on its cage.
    b. A student drives within the speed limit to avoid getting another parking ticket.
    c. A dog rolls over for a dog biscuit.
    d. A student's blood pressure increases when she anticipates speaking with her chemistry professor.

26. When we continue to act in a manner that will lead to pleasing consequences, we behave according to the:
    a. law of frequency.
    b. principle of similarity.
    c. law of effect.
    d. principle of contiguity.

27. Which name below is **not** associated with classical conditioning or operant conditioning?
    a. Pavlov
    b. Skinner
    c. Wertheimer
    d. Thorndike

28. The distinction between primary reinforcers and secondary reinforcers is that:
    a. primary reinforcers satisfy some biological need; secondary reinforcers are effective because of their association with primary reinforcers.
    b. organisms prefer primary reinforcers to secondary reinforcers.
    c. primary reinforcers are not effective with all organisms.
    d. primary reinforcers depend upon the past conditioning of the organism; secondary reinforcers have a biological basis.

29. Typically, food is a _____, whereas money is a _____.
    a. discriminative stimulus; conditioned reinforcer
    b. need; motive
    c. primary reinforcer; secondary reinforcer
    d. drive reducer; natural reinforcer

30. Any stimulus that increases the likelihood that a preceding behavior be repeated is called:
    a. a punisher.
    b. a reinforcer.
    c. a response.
    d. an operant.

31. According to the definition given in the text, which of the following is most likely to be considered a primary reinforcer?
    a. money
    b. water
    c. good grades
    d. a hammer

32. Negative reinforcement:
    a. is a special form of punishment.
    b. is a phenomenon that results when reward is withheld.
    c. involves the decrease or removal of an aversive stimulus.
    d. occurs in both classical and instrumental conditioning.

33. According to the text, in which of the following situations would the use of punishment be most effective in reducing the undesired behavior?
    a. An employee is demoted for misfiling a report.
    b. A child is spanked for hitting her sister.
    c. A teenager is denied the opportunity to attend the Friday dance for staying out late on Monday.
    d. A child is spanked for running into the street.

34. Under variable schedules of reinforcement, the response rate is:
    a. always high.
    b. always constant and low.
    c. easily extinguished.
    d. highly resistant to extinction.

35. Piecework in a factory, where a worker is paid for three pieces made, is an example of a:
    a. fixed-interval schedule of reinforcement.
    b. variable-interval schedule of reinforcement.
    c. variable-ratio schedule of reinforcement.
    d. fixed-ratio schedule of reinforcement.

36. Since the number of responses made by a door-to-door salesperson before reinforcement in the form of a sale is not certain, he or she is working on a:
    a. variable-ratio schedule.
    b. fixed-ratio schedule.
    c. variable-interval schedule.
    d. fixed-interval schedule.

37. With a fixed-interval schedule, especially in the period just after reinforcement, response rates are:
    a. speeded up.
    b. extinguished.
    c. relatively unchanged
    d. relatively low.

38. The typical study pattern of a college student that "crams" right before the examinations looks most like the response rate that is observed in a:
    a. fixed-interval schedule of reinforcement.
    b. variable-interval schedule of reinforcement.
    c. variable-ratio schedule of reinforcement.
    d. fixed-ratio schedule of reinforcement.

39. Superstitious behavior is thought to arise because of:
    a. continuously reinforced patterns of behavior that have led to results related to the behavior.
    b. universal biological constraints that guide specific kinds of behavior.
    c. religious dogma.
    d. partial reinforcement of the connection of incidental events to a specific consequence.

40. Rewarding each step toward a desired behavior _____ the new response pattern.
    a. inhibits
    b. shapes
    c. disrupts
    d. eliminates

41. Which alternative below is probably **not** good advice in selecting materials for computer-assisted programmed instruction?
    a. Determine if the materials use shaping procedures when incorrect answers are given.
    b. Establish that the programs provide appropriate reinforcement for correct answers.
    c. Determine whether the materials have been field-tested.
    d. Ensure that the developers of the materials have taken courses in learning and memory.

42. Which of the following is a limitation of programmed instruction?
    a. The user cannot ask questions beyond those programmed into the computer.
    b. There is no provision for error analysis.
    c. Reinforcement is routinely delayed.
    d. Computers are not generally available.

43. A new generation of computers can teach themselves to learn through the technology of:
    a. programmed instruction.
    b. neural networks.
    c. partial reinforcement.
    d. multiaxial connections.

44. _____ constitute built-in hereditary limitations to conditioning.
    a. Fixed action patterns
    b. Biofeedback mechanisms
    c. Cognitive maps
    d. Biological constraints

45. Psychologists who emphasize unseen mental processes that intervene in learning are would be called:
    a. personality psychologists.
    b. sensory psychologists.
    c. cognitive psychologists.
    d. biopsychologists.

46. Which of the following is especially effective in situations where shaping may be inappropriate or unethical (like neurosurgery, race car driving, and parenting)?
    a. classical conditioning
    b. learned helplessness
    c. observational learning
    d. insight

47. People who exhibit learned helplessness feel that they:
    a. are unable to learn anything new.
    b. have no control over their environment.
    c. can learn only if new behaviors are shaped.
    d. have no control over their behavior.

ESSAY QUESTIONS

Recite and Review: ❏

Essay Question 7.1: *Using Physical Punishment*

The use of physical punishment has become quite controversial. Most school systems now outlaw its use, and many parents try to find alternatives to it. Define the issues related to the use of punishment, and answer the question, "Is it wrong to use physical punishment to discipline children?" As you answer, consider whether there are circumstances that may require routine use, or should it be rare. Describe alternatives for use in normal disciplining of children.

_____

_____

_____

_____

_____

_____

_____

_____

_____

_____

_____

_____

_____

_____

_____

_____

_____

_____

Essay Question 7.2: *Which Approach Is Correct?*

Three approaches to learning are described in the text. Classical and operant conditioning rely on external determinants of behavior, and cognitive learning depends in part on internal, mental activity. How can the differences between these three approaches be reconciled?

_____

_____

_____

_____

_____

_____

_____

_____

_____

_____

_____

_____

_____

_____

_____

_____

ACTIVITIES AND PROJECTS

1. Either write about or discuss with a friend a fear that you have—a fear of cats, mice, dogs, insects, spiders, heights, being home alone, or any other fear. How did you acquire the fear? Can you see any connection between acquiring the fear and the principles of classical conditioning? How might the fear be explained through conditioning? Has the fear extended to other stimuli through higher-order conditioning or through stimulus generalization? Why has your fear not been extinguished?

2. Keep a record for several days of the activities that you undertake and the kinds of rewards and other reinforcements you give yourself or receive from others. Include the time you do the activity and whether anyone was with you. After several days, review the list and the related reinforcement. Are there any patterns? Do you tend to accept offers to do things that distract you from study (like going for pizza, going to the game room, or watching television or a movie) more readily than offers that distract you from other activities? What other patterns do you find? Do you reinforce your study time with food or with some other form of relaxation?

8

MEMORY

DETAILED OUTLINE

Survey: ☐

This detailed outline contains all the headings in Chapter 8: Memory. If you are using the SQ3R method, then an examination of the outline is the best way to begin your survey of the chapter.

Prologue: Pamilla Smith
Looking Ahead

Encoding, Storage, and Retrieval of Memory
   The three stages of memory: The storehouses of memory
      Sensory memory
      Short-term memory: Our working memory
      Rehearsal
      Long-term memory: The final storehouse
      Episodic and semantic memories
   The Cutting Edge Implicit Memory: Retention without Remembering
      Storage in long-term memory
   Levels of processing
   ● **Recap and Review I**

Recalling Long-Term Memories
   Flashbulb memories
   Constructive processes in memory: Rebuilding the past
Psychology at Work Memory on Trial: The Fallibility of Witnesses
   Autobiographical memory: Where past meets present
   Everyday memory: Different in the laboratory?
   ● **Recap and Review II**

Forgetting: When Memory Fails
   Proactive and retroactive interference: The before and after of forgetting
   The biological bases of memory: The search for the engram
   Memory dysfunctions: Afflictions of forgetting
The Informed Consumer of Psychology Improving Your Memory
   ● **Recap and Review III**

Looking Back
Key Terms and Concepts

➤ Now that you have surveyed the chapter, read **Looking Ahead**, pages 242–243. *Question:* ☐
Focus on the questions on pages 242–243. *Read:* ☐

CONCEPTS AND LEARNING OBJECTIVES

Survey: ☐

These are the concepts and the learning objects for Chapter 8. Read them carefully as part of your preliminary survey of the chapter.

Concept 1: Memory's role in human behavior is to aid in the management of information. Memory involves three processes: encoding, storage, and retrieval. There are also three main types of memory: sensory, short-term, and long-term, and these types are distinguished according to how long the information stays in them (storage), how they are acquired (encoded), and how they are recalled (retrieval).

1. Define memory and the basic processes of encoding, storing, and retrieving information. (pp. 242-244)

2. Describe the three stages of memory, and discuss sensory memory. (pp. 244-246)

3. Describe the characteristics and limitations of short-term memory. (pp. 246-249)

4. Describe the characteristics of long-term memory and the way information is stored in and retrieved from long-term memory, and distinguish implicit and explicit memory. (pp. 249-252)

5. Distinguish the levels of processing theory from the three stages of sensory, short-term, and long-term memory. (pp. 252-253)

Concept 2: Recollection from long-term memory presents a number of issues regarding the accuracy of the memory, the way it was stored, and its specific nature.

6. Define the means of recalling information from long-term memory and the characteristics of memory that improve recall. (pp. 254-257)

7. Define constructive processes and discuss how schemas, serial production, and the soap opera effect construct memories as well as issues regarding the accuracy of constructed memory. (pp. 257-260)

8. Describe autobiographical and everyday memory. (pp. 260-262)

Concept 3: Forgetting is a normal process of memory, and it is required in order to make memory more efficient. The major forms of forgetting include the decay theory and the concept of interference. Memory dysfunctions can have biological and psychological causes.

9. Discuss how memories are forgotten, especially the role of proactive and retroactive interference. (pp. 262-265)

10. Describe the biological basis of memory processes. (pp. 265-266)

11. Discuss the common memory dysfunctions. (pp. 266-267)

12. Describe techniques for improving memory skills. (pp. 268-270)

CHAPTER SUMMARY

There are several ways you can use this summary as part of your systematic study plan. You may read each concept summary and then read the corresponding pages in the text, or you may read the entire summary and then read the entire chapter in the text. As you finish each section, complete the **Recap and Review** questions that are supplied in the text.

CONCEPT 1: Prologue and Looking Ahead
　　　　　　Encoding, Storage, and Retrieval of Memory

Survey: ☐
Read: ☐

Pages 242-254

The case of Pamilla Smith described in the Prologue illustrates the importance of memory to daily life. Her loss of the ability to form new memories also illustrates the close connection between the biological foundation of memory and its proper function.

Three processes comprise memory. **Encoding** is the process of placing information in a form that can be used by memory. **Storage** is the process of retaining information for later use. **Retrieval** is the process of recovering information from storage. By definition, then, **memory** is the sum of these three processes. Forgetting is an important part of memory because it allows us to make generalizations and abstractions from daily life.

The memory system is typically divided into three storage components or stages. The initial stage is that of **sensory memory**, where momentary storage of sensory information occurs. **Short-term memory** includes information that has been given some form of meaning, and it lasts for fifteen to twenty-five seconds. **Long-term memory** is the relatively permanent storage of memory. While there are no locations in the brain of these memory stages, they are considered abstract memory systems with different characteristics.

Sensory memories are considered to differ according to the kind of sensory information, and the sensory memory is thought of as several types of sensory memories based on the source of the sensory messages. Visual sensory memory is called **iconic memory**, and its source is the visual sensory system; and auditory sensory memory is called **echoic memory**, and its source is the auditory sensory system. Sensory memory stores information for a very short time. Iconic memory may last no more than a second, and echoic memory may last for three to four seconds. The duration of iconic memory was established by George Sperling's classic experiment in which subjects were unable to recall an entire array of letters but could, on a cue after the array was shown for one-twentieth of a second, recall any part of the array. Unless the information taken into the sensory memories is somehow transferred to another memory system, they are quickly lost.

Sensory memories are raw information without meaning. In order to be transferred to the long-term memory, these sensory memories must be given meaning and placed in short-term memory. One view of this process suggests that the short-term memory is composed of verbal representations that have a very short duration. George Miller has identified the capacity of short-term memory as seven plus or minus two **chunks**, or meaningful groups of stimuli that are stored as a unit in the short-term memory. Chunks can be several letters or numbers or can be complicated patterns, like the patterns of pieces on a chessboard. However, to be placed in a chunk, the board must represent a real or possible game even for chess masters to be able to make a chunk.

Memory can be held in short-term memory longer by **rehearsal**, the repetition of information already in the short-term memory. Rehearsal is also the beginning of transferring memory into long-term memory. The kind of rehearsal influences the effectiveness of the transfer to long-term memory. Elaborative rehearsal occurs whenever the material is associated with other information through placement in a logical framework, connection with another memory, the formation of an image, or some other transformation. The strategies for organizing memories are called **mnemonics**. Mnemonics are formal techniques for organizing information so that recall is more likely.

The evidence for the existence of a separate long-term memory system comes from cases like that of Pamilla Smith and others who have damage that allows short-term memories but not the creation of new long-term memories. Experiments have demonstrated that if new information is not allowed to be processed, then after a period of time, the information is lost.

Two kinds of long-term memory have been identified. **Episodic memories** are memories of specific events related to individual experiences. **Semantic memories** are those that consist of abstract knowledge and facts about the world. Psychologists use the **associative model** to suggest that semantic memories represent the associations between mental representations of various pieces of information. When we think about a particular thing, related ideas are activated because of the association. **Priming** refers to the activation of one item, thereby making recall of related items easier. **Explicit memory** refers to intentional or conscious effort to recall memory, and **implicit memory** refers to memories of which people are not consciously aware but nevertheless affect later performance and behavior. Implicit memory is illustrated by a tendency for surgical patients to use words in an association test that were spoken during the surgery when they were under anaesthesia.

One of the main ways memories are stored in long-term memory is through the **linguistic code**, that is, language. We also store information in an **imaginal code**, or visual images, and a third way is through the **motor code**, or physical activity.

An alternative to the three-stage view of memory is the **levels-of-processing theory**. This theory suggests that the difference in memories depends on the depth to which particular information is processed, that is, the degree to which information is analyzed and considered. The more attention information is given, the deeper it is stored and the less likely it is to be forgotten. Superficial aspects of information are given shallow processing, and when meaning is given, the processing is at its deepest level. The levels-of-processing approach suggests that memory requires more active mental processing than does the three-stage approach.

CONCEPT 2: Recalling Long-Term Memories

Survey: ☐
Read: ☐

Pages 254-262

Retrieving information from long-term memory may be influenced by many factors. The **tip-of-the-tongue** phenomenon, where one is certain of knowing something but cannot recall it, represents one difficulty. The simple number of items of information that has been stored may influence recall. We sort through this quantity with the help of **retrieval cues**. These are stimuli that allow recall from long-term memory. **Recall** consists of a series of processes—a search through memory, retrieval of potentially relevant information, then a decision whether the information is accurate, and a continuation of these steps until the right information is found. In contrast, **recognition** involves determining whether a stimulus that has been presented is correct, such as the selection of the stimulus from a list or determining whether the stimulus has been seen before.

In particularly intense events, we may develop flashbulb memories, where due to a specific, important or surprising event memories are so vivid that they appear as if a snapshot of the event. Research regarding flashbulb memories concerning President Kennedy's assassination has revealed common details, such as where the person was, who told the person, the person's own emotions, and some personal detail of the event. Harsh and Neisser asked students the day after the *Challenger* accident how they had heard about it, and then asked the same question three years later. One-third were wrong, a result suggesting that flashbulb memories may be inaccurate. Memories that are exceptional may be more easily retrieved than commonplace information. The **von Restorff effect** refers to the increase in likelihood of recall with the increase in distinctiveness of information.

Our memories reflect **constructive processes**, processes in which memories are influenced by the meaning we have attached to them. Guesses and inferences thus influence memory. Sir Frederic Bartlett first suggested that people remember in terms of **schemas** which are general themes without specific details and that these schemas were based on understanding of the event, expectations, and an understanding of the motivation of others. The process of **serial reproduction**, a process that requires people to pass information from one to another in a sequence, has shown the effect of schemas. The final story is much changed in comparison to the original version, and it reflects the expectations of those retelling the story. Apparently, prior knowledge and expectations influence how we initially store the information. How we understand peoples' motivation also influences memory. In the **soap opera effect**, knowledge about a person's motivation leads to an elaboration of past events involving that person.

The imperfection of memory has led to research into the accuracy of eye-witness testimony. The mistaken identification of individuals can lead to imprisonment. When a weapon is involved, the weapon draws attention away from other details. In research involving staged crimes, witnesses vary significantly in their judgment of the height of the perpetrator, with judgments differing by as much as two feet. The wording of questions can influence testimony. Children are especially prone to unreliable recollections.

Autobiographical memories are our collections of information about our lives. People tend to forget information about the past that is incongruent with the way they currently see themselves. Depressed people tend to recall sad events more readily than happy ones from their past. More recent information also appears to be more affected than recollections from earlier times.

Everyday memory differs from memories studied in a laboratory. In one study, a researcher and a companion took a bicycle tour of Europe, and the researcher recorded daily details. After the trip, the companion was able to recall the frequency of events with accuracy. Critics of this naturalistic study argue that it is difficult to generalize results from this kind of study. The middle ground is to suggest that research depends upon the care taken, not where it is done.

CONCEPT 3: Forgetting: When Memory Fails

Survey: ☐
Read: ☐

Pages 262-270

Herman Ebbinghaus studied forgetting by learning a list of nonsense syllables and then timing how long it took him, at a later trial, to relearn the list. The most rapid forgetting occurs in the first nine hours. Two views concerning the forgetting of information have been developed. One theory explains forgetting by **decay**, or the loss of information through nonuse. When a memory is formed, a **memory trace**, or **engram**, occurs. An engram is an actual physical change in the brain. The decay theory assumes that memories become more decayed with time, but the evidence does not support this happening, though there is support for the existence of decay. The other theory proposes that **interference** between bits of information leads to forgetting. In interference, information blocks or displaces other information, preventing recall. Most forgetting appears to be the result of interference.

There are two kinds of interference. One is called **proactive interference** which occurs when previously learned information blocks the recall of newer information. **Retroactive interference** is when new information blocks the recall of old information. Most research suggests that information that has been blocked by interference can eventually be recalled if appropriate stimuli are used.

It was originally thought that memories were evenly distributed throughout the brain. However, the current view suggests that the areas of the brain that are responsible for processing information about the world also store that information. The appearance of the even distribution of information is probably the result of the fact that every memory is composed of a variety of information about particular events or skills, thus several areas of the brain must be involved in every memory. Evidence also suggests that the hippocampus plays a central role in the formation of memories by transforming sensory information into the form that eventually becomes the long-term memory. Neurotransmitters and glucose in the blood also have an influence on memory.

Alzheimer's disease has severe memory problems as one of its many symptoms. Initially, the symptoms appear as simple forgetfulness, progressing to more profound loss of memory, even failure to recognize one's own name and the loss of language abilities. The protein beta amyloid, important for maintaining neural connections, has been implicated in the progress of the disease. **Amnesia** is another memory problem. Amnesia is a loss of memory occurring without apparent loss of mental function. **Retrograde amnesia** is memory loss for memories that preceded a traumatic event. **Anterograde amnesia** is a loss for memories that follow a traumatic event. Long-term alcoholics who develop **Korsakoff's syndrome** also have amnesia. Korsakoff's syndrome is related to thiamine deficiency. A perfect memory, one with total recall, might actually be very discomforting. A case studied by Luria of a man with total recall reveals that the inability to forget becomes debilitating.

The *Informed Consumer of Psychology* section outlines several mnemonic techniques and how they can be applied to taking tests. They include the **keyword technique**, in which one pairs a word with a mental image, or in the case of learning a foreign language, the foreign word with a similar sounding English word. The **method of loci** requires that one imagine items to be remembered as being placed in particular locations. Another phenomenon that affects memory is called **encoding specificity**. Recall is best when it is attempted in conditions that are similar to the conditions under which the information was originally learned. The organization of text and lecture material may enhance memory of it. Practice and rehearsal also improve long-term recall. Rehearsal to the point of mastery is called **overlearning**. It should be noted that cramming for exams is an ineffective technique, and the better approach is to distribute practice over many sessions.

➤ Now that you have surveyed, questioned, and read the chapter and completed
    the **Recap and Review** questions, review **Looking Back**, pages 271–272.   *Review:* ☐

➤ For additional practice through recitation and review, test your knowledge of the chapter material by answering the questions in the ***Key Word Drill***, the ***Practice Questions***, and the ***Essay Questions***.

KEY WORD DRILL   *Recite:* ☐

The following **Fill in the Blank** and **Matching Questions** test key words from the text. Check your answers with the Answer Key in the back of the *Study Guide*.

FILL IN THE BLANK

1. _____ is defined as the capacity to record, retain, and retrieve information.

2. In short term-memory, a meaningful grouping of stimuli would be stored as a _____.

3. _____ refers to the formal techniques for organizing material to increase the likelihood of its being remembered.

4. Intentional or conscious recollection of information is called _____ memory and memories of which people are not consciously aware, but which can improve subsequent performance and behavior is called _____ memory.

5. The _____ -of- _____ theory suggests that the way information is initially perceived and learned determines how difficult it is to recall.

6. Whenever you experience an inability to recall information, but you realize that you know it, the _____ -of-the- _____ _____ has probably resulted because of the difficulty of retrieving information from long-term memory.

7. _____ _____ result when memories are influenced by the interpretation and meaning we give to events.

8. When we remember situations in terms of general themes, we are using _____.

9. Information is lost through _____ when it is not used.

10. The phenomenon called _____ refers to occasions when recall is hindered because of other information in memory which displaces or blocks it out.

MATCHING QUESTIONS

_____ 11. encoding

_____ 12. storage

_____ 13. retrieval

_____ 14. sensory memory

_____ 15. short-term memory

_____ 16. long-term memory

a. Locating and using information stored in memory.

b. Relatively permanent memory.

c. Information recorded as a meaningless stimulus.

d. Recording information in a form usable to memory.

e. Working memory that lasts about fifteen to twenty-five seconds.

f. The location where information is saved.

_____ 17. iconic memory

_____ 18. echoic memory

_____ 19. episodic memories

_____ 20. semantic memories

_____ 21. motor code

a. Memory storage based on physical activities.

b. Stored information relating to personal experiences.

c. Stored, organized facts about the world (e.g., mathematical and historical data).

d. The storage of information obtained from the sense of hearing.

e. The storage of visual information.

_____ 22. retrieval cue

_____ 23. recall

_____ 24. recognition

_____ 25. flashbulb memories

_____ 26. von Restorff effect

_____ 27. serial reproduction

_____ 28. soap opera effect

a. Drawing from memory a specific piece of information for a specific purpose.

b. The phenomenon by which distinctive stimuli are recalled more readily than less distinctive ones.

c. The phenomenon by which memory of a prior event involving a person is more reliable when we understand that person's motivations.

d. Memories of a specific event that are so clear they seem like "snapshots" of the event.

e. Acknowledging prior exposure to a given stimulus, rather than recalling the information from memory.

f. A stimulus such as a word, smell, or sound that aids recall of information located in long-term memory.

g. The passage of interpretive information from person to person, often resulting in inaccuracy through personal bias and misinterpretation.

_____ 29. memory trace

_____ 30. proactive interference

_____ 31. retroactive interference

_____ 32. keyword technique

_____ 33. method of loci

_____ 34. encoding specificity

_____ 35. overlearning

a. The pairing of a foreign word with a common, similar sounding English word to aid in remembering the new word.

b. A physical change in the brain corresponding to the memory of material.

c. New information interferes with the recall of information learned earlier.

d. Rehearsing material beyond the point of mastery to improve long-term recall.

e. Assigning words or ideas to places, thereby improving recall of the words by envisioning those places.

f. Memory of information is enhanced when recalled under the same conditions as when it was learned.

g. Information stored in memory interferes with recall of material learned later.

_____ 36. rehearsal

_____ 37. associative models

_____ 38. priming

_____ 39. linguistic code

_____ 40. imaginal code

_____ 41. autobiographical memory

_____ 42. engram

a. A technique of recalling information by having been exposed to related information at an earlier time.

b. Memory storage based on visual images.

c. The transfer of material from short- to long-term memory by repetition.

d. Memory storage relying on language.

e. Recollections of the facts about our own lives.

f. A physical change in the brain corresponding to the memory of material.

g. A technique of recalling information by thinking about related information.

_____ 43. Alzheimer's disease

_____ 44. amnesia

_____ 45. retrograde amnesia

_____ 46. anterograde amnesia

_____ 47. Korsakoff's syndrome

a. An illness associated with aging that includes severe memory loss and loss of language abilities.

b. A memory impairment disease among alcoholics.

c. Memory loss unaccompanied by other mental difficulties.

d. Memory loss of the events following an injury.

e. Memory loss of occurrences prior to some event.

PRACTICE QUESTIONS

Recite and Review: ☐

Test your knowledge of the chapter material by answering these **True-False** and **Multiple Choice Questions**. Check your answers with the Answer Key in the back of the *Study Guide*.

TRUE-FALSE QUESTIONS

T   F   1.   It is probably difficult for the average person to store phone numbers of ten digits or more in short-term memory.

T   F   2.   In order for information to reach long-term memory, it must first be transferred from sensory memory to short-term memory.

T   F   3.   A psychology student's understanding of the concept of semantic memory is likely to be stored in memory as an imaginal code.

T   F   4.   Flashbulb memories are memories that are centered around a specific, important event.

T   F   5.   Heather is having difficulty recalling the name of a favorite restaurant in a nearby city. As she drives into that town, however, the name suddenly comes to mind. This phenomenon is called serial reproduction.

T   F   6.   Using the process of serial reproduction, memory researchers have found that people are remarkably accurate in their descriptions of incidents.

T   F   7.   We fail to remember events mainly because of the passage of time between our first exposure and recall.

T   F   8.   Most of forgetting is due to decay of the memory trace.

T   F   9.   It would be very advantageous to have a type of memory in which nothing is ever forgotten.

T   F   10.   Korsakoff's syndrome is a disease of unknown cause, resulting in memory loss and confusion.

MULTIPLE CHOICE QUESTIONS

1. The process of recording information in a form that can be recalled is:
   a. encoding.
   b. storage.
   c. decoding.
   d. retrieval.

2. Recording information in the memory system is referred to as:
   a. encoding.
   b. storage.
   c. decoding.
   d. retrieval.

3. The process of identifying and using information stored in memory is referred to as:
   a. storage.
   b. retrieval.
   c. recording.
   d. learning.

4. The stage of momentary storage of information, lasting only an instant and consisting only of raw stimuli, is called:
   a. sensory memory.
   b. short-term memory.
   c. episodic memory.
   d. long-term memory.

5. _____ stores information for approximately fifteen to twenty seconds.
   a. Sensory memory
   b. Short-term memory
   c. Iconic memory
   d. Long-term memory

6. As Mark listened to the television news, his young son talked excitedly about the new puppy next door. Somewhat frustrated, the boy exclaimed, "You're not paying attention to me!" At this point, Mark diverted his attention to his son and recited the last few things the boy had said. Which memory system is responsible for this ability?
   a. episodic memory
   b. echoic memory
   c. iconic memory
   d. short-term memory

7. Which of the following statements about sensory memory is true?
   a. The information is held until it is replaced by new information.
   b. The information is an accurate representation of the stimulus.
   c. The information is an incomplete representation of the stimulus.
   d. The information is lost if it is not meaningful.

8. Information in short-term memory is stored according to its:
   a. meaning.
   b. intensity.
   c. length.
   d. sense.

9. Short-term memory can hold approximately:
   a. five items.
   b. seven items.
   c. ten items.
   d. eighteen items.

10. The process of grouping information into units for storage in short-term memory is called:
    a. similarity.
    b. priming.
    c. chunking.
    d. closure.

11.   One purpose of rehearsal is:
   a.   to attach linguistic codes to echoic memory.
   b.   to maintain information in short-term memory.
   c.   to transfer information from sensory to short-term memory.
   d.   to organize material for chunking.

12.   In order to enhance transferral to long-term memory, _____ may be necessary while information is in the short-term stage.
   a.   massed practice   c.   interpolation
   b.   elaborative rehearsal   d.   interference

13.   Which is **not** a characteristic of long-term memory?
   a.   It has almost unlimited storage capacity.
   b.   Memories recalled are highly accurate, faithful, and almost verbatim reproductions of the original information.
   c.   This stage of memory is nonexistent in some patients with brain injury.
   d.   It retains memories for years.

14.   Recalling what we have done and the kinds of experiences we have had best illustrates:
   a.   periodic memory.   c.   semantic memory.
   b.   episodic memory.   d.   serial production memory.

15.   Knowledge about grammar, spelling, historical dates, and other knowledge about the world best illustrates:
   a.   periodic memory.   c.   semantic memory.
   b.   episodic memory.   d.   serial production memory.

16.   Episodic memories are different from semantic memories in that:
   a.   episodic memories deal with personal experiences.
   b.   episodic memories deal with thought and language.
   c.   episodic memories exist in long-term memory, whereas semantic memories exist only in short-term memory.
   d.   the number of episodic memories is restricted.

17.   Which codes would most likely be used to establish a cognitive map?
   a.   semantic codes   c.   linguistic codes
   b.   imaginal codes   d.   mnemonic codes

18.   Your memory of how to skate is probably based on:
   a.   a motor code.   c.   elaborative rehearsal.
   b.   semantic memory.   d.   an imaginal code.

19.   Memory storage based on mental, visual representation is called:
   a.   a linguistic code.   c.   an imaginal code.
   b.   a semantic code.   d.   a motor code.

20.   Storage of verbal material in long-term memory without visual imagery is accomplished through:
   a.   an imaginal code.   c.   a sensory code.
   b.   a motor code.   d.   a linguistic code.

21. Linguistic, imaginal, and motor codes are ways that information is:
    a. introduced to short-term memory.
    b. shifted from long-term to short-term memory.
    c. stored in long-term memory.
    d. transferred from sensory to long-term memory.

22. According to the levels-of-processing model, what determines how well specific information is remembered?
    a. the stage attained
    b. the meaning of the information
    c. the quality of the information
    d. the depth of processing

23. Which alternative below is **not** a distinguishing feature of the levels-of-processing approach?
    a. It maintains the distinction between short-term and long-term memory stages.
    b. It suggests that the way information is processed initially greatly influences how well that information is remembered.
    c. It suggests that relating initial information to other memories will improve recall.
    d. It suggests that examination of various strategies for how initial information is processed (such as shape or meaning) will provide a useful understanding of memory.

24. Information from long-term memory is easier to access with the aid of:
    a. a retrieval cue.
    b. distractors.
    c. interpolated material.
    d. a sensory code.

25. Finding the correct answer on a multiple choice test depends on:
    a. serial search.
    b. recall.
    c. mnemonics.
    d. recognition.

26. The tip-of-the-tongue phenomenon exemplifies difficulties in:
    a. encoding.
    b. decoding.
    c. storage.
    d. retrieval.

27. The detailed, vivid account of what you were doing when you learned of the Challenger disaster represents a:
    a. cognitive map.
    b. schema.
    c. flashbulb memory.
    d. seizure.

28. Constructive processes are associated with all of the following **except**:
    a. memorization.
    b. motivation.
    c. expectation.
    d. organization.

29. Which of the following experiences would be **least** influenced by the von Restorff effect?
    a. You recall almost word for word what your psychology professor said to you and your class of over 100 peers about your exceptional term paper on neuropsychology.
    b. During a memory experiment, you remember the random number 6701 from a list of four-digit numbers.
    c. You remember to stop at the cleaners after buying groceries because your roommate included the word "cleaners" on your grocery list with a smiling face beside it.
    d. You remember the shape of the customized tail fins on your 1957 Chevy because you designed them and did the body work yourself.

30. After memorizing a series of nonsense syllables, Ebbinghaus discovered that forgetting was most dramatic _____ following learning.
    a. two days
    b. an hour
    c. ten days
    d. one day

31. Which explanation has **not** been offered to account for how we forget information that was learned?
    a. decay
    b. interference
    c. spontaneous inhibition
    d. inadequate processing during learning

32. You are asked to write a definition of psychology that is based on text and lecture materials in your course. Instead, you write a definition based on materials learned prior to the course. You are experiencing:
    a. retroactive interference.
    b. fugue.
    c. amnesia.
    d. proactive interference.

33. John learns the word-processing program "Easy Word" on his personal computer. Then he learns a second program, "Perfect Word," at work. He now finds it difficult to remember some of the commands when he uses his word processor at home. This is an example of:
    a. work-induced interference.
    b. retroactive interference.
    c. proactive interference.
    d. spontaneous interference.

34. Susan first learned to drive an automobile with a manual transmission and clutch. Now she has a car with an automatic transmission. From time to time, she finds herself trying to "push in the clutch" on the new car. This is an example of:
    a. proactive interference.
    b. work-induced interference.
    c. spontaneous interference.
    d. retroactive interference.

35. Current research indicates that:
    a. most neural traces are located in the left hemisphere.
    b. most neural traces are located in the right hemisphere.
    c. the location of the neural trace depends on the nature of the material being learned.
    d. there does not appear to be any physical area where traces are located.

36. All of the following have been associated with the biological basis of memory **except**:
    a. the hippocampus.
    b. carrots.
    c. protein synthesis.
    d. highly sweetened lemonade.

37. Which of the following statements about Alzheimer's disease is **not** correct?
    a. Initially, the afflicted individual simply appears to be forgetful.
    b. Alzheimer's disease affects primarily older people.
    c. The disease usually results in marked impairments in memory.
    d. The disease usually can be effectively treated with medication.

38. Alzheimer's disease is associated with deterioration of:
    a. the neurological connection between the spinal cord and muscles.
    b. the connection between the hemispheres.
    c. the manufacture of beta amyloid.
    d. the basal ganglia and lower brain structures.

39. Which statement about memory is **not** true?
    a. Recent studies of memory have substantiated Ebbinghaus's curve of forgetting.
    b. Women appear to be superior to men in their ability to learn a variety of information.
    c. After something is forgotten, it is easier to learn it the second time than it was initially.
    d. The savings associated with the relearning of forgotten information apply to memories as diverse as motor skills and academic information.

40. Which situation below is characteristic of anterograde amnesia?
    a. A person has loss of memory for events prior to some critical event.
    b. A person receives a physical trauma to the head and has difficulty remembering things after the accident.
    c. A person forgets simple skills such as how to dial a telephone.
    d. A person begins to experience difficulties in remembering appointments and relevant dates such as birthdays.

41. Which of the following syndromes is the **least** common?
    a. retrograde amnesia
    b. anterograde amnesia
    c. Alzheimer's disease
    d. Korsakoff's syndrome

42. Which situation below is most characteristic of retrograde amnesia?
    a. A person begins to experience difficulties in remembering appointments and relevant dates such as birthdays.
    b. A person receives a physical trauma to the head and has difficulty remembering things after the accident.
    c. A person forgets simple skills such as how to dial a telephone.
    d. A person has loss of memory for events prior to some critical event.

43. The keyword technique is a memory aid that can be helpful in learning a foreign language. The first step is to identify:
    a. a word that has similar meaning in a familiar language and pair it with the foreign word to be learned.
    b. a word that has a similar sound in a familiar language to at least part of the foreign word and pair it with the foreign word to be learned.
    c. a word that suggests similar imagery in a familiar language and pair it with the foreign word to be learned.
    d. the first word to come to mind in a familiar language and pair it with the foreign word to be learned.

44. Kevin is preparing a long speech. He associates the main body of the speech with walking into his living room. This technique is called:
    a. the method of loci.
    b. serial production memory.
    c. the keyword technique.
    d. retroactive interference.

45. Which alternative below is **least** likely to help you do well on your next psychology quiz?
    a. Use a prioritized strategy by studying the material only the day before the quiz and avoiding any other subjects which might interfere.
    b. Overlearn the material.
    c. Take brief lecture notes that focus on major points and that emphasize organization.
    d. Ask yourself questions about the material as you study.

| ESSAY QUESTIONS | *Recite and Review:* ☐ |

Essay Question 8.1: *Writing about Eyewitness Testimony*

What role should psychologists play in helping the courts deal with witness fallibility? Consider both the advantages and disadvantages of the answer you give.

_____

_____

_____

_____

_____

_____

_____

_____

_____

_____

_____

_____

_____

_____

_____

_____

_____

_____

Essay Question 8.2: *Comparing the Laboratory and Real Life*

Compare memory research that takes place in the laboratory with research that takes place in natural surroundings. What are the advantages and disadvantages of each? How would the "middle ground" between these two approaches be able to have the advantages of each but not the disadvantages?

_____

_____

_____

_____

_____

_____

_____

_____

_____

_____

_____

_____

_____

_____

_____

_____

_____

ACTIVITIES AND PROJECTS

1.   If you are currently studying a foreign language, use the keyword technique to memorize ten words in the language. Learn an additional ten words using the methods you normally use. Either test yourself, or try this prior to a vocabulary test in your language class. Which method is more effective? Does the key word make the foreign term easier to recall? Which set of words did you remember better on the test? Remember, in the keyword system, pair the foreign word with a common, similar sounding English word to enhance your memory of the foreign word.

2.   Try to remember what you were doing one year ago on this date. This task may seem impossible at first, but when you begin thinking about it, you will probably be able to reconstruct the memory. Verbalize out loud the processes that you are using to remember what you were doing that day. This verbalization should help you understand the steps you are taking as you reconstruct the memory. Ask a friend to try the same.

3.   With other members of your psychology class, construct lists of nonsense syllables in order to replicate the research done by Ebbinghaus. The lists should be fourteen to twenty-one "words" long. Now each person should rehearse a list until it is comfortably memorized. Test each other through the day and record the number of forgotten items and how many hours since the list was memorized. Do not review the list. The forgetting curve can be charted based on the gradual decline in the number of "words" remembered correctly. Several variations of this can be attempted—be creative!

CHAPTER

9

COGNITION AND LANGUAGE

143

● **Recap and Review III**

Looking Back
Key Terms and Concepts

➤ Now that you have surveyed the chapter, read **Looking Ahead**, pages 276–277.   ***Question:*** ☐
Focus on the questions on page 277.   ***Read:*** ☐

CONCEPTS AND LEARNING OBJECTIVES   *Survey:* ☐

These are the concepts and the learning objects for Chapter 9. Read them carefully as part of your preliminary survey of the chapter.

Concept 1: Cognitive psychology is focused on the study of processes we typically identify with thinking. Central to our ability to think is the process of forming concepts, the placing of these concepts in categories, and the processes of decision making.

1. Define cognition and the processes of thinking, reasoning, and conceptualizing. (pp. 276-278)

2. Describe the processes that are involved in decision making, including deductive reasoning and syllogistic logic. (pp. 278-281)

3. Discuss how algorithms and heuristics influence our judgments and decision making. (pp. 281-283)

Concept 2: Problem solving is also a central process related to thinking. We have both systematic and nonsystematic ways of approaching and understanding problems.

4. Explain the importance of understanding and diagnosing problems as the first step in effective problem solving. (pp. 284-288)

5. Describe the heuristic at work in generating possible solutions to problems and how solutions should be evaluated. (pp. 288-291)

6. Illustrate how efforts to develop solutions can be blocked by functional fixedness, mental set, and confirmation bias. (pp. 291-292)

7. Describe the factors that contribute to creativity and the role of creativity in problem solving and critical thinking. (pp. 292-294)

Concept 3: Language is the means by which thoughts can be represented to others and by which objects and events in the world around us can be processed mentally and stored for later use. The relationship between thought and language continues to be of concern for psychology.

8. Define the basic components of language, grammar, and syntax. (pp. 295-297)

9. Discuss the developmental processes of language and the theories of language acquisition. (pp. 297-299)

10. Identify the issues that arise with animal language, the linguistic relativity hypothesis, and bilingual education. (pp. 299-302)

CHAPTER SUMMARY

There are several ways you can use this summary as part of your systematic study plan. You may read each concept summary and then read the corresponding pages in the text, or you may read the entire summary and then read the entire chapter in the text. As you finish each section, complete the **Recap and Review** questions that are supplied in the text.

CONCEPT 1: **Prologue and Looking Ahead**
Thinking and Reasoning

Survey: ☐
Read: ☐

Pages 276-284

The branch of psychology that studies problem solving and other aspect of thinking is called **cognitive psychology**. The term **cognition** brings together the higher mental processes of humans, including understanding the world, processing information, making judgments and decisions, and describing knowledge.

Thinking is the manipulation of mental representations—words, images, sounds, or data in any other modality—of information. Thinking transforms the representation in order to achieve some goal or solve some problem. **Concepts** are categorizations of objects, events, or people that share common properties. Because we have concepts, we are able to classify newly encountered material on the basis of our past experiences. **Artificial concepts** are those that are defined by a clear set of properties and features. **Natural concepts** represent common objects which share characteristic features; however, they have features that vary and are not necessarily universal. Natural concepts are usually represented by **prototypes** which are typical, highly representative examples of a concept. Concepts provide an efficient way of understanding events and objects as they occur in the complex world.

Decision making is one of the most complex forms of thinking. Formal reasoning procedures have been studied as a way of understanding decision making. Deductive and inductive reasoning are the two major forms of formal reasoning. **Deductive reasoning** involves the application of inferences and implications from a set of assumptions to specific cases. The technique for studying deductive reasoning is called the syllogism. The **syllogism** presents two assumptions and a conclusion derived from them. If the assumptions are true, then the conclusion must be true. It is possible to have logically valid conclusions even if the premises are untrue. The use of formal deductive reasoning may not succeed because of inaccurate assumptions, erroneous conclusions, or the failure to apply formal logic. **Inductive reasoning** infers general rules from specific cases. The problem with inductive reasoning is that conclusions may be biased by insufficient or invalid evidence.

An **algorithm** is a rule that guarantees a solution if it is properly followed. Applying mathematical rules to equations will give us the answer even when we do not know why it works. A **heuristic** is a rule of thumb or some other shortcut that may lead to a solution. Heuristics can help but they often lead to erroneous solutions. People often use a **representativeness heuristic** to determine whether something belongs to a category or not. The decision is based on whether an observed characteristic belongs in the category. The availability heuristic judges the probability of an event on how easily the event can be recalled from memory. We assume that events that are easier to remember must have happened more often and that similar events are more likely to recur. When heuristics are misapplied, they can become hindrances to decision making.

CONCEPT 2: Problem Solving

Survey: ☐
Read: ☐

Pages 284-295

Problem solving typically involves three major steps: preparation, production of solutions, and evaluation of solutions. Problems are distinguished as either well-defined or ill-defined. In a **well-defined problem** the problem itself is clearly understood and the information needed to solve it is clearly understood. The appropriate solution is thus easily identified. In an **ill-defined problem**, both the problem and what information is needed may be unclear.

There are three categories of problem types. **Arrangement problems** require the recombination or reorganization of a group of elements in order to solve the problem. Jigsaw puzzles are a common example. With **problems of inducing structure**, the problem solver must identify a relationship between elements and then construct a new relationship among them. A common example is number sequence problems where a test taker may be asked to supply the next number in the sequence. The third kind of problem is **transformation problems**. Transformation problems have a desired goal and require a series of steps or changes to take place in order to reach the goal. The Tower of Hanoi problem described in the text is a transformation problem. Once the category of problem is understood, it is easier to determine how to represent the problem and how to organize it.

The creation of solutions may proceed at the simplest level as trial and error, but this approach may be inadequate for problems that have a large number of possible configurations. The use of heuristics aids in the simplification of problems. The heuristic of **means-ends analysis** proceeds by testing the difference between the current status and the desired outcome, and with each test it tries to reduce the difference. This strategy is effective only if there is a direct solution. In cases where indirect approaches are necessary, the means-ends analysis would require avoiding these indirect paths and so become a hindrance. Another heuristic divides the goal into intermediate steps, or **subgoals**, and works on each one individually. The problem here is that sometimes problems cannot be subdivided, and this approach may make the problem bigger than it was. The use of **insight** takes a slightly different approach to problem solving, requiring a reorganization of the entire problem in order to achieve a solution. The reorganization of existing elements requires prior experience with the elements.

The final step of problem solving is to evaluate the adequacy of a solution. If the solution is not clear, criteria to judge the solution must be made clear.

In the progress toward a solution, there are several obstacles that can be met. **Functional fixedness** refers to the tendency to think of an object according to its given function or typical use. Such a block may prevent us from realizing new uses for an object. Functional fixedness is an example of a large phenomenon called mental set. **Mental set** is the tendency for old patterns of solutions to persist. The Luchin's jar problem is an example of mental set. In the first trials, a set of combinations is required to solve the problem of filling a jar. The final problem is straightforward, but the problem solver usually attempts to use the solutions applied to the previous trials. Sometimes people inaccurately evaluate solutions and act on the wrong solution because they ignore contradictory evidence. This tendency to ignore contradictory evidence is called the **confirmation bias**, where an initial hypothesis is favored and alternatives are ignored.

Problems often require creative solutions. Cognitive psychologists have tried to identify the factors that constitute creativity for a long time. **Creativity** is usually defined as the combining of responses or ideas in novel ways. One of the factors thought to be related to creativity is divergent thinking. **Divergent thinking** refers to the ability to generate unusual yet appropriate responses to problems. **Convergent thinking** produces responses that are based primarily on knowledge or logic. Cognitive complexity is another factor in creativity. Cognitive complexity is the use of elaborate, intricate, and complex stimuli and thinking patterns. Humor can increase creative output as well. Apparently intelligence is not related to creativity, perhaps because the tests for intelligence test convergent thinking rather than divergent thinking.

Creativity and problem solving can be improved by engaging in one or more of the following: redefine problems, use fractionation (braking a concept into its parts), adopt a critical perspective, use analogies, think divergently, take the perspective of others, use heuristics, and experiment with different solutions.

CONCEPT 3: Language

Survey: ☐
Read: ☐

Pages 295-303

Language is the systematic, meaningful arrangement of symbols. It is important for cognition and for communication with others. The basic structure of language is **grammar**, the framework of rules that determine how thoughts are expressed. The three components of grammar are: **phonology**, the smallest units of sound, called phonemes, that affect the meaning of speech and how words are formed; **syntax**, the rules that govern how words and phrases are combined to form sentences; and **semantics**, the rules governing meaning of words and sentences.

Language develops through set stages. At first children **babble**, producing speechlike but meaningless sounds. Babbling gradually sounds like actual speech, and by one year, sounds that are not part of the language disappear. After the first year, children produce short, two-word combinations followed by short sentences. **Telegraphic speech** refers to the short sentences that contain a critical message but sound as if written as a telegram, with noncritical words left out. As children begin to learn speech rules, they will apply them without flexibility, a phenomenon known as **overregularization**, where an "ed" might be applied to every past tense construction. Adults speak to children slowly, using primitive vocabulary, substituting nouns for pronouns, and with simpler sentence structure. By the age of 5, most children have acquired the rules of language.

The **learning-theory approach** to language acquisition suggests that the reinforcement and conditioning principles are responsible for language development. Praise for saying a word like "mama" reinforces the word and increases the likelihood of its being repeated. Shaping then makes child language become more adultlike. This approach has difficulty explaining the acquisition of language rules, because children are also reinforced when their language is incorrect. An alternative proposed by Noam Chomsky suggests that there exist **innate mechanisms** responsible for the acquisition of language. All human languages have a similar underlying structure he calls **universal grammar**, and a neural system in the brain, the **language-acquisition device**, is responsible for the development of language.

Whether animals use language depends on demonstrating whether they can create unique meanings that use a grammar system. Many animals as well as insects have communication systems, but they do not qualify as language. Psychologists have taught chimps to use language at the level of 2-year-old humans. Critics suggest that the language is not sophisticated enough to be considered language. In either case, humans are much better equipped for language.

Psychologists are also concerned whether the structure of language influences the structure of thought or whether thought influences language. The **linguistic-relativity hypothesis** suggests that language shapes thought, determining how people of a particular culture perceive and understand the world. In an alternative view, language may reflect the different ways we have of thinking about the world, essentially that thought produces language. A study by Eleanor Rosch concerning color perception of the Dani of New Guinea found that even though the Dani have only two color words, they could distinguish colors as well as English-speaking people who have hundreds of color words. In this respect, the linguistic-relativity hypothesis is considered to be unsupported. However, language does influence how we store memories and form categories.

Children who enter school as nonnative speakers of English face a number of hardships. The debate over whether to take a bilingual approach or whether all instruction should be in English is a major controversy. Evidence suggests that bilingual children have cognitive advantages, being more flexible, more aware of the rules of language, and higher scores on verbal and nonverbal intelligence tests. Evidence also suggests that initial instruction in the native language may enhance the acquisition of the second language.

▶ Now that you have surveyed, questioned, and read the chapter and completed

the **Recap and Review** questions, review **Looking Back**, page 303–304.　　*Review:* ☐

▶ For additional practice through recitation and review, test your knowledge of the chapter material by answering the questions in the *Key Word Drill*, the *Practice Questions*, and the *Essay Questions*.

KEY WORD DRILL　　　　　　　　　　　　　　　　*Recite:* ☐

The following **Fill in the Blank** and **Matching Questions** test key words from the text. Check your answers with the Answer Key in the back of the *Study Guide*.

FILL IN THE BLANK

1. _____ encompasses the higher mental processes by which we understand the world, process information, make judgments and decisions, and communicate knowledge to others.

2. The manipulation of mental representations of information refers to _____.

3. _____ are categorizations of objects, events, or people that share common properties.

4. The reasoning process whereby inferences and implications are drawn from a set of assumptions and

    applied to specific cases is called _____ reasoning, and the reasoning process whereby a general rule is inferred from specific cases, using observation, knowledge, and experience

    is called _____ reasoning.

5. A problem whose nature is clear, and the information needed to solve it is available is considered a

_____-_____ problem, while a problem whose specific nature is unclear, and the information required to solve it is not obvious is called an

_____-_____ problem.

6. _____ _____ refers to the tendency to think of an object in terms of its most typical use.

7. _____ is both essential for communication and reflects the way we think about and understand the world because of its close link with thought.

8. According to the _____-_____ approach, language acquisition follows the principles of reinforcement and conditioning.

9. The _____-_____ _____ claims that language shapes and may even determine the way people perceive and understand the world.

10. The use of and preference for elaborate, intricate, and complex stimuli and thinking patterns is a sign

of _____ _____ and is closely related to creativity.

MATCHING QUESTIONS

_____ 11. syllogism

_____ 12. algorithm

_____ 13. heuristic

_____ 14. representativeness heuristic

_____ 15. availability heuristic

a. A rule in which people and things are judged by the degree to which they represent a certain category.

b. A set of rules that, if followed, guarantee a solution, though the reason they work may not be understood by the person using them.

c. A rule for judging the probability that an event will occur by the ease with which it can be recalled from memory.

d. A rule of thumb that may bring about a solution to a problem but is not guaranteed to do so.

e. A major technique for studying deductive reasoning, in which a series of two assumptions are used to derive a conclusion.

_____ 16. arrangement problems

_____ 17. problems of inducing structure

_____ 18. transformation problems

_____ 19. means-ends analysis

_____ 20. subgoals

a. Problems to be solved using a series of methods to change an initial state into a goal state.

b. A commonly used heuristic to divide a problem into intermediate steps and to solve each one of them.

c. Problems whose solution requires the identification of existing relationships among elements presented so as to construct a new relationship among them.

d. Problems whose solution requires the rearrangement of a group of elements in order to satisfy a certain criterion.

e. Repeated testing to determine and reduce the distance between the desired outcome and what currently exists in problem solving.

_____

_____ 21. insight

_____ 22. mental set

_____ 23. confirmation bias

_____ 24. creativity

_____ 25. divergent thinking

_____ 26. convergent thinking

a. The tendency for patterns of problem solving to persist.

b. Sudden awareness of the relationships among various elements that had previously appeared to be independent of one another.

c. A type of thinking which produces responses based on knowledge and logic.

d. The ability to generate unusual but appropriate responses to problems or questions.

e. A bias favoring an initial hypothesis and disregarding contradictory information suggesting alternative solutions.

f. The combining of responses or ideas in novel ways.

_____

_____ 27. grammar

_____ 28. phonology

_____ 29. phonemes

_____ 30. syntax

_____ 31. semantics

a. The framework of rules that determine how our thoughts can be expressed.

b. The rules governing the meaning of words and sentences.

c. The rules that indicate how words are joined to form sentences.

d. The study of how we use those sounds to produce meaning by forming them into words.

e. The smallest units of sound used to form words.

_____ 32. telegraphic speech

_____ 33. overregularization

_____ 34. innate mechanism

_____ 35. universal grammar

_____ 36. language-acquisition device

a. A neural system of the brain hypothesized to permit understanding of language.

b. Sentences containing only the most essential words.

c. Applying rules of speech in instances in which they are inappropriate.

d. An underlying structure shared by all languages, according to Chomsky's theory that certain language characteristics are based in the brain's structure and are therefore common to all people.

e. According to Chomsky, the innate linguistic capability in humans that emerges as a function of maturation.

_____ 37. cognitive psychology

_____ 38. artificial concepts

_____ 39. natural concepts

_____ 40. prototypes

a. Concepts that are defined by a set of general, relatively loose characteristic features, such as prototypes.

b. Concepts that are clearly defined by a unique set of properties or features.

c. Typical, highly representative examples of a concept.

d. The branch of psychology that specializes in the study of cognition.

| PRACTICE QUESTIONS |

Recite and Review: ☐

Test your knowledge of the chapter material by answering these **True-False** and **Multiple Choice Questions.** Check your answers with the Answer Key in the back of the *Study Guide.*

TRUE-FALSE QUESTIONS

T   F   1.   Algorithms and heuristics rarely lead to the wrong solutions to problems.

T   F   2.   An algorithm always guarantees a solution to a problem, but the solution may be wrong if the algorithm is misapplied.

T   F   3.   The representativeness heuristic is based on the principle of overgeneralization.

T   F   4.   The organization and representation of a problem are often critical in determining whether the problem will be solved.

T   F   5. Insight depends on previous experience with the elements involved in a problem.

T   F   6. Unfortunately, the person who evaluates the quality of a solution to a problem may not be making as objective and valid an evaluation as he or she thinks.

T   F   7. Sometimes, there are a number of identifiable factors in problem solving which limit the development of creative, appropriate, and accurate solutions.

T   F   8. Bill is considering voting for a particular candidate. He then learns additional information that supports his decision. This illustrates confirmation bias.

T   F   9. Intelligence tests provide good measures of a person's ability to think creatively.

T   F   10. Creative problem solvers tend to rely on heuristics and unusual strategies rather than on algorithms and established rules.

T   F   11. According to the text, language production precedes language comprehension.

T   F   12. Saying "I falled down" instead of "I fell down" is an example of telegraphic speech.

MULTIPLE CHOICE QUESTIONS

1. Which alternative below does not fit within your text's definition of cognition?
    a. the higher mental processes of humans
    b. how people know and understand the world
    c. how people communicate their knowledge and understanding to others
    d. how people's eyes and ears process the information they receive

2. The study of higher mental processes in humans is called:
    a. perception.
    b. cognition.
    c. linguistics.
    d. semantics.

3. Cognitive psychologists study all of the following **except**:
    a. how the sensory system takes in information.
    b. how people understand the world.
    c. how people process information.
    d. how people make judgments.

4. A concept is defined as:
    a. an idea or thought about a new procedure or product.
    b. a group of attitudes which define an object, event, or person.
    c. a categorization of people, objects, or events that share certain properties.
    d. one of many facts which collectively define the subject matter for a specific area of knowledge (such as psychology).

5. Prototypes of concepts are:
   a. new concepts to describe newly emerging phenomena.
   b. new concepts which emerge within a language spontaneously and then are retained or discarded.
   c. representative examples of concepts.
   d. concepts from other languages which are incorporated into a native language if they appear useful.

6. Concepts are similar to perceptual processes in that:
   a. concepts, like visual illusions, can produce errors in interpretation.
   b. concepts allow us to simplify and manage our world.
   c. concepts are to language what figure-ground relationships are to perception.
   d. some concepts and perceptual processes are innate.

7. Drawing inferences and implications from a set of assumptions and then applying them to specific cases is the definition of:
   a. decision making.
   b. algorithms.
   c. heuristic.
   d. deductive reasoning.

8. A syllogism is defined as:
   a. a reasoning error made when the decision makers fail to use systematic techniques.
   b. any time a representativeness heuristic is used in a humorous manner.
   c. a series of two assumptions that is used to derive a conclusion.
   d. an analogy concerning the relationship between two sets of paired items, like "A is to B as C is to D."

9. The use of inaccurate premises, coming to erroneous conclusions, and simply failing to use formal reasoning are all errors related specifically to the use of:
   a. deductive reasoning.
   b. inductive reasoning.
   c. availability heuristics.
   d. algorithms.

10. If you fail to solve a problem because you misapply a category or set of categories, you have relied on:
    a. an availability heuristic.
    b. a mental set.
    c. functional fixedness.
    d. a representativeness heuristic.

11. You have had a number of troublesome, time-consuming, expensive, and emotionally trying experiences with people who sell used cars. Then you find out that your roommate for next term is a part-time used-car dealer. You are convinced, even without meeting your future roommate, that you should not be paired with this person. You have used the _____ heuristic to arrive at your conclusion.
    a. means-ends
    b. representativeness
    c. availability
    d. personality

12. Which alternative below is **not** a major step in problem solving?
    a. evaluation of solutions generated
    b. preparation for the creation of solutions
    c. documentation of all solutions
    d. production of solutions

13. According to your text, problems fall into one of three categories. Which of the following is **not** one of them?
    - a. arrangement
    - b. affability
    - c. structure
    - d. transformation

14. According to the text, an ill-defined problem is one that:
    - a. has many solutions.
    - b. has no solution.
    - c. depends on unavailable information for its solution.
    - d. is vague in nature.

15. Identifying existing relationships among elements and constructing a new relationship is an example of:
    - a. an inducing-structure problem.
    - b. an organization problem.
    - c. an arrangement problem.
    - d. a transformation problem.

16. According to the text, which of the following is perhaps the most frequently used heuristic technique for solving problems?
    - a. the availability heuristic
    - b. categorical processing
    - c. the representativeness heuristic
    - d. means-ends analysis

17. According to the text, the elements of the problem undergo changes in state in:
    - a. problems of inducing structure.
    - b. representation problems.
    - c. arrangement problems.
    - d. transformation problems.

18. According to the text, which of the following is **not** associated with defining and understanding a problem?
    - a. discarding inessential information
    - b. simplifying essential information
    - c. dividing the problem into parts
    - d. clarifying the solution

19. Breaking down a complex issue into a sequence of steps illustrates the heuristic called:
    - a. insight.
    - b. subgoal analysis.
    - c. availability heuristic.
    - d. means-ends analysis.

20. Insight is a:
    - a. sudden awareness of the relationships among various elements in a problem that previously appeared to be independent of one another.
    - b. sudden awareness of the solution to a problem with which one has had no prior involvement or experience.
    - c. sudden awareness of a particular algorithm that can be used to solve a problem.
    - d. spontaneous procedure for generating a variety of possible solutions to a problem.

21. Which of the following statements about insight is true?
    - a. It is an unexplained discovery of a solution without prior experience with any elements of the problem.
    - b. It results from a methodical trial-and-error process.
    - c. It is a sudden realization of relationships among seemingly independent elements.
    - d. It is a solution that is independent of trial and error and experience.

22. The tendency for old patterns of problem solving to persist is called:
    a. both functional fixedness and convergent thinking.
    b. both mental set and divergent thinking.
    c. both convergent thinking and divergent thinking.
    d. both mental set and functional fixedness.

23. An obstacle to problem solving that is based on the tendency to think of an object in terms of its typical use is called:
    a. functional fixedness.
    b. means-ends analysis.
    c. mental set.
    d. subgoal analysis.

24. Thinking of a wrench in conventional terms may handicap your efforts to solve a problem when a possible solution involves using the wrench for a novel use. This phenomenon is called:
    a. functional fixedness.
    b. insight.
    c. awareness.
    d. preparation.

25. Which kind of thinking is exemplified by logic and knowledge?
    a. creative
    b. convergent
    c. divergent
    d. imaginal

26. Which of the following is characteristic of a creative thinker?
    a. convergent thought
    b. divergent thought
    c. high intelligence
    d. recurrent thought

27. The ability to conceive and implement alternate, unique solutions to a problem is called:
    a. deductive reasoning.
    b. cognitive reflection.
    c. divergent thinking.
    d. retroactive diversity.

28. The order of the words forming a sentence is generated by:
    a. synthetics.
    b. semantics.
    c. syntax.
    d. systematics.

29. The syntax of a language is the framework of rules that determine:
    a. the meaning of words and phrases.
    b. how words and phrases are combined to form sentences.
    c. the sounds of letters, phrases, and words.
    d. how thoughts can be translated into words.

30. The slight difference in meaning between the sentences "The truck hit the pole" and "The pole was hit by the truck" is determined by the rules of:
    a. grammar.
    b. phonology.
    c. syntax.
    d. semantics.

31. It is **not** true that babbling:
    a. occurs from 3 to 6 months of age.
    b. includes words such as "dada" and "mama."
    c. is speechlike.
    d. produces sounds found in all languages.

32. Of the following, which is the first refinement in the infant's learning of language?
    a. production of short words that begin with a consonant.
    b. disappearance of sounds that are not in the native language.
    c. emergence of sounds that resemble words.
    d. production of two-word combinations.

33. Telegraphic speech in young children refers to the fact that:
    a. speech is very rapid.
    b. seemingly nonessential words are omitted from phrases and sentences.
    c. the tonal quality of speech is limited.
    d. speech may speed up, slow down, or contain pauses.

34. In the English language, the fact that "mama" and "dada" are among the first words spoken:
    a. is unusual, since these words do not contain the first sounds a child can make.
    b. suggests that they are responses the child is born with.
    c. is not surprising, since these words are easy to pronounce, and the sound capabilities of the young child are limited.
    d. demonstrates that the sounds heard most frequently are the sounds spoken first.

35. Generalizing from information presented in the text, which of the following two-word combinations is **least** likely to be spoken by a 2-year-old?
    a. Daddy up.   c. I'm big.
    b. Mommy cookie.   d. More, more.

36. A child exhibits a speech pattern characterized by short sentences, with many noncritical words missing. Which of the following is **not** true?
    a. The child is between 2 and 3 years old.
    b. The child is exhibiting telegraphic speech.
    c. The child is building complexity of speech.
    d. The child is using overregularization.

37. According to the text, a child acquires most of the basic rules of grammar by:
    a. 2 years of age.   c. 4 years of age.
    b. 3 years of age.   d. 5 years of age.

38. According to Noam Chomsky, the brain contains a neural system designed for understanding and learning language called the:
    a. linguistic relativity system.   c. limbic system.
    b. language acquisition device.   d. phonological linguistic device.

39. Which alternative below is **not** associated with current ideas about how language is acquired?
    a. consonant drift   c. innate processes
    b. shaping   d. reinforcement

40. Which of the following statements does **not** reflect Chomsky's view of language acquisition?
    a. All languages share universal grammar.
    b. The main determinant of language is reinforcement.
    c. The brain has a language acquisition device.
    d. Language is a uniquely human phenomenon.

41. Learning theorists view the learning of language as a process of:
    a. classical conditioning.   c. shaping.
    b. stimulus generalization.   d. chaining.

42. Psychologists who argue that the language of the child depends on exposure to the language of the parents would say that language is acquired through:
    a. classical conditioning.   c. universal grammar.
    b. shaping.   d. biological unfolding.

43. Which statement below is **not** true about the language skills of humans and apes?
    a. Many critics feel that the language skills acquired by chimps and gorillas are no different from a dog learning to sit on command.
    b. The language skills of chimps and gorillas are about equal to those of a 5-year-old human child.
    c. Sign language and response panels with different-shaped symbols have been used to teach chimps and gorillas language skills.
    d. Humans are probably better equipped than apes to produce and organize language into meaningful sentences.

44. Eskimos have several verbal expressions to identify snow. This fact has been used to support:
    a. the theory that language determines thought.
    b. the theory that thought determines language.
    c. the existence of the language acquisition device.
    d. development of the nativistic position.

45. Rosch's study with the Dani tribe of New Guinea showed that:
    a. English speakers perceived colors differently from the Dani.
    b. the number of categories in a language depends on perception.
    c. language does not limit the way that colors are perceived.
    d. the number of color names available determines the perception of color.

46. The linguistic relativity hypothesis might be paraphrased as:
    a. "Without thought there is no language."
    b. "Thought creates language."
    c. "Language and thought are synonymous."
    d. "Language determines thought."

47. The notion that language shapes the way that people of a particular culture perceive and think about the world is called the:
    a. semantic-reasoning theory.   c. prototypical hypothesis.
    b. cultural-language law.   d. linguistic-relativity theory.

| **ESSAY QUESTIONS** | *Recite and Review:* ☐ |

Essay Question 9.1: *Problem Solving*

Identify a major challenge that you anticipate facing in the next several years. It can involve choosing a career, getting married, selecting a major, choosing a graduate school, or one of many others. Describe the problem or challenge briefly, then describe how you would apply the problem-solving steps presented in the text to the problem to generate solutions that you might try.

_____

_____

_____

_____

_____

_____

_____

_____

_____

_____

_____

_____

_____

_____

_____

_____

_____

Essay Question 9.2: *Is Language Uniquely Human?*

Some consider language to be the capability that uniquely distinguishes us as human. Weigh the arguments for the language skills of specially trained chimpanzees and develop your position on this issue. Is language unique to humans? If so, how would you characterize the communication skills of chimpanzees? If not, then what capability does distinguish us from other animals?

_____

_____

_____

_____

_____

_____

_____

_____

_____

_____

_____

_____

_____

_____

_____

_____

_____

_____

ACTIVITIES AND PROJECTS

1. To counteract functional fixedness and to foster creativity, record as many uses as you can for a paper clip. Limit yourself to three minutes. Repeat the exercise with a brick and a coat hanger. Ask a friend to do the same thing and then compare the number of unique items each of you have. Consider the extent to which this exercise reflects intelligence (and what kind of intelligence) and creativity. Are the types of uses you identified specific to one or two of Gardner's types of intelligence? If you have a high number of uses, does this indicate strength in practical intelligence? Is the exercise dependent on linguistic or cultural skills? (A particularly interesting variation is to ask a friend from another culture or ethnic group to do the exercise and then determine whether some of the uses are unique as a result of cultural experience.)

2. Select several common nouns like "house," "tree," and "dog." Then ask people in the following age groups to give you a definition:

   Child, age 3 to 4 years old
   Child, age 9 to 10 years old
   Teenager
   Adult

   To vary the activity, you may ask a young child to describe the size or some other feature of one or more of the common objects. These descriptions will reflect the child's conception of the object ("a star is about twenty feet bigger than a house"). Be sure to ask the adult and teenager for a description of the same object.

3. Observe and record (with a tape recorder or on a note pad) examples of language production in one or more children between the ages of six months and four years. Then compare the examples with those given in the text. Which of the basic concepts of language acquisition were you able to observe?

10

INTELLIGENCE

DETAILED OUTLINE

Survey: ☐

This detailed outline contains all the headings in Chapter 10: Intelligence. If you are using the SQ3R method, then an examination of the outline is the best way to begin your survey of the chapter.

Prologue: Leslie Lemke
Looking Ahead

Defining Intelligent Behavior
    Measuring intelligence
    Measuring IQ
    Achievement and aptitude tests
    Alternative formulations of intelligence
   The Cutting Edge Emotional Intelligence: Getting Smart about Emotions
    Is information processing intelligence? Contemporary approaches
   Psychology at Work Is Practical Intelligence Different from School Intelligence?
   The Informed Consumer of Psychology Can You Do Better on Standardized Tests?
● **Recap and Review I**

Variations in Intellectual Ability
    Mental retardation
    The intellectually gifted
● **Recap and Review II**

Individual Differences in Intelligence: Heredity, Environment—or Both?
    The basic controversy: The relative influence of heredity and of environment
    Placing the heredity/environment question in perspective
● **Recap and Review III**

Looking Back
Key Terms and Concepts

➤ Now that you have surveyed the chapter, read **Looking Ahead**, pages 308–309.

Question: ☐
Read: ☐

Focus on the questions on page 309.

CONCEPTS AND LEARNING OBJECTIVES

Survey: ☐

These are the concepts and the learning objects for Chapter 10. Read them carefully as part of your preliminary survey of the chapter.

Concept 1: Intelligence is understood as a predictor of school success, and it is also viewed as a limited expression of the cognitive capacity of individuals. Alternative views of intelligence include the view that there exist many intelligences, including practical intelligence, which is made up of the skills needed to survive in cultural and social settings.

1. Define intelligence and the issues related to its definition. (pp. 308-311)

2. Discuss how intelligence is measured, define intelligence quotient, and describe how achievement and aptitude differ from intelligence. (pp. 311-314)

3. Describe the alternative views of intelligence. (pp. 314-316)

4. Explain how cognitive psychology uses information processing to define intelligence. (pp. 316-317)

5. Describe the concept of practical intelligence and discuss whether performance on achievement tests can be improved with training. (pp. 318-320)

Concept 2: The extremes in intellectual function lead to distinctions of mental retardation and giftedness. The basic challenge for identifying these two groups is to identify and utilize educational resources in order to best serve the two populations.

6. Define and describe mental retardation and its causes. (pp. 321-323)

7. Define and describe intellectual giftedness. (pp. 323-324)

Concept 3: The major debate in intelligence is over the relative influence on intelligence of heredity and environment, and the extent to which these two influences can be understood in order to improve intellectual potential.

8. Analyze the issues related to the heredity versus environment debate, and discuss the problem of cultural bias in intelligence tests. (pp. 325-329)

CHAPTER SUMMARY

There are several ways you can use this summary as part of your systematic study plan. You may read each concept summary and then read the corresponding pages in the text, or you may read the entire summary and then read the entire chapter in the text. As you finish each section, complete the **Recap and Review** questions that are supplied in the text.

**CONCEPT 1: Prologue and Looking Ahead
Defining Intelligent Behavior**

The Prologue describes Leslie Lemke, a blind, crippled, and mentally retarded individual with an exceptional musical talent. Leslie Lemke's condition is called the "savant syndrome," a condition in which an otherwise handicapped individual has an exceptional talent in a very specific area, like Lemke's ability to play the piano.

Intelligence has many different meanings, depending upon whether it is applied to behavior in a Pacific culture like that of the Trukese who can navigate in open sea without any equipment or to someone who can get around the New York subway system. In the examples in the text, the common theme is that intelligent people can use their resources more effectively than others in accomplishing whatever task is at hand. In a survey of laypersons, three major components of intelligence were identified: (1) problem-solving ability, (2) verbal ability, and (3) social competence. **Intelligence** has been defined by psychologists as the capacity to understand the world, think rationally, and use resources effectively. Intelligence remains difficult to determine, though intelligence tests have been successful in identifying individuals who need help in school, who have cognitive difficulties, and who need help making choices about school.

Alfred Binet developed the first formal intelligence test to identify the "dullest" students in the Parisian school system. His test was able to distinguish the "bright" from the "dull" and eventually made distinctions between age groups. The original test became the **Stanford-Binet test**, and it is based on items that vary according to the age of the subject. An IQ score is determined by the level at which a person performs on the test in relation to others of the same age. Other IQ tests given in America are the **Weschler Adult Intelligence Scale—Revised**, the **WAIS—R**, and the **Weschler Intelligence Scale for Children—III**, the **WISC—III**. The WAIS—R and the WISC—III have verbal and performance scales. The two scales allow a more accurate picture of the person's abilities. The Stanford-Binet, the WISC—R, and WISC—III require individual administration. A number of "paper and pencil" tests have been developed, but they sacrifice flexibility and fail to motivate the test taker. Also, they are not easily given to children or to people with low IQs.

The **achievement test** is a test meant to determine the level of achievement of an individual, that is, what the person has actually learned. An **aptitude test** measures and predicts an individual's ability in a particular area. The SAT is an exam that predicts how well a student will do in college. There is quite a bit of overlap among the IQ, achievement, and aptitude tests.

In the two dominant tests, the score is considered to be a reflection of the intelligence of the person. It remains unclear whether intelligence is a single factor or a combination of factors. The single-factor view suggests that there is a general factor for mental ability called **g**, or **g-factor**. Recently, two factors have been accepted by most. They are **fluid intelligence**, the ability to deal with new problems and situations, and **crystallized intelligence**, the store of information, skills, and strategies acquired through experience. Fluid intelligence is thought to decline in the elderly. In an alternate formulation, Howard Gardner has proposed the existence of seven multiple intelligences: (1) musical intelligence, (2) bodily-kinesthetic intelligence, (3) logical-mathematical intelligence, (4) linguistic intelligence, (5) spatial intelligence, (6) interpersonal intelligence, and (7) intrapersonal intelligence. Gardner suggests that these separate intelligences do not operate in isolation. Results from Gardner's work include the acceptance of more than one answer as correct on a test. Other kinds of intelligence include emotional intelligence, the set of skills that underlie the accurate assessment, evaluation, expression, and regulation of emotions. Emotional intelligence allows people to use emotions to achieve goals.

The information processing approach to intelligence views intelligence as the ability to process information. Effective problem solvers have traditionally been those who also score high on intelligence tests. In solving an analogy problem, a bright student will go through a series of steps, first encoding the information in a useful way, then making inferences about the analogy relationship, then mapping the relationship from the first half of the analogy to the second half, then applying the relationship to test answers, then responding with a solution. People with higher intelligence levels tends to get the right answer and to have qualitatively different methods for solving problems. High scorers spend more of their time on the initial stage of encoding, identifying parts of the problems, and retrieval from memory.

Robert Sternberg has proposed a **triarchic theory of intelligence**. The three components are: componential aspect that focuses on rational behavior, the experiential aspect that focuses on how prior experience is applied, and the contextual aspect that focuses on how successful people respond to the demands of the everyday environment. **Practical intelligence** grows from Sternberg's attention to the practical demands of everyday life. One of the problems is that though IQ tests predict performance in school, they do not correlate with career success. Several tests have been designed that measure practical intelligence in the business world.

There are many coaching services that claim to help students improve their scores on the Scholastic Aptitude Test. Though the service that produces the test originally argued that these were not helpful, it now has accepted that some coaching may help. One must determine what is sought from the coaching in selecting a type of coaching. Hints for improving testing include: previewing the section of the test as soon as you begin, timing yourself carefully, checking the scoring to see if you will be penalized for wrong answers (if so, then do not guess), and completing the answer sheets accurately.

SECTION 2: Variations in Intellectual Ability

Survey: ☐
Read: ☐

Pages 321-325

About 6.5 million people in the United States are classified as mentally retarded, and the populations that comprise the mentally retarded and the exceptionally gifted require special attention in order to reach their potential.

Mental retardation is defined by the American Association on Mental Deficiency as when there is "significantly subaverage general intellectual functioning existing concurrently with deficits in adaptive behavior and manifested during the developmental period." This definition includes mild to severe retardation. **Mild retardation** includes individuals whose IQ scores fall in the 55 to 69 range. This comprises about 90 percent of the people with mental retardation. **Moderate retardation**, with scores ranging from 40 to 54, **severe retardation**, with scores from 25 to 39, and **profound retardation**, with scores below 25, have difficulties that become more pronounced the lower the IQ score. The moderately retarded require some supervision during their entire lives, and the severe and profound groups require institutionalization. One-third of the people classified as retarded suffer from biological causes of retardation, mostly from **Down syndrome**, a genetic disorder caused by an extra chromosome. **Familial retardation** occurs in cases when there is no biological cause but instead may be linked with a family history of retardation. This may be caused by environmental factors like severe poverty, malnutrition, and possibly a genetic factor that cannot be determined. In 1975, Congress passed a law that entitles mentally retarded individuals to a full education and to education and training in the **least-restrictive environment**. This law leads to a process of returning individuals to regular classrooms, a process called **mainstreaming**. The view is that by mainstreaming individuals, they interact with non-retarded individuals and benefit from the interaction.

The **intellectually gifted** comprise about 2 to 4 percent of the population. This group is generally identified as those individuals with IQ scores higher than 130. Contrary to the stereotype, these individuals are usually outgoing, well-adjusted, popular people who do most things better than the average person. Lewis Terman conducted a well-known longitudinal study following 1500 gifted children (with IQs above 140). They have an impressive record of accomplishments, though being gifted does not guarantee success.

CONCEPT 3:   Individual Differences in Intelligence: Heredity, Environment—or Both?

Survey: ☐
Read: ☐

Pages 325–330

In the determination of the causes of individual differences, cultural differences in the framing of questions on the test can play an important role. Adrian Dove has developed a test that illustrates how foreign culture-specific tests can be by asking questions drawn from the experience of inner-city black populations. On standard intelligence tests, some culture and ethnic groups score lower than others, as with blacks, who tend to score fifteen points lower than whites. Because of the possibility of bias and discrimination, some states have banned the use of traditional intelligence tests.

Attempts to develop a **culture-fair IQ test** that does not discriminate have led in some cases to even greater disparities in scores. The controversy based on ethnic and minority differences in intelligence tests reflects a greater concern of whether intelligence is predominantly a result of heredity or of environmental forces. On the heredity side, the explanation for lower performance by a population would be that they are less intelligent as a result of genetics. The debate reached a major peak when Arthur Jensen argued that the difference between white and black IQ scores could not be explained by environmental differences because even when socioeconomic factors were considered, the difference did not disappear. Intelligence does show a high degree of **heritability**, the measure of the extent to which a characteristic is related to genetic, inherited factors. The closer two people are linked genetically, the closer their IQ scores are likely to be. Jensen argued that 75 to 80 percent of the variability in IQ scores was a result of genetics. Critics of Jensen have argued, with the support of most of the psychological community, that such a factor as socioeconomic status is itself a highly variable factor, with wide variations from one household to another. Other research has demonstrated that blacks raised in enriched environments similar to whites do not have lower IQ scores. The real differences between IQ scores cannot be between the means of groups but must be understood as the difference between individuals.

The issue of heredity and environment is one in which experimental research that might establish causal relationships cannot be devised because of ethical issues. A question that should be of concern is how can we maximize the potential intellectual development of individuals.

➤ Now that you have surveyed, questioned, and read the chapter and completed the **Recap and Review** questions, review **Looking Back**, pages 330–331.   *Review:* ☐

➤ For additional practice through recitation and review, test your knowledge of the chapter material by answering the questions in the *Key Word Drill*, the *Practice Questions*, and the *Essay Questions*.

KEY WORD DRILL   *Recite:* ☐

The following **Fill in the Blank** and **Matching Questions** test key words from the text. Check your answers with the Answer Key in the back of the *Study Guide*.

FILL IN THE BLANK

1. When we speak of _____, we are referring to our capacity to understand the world, think rationally, and use resources effectively when faced with challenges.

2. In order to compare a person's performance on an IQ test to the performance of others, a means

   of calculating the IQ score called the _____ _____

   _____ is used.

3. An _____ test is intended to determine a person's level of knowledge in a

   given subject, while an _____ test is designed to predict a person's ability in a particular line of work.

4. Early psychologists assumed the existence of a _____-_____, a theoretical single general factor accounting for mental ability and thought to underlie performance on every aspect of intelligence.

5. The _____ theory of intelligence suggests the existence of three major aspects of intelligence: the componential, the experiential, and the contextual.

6. _____ _____ is defined by a significantly subaverage level of intellectual functioning that is also accompanied by deficits in adaptive behavior.

7. The official phrase from PL94-142, _____-_____

   _____, refers to the guarantee of the right of full education for retarded people in an environment that is most similar to the educational environment of typical children.

8. The integration of retarded people into regular classroom situations has been called

   _____.

9. Psychologists have tried to devise tests that assess experiences common to all cultures; these

   _____-_____ IQ tests are designed to avoid discrimination against members of any minority culture group.

10. _____ is a measure of the degree to which a characteristic is related to genetic, inherited factors as opposed to environmental factors.

MATCHING QUESTIONS

_____ 11. intelligence tests

_____ 12. Stanford-Binet test

_____ 13. Wechsler Adult Intelligence Scale—Revised (WAIS-R)

_____ 14. Wechsler Intelligence Scale for Children—III (WISC-III)

a. A test of intelligence consisting of verbal and nonverbal performance sections, providing a relatively precise picture of a person's specific abilities.

b. A test of intelligence that includes a series of items varying in nature according to the age of the person being tested.

c. A battery of measures to determine a person's level of intelligence.

d. An intelligence test for children; see Wechsler Adult Intelligence Scale—Revised.

_____ 15. mild retardation

_____ 16. moderate retardation

_____ 17. severe retardation

_____ 18. profound retardation

_____ 19. Down syndrome

_____ 20. familial retardation

_____ 21. intellectually gifted

a. Characterized by an IQ between 25 and 39 and difficulty in functioning independently.

b. Mental retardation in which there is a history of retardation in a family but no evidence of biological causes.

c. Characterized by higher-than-average intelligence, with IQ scores above 130.

d. A common cause of mental retardation, brought about by the presence of an extra chromosome.

e. Characterized by an IQ below 25 and an inability to function independently.

f. Characterized by an IQ between 55 and 69 and the ability to function independently.

g. Characterized by an IQ between 40 and 54.

_____ 22. mental age

_____ 23. chronological age

_____ 24. intelligence quotient (IQ) score

_____ 25. fluid intelligence

_____ 26. crystallized intelligence

_____ 27. practical intelligence

a. Intelligence related to overall success in living, rather than to intellectual and academic performance.

b. A measure of intelligence that takes into account an individual's mental and chronological ages.

c. The store of specific information, skills, and strategies that people have acquired through experience.

d. The typical intelligence level found for people at a given chronological age.

e. The ability to deal with new problems and encounters.

f. A person's physical age.

| PRACTICE QUESTIONS | *Recite and Review:* ☐ |

Test your knowledge of the chapter material by answering these **True-False** and **Multiple Choice Questions**. Check your answers with the Answer Key in the back of the *Study Guide*.

TRUE-FALSE QUESTIONS

T   F   1. A 16-year-old adolescent with a mental age of 15 would have an IQ score under 100.

T   F   2. The majority of people who take intelligence tests fall within 15 IQ points of the average score.

T   F   3. The Stanford-Binet and the Wechsler intelligence tests can be administered to a group of people.

T   F   4. An aptitude test measures what a person has actually learned.

T   F   5. The Stanford-Binet intelligence test is administered as a paper-and-pencil test.

T   F   6. Some psychologists feel that tests such as the Stanford-Binet and the Wechsler (WAIS-R or WISC-R) give little information about the nature of intelligence.

T   F   7. Cognitive psychologists use an information-processing model to understand intelligence.

T   F   8. Traditional measures of intelligence are very good predictors of career success.

T   F   9. The process of mainstreaming usually places children of normal intelligence among mentally retarded children in special education classrooms.

T   F   10.   Some culture-fair intelligence tests produce larger differences in average scores between the majority and minority groups.

MULTIPLE CHOICE QUESTIONS

1. A person who is diagnosed as having _____ may exhibit extraordinary talents yet be mentally retarded.
   a. Down syndrome
   b. the symptoms of Alzheimer's disease
   c. Kleinfelter's syndrome
   d. savant syndrome

2. The feature or ability common to virtually all definitions of intelligence is:
   a. high score on a written test.
   b. verbal proficiency.
   c. mastery of logical thought.
   d. effective use of environmental resources.

3. Your textbook defines intelligence as:
   a. the ability to understand subject matters from different disciplines in an academic setting.
   b. a complex capability in humans and animals that allows them to think, act, and function adaptively.
   c. the capacity to understand the world, think rationally, and use resources effectively when faced with challenges.
   d. a multidimensional human capability which is determined by a person's heredity and environment.

4. In order to distinguish more intelligent from less intelligent people, psychologists generally have relied on:
   a. intelligence tests.
   b. genealogy.
   c. achievement tests.
   d. projective tests.

5. According to Binet, a retarded person's mental age would be _____ the person's chronological age.
   a. lower than
   b. higher than
   c. the same as
   d. unrelated to

6. The measure of intelligence that takes into consideration both mental and chronological age is called the:
   a. achievement scale.
   b. aptitude level.
   c. intelligence quotient.
   d. g-factor.

7. The intelligence quotient was developed to:
   a. increase the reliability of the early intelligence tests.
   b. provide a way to compare the performance of French and American children on intelligence tests.
   c. permit meaningful comparisons of intelligence among people of different ages.
   d. correct a systematic scoring error in the first American intelligence tests.

8. If an 8-year-old child receives a score on an IQ test that is usually achieved by a typical 10-year-old, the child's IQ is:
   a. 80.
   b. 100.
   c. 125.
   d. 180.

9. Using standard testing procedures and the IQ formula, which of the following will have the highest IQ?
   a. a 12-year-old with a mental age of 10
   b. a 10-year-old with a mental age of 12
   c. a 25-year-old with a mental age of 23
   d. a 23-year-old with a mental age of 25

10. If a 12-year-old child receives a score on an IQ test that is usually achieved by a typical 9-year-old, the child's mental age is:
    a. 9.
    b. 12.
    c. 10 and a half.
    d. not determined without further investigation.

11. The formula _____ is used to calculate ratio IQ.
    a. $CA \div MA \times 100 = IQ$.
    b. $CA \div MA \times .01 = IQ$.
    c. $MA + CA \times 100 = IQ$.
    d. $(MA - CA) \div 100 = IQ$.

12. The first intelligence test was designed and used by:
    a. Alfred Binet.
    b. David Wechsler.
    c. Howard Gardner.
    d. Sigmund Freud.

13. Which alternative about the first intelligence test is **not** correct?
    a. It was designed to identify the "gifted" children in the school system.
    b. It was developed by Alfred Binet in France.
    c. It assumed that performance on certain items and tasks improved with age.
    d. Many items were selected for the test when "bright" and "dull" students scored differently on them.

14. About two-thirds of all people have IQ scores of:
    a. 95-105.
    b. 90-110.
    c. 85-115.
    d. 70-110.

15. The two major categories of the Wechsler intelligence tests are:
    a. visual and conceptual.
    b. spatial and verbal.
    c. performance and verbal.
    d. performance and spatial.

16. Of the following, which IQ range has the lowest percentage of individuals in it?
    a. 55-70
    b. 70-85
    c. 85-100
    d. 100-115

17. The administration of the Stanford-Binet test is ended when:
    a. all items have been administered.
    b. the person misses a total of five items.
    c. the person misses a total of ten items.
    d. the person cannot answer any more questions.

18. Which of the following is **not** one of the verbal subtests on the Wechsler intelligence scale?
    a. information
    b. similarities
    c. block design
    d. vocabulary

19. Which of the following is **not** one of the performance subtests on the Wechsler intelligence scale?
    a. comprehension
    b. picture completion
    c. picture arrangement
    d. digit symbol

20. Which of the following types of tests was designed to measure a person's level of knowledge in a given subject area?
    a. motor skills tests
    b. personality tests
    c. aptitude tests
    d. achievement tests

21. Aptitude tests are designed to:
    a. predict future performance.
    b. measure achievement in a certain area.
    c. measure intelligence.
    d. calculate the G-factor.

22. Crystallized intelligence is dependent on _____ for its development.
    a. heredity
    b. nutrition and diet
    c. fluid intelligence
    d. native intelligence

23. If you were asked to solve a problem using your own experience as a basis for the solution, you would be using:
    a. availability heuristics.
    b. crystallized intelligence.
    c. fluid intelligence.
    d. g-factors.

24. _____ is the most detailed perspective of intelligence to date.
    a. Spearman's G-factor
    b. Thurstone's primary abilities
    c. Cattell's fluid and crystallized intelligence
    d. Gardner's multiple intelligences

25. Gardner suggested that we have seven types of intelligence. Which of the following is **not** among them?
    a. general information intelligence
    b. musical intelligence
    c. spatial intelligence
    d. interpersonal intelligence

26. Gardner asserts that there are seven types of intelligence. Which alternative below is **not** one of them?
    a. technical
    b. interpersonal
    c. linguistic
    d. logical-mathematical

27. Among Gardner's suggested intelligences, which intelligence is described as "skill in interacting with others such as sensitivity to moods"?
    a. linguistic
    b. bodily-kinesthetic
    c. interpersonal
    d. intrapersonal

28. Cognitive psychologists use the _____ approach to understand intelligence.
    a. structure-of-intellect
    b. deviation IQ
    c. aptitude-testing
    d. information-processing

29. The _____ approach to understanding intelligence emphasizes processes.
    a. cognitive
    b. learning
    c. environmental
    d. physiological

30. To find out if you are particularly well suited to a career in business, you would be best advised to take the intelligence test devised by:
    a. Alfred Binet.
    b. Robert Sternberg.
    c. Raymond Cattell.
    d. Seymour Epstein.

31. According to Sternberg, intelligence and success in business:
    a. are strongly correlated.
    b. are minimally correlated.
    c. cannot be correlated.
    d. are inversely correlated.

32. Mental retardation is primarily defined by:
    a. ability to get along in the world and with other people.
    b. deficits in intellectual functioning and adaptive behavior.
    c. ability to perform in school.
    d. ability to perform on intelligence tests.

33. A significantly subaverage level of intellectual functioning accompanied by deficits in adaptive behavior defines:
    a. savant syndrome.
    b. profound retardation.
    c. mental retardation.
    d. severe retardation.

34. IQ scores falling below _____ fit the criterion for mental retardation.
    a. 80
    b. 70
    c. 60
    d. 50

35. The most common form of mental retardation that is clearly biologically based is:
    a. profoundly disabled.
    b. familial.
    c. savant syndrome.
    d. Down syndrome.

36. Which of the following statements about mental retardation is **not** true?
    a. Retardation often runs in families.
    b. Retardation is often caused by genetic defects.
    c. Retarded children are mainstreamed whenever possible.
    d. Profoundly retarded children are placed in special-education classes.

37. Most cases of mental retardation are classified as being caused by:
    a. Down syndrome.
    b. familial retardation.
    c. Kleinfelter's syndrome.
    d. traumatic injury.

38. Familial retardation:
    a. results from hereditary factors.
    b. results from environmental factors.
    c. is a paradox, since there are no known hereditary or environmental causes.
    d. may result from either hereditary or environmental factors, although there are no known biological causes.

39. According to the terminology used in the text, people with unusually low IQs (such as 42) are referred to as _____, whereas people with unusually high IQs (such as 164) are referred to as _____.
    a. mental defectives; geniuses
    b. the mentally retarded; the intellectually gifted
    c. the slow; the gifted
    d. the congenitally retarded; the intellectually superior

40. For the retarded youngster, mainstreaming means:
    a. more opportunities to relate to other retarded students.
    b. increased opportunities for education and socialization.
    c. the exclusion of other retarded students from the classroom.
    d. separating retarded and normal students.

41. Legislation designed to protect the rights of the mentally retarded, including providing a "least restrictive environment," has led to:
    a. mainstreaming.
    b. special-education classrooms.
    c. resource classrooms.
    d. mandatory IQ testing for all students with suspected deficits.

42. An intellectually gifted person:
    a. has an IQ higher than 130.   c. is antisocial.
    b. is very shy.   d. is successful in everything.

43. Youngsters with very high IQs:
    a. are gifted in every academic subject.
    b. have adjustment problems later in life.
    c. should not be mainstreamed.
    d. show better social adjustment in school than others.

44. A culture-unfair intelligence test is one in which the information being tested:
    a. is strictly academic.
    b. is cultural in nature.
    c. is easier for members of a particular culture.
    d. ignores all aspects of culture.

45. A _____ measure of intelligence does not favor any particular cultural group over another.
    a. quantitative   c. verbal
    b. conventional   d. culture-fair

46. What percentage of the variation in intelligence from one person to another did Arthur Jensen argue was inherited?
    a. 25   c. 75
    b. 50   d. 100

ESSAY QUESTIONS

Essay Question 10.1: *Defining Intelligence*

Describe and outline the definitions of intelligence offered in the text. Which of these do you find most acceptable? Support your view with examples or other evidence. What additional evidence would be required to strengthen the validity of the definition you have chosen?

_____

_____

_____

_____

_____

_____

_____

_____

_____

_____

_____

_____

_____

_____

_____

_____

_____

_____

Essay Question 10.2: *The Heredity/Environment Question*

Outline the basic issues involved in the heredity versus environment debate. The text suggests that the more important concern is how to maximize intelligence. Considering the concepts introduced so far on the text, what methods ought to be considered in our efforts to reach our fullest intelligence potential?

_____

_____

_____

_____

_____

_____

_____

_____

_____

_____

_____

_____

_____

_____

_____

_____

_____

_____

_____

ACTIVITIES AND PROJECTS

1. Survey your friends and classmates regarding their views of what makes a person intelligent. Your questions may include items regarding whether intelligence necessarily correlates with success in school or work; items concerning the existence of emotional and practical intelligence, as well as the seven types of intelligence defined by Howard Gardner (page 315 in the text). Your objective should be to determine the preconceived, commonly held attitudes about intelligence. For instance, you may also include questions regarding the social skills of very bright and gifted people, and the view that many intelligent people lack common sense.

2. It is also interesting to explore the views and attitudes concerning the role of genetic inheritance on intelligence and related factors like personality. Do intelligent people view themselves as having their intelligence as a result of their genetic make-up? Do they expect their children to be as intelligent as they are? (This could be a sign of their tacitly holding the view that intelligence is inherited to a large extent.)

11

MOTIVATION
AND EMOTION

DETAILED OUTLINE	*Survey:* ☐

This detailed outline contains all the headings in Chapter 11: Motivation and Emotion. If you are using the SQ3R method, then an examination of the outline is the best way to begin your survey of the chapter.

Deciphering Our Own Emotions

The James-Lange theory: Do gut reactions equal emotions?

The Cannon-Bard theory: Physiological reactions as the result of emotions

The Schachter-Singer theory: Emotions as labels

Summing up the theories of emotion

The truth about lies: Using emotional responses to separate the dishonest from the honest

● **Recap and Review III**

Nonverbal Behavior and the Expression of Emotions

Universality in emotional expressivity

The facial-feedback hypothesis: Smile, though you're feeling blue

The Cutting Edge Why Don't We Smile When We're Sad? The Bloodlines of Emotions

● **Recap and Review IV**

Looking Back
Key Terms and Concepts

➤ Now that you have surveyed the chapter, read **Looking Ahead**, pages 334–335.   *Question:* ☐

Focus on the questions on page 335.   *Read:* ☐

CONCEPTS AND LEARNING OBJECTIVES   *Survey:* ☐

These are the concepts and the learning objects for Chapter 11. Read them carefully as part of your preliminary survey of the chapter.

Concept 1: The theories of motivation examine basic instincts, drives, levels of arousal, expectations, and self-realization as possible sources for motives. Many of the approaches may actually be complementary, each explaining an aspect of the forces that direct and energize behavior.

1. Define motivation and emotions, and discuss the role of each in behavior. (pp. 334-335)

2. Describe and distinguish the instinct, drive reduction, and arousal theories of motivation. (pp. 335-338)

3. Describe incentive theory and opponent process theory of motivation. (pp. 338-340)

4. Describe how cognitive theory accounts for motivation, and discuss Maslow's hierarchy of motivation. (pp. 341-343)

Concept 2: Thirst and hunger are two motives that have a physiological basis, and the needs for achievement, affiliation, and power are learned motives.

5. Outline and describe the processes involved in the physiological motivations of thirst and hunger. (pp. 344-353)

6. Describe and distinguish achievement, affiliation, and power motivation. (pp. 353-356)

Concept 3: Emotions are highly complex experiences that combine physiological arousal, situational conditions, and cognitive understanding. Emotions also serve a number of functions related to preparing for action, shaping behavior, and regulating interaction. Three major theories of emotion are the James-Lange theory, the Cannon-Bard theory, and the Schachter-Singer theory.

7. Describe the functions of emotions and the range of emotional expression. (pp. 358-362)

8. Identify the key points of each theory of emotions—the James-Lange theory, the Cannon Bard theory, and the Schachter-Singer theory—and distinguish each theory from the others. (pp. 362-366)

9. Describe how lying is detected. (pp. 366-367)

Concept 4: Expression of the primary emotions is recognized across cultures. The similarity of facial expression has suggested the facial feedback hypothesis that states that facial expressions made determine how emotions are experienced and may influence blood flow to different parts of the brain, causing different experiences.

10. Discuss the evidence for the universality of emotional experience and expression. (pp. 367-369)

11. Explain how the facial feedback hypothesis helps account for emotional experience and expression. (pp. 369-371)

CHAPTER SUMMARY

There are several ways you can use this summary as part of your systematic study plan. You may read each concept summary and then read the corresponding pages in the text, or you may read the entire summary and then read the entire chapter in the text. As you finish each section, complete the **Recap and Review** questions that are supplied in the text.

CONCEPT 1: Prologue and Looking Ahead   *Survey:* ☐
              Formulations of Motivation   *Read:* ☐

Pages 334-344

The story of Peter Potterfield in the Prologue describes the importance and necessity of simple biological needs like fluid, and the ways in which individuals can be affected by basic needs. These factors that direct and energize behavior comprise the major focus of the study of **motivation**. **Motives** are the desired goals that underlie behavior. Psychologists who study motivation seek to understand why people do the things they do. The study of **emotions** includes the internal experience at any given moment.

There are a number of approaches to understanding motivation. An early approach focused on instincts as inborn, biologically determined patterns of behavior. The instinct theories argue that there exist preprogrammed patterns of behavior. The problems with these theories include the difficulty in determining a set of instincts, and the fact that instinct theories do not explain why a behavior occurs. Also, they are unable to account for the variety of behavior.

Drive-reduction theories focus on behavior as an attempt to remedy the shortage of some basic biological requirement. In this view, a **drive** is a motivational arousal that energizes a behavior to fulfill a need. **Primary drives** meet biological requirements, while **secondary drives** have no obvious biological basis. The need to achieve, for instance, is not a biological need. Primary drives are resolved by reducing the need that underlies them. Primary drives are also governed by a basic motivational phenomenon of **homeostasis**, the goal of maintaining optimal biological functioning. Drive reduction theories have difficulty explaining behavior that is not directed at reducing a need, but may be directed instead at maintaining or increasing arousal. Also, behavior appears to be motivated occasionally by curiosity as well.

The theory that explains motivation as being directed toward maintaining or increasing excitement is the **arousal theory**. If the levels of stimulation are too low, arousal theory says that we will try to increase the levels. The **Yerkes-Dodson law** suggests that each kind of task has an optimum level of arousal. Performance on simple tasks benefits from higher levels of arousal than the optimum level for complex tasks. However, if arousal is too high, both complex and simple tasks suffer. Arousal theory has been applied in many fields. If students are highly aroused, their performance on tests may be hampered.

In motivational terms the reward is the **incentive**. Incentive theory explains why behavior may be motivated by external stimuli. The properties of the incentive direct and energize behavior. External incentives can be powerful enough to overcome the lack of internal stimuli drives. This view is compatible with the drive reduction theory, as incentives work to "pull" and drives to "push" behavior.

According to another theory, the **opponent-process theory of motivation**, the stimuli that produce arousal also cause a later, opposite response as the body tries to calm down. Also, each time the stimuli recur, the second, opponent response gets stronger. This theory explains drug addiction: each time the second response strengthens, more of the drug must be taken in order to increase the initial response. When the initial response is negative, like the terror of sky-diving, the opponent process will be positive, and it will strengthen even if the initial fright weakens.

Cognitive theories of motivation focus on our thoughts, expectations, and understandings of the world. For instance, **expectancy-value theory** combines our expectations of reaching a goal with the value we place on it to account for the degree of motivation. **Intrinsic motivation** refers to the value an activity has in the enjoyment of participating in it, and extrinsic motivation refers to behavior that is done for a tangible reward. We work harder for a task that has intrinsic motivation. Also, as tangible rewards become available, intrinsic motivation declines and extrinsic motivation increases.

Abraham Maslow conceptualized motivational needs as fitting in a hierarchy from basic to higher-order. The first level of needs is that of the basic physiological needs of water, food, sleep, and sex. The second level is that of safety, having a secure and safe environment. The third level, the first of the higher-order needs, is that of love and belongingness. The fourth level is that of self-esteem, and the final level is that of self-actualization. **Self-actualization** is a state of fulfillment where people realize their potential.

CONCEPT 2: Human Needs and Motivation: Eat, Drink, and Be Daring

Survey: ☐
Read: ☐

Pages 344-357

Thirst signals one of the most important of human needs. Without water we will die in a few days. Three mechanisms produce thirst. The first is the variation of the salt concentration in the body. When it reaches certain levels, it triggers the hypothalamus. The second is the total volume of fluid in the circulatory system. The third is a rise in body temperature or an increase in energy use. The mouth and the stomach apparently work together to indicate when enough fluid has been taken in to restore the proper balance.

One-quarter of Americans are considered more than 20 percent overweight and thus suffering from **obesity**. Most nonhumans will regulate their intake of food even when it is abundant. Animals will also seek specific kinds of foods of which they have been deprived. Hunger is apparently quite complex, consisting of a number of mechanisms that signal changes in the body. One is the level of the sugar glucose in the blood. The higher the level of glucose, the less hunger is experienced. The **hypothalamus** monitors the blood chemistry. A rat with its **lateral hypothalamus** damaged will starve itself to death, and one with the **ventromedial hypothalamus** damaged will experience extreme overeating. One theory suggests that the body maintains a **weight set point**. This set point controls whether the hypothalamus calls for more or less food intake.

Internal biological factors do not explain our eating behavior fully. For instance, we eat meals on a customary schedule and thus feel hungry on that schedule. We eat about the same amount even if our exercise has changed, and we prefer certain types of food. Oversensitivity to external cues and insensitivity to internal cues are related to obesity. Also, reports of hunger in obese people do not correspond with the period of time deprived of food.

Weight set point has been implicated as a cause for obesity. Overweight people may have higher set points than normal weight people. The size and number of fat cells may account for the high set points. Differences in people's metabolism may also account for being overweight. **Metabolism** is the rate at which energy is produced and expended. People with high metabolic rates can eat as much food as they want and not gain weight. People with low metabolism eat little and still gain. There is evidence that people may be born to be fat, that weight is controlled genetically. Children may learn that food is a form of consolation if they are given food after being upset; thus, food becomes a treatment for emotional difficulties.

Anorexia nervosa is a disease that afflicts primarily females. Sufferers refuse to eat and may actually starve themselves to death. **Bulimia** is a condition in which individuals will binge on large quantities of food and then purge themselves with vomiting or laxatives. People suffering from bulimia are treated by being taught to eat foods they enjoy and to have control over their eating. Anorexia is treated by reinforcing weight gain, that is, giving privileges for success. The causes of these eating disorders are thought by some to be a chemical imbalance and by others to be the societal expectations placed on the sufferers of the disorders.

The Informed Consumer of Psychology addresses techniques for effective dieting. The recommendations include remembering that there is no easy way to lose weight, that reasonable goals must be set, that exercise must be included, that attention must be given to internal cues, that fad diets should be avoided, and that to maintain the weight level when it is reached one must establish appropriate habits.

The **need for achievement** is a learned characteristic involving the sustained striving for and attainment of a level of excellence. People with high needs for achievement seek out opportunities to compete and succeed. People with low needs for achievement are motivated by the desire to avoid failure.

The **Thematic Apperception Test** (**TAT**) is used to test achievement motivation. It requires that the person look at a series of ambiguous pictures and then write a story that tells what is going on and what will happen next. The stories are then scored for the amount of achievement imagery used in the story—the amount of striving to win or working hard images that suggest an achievement orientation. The achievement levels of societies have been analyzed by examining the achievement imagery in children's stories.

It is believed that people learn the need for achievement through high standards set by parents, who also praise success and encourage their children warmly. The question of whether achievement can be trained in adults has been explored by McClelland and Winter in a village in India. They asked the experimental group to imagine themselves as more successful and then to make concrete step-by-step plans for achievement. The experiment was a success, as the experimental group increased their business activity and created new jobs.

The **need for affiliation** refers to the needs we have of establishing and maintaining relationships with others. People high in affiliation needs tend to be more concerned with relationships and to be with their friends more. The **need for power** is a tendency to seek impact, control, or influence over others.

CONCEPT 3: Understanding Emotional Experiences
Deciphering Our Own Emotions

Survey: ☐
Read: ☐

Pages 358-367

Though difficult to define, **emotions** are understood to be the feelings that have both physiological and cognitive aspects and influence behavior. Physical changes occur whenever we experience an emotion, and we identify these changes as emotions. Some psychologists argue that separate systems account for the cognitive responses and the emotional responses. A current controversy involves whether emotions take precedence over cognitions. Finally, some argue that we first have cognitions and then emotional responses follow.

A number of important functions of emotions have been identified. They include preparing us for action by preparing effective responses to a variety of situations. They shape our future behavior by promoting learning that will influence making appropriate responses in the future by leading to the repetition of responses that lead to satisfying emotional feelings. They also help regulate interactions with others.

Psychologists have been attempting to identify the most important fundamental emotions. Robert Plutchik has identified a list of eight fundamental emotions. They are: joy, acceptance, fear, surprise, sadness, disgust, anger, and anticipation. Others have suggested that there may be fewer or that the emotions should be understood through their component parts.

We have many ways to describe the experiences of emotion that we have. The physiological reactions that accompany fear are associated with the activation of the autonomic nervous system. They include: an increase in breathing rate, an increase in heart rate, a widening of the pupils, a cessation of the functions of the digestive system, and a contraction of the muscles below the surface of your skin. Though these changes occur without awareness, the emotional experience of fear can be felt intensely. Whether these physiological responses are the cause of the experience or the result of the experience of emotion remains unclear.

The **James-Lange theory of emotion** states that emotions are the perceived physiological reactions that occur in the internal organs. They called this **visceral experience**. One of the problems with this view is that in order for this theory to be valid, the visceral changes would have to be fairly rapid, whereas emotional experiences often occur before visceral changes can take place. Another problem is that physiological arousal does not invariably produce emotional experience. Finally, internal organs produce limited sensations.

The **Cannon-Bard theory of emotion** rejects the view that physiological arousal alone leads to the perception of emotion. In their theory, the emotion producing stimuli is first perceived, then the thalamus activates the viscera and at the same time a message is sent to the cortex. The difference between emotional experiences depends upon the message received by the cortex.

The **Schachter-Singer theory of emotion** emphasizes that the emotion experienced depends on the environment and on comparing ourselves with others. Schachter and Singer conducted a classic experiment in which subjects were injected with epinephrine to cause physiological arousal. One group was informed about the effects and another was kept uninformed. These two groups were then exposed to either a situation in which a confederate of the experimenter was acting angry and hostile or in which the confederate was acting euphoric. The informed subjects were not affected by the situation because they accounted for their arousal as the effects of the drug, but the uninformed subjects accounted for their physiological arousal according to the situation. The experiment then supports the cognitive view of emotions that emotions depend on general arousal that is labeled according to cues in the environment. The Schachter-Singer theory of emotions has been applied to other circumstances, one of which involved an attractive female as subject who asked males a series of questions and then gave them her telephone number so they could get the results of the survey. Two groups of men were involved. One group had just crossed a 450-foot suspension bridge over a deep canyon and the other crossed a stable bridge over a shallow stream. Those who crossed the canyon reported a stronger attraction to the woman, accounting for their arousal the presence of the female rather than the fear of the canyon.

For each of the three major theories, there is some contradictory evidence. Emotions are complex phenomena that no single theory can yet explain adequately.

The lie detector, or **polygraph**, indicates when someone is most likely telling lies because of the arousal of the autonomic nervous system that signals an increase in emotionality. The polygraph detects a number of physiological indicators, including irregularity of breathing patterns, heart rate and blood pressure, and an increase in sweating. The drawbacks include the fact that some people react emotionally to being questioned and that some people can fool the polygraph. The American Psychological Association has adopted a position that states that the polygraph is still unsatisfactory in its effectiveness.

CONCEPT 4: Nonverbal Behavior and the Expression of Emotions

Survey: ☐
Read: ☐

Pages 367-372

Emotions are communicated in nonverbal ways through a variety of paths of communication called **channels**. Each channel—eye contact, body movement, tone of voice, and even eyebrow position—is capable of carrying a different message.

Facial expressions have been used to define six categories of emotional expression: happiness, anger, sadness, surprise, disgust, and fear. Paul Ekman has found that members of a jungle tribe were able to identify these emotions. He told the tribal members a story and then showed them pictures of three westerners and asked them to identify which face represented the most reasonable expression. Only fearful faces were confused with another emotion, and that was surprise. Other natives were told the same stories and then asked to give the correct facial expression for the emotion. These faces were then shown to westerners who correctly identified them, with the exception of fear and surprise. One explanation for this similarity is the hypothesis that a **facial-effect program** exists at birth. The program is set in motion when the emotion is experienced and then the appropriate expression is produced.

The **facial-feedback hypothesis** argues that faces both reflect emotional experience and help determine how emotions are experienced. In a classic experiment, actors were asked to make facial expressions of emotions by describing the facial posture without mention of the actual emotion. When making the face for fear, the actors experienced an increase in heart rate and a decline in body temperature consistent with the experience of fear.

Robert Zajonc has proposed that facial expressions change the flow of blood to the brain and thus influence emotional experience. The theory is called the **vascular theory of emotions**. Facial expressions affect the temperature of the blood. The cooler blood experienced during a smile accounts for the pleasure that is experienced. This also accounts for meditation and relaxation techniques because they require breathing through the nose, which cools the blood.

➤ Now that you have surveyed, questioned, and read the chapter and completed
the **Recap and Review** questions, review **Looking Back**, page 372–373.   *Review:* ☐

➤ For additional practice through recitation and review, test your knowledge of the chapter material by
answering the questions in the **Key Word Drill**, the **Practice Questions**, and the **Essay
Questions**.

KEY WORD DRILL

Recite: ☐

The following **Fill in the Blank** and **Matching Questions** test key words from the text. Check your
answers with the Answer Key in the back of the *Study Guide*.

FILL IN THE BLANK

1. _____ includes all the factors that direct and energize behavior.

2. An organism tries to maintain an internal biological balance, or "steady state," through

   _____.

3. The _____ is an external stimulus that directs and energizes behavior by being
   anticipated as a reward.

4. _____ is defined as being more than _____ percent
   above the average weight for a person of a particular height.

5. The body strives to maintain weight at the _____ _____

   _____.

6. The eating disorder with symptoms that include various degrees of self-starvation in an attempt to

   avoid obesity is called _____ _____, and the eating
   disorder characterized by vast intake of food that may be followed by self-induced vomiting is called

   _____.

7. The _____ _____ _____ consists
   of a series of ambiguous pictures about which a person is asked to write a story.

8. Feelings such as happiness, despair, and sorrow that generally have both physiological and cognitive

   elements and that influence behavior are called _____.

9. The _____ is an electronic device that measures bodily changes which may
   signal that a person is lying.

10. _____ are paths along which verbal and nonverbal behavioral messages, such as facial expressions, eye contact, body movements, are communicated.

MATCHING QUESTIONS

_____ 11. motives

_____ 12. emotions

_____ 13. instinct

_____ 14. drive

_____ 15. primary drives

_____ 16. secondary drives

_____ 17. intrinsic motivation

_____ 18. extrinsic motivation

a. An inborn pattern of behavior that is biologically determined.

b. Motivation causing people to participate in an activity for a tangible reward.

c. Motivation causing people to participate in an activity for their own enjoyment, not for the reward it will get them.

d. Desired goals that prompt behavior.

e. The internal feelings experienced at any given moment.

f. Biological needs such as hunger, thirst, fatigue, and sex.

g. Drives in which no biological need is fulfilled.

h. A motivational tension or arousal that energizes behavior in order to fulfill a need.

_____ 19. drive-reduction theory

_____ 20. arousal theory

_____ 21. Yerkes-Dodson law

_____ 22. incentive theory

_____ 23. opponent-process theory of motivation

_____ 24. cognitive theories of motivation

a. Theories explaining motivation by focusing on the role of an individual's thoughts, expectations, and understanding of the world.

b. The theory which claims that drives are produced to obtain our basic biological requirements.

c. The theory which postulates that increases in arousal ultimately produce a calming reaction in the nervous system, and vice versa.

d. The belief that we try to maintain certain levels of stimulation and activity, increasing or reducing them as necessary.

e. The theory explaining motivation in terms of external stimuli.

f. The theory that a particular level of motivational arousal produces optimal performance of a task.

_____ 25. expectancy-value theory

_____ 26. self-actualization

_____ 27. need for achievement

_____ 28. need for affiliation

_____ 29. need for power

a. A tendency to want to seek impact, control, or influence on others in order to be seen as a powerful individual.

b. A need to establish and maintain relationships with other people.

c. A stable, learned characteristic in which satisfaction comes from striving for and achieving a level of excellence.

d. A state of self-fulfillment in which people realize their highest potential.

e. A view that suggests that people are motivated by expectations that certain behaviors will accomplish a goal and their understanding of the importance of the goal.

_____ 30. hypothalamus

_____ 31. lateral hypothalamus

_____ 32. ventromedial hypothalamus

_____ 33. metabolism

_____ 34. visceral experience

_____ 35. facial-affect program

_____ 36. facial-feedback hypothesis

a. The part of the brain which, when damaged, results in an organism's starving to death.

b. The "gut" reaction experienced internally, triggering an emotion.

c. The notion that facial expressions not only reflect, but also determine and help people identify, the experience of emotions.

d. The part of the brain which, when injured, results in extreme overeating.

e. The activation of a set of nerve impulses that make the face display the appropriate expression.

f. The structure in the brain that is primarily responsible for regulating food intake.

g. The rate at which energy is produced and expended by the body.

_____ 37. James-Lange theory of emotion

_____ 38. Cannon-Bard theory of emotion

_____ 39. Schachter-Singer theory of emotion

_____ 40. vascular theory of emotions

a. The belief that emotions are determined jointly by a nonspecific kind of physiological arousal and its interpretation, based on environmental cues.

b. The belief that emotional experience is a reaction to bodily events occurring as a result of an external situation.

c. The theory that there is a link between particular facial expressions and the temperature of the blood flow to the brain, which in turn affects the experience of emotions.

d. The belief that both physiological and emotional arousal are produced simultaneously by the same nerve impulse.

| **PRACTICE QUESTIONS** | *Recite and Review:* ☐ |

Test your knowledge of the chapter material by answering these **True-False** and **Multiple Choice Questions**. Check your answers with the Answer Key in the back of the *Study Guide*.

TRUE-FALSE QUESTIONS

T   F   1. Motivation is studied only in humans, since it is rarely observed in lower animals.

T   F   2. Curiosity has been demonstrated in both humans and animals.

T   F   3. Drive-reduction theories are adequate to explain behaviors in which the goal is to maintain a particular level of excitement.

T   F   4. Maslow's theory of self-actualization applies only to people who have exceptional accomplishments and distinctions.

T   F   5. Self-actualization can be attained more readily if no attention is paid to lower motivational states.

T   F   6. Bulimia, an eating disorder, affects men and women in equal numbers.

T   F   7. People with low achievement motivation tend mainly to be motivated by the desire to avoid failure.

T   F   8. Emotions prepare us for action, shape our future, and help us regulate our behavior.

T   F   9. According to the text, polygraphs can validly be used to screen job applicants for employment.

T   F   10. According to the vascular theory of emotions, when the blood supply to the brain is cooled, we have more positive feelings.

MULTIPLE CHOICE QUESTIONS

1. The study of motivation seeks ways of:
    a. identifying why people behave the way they do.
    b. discussing the relationship between people's past experiences and their emotions.
    c. understanding genetic inheritance.
    d. identifying social pressures affecting an individual's emotions.

2. According to the text, the main function of motivation is to:
    a. create tension.   c. promote learning of survival behaviors.
    b. provide feeling.   d. provide direction to behavior.

3. The story of Peter Potterfield, who survived on a narrow crest of Chimney Rock, illustrates how:
    a. physical training required for mountain climbing was responsible for his survival.
    b. preparation before the accident provided Potterfield with the minimal nutrition he needed to survive.
    c. survival was the complex result of biological and other factors.
    d. prudent actions preserved his life, but the accident ended his mountain climbing career.

4. Primary drives are motives that:
    a. people rate as being most important to them.
    b. seem to motivate an organism the most.
    c. are least likely to be satisfied before self-actualization can occur.
    d. have a biological basis and are universal.

5. Which of the following is the best example of a drive that is common to both humans and animals?
    a. power   c. cognition
    b. hunger   d. achievement

6. The process by which an organism tries to maintain an optimal level of internal biological functioning is called:
    a. primary drive equilibrium.   c. drive reduction.
    b. homeostasis.   d. opponent-process theory.

7. The compensatory activity of the autonomic nervous system, which returns the body to normal levels of functioning after a trauma, is called:
    a. homeostasis.   c. biofeedback.
    b. biorhythmicity.   d. transference.

8. According to the text, a motivation behind behavior in which no obvious biological need is being fulfilled is the definition of:
    a. a primary drive.   c. a secondary drive.
    b. an achievement.   d. instinct.

9. Which of the following would be considered a secondary drive?
   a. power
   b. hunger
   c. thirst
   d. sleep

10. The basic premise of the Yerkes-Dodson law is that:
    a. instincts are the primary motivational force for behavior.
    b. there is an optimal level of arousal for task performance.
    c. secondary drives are brought about by experience and learning.
    d. homeostatic balance is maintained by compensation for deviations.

11. According to the Yerkes-Dodson law, the effect of a high level of arousal on performance of a complex task would be:
    a. enhancement of performance.
    b. impairment of performance.
    c. irrelevant to performance.
    d. to accelerate performance.

12. The major prediction from the Yerkes-Dodson law is that:
    a. performance of simple tasks will be enhanced by greater levels of arousal; performance of complex tasks will be enhanced by lower levels of arousal.
    b. increasing levels of arousal result in decreased task performance.
    c. different people have different curves at different times.
    d. the particular level of arousal that leads to optimal performance of a task is determined by the combined strengths of other drives (such as hunger and fatigue).

13. The incentive theory of motivation focuses on:
    a. instincts.
    b. the characteristics of external stimuli.
    c. drive reduction.
    d. the rewarding quality of various behaviors which are motivated by arousal.

14. According to the text, some psychologists feel that the incentive theory of motivation is strengthened when combined with complementary concepts drawn from:
    a. instinct theory.
    b. drive-reduction theory.
    c. arousal theory.
    d. opponent-process theory.

15. Which of the following theories of motivation specifically seeks to explain both drug addiction and the physiological and emotional reactions that occur in situations involving extreme danger?
    a. arousal
    b. drive-reduction
    c. cognitive
    d. opponent-process

16. According to the text, which motivation theory attempts to explain motivation in terms of the external stimuli which direct and energize behavior?
    a. incentive
    b. opponent-process
    c. arousal
    d. cognitive

17. Our hopes that a behavior will cause us to reach a certain goal and our understanding that the goal will be meaningful or important to us are combined in:
   a.   the expectancy-value theory of motivation.
   b.   the drive-reduction theory of motivation.
   c.   Maslow's hierarchy of motivation.
   d.   theory of extrinsic motivation.

18. Advertisements for a job boast that it offers $4 more than minimum wage, a guaranteed cash bonus after thirty days, and a paid vacation. This advertisement emphasizes the concept of:
   a.   opponent-process motivation.   c.   drive-reduction motivation.
   b.   arousal motivation.   d.   extrinsic motivation.

19. Motivation that causes a person to behave in a particular manner for a reward is called:
   a.   intrinsic motivation.   c.   achievement motivation.
   b.   extrinsic motivation.   d.   instinctual motivation.

20. Which theory is **least** tied to biological mechanisms?
   a.   instinct theory   c.   drive-reduction theory
   b.   cognitive theory   d.   arousal theory

21. According to Maslow, which of the following must be met before people can fulfill any higher-order motivations?
   a.   extrinsic needs   c.   primary drives
   b.   intrinsic needs   d.   secondary drives

22. According to Maslow, which of the following is the highest state of self-fulfillment?
   a.   self-esteem   c.   self-satisfaction
   b.   self-actualization   d.   self-centeredness

23. Which alternative below is **not** associated with thirst?
   a.   changes in the salt concentration in the cells of the body
   b.   changes in total volume of fluid in the circulatory system
   c.   a significant decrease in body weight
   d.   an increase in body temperature

24. According to the text, which of the following is thought to be primarily involved in the physiological regulation of eating behavior?
   a.   cortex   c.   hypothalamus
   b.   amygdala   d.   hippocampus

25. For the American public, which factor appears to play the **least** significant role in hunger?
   a.   blood chemistry   c.   number and size of fat cells
   b.   stomach contractions   d.   weight set point

26. Which alternative below is correct about nonobese versus obese individuals?
    a. Small tumors in the hypothalamus account for about 60 percent of all cases of obesity.
    b. Obese individuals will work harder than nonobese individuals so that they can consume food.
    c. Obese individuals seem less responsive to internal hunger cues than nonobese individuals.
    d. Nonobese individuals are more critical and rejecting of unpleasant-tasting food than are obese individuals.

27. At which of the following ages does the amount of fat cells in the body usually stop declining?
    a. 24 years of age
    b. 20 years of age
    c. 12 years of age
    d. 2 years of age

28. Which of the following mechanisms may underlie obesity?
    a. The fat cells may be too small.
    b. The weight set point may be too high.
    c. The metabolic rate may be too high.
    d. The number of fat cells may have been increased after puberty.

29. Which of the following is an eating disorder usually affecting attractive, successful females between the ages of 12 and 20 who refuse to eat and sometimes literally starve themselves to death?
    a. metabolic malfunction
    b. bulimia
    c. anorexia nervosa
    d. obesity

30. Sonya developed a cycle of binge eating, during which she consumed a variety of gourmet foods and wines and then induced vomiting afterward. Her doctor told Sonya that she could do permanent damage to her health if she continued the behavior and that if she continued she could become:
    a. ischemic.
    b. depressed.
    c. volumetric.
    d. bulimic.

31. According to the text, which alternative below is **not** good advice for a person trying to lose weight?
    a. Exercise regularly.
    b. Reduce the influence of external cues and social behavior on your eating.
    c. Choose a diet program that gives rather rapid weight losses so that you will stay motivated.
    d. Remember, when you reach your desired goal, you're not finished!

32. Jane finished her college degree with honors and received a variety of excellent job offers. Instead, she decided to enter graduate school to acquire more advanced skills and get even better job offers. Jane is demonstrating her:
    a. need for affiliation.
    b. need for achievement.
    c. fear of failure.
    d. need for power.

33. Which alternative below is **not** true of the need for achievement?
    a. Individuals with a high need for achievement choose situations in which they are likely to succeed easily.
    b. It is a learned motive.
    c. Satisfaction is obtained by striving for and attaining a level of excellence.
    d. High need for achievement is related to economic and occupational success.

34. Which of the following statements is true of people with high achievement motivation?
    a. They choose tasks which they can do easily.
    b. They choose difficult tasks for the challenge.
    c. They choose tasks at which they can compete against a standard.
    d. They choose friends who have low achievement motivation.

35. The _____ is used to measure an individual's need for achievement.
    a. Scholastic Aptitude Test
    b. Intelligence Quotient Test
    c. Yerkes-Dodson Achievement Analysis
    d. Thematic Apperception Test

36. According to the text, women, as opposed to men, tend to channel their need for power through:
    a. socially responsible ways
    b. questionable means
    c. quietly aggressive ways
    d. uncharted, high-risk opportunities

37. According to the text, emotions play an important role in all of the following **except**:
    a. making life interesting.
    b. helping us to regulate social interaction.
    c. informing us of internal bodily needs.
    d. preparing us for action in response to the external environment.

38. According to the text, which of the following functions of emotion involves the activation of the sympathetic nervous system in order to make our response to situations more effective?
    a. preparation for action
    b. regulation of social interactions
    c. labeling feelings
    d. making us feel sad

39. William James and Walter Lange suggested that major emotions correlate with particular "gut reactions" of internal organs. They called this internal response:
    a. a physiological pattern.   c. an autonomic response.
    b. a psychological experience.   d. a visceral experience.

40. According to the James-Lange theory of emotion, _____ determines the emotional experience.
    a. physiological change   c. an instinctive process
    b. a cognitive process   d. the environment

41. Which theory postulates that emotions are identified by observing the environment and comparing ourselves with others?
    a. Schachter-Singer theory   c. James-Lange theory
    b. Cannon-Bard theory   d. Plutchik's theory

42. A polygraph is an electronic device that detects lying by measuring:
    a. brain waves.
    b. heart rate and sweating.
    c. breathing patterns and sweating.
    d. breathing patterns and brain waves.

43. Which of the following is **not** one of the six basic categories of nonverbal emotion identified by Ekman?
    a. happiness
    b. love
    c. anger
    d. surprise

44. According to the text, when asked to choose a "reasonable" facial expression after hearing a story, New Guineans differed from westerners only in identifying:
    a. happy faces.
    b. angry faces.
    c. fearful faces.
    d. sad faces.

45. There is convincing evidence that the way in which basic emotions are displayed and interpreted is:
    a. culture-specific.
    b. universal.
    c. gender-specific.
    d. learned.

46. The facial-affect program is:
    a. developed during early childhood.
    b. unique to American culture.
    c. a technological breakthrough.
    d. the activation of nerve impulses.

47. When you are feeling down yet continue to smile, you will begin to feel better according to the:
    a. facial-feedback hypothesis.
    b. James-Lange theory of emotions.
    c. facial-affect program.
    d. Cannon-Bard theory of emotions.

ESSAY QUESTIONS

Essay Question 11.1: *Theories of Motivation*

Describe each of the main theories of motivation and attempt to explain a single behavior from the point of view of each theory.

_____

_____

_____

_____

_____

_____

_____

_____

_____

_____

_____

_____

_____

_____

_____

_____

_____

Essay Question 11.2: *The Polygraph*

Under what conditions might a polygraph test be considered fair? Outline the possible ethical and scientific concerns that arise from the use of the polygraph in support of your answer.

_____

_____

_____

_____

_____

_____

_____

_____

_____

_____

_____

_____

_____

_____

_____

_____

_____

_____

ACTIVITIES AND PROJECTS
---

1. The next time you experience an emotion that is clear enough for you to give it a label, take time afterward to analyze which theory of emotion best applies to your particular emotional experience. For example, would the James-Lange theory apply? Did your experience follow from physiological cues? Or did these processes happen simultaneously as suggested by the Cannon-Bard theory? Or did cognitive processes and labeling on the basis of context play a major role in your experience of the emotion?

2. Determine where you believe that you fit on Maslow's hierarchy of needs. How do you know that you are at that particular level? What types of thought patterns and behaviors might you engage in during your striving to the next level in the hierarchy? You may also identify your specific concerns and behaviors as they fit each of the levels of Maslow's hierarchy. What behaviors would you identify with your eventual self-actualization?

12

SEXUALITY AND GENDER

The Informed Consumer of Psychology Recognizing the Promises and Pitfalls of Sex Therapy
● **Recap and Review IV**

Looking Back
Key Terms and Concepts

➤ Now that you have surveyed the chapter, read **Looking Ahead**, pages 376–377. *Question:* ☐
Focus on the questions on pages 376–377. *Read:* ☐

CONCEPTS AND LEARNING OBJECTIVES

Survey: ☐

These are the concepts and the learning objects for Chapter 12. Read them carefully as part of your preliminary survey of the chapter.

Concept 1: Gender differences are primarily a result of social expectations and cultural patterns. Minor differences have been described in personality and cognitive skills.

1. Describe the bases of sexuality and gender, and discuss the sources of our typical attitudes toward them. (pp. 376-379)

2. Discuss the roles of personality and cognition in the development and perception of gender and sexuality. (pp. 380-382)

3. Identify the biological and environmental sources of gender and sexual schemas. (pp. 382-384)

Concept 2: The human sexual response is unique among animals because it is not tied to a monthly cycle. The physiological response does follow a pattern. Erotic material is socially and culturally defined.

4. Describe the biological and psychological aspects of sexual behavior, especially the concept of sex drive and the experience of sexual response. (pp. 385-387)

5. Outline and describe the sexual response, and distinguish the female and the male response. (pp. 387-391)

Concept 3: The variety of sexual behavior includes masturbation; premarital, marital, and extramarital heterosexual activity; and homosexual and bisexual activity.

6. Describe how sexual normality is understood and defined by society, and discuss whether masturbation is normal. (pp. 391-394)

7. Describe the heterosexual patterns of sexual behavior, including premarital sex, marital sex, and extramarital sex. (pp. 394-398)

8. Describe the similarities and differences between normal sexuality and homosexual and bisexual behavior. (pp. 398-400)

Concept 4: Sexual crimes are perhaps the most frightening because of the violence they do to the victim. They include rape, date rape, and child sexual abuse. Problems related to sexual behavior include the transmission of series diseases like AIDS and the development of sexual problems.

9.   Describe the common patterns of rape, including date rape, and abuse. (pp. 400-403)

10.   Identify the common sexually transmitted diseases (STDs). (pp. 404-406)

11.   Describe the sexual problems most commonly experienced and the treatment approaches available. (pp. 406-409)

CHAPTER SUMMARY

There are several ways you can use this summary as part of your systematic study plan. You may read each concept summary and then read the corresponding pages in the text, or you may read the entire summary and then read the entire chapter in the text. As you finish each section, complete the **Recap and Review** questions that are supplied in the text.

CONCEPT 1: Prologue and Looking Ahead
Gender and Sex

Survey: ☐
Read: ☐

Pages 376-384

The Prologue illustrates the crime of date rape, a growing phenomenon on college campuses and elsewhere. Date rape is one of many issues examined in the chapter. Human sexuality is studied by a wide variety of psychologists, ranging from biopsychologists to social psychologists. **Gender** is the sense of being male or female.

From the very beginning of life the child is exposed to societal expectations that lead to the formation of a **gender role**, defined as the set of expectations that indicate appropriate behavior for men and women. The expectations differ significantly, and the result is that one sex stereotypes the other. **Stereotyping** is the process of forming beliefs and expectations about members of a group based on membership in the group. Stereotypes based on gender roles result in sexism, which consists of negative attitudes and behavior toward a person based on that person's sex. In our society, the stereotype of the male is that he must be competent, and the stereotype of the female is that she must be warm and expressive. We also hold competence in higher esteem than warmth and expressiveness, creating a bias based on sex. Apparently, our attitudes have changed little since this topic was first studied by Broverman twenty years ago. Women continue to be discriminated against in occupations, and the attitudes in the workplace contribute to the occurrence of sexual harassment, which is defined by unwanted sexual advances, coercion forcing an employee to participate in a relationship, physical conduct where the employee is touched or the recipient of threatening gestures, or visual harassment in which pornographic materials are displayed. Women continue to select careers that are traditionally female-dominated.

The actual differences between men's and women's behavior is quite small. Also, what differences do exist are based on the difference between the average group differences, not the differences between individuals. Though males as a group may be more aggressive than females, there are many males less aggressive than many females.

In addition to expressing less aggression, women tend to feel greater anxiety and guilt when they are aggressive. Women tend to have lower levels of self-esteem, and they tend to have lower confidence levels concerning how they will do on future tasks. The lower self-esteem and lower aggressiveness may explain why women are reluctant to enter high-prestige professions. Contrary to the stereotype, men apparently talk more than women, though women have more precise speech. Female speech is less assertive and more tentative. Men and women also differ in their nonverbal behavior. Males communicate power and dominance, and females communicate less power. Men are also more likely to touch others, while women are more likely to be touched.

The major cognitive difference that has been identified is that of boys having better quantitative and spatial abilities than girls. Recent studies have shown that the major difference has resulted in slightly better performance on high school mathematics problem solving. Recent studies have also shown that the difference on verbal skills is insignificant. Even though the difference on mathematics performance is insignificant, the high scorers on the mathematics sections of the Scholastic Aptitude Test are predominantly male.

Both biological and environmental factors contribute to gender and sex differences. Hormones may play a role in the differences between male and female brains. Prenatal exposure to androgens, the male sex hormones, may slow the growth of the left hemisphere. The right hemisphere, responsible for mathematical problem solving, may then be strengthened. When **estrogen**, the female sex hormone, levels are high, women perform better on tasks requiring verbal skill and muscle coordination.

Environmental causes of gender differences include the amount and kind of interaction between parents and their children. Fathers play more roughly with their infant sons than daughters, and middle class mothers talk more to their daughters. These differences lead to different experiences of the socialization process. **Socialization** is the way individuals learn the rules and norms of socially appropriate behavior. The socialization process includes information gained from television and the educational system. Boys are more likely to receive attention from teachers. Sandra Bem has suggested that socialization produces **gender schema**, cognitive frameworks that organize and guide a child's understanding of gender-relevant information. In order to get around gender schemas, society must encourage **androgynous** activity, in which the gender roles include both male and female characteristics.

CONCEPT 2: Understanding Human Sexual Response: The Facts of Life

Survey: ☐
Read: ☐

Pages 385-391

Sexual behavior in humans is filled with meaning, values, and feelings. The basic biology of the sexual response helps us understand the importance of sexual behavior. Human sexual behavior is not governed by the genetic control that other animals experience. In males, the **testes**, part of the male **genitals**, secrete androgen beginning at puberty. Androgen increases the sex drive and produces secondary sex characteristics like body hair and voice change. When women reach puberty, the **ovaries**, the female reproductive organs produce estrogen, the female sex hormone. Estrogen reaches it highest levels during **ovulation**, the release of eggs from the ovaries. In many animals, the period of ovulation is the only time they are receptive to sex. Women remain receptive throughout their cycles. Though biological factors are important, we are also conditioned to respond to a wide range of stimuli that lead to arousal.

The external stimuli that lead to sexual arousal are called **erotic** stimuli. No areas of the body automatically lead to sexual arousal when touched. The erogenous zones, areas of the body that are dense ion nerve endings, are sensitive to all kinds of touch, and what differs from one touch to another is the interpretation given to it. What is considered erotic by one culture may not be erotic to another. In some cultures the tattooed thigh of a woman is erotic; in another, fat women are erotic. The female preferences in our culture are for men to have small buttocks and moderately sized breasts. Fantasy also plays a role in arousal, and 60 percent of all people have fantasies during sexual intercourse. Fantasies differ little between men and women on content and quantity.

The phases of the sexual response are: (1) The **excitement phase**, during which the **penis** becomes erect and the **clitoris** swells. The **vagina** also becomes lubricated. (2) The **plateau phase**, during which the body prepares for orgasm, with a maximum level of arousal being reached. In women, the breasts and the vagina swell. Heartbeat and pulse rate increase. (3) **Orgasm**, though the sensation is difficult to describe, the physical process is a rhythmic muscular contraction. Males expel **semen**, the fluid containing sperm, in a process known as **ejaculation**. (4) The final phase is the **resolution stage** during which the body returns to normal. In males, a period called the **refractory period** occurs during which the males are unable to be aroused. Orgasm and ejaculation are controlled by separate parts of the nervous system, so it is possible for some males to have multiple orgasms prior to ejaculation.

CONCEPT 3: The Varieties of Sexual Behavior: Different Strokes for Different Folks

Survey: ☐
Read: ☐

Pages 391-400

Sexual behavior is influenced by expectations, attitudes, beliefs, and the state of medical and biological knowledge. Normal sexual behavior is described by the range of behaviors from traditional marital sexual intercourse to bizarre behaviors. Defining what is normal can be approached by determining the deviation for an average or typical behavior, though there are many behaviors that are unusual statistically but not abnormal. Another approach is to compare behavior against a standard or ideal form. However, the selection of a standard is difficult, since it must be universally acceptable. A reasonable approach to defining sexual normality is to consider the psychological consequences of the behavior. If it produces a sense of distress, anxiety, or guilt or is harmful to a person, then it should be considered abnormal. Until Albert Kinsey undertook his study of sexual behavior, little was known about sexual behavior of typical Americans. Kinsey collected a large number of sexual histories. One criticism of his approach is with regard to his sampling techniques which led him to interview a large proportion of college students and well-educated individuals. Also, since the surveys were based on volunteers, it is uncertain whether the attitudes of individuals willing to share sensitive information are different from those who did not volunteer. Kinsey's work has led to a number of other national surveys.

Masturbation is sexual self-stimulation, and its practice is quite common. Males masturbate more often than females, with males beginning in early teens, though females start later and reach a maximum frequency later. Though thought of as an activity to be done when other sexual partners are unavailable, almost three-quarters of married men masturbate. Negative attitudes about masturbation continue, though it is perfectly healthy and harmless.

Heterosexuality refers to sexual behavior between men and women. It includes all aspects of sexual contact—kissing, caressing, sex play, and intercourse. Premarital sex continues to be viewed through a **double standard**, as something acceptable for males but unacceptable for females. However, sexual activity among unmarried women is high according to several surveys. When younger and older females are compared, there appears to be an increase in premarital sexual activity. Males have shown a similar increase in activity, though it is not as dramatic. The double standard appears to be changing to an attitude of permissiveness with affection, meaning that premarital intercourse is permissible if affection exists between the two persons. There are major cultural differences.

The average married couple has intercourse six times a month, and the longer a couple is married, the less frequently intercourse occurs. The frequency of sexual intercourse has increased with the availability of contraceptives and of abortion. Sex is more openly in the media, and the notion that female sexuality is acceptable have all contributed to the increase in activity. The frequency of sexual intercourse is not a predictor of happiness in the marriage. With the increase in marital intercourse there has also been an increase in extramarital sex, or sexual activity between a married person and someone other than the spouse. Extramarital sex remains something that is consistently disapproved.

Humans are not born with an innate attraction to the opposite sex. Homosexuality refers to sexual attraction for members of the same sex, while bisexuality refers to sexual attraction for both sexes. At least 20 to 25 percent of males and about 15 percent of females have had an adulthood homosexual experience and between 5 and 10 percent of both males and females are exclusively homosexual. Though people view homosexuality and heterosexuality as distinct orientations, Kinsey places the two orientations on a scale. There are a number of theories accounting for sexual orientation, with some focusing on biological factors and others on social factors. Recent evidence suggests that there may be a physical difference in the anterior hypothalamus of heterosexual and homosexual males. Other theories focus on childhood and family background. Psychoanalysts suggest that male homosexuals have overprotective and dominant mothers and passive fathers. Learning theory suggests that sexual orientation is learned through rewards and punishments. Experiences with unpleasant outcomes would lead to linking the unpleasant experience with the opposite sex. Rewarding experiences would be incorporated into sexual fantasies. These fantasies are then positively reinforced by the pleasure of orgasm. The problem with learning theory is that the expected punishments of homosexuality from society should outweigh the rewards and prevent the learning. Most researchers believe that a combination of factors must be at work.

Concept 4: Sexual Difficulties and Treatment: When Sex Goes Wrong

Survey: ☐
Read: ☐

Pages 400-409

Sexual crimes have profound and long-lasting psychological consequences. **Rape** occurs when one person forces another to submit to sexual activity such as intercourse or oral-genital sex. Though rape is thought of by most as a crime committed by strangers, **date rape** occurs when an acquaintance or first or casual date rapes an individual. Date rape is statistically more likely than rape by a stranger. In some cases rape is a means for an individual to express power and control over the victim. Other rapes occur as an expression of anger and often include physical violence and degrading acts toward women. Of course, some rapes are committed for sexual gratification. There is a common, though unfounded, belief that resistance is meant to be token and that women really want sex when they say "no." The risk of date rape can be lowered when women set clear limits, assert themselves when someone is pressuring them, and remain aware of risky situations. Men should be aware of their dates' views on sexual behavior, should not see a date as a possible "score," should understand "no" to mean "no," and should not assume that certain kinds of dress and behavior are an invitation to sex. Both men and women should realize that alcohol and drugs affect judgment and communication.

The frequency of child sexual abuse is difficult to judge because only the extreme cases become public, making the crime a secret crime. One survey found that as many as 22 percent of adult Americans had experienced some form of child sexual abuse. Most cases of abuse are committed by a relative or an acquaintance and only about a quarter by a stranger. The consequences of abuse are negative and include increases of fear, anxiety, depression, anger, hostility, and aggression. Sexual behavior can be disturbed as well. Long-term effects include self-destructive behavior, anxiety, feelings of isolation, poor self-esteem, and sexual maladjustment.

Sexual behavior in the last decade has changed due to **acquired immune deficiency syndrome (AIDS)** which is classified as a **sexually transmitted disease (STD)** because it is transmitted through sexual contact. Though AIDS was transmitted early among homosexuals, it now affects most populations. Casual sex is now less likely, and people use condoms more frequently. The only sure way to avoid getting AIDS from sexual activity is not to have any. The psychological challenges raised by AIDS include helping the individual with the disease to cope with it, helping those who have a chance of coming down with the disease, reducing the fear that people have of catching AIDS, and preventing people from taking extreme measures against its victims. Psychologists can also contribute by finding ways to change behaviors that increase the risk for transmission of the disease.

There are other STDs. **Chlamydia** is a disease that produces no symptoms initially in women but a burning sensation during urination for men. **Genital herpes** is a virus related to cold sores. Small sores appear around the genitals and can break open and cause pain. **Gonorrhea** can lead to fertility problems and infection, and untreated **syphilis** can lead to brain and heart disease, can affect a fetus, and can be fatal. **Genital warts** are small lumpy warts on the genitals.

Almost everyone will at some time in their lives experience a sexual problem. For males, one of the most common is **erectile failure**, or the inability to achieve or maintain an erection. **Primary erectile failure** is when the man has never had an erection, and **secondary erectile failure** occurs when a man has been able to have erections in the past and now can no longer do so. **Premature ejaculation** refers to the inability of a male to delay orgasm as long as he wishes. **Inhibited ejaculation** occurs when a man is unable to ejaculate. Women experience **anorgasmia**, or the lack of an orgasm. **Primary orgasmic dysfunction** refers to women who have never experienced an orgasm, and **secondary orgasmic dysfunction** refers to women who are currently unable to experience orgasm but have done so in the past. Both males and females can experience **inhibited sexual desire**, which is described as a loss of motivation for sexual activity.

Sex therapy is a means of solving these sexual problems. A sex therapist must have appropriate credentials, and therapy should never involve sexual activity with the therapist. Not all sexual difficulties are problems; they may be conflicts in sexual standards. Also, a good sex life does not cure a bad relationship. Sexual problems usually indicate other problems in the relationship.

▶ Now that you have surveyed, questioned, and read the chapter and completed

the **Recap and Review** questions, review **Looking Back**, pages 409–410.   *Review:* ☐

▶ For additional practice through recitation and review, test your knowledge of the chapter material by answering the questions in the *Key Word Drill*, the *Practice Questions*, and the *Essay Questions*.

KEY WORD DRILL

Recite: ☐

The following **Fill in the Blank** and **Matching Questions** test key words from the text. Check your answers with the Answer Key in the back of the *Study Guide*.

FILL IN THE BLANK

1. Our _____ is our sense of being male or female.

2. _____ are male sex hormones, and _____ are the female sex hormone.

3. Individuals learn what society deems appropriate behavior, including gender roles, through the process called _____.

4. _____ _____ refers to areas of the body that are particularly sensitive because of an unusually rich array of nerve receptors, while _____ refers to anything that is sexually stimulating.

5. _____ is the term for sexual self-stimulation.

6. _____ is ejaculated through the _____ during orgasm.

7. The _____ _____ holds that premarital sex is permissible for males but not for females.

8. According to the view called _____ _____ _____, premarital sex is permissible for both men and women if it occurs within a long-term or loving relationship.

9. _____ refers to one person forcing another to submit to sexual activity, and _____ _____ involves forced sexual activity with either a date or an acquaintance.

10. The abbreviation ___ ___ ___ refers to any disease spread primarily through sexual contact.

MATCHING QUESTIONS

_____ 11. gender roles

_____ 12. stereotyping

_____ 13. sexism

_____ 14. gender schema

_____ 15. androgynous

a. Societal expectations about appropriate behavior for women and men.

b. A cognitive framework that organizes and guides a child's understanding of gender.

c. Beliefs and expectations about members of a group based on their membership in that group.

d. A state in which gender roles encompass characteristics thought typical of both sexes.

e. Negative attitudes toward a person based on that person's sex.

_____ 16. testes

_____ 17. genitals

_____ 18. ovaries

_____ 19. ovulation

_____ 20. clitoris

_____ 21. vagina

a. The female canal into which the penis enters during sexual intercourse.

b. The monthly release of an egg from an ovary.

c. The female reproductive organs.

d. The male reproductive organs responsible for secreting androgens.

e. The small and very sensitive organ in the female's external genitals.

f. The male and female sex organs.

_____ 22. excitement phase

_____ 23. plateau phase

_____ 24. orgasm

_____ 25. ejaculation

_____ 26. resolution stage

_____ 27. refractory period

a. The peak of sexual excitement during which time rhythmic muscular contractions occur in the genitals.

b. Entered by a male after the resolution stage, a temporary period during which he cannot be sexually aroused again.

c. The final stage of sexual arousal during which the body returns to its normal state.

d. The expulsion of semen through the penis.

e. A period during which the body prepares for sexual intercourse.

f. A period in which the maximum level of arousal is attained, the penis and clitoris swell with blood, and the body prepares for orgasm.

_____ 28. heterosexuality

_____ 29. extramarital sex

_____ 30. homosexuality

_____ 31. bisexuality

a. A sexual attraction to a member of one's own sex.

b. Sexual behavior between a man and a woman.

c. Sexual activity between a married person and someone who is not his or her spouse.

d. A sexual attraction to members of both sexes.

_____ 32. acquired immune deficiency syndrome

_____ 33. chlamydia

_____ 34. genital herpes

_____ 35. gonorrhea

_____ 36. syphilis

_____ 37. genital warts

a. An STD which, if untreated, may affect brain, heart, and developing fetus, and can be fatal.

b. An STD which leads to infertility and infection.

c. A noncurable virus producing small blisters or sores around the genitals; symptoms disappear but often recur.

d. A fatal, sexually transmitted disease that is caused by a virus that destroys the body's immune system and has no known cure.

e. An STD which initially produces no symptoms in women but which can lead to pelvic inflammation and sterility, and produces in men painful urination and discharge from the penis.

f. An STD that causes small lumpy warts to form on or near the penis or vagina.

_____ 38. erectile failure

_____ 39. primary erectile failure

_____ 40. secondary erectile failure

_____ 41. premature ejaculation

_____ 42. inhibited ejaculation

a. A male's temporary inability to achieve or maintain an erection.

b. A male's inability to ejaculate when he wants to, if at all.

c. A male's inability to achieve or maintain an erection.

d. A male's inability to delay ejaculation.

e. A long-term inability to achieve or maintain an erection.

_____ 43. anorgasmia

_____ 44. primary orgasmic dysfunction

_____ 45. secondary orgasmic dysfunction

_____ 46. inhibited sexual desire

a. A female's long-term inability to achieve orgasm.

b. A condition in which the motivation for sexual activity is restrained or lacking.

c. A female's temporary inability to achieve orgasm or her ability to achieve orgasm only under certain conditions (such as masturbation).

d. A female's lack of orgasm.

| PRACTICE QUESTIONS | *Recite and Review:* ☐ |

Test your knowledge of the chapter material by answering these **True-False** and **Multiple Choice Questions**. Check your answers with the Answer Key in the back of the *Study Guide*.

TRUE-FALSE QUESTIONS

T F 1. With the large increase in women entering the work force, career stereotypes are changing dramatically.

T F 2. According to Hyde and her colleagues, the differences between men and women in terms of cognitive skills are negligible.

T F 3. Male students receive more attention, help, and eye contact in the classroom than do female students.

T F 4. Men and women differ very little in their use of fantasies while engaged in sexual behavior.

T F 5. Written descriptions of male and female sexual orgasms are distinguishable by the sex of the writer.

T F 6. There are rather clear classes of behavior which experts agree constitute normal and abnormal sexual behavior.

T F 7. At one time masturbation was thought to lead to insanity.

T F 8. Alfred Kinsey made the first systematic attempt at scientific, quantitative research about human sexual behavior.

T F 9. The frequency of marital sex today is lower than in earlier decades because of women's increasing role and time commitments outside the home.

T F 10. Homosexuals and bisexuals are as well adjusted as heterosexuals.

MULTIPLE CHOICE QUESTIONS

1. Gender roles are based on:
   a. what men and women have the physical ability to do.
   b. biologically determined norms.
   c. learned abilities.
   d. culturally determined expectations.

2. Suzy's father always longed for a son. In fact, she had been expected to be her father's first son. As Suzy grew older, she was competitive and aggressive and liked playing sports, going fishing, mowing the lawn, and repairing automobiles. Suzy's behavior is consistent with her father's:
    a. stereotype for her.
    b. sexism toward her.
    c. sex role for her.
    d. gender role for her.

3. The negative stereotype about someone that is based on that individual's sex is called:
    a. gender role.
    b. sexism.
    c. psychosexual bias.
    d. gender schema.

4. Sexism produces:
    a. negative attitudes and behavior toward a group.
    b. positive attitudes and behavior toward a group.
    c. positive and negative attitudes and behavior toward a group.
    d. negative attitudes and positive behavior toward a group.

5. Which of the following is the best example of a culturally determined stereotype?
    a. Redheads have short tempers.
    b. Men are taller than women.
    c. Advanced education leads to greater income.
    d. Computers will be used more and more in the future.

6. According to Broverman's study of stereotypes, which of the following traits is more typically male than female?
    a. tactful
    b. gentle
    c. religious
    d. independent

7. Long-term research attempting to determine differences between males and females on measures of intelligence showed that males score higher than females in:
    a. high school mathematics.
    b. grammar and language arts.
    c. diction and pronunciation of words.
    d. music courses.

8. Which alternative below best summarizes current thinking on differences in verbal skills between men and women?
    a. Men are superior to women in verbal skills.
    b. Women are superior to men in verbal skills.
    c. There are no differences in verbal skills between men and women.
    d. Men are superior in verbal skills until adolescence, when women gain superiority for the rest of their lives.

9. Gender differences are determined by _____ forces.
    a. societal
    b. cultural
    c. biological sex
    d. biological and environmental

10. Socialization refers to the process by which an individual:
    a. learns the rules and norms for appropriate behavior.
    b. enters into relationships with other males and females.
    c. learns the roles and behaviors that are appropriate for sexual encounters.
    d. behaves in a cooperative and understanding manner to promote harmony in social situations.

11. According to Sandra Bem, the cognitive framework that organizes and guides a child's understanding of gender is called:
   a. sex role.
   b. gender role.
   c. gender schema.
   d. stereotyping.

12. According to Sandra Bem, androgyny is:
   a. damaging to American youth.
   b. restricting the flexibility with which men and women can behave.
   c. behavior which encompasses both typical masculine and feminine roles.
   d. an inherited predisposition.

13. Because he must show resolve and affection, assertiveness and love, a single male parent may develop:
   a. bisexuality.
   b. androgyny.
   c. sexism.
   d. gender schema.

14. The name for the male reproductive organ(s) is:
   a. androgen.
   b. prostate.
   c. the penis.
   d. the testes.

15. At what point in life does the human male secrete the greatest amount of androgen?
   a. just after birth
   b. just after puberty
   c. upon entering young adulthood
   d. upon entering middle adulthood

16. Estrogen is _____, whereas androgen is _____ .
   a. a male hormone; a female hormone
   b. part of the estrus cycle; a synthetic male hormone
   c. produced cyclically; released in a relatively constant way
   d. released prenatally; released after delivering a baby

17. Which alternative below is correct about the role of biological factors in the female sex drive?
   a. The female sex drive is related to the level of estrogen, which is greatest when a woman is 25 to 38 years old; sex drive is lower before and after this period.
   b. Estrogen levels vary dramatically each month; however, female sex drive occurs anytime during the month and appears greatly influenced by psychological and situational factors.
   c. The sex drive is related to the level of estrogen, which is greatest soon after sexual maturity; short-term variations in estrogen are minor.
   d. The female sex hormone, estrogen, fluctuates each month; female sex drive is usually strongest midcycle, when levels are greatest.

18. Human sexual behavior is unique compared with many nonhuman species in that:
   a. males reach their sexual peak much later than females.
   b. sexual drive is not cyclical.
   c. sexual behavior is confined to days 12 through 18 of the estrus cycle.
   d. resolution may be achieved prior to orgasm.

19. Erogenous zones are:
    a. areas of the body especially sensitive to sexual arousal.
    b. areas of the body with a rich array of nerve receptors.
    c. the same as erotic zones.
    d. necessarily stimulated in order for excitement to occur.

20. According to the text, the erotic character of a stimulus is determined for the most part by:
    a. genetic history.   c. society.
    b. whether or not it depicts nudity.   d. hereditary factors.

21. According to the text, which of the following is **not** true about sexual arousal?
    a. What people find to be sexually arousing changes with history.
    b. What people find to be sexually arousing changes with culture.
    c. Only in western culture do men find large breasts to be arousing.
    d. In America, women find a large male chest to be arousing.

22. During the excitement and plateau phases, the penis and clitoris swell with:
    a. semen.   c. blood.
    b. androgen.   d. estrogen.

23. According to Masters and Johnson, an intense, highly pleasurable sexual experience that defies description occurs in the:
    a. resolution phase.   c. excitement phase.
    b. orgasm phase.   d. plateau phase.

24. The stage of sexual response characterized by rhythmic muscular contractions in the genitals is called:
    a. excitement.   c. orgasm.
    b. plateau.   d. resolution.

25. Men are unable to be aroused or have orgasms during the:
    a. plateau phase of sexual response.   c. orgasm phase of sexual response.
    b. excitement phase of sexual response. d. resolution phase of sexual response.

26. Lisa frequently experiences several orgasms, many of which occur by cycling from the:
    a. excitement to the resolution stage.   c. orgasmic to the excitement stage.
    b. plateau to the orgasmic stage.   d. resolution to the orgasmic stage.

27. Which alternative below is **not** a criterion for sexual abnormality?
    a. a standard or ideal   c. deviation from the average
    b. frequency of the behavior   d. psychological consequences

28. J. B. is 30 years old and is having sexual fantasies of being irresistible and having oral sex. J. B. is likely to be:
    a. a man.   c. a transvestite.
    b. a woman.   d. male or female.

29. Which of the following statements about masturbation is true?
    a. Most of society views masturbation as a healthy, normal activity.
    b. The majority of people surveyed have masturbated at least once.
    c. Males and females begin masturbation at puberty.
    d. Psychologists view people who masturbate as poorly adjusted.

30. Masturbation is:
    a. usually viewed as inappropriate behavior.
    b. practiced more by men than women.
    c. more common in older men than younger men.
    d. commonly regarded by experts as counterproductive to learning about one's sexuality.

31. The double standard for premarital sex means:
    a. twice as many men have premarital sex as women.
    b. premarital sex is discouraged for both men and women.
    c. even people who are marrying for a second time should refrain from sex before their remarriage.
    d. premarital sex is discouraged for women but not for men.

32. Which of the following trends was most pronounced between the mid-1960s and mid-1980s in America?
    a. An increased percentage of females engaged in premarital sex.
    b. An increased percentage of males engaged in extramarital sex.
    c. A decreased percentage of males engaged in premarital sex.
    d. A decreased percentage of females engaged in extramarital sex.

33. Which statement about marital sexual intercourse is correct?
    a. There are few differences in the frequency of marital sex for younger and older couples.
    b. The average frequency of marital sex is 1.3 times per week.
    c. The frequency of marital sex is closely related to happiness in the marriage.
    d. The frequency of marital sex today is higher than ever before.

34. Which alternative below is correct about homosexuality?
    a. Homosexuality appears to result entirely from environmental factors.
    b. Genetic and hormonal factors seem to be the predictors of who will become homosexual.
    c. Hormonal differences in people cause them to be attracted to individuals of their own sex.
    d. Homosexuals are as well-adjusted as heterosexuals.

35. Which of the following is **least** likely to represent the motivations of a rapist?
    a. the desire for sexual gratification.
    b. revenge for past mistreatment by a member of the opposite sex.
    c. demonstration of power or control over the victim.
    d. the notion that women want forced sex.

36. Which of the following is **not** characteristic of child molestation and sexual abuse?
    a. The child abuser is generally a man 50 years of age or older.
    b. Most children are molested when they are about 10 years old.
    c. The abuser is more likely to be an acquaintance than a relative or a stranger.
    d. Sexual intercourse is a more common activity during molestation than just fondling.

37. Which alternative is **not** a factor that is especially damaging in experiences of child molestation and sexual abuse?
    a. The initial molestation occurs soon after puberty.
    b. The abuse involves genital contact.
    c. The abuser is the child's parent.
    d. The abuse involves force.

38. According to the text's description, depression, self-destructive behavior, anxiety, feelings of isolation and stigma, and poor self-esteem are the common, long-term effects of:
    a. childhood sexual abuse.
    b. frequent extra-marital affairs.
    c. typical homosexual experiences.
    d. chlamydia.

39. The AIDS virus is **not** transmitted through:
    a. the blood.
    b. semen.
    c. exchange of bodily fluids.
    d. the genes.

40. Which alternative is **not** correct about AIDS?
    a. AIDS can be contracted by contact with infected blood.
    b. Sexual contact can spread AIDS.
    c. There is no cure for AIDS; it is usually fatal.
    d. AIDS can be contracted by living or working closely with an individual afflicted with the disease.

41. AIDS has affected sexual behavior in general in that there has been:
    a. a decrease in casual sex.
    b. an increase in the requirement of blood checks before sex.
    c. an increase in nonconsenting sex.
    d. a decrease in extramarital sex.

42. According to the text, the threat of AIDS has prompted several large-scale changes in sexual behavior. Which alternative is **not** one of them?
    a. People are less likely to engage in casual sex with new acquaintances.
    b. Use of condoms during sexual intercourse has increased.
    c. The practice of celibacy is more common.
    d. The frequency of rape has decreased.

43. Which alternative is **not** a practice consistent with "safe sex"?
    a. Avoid intercourse and engage in anal sex or oral-genital sex.
    b. Use condoms.
    c. Know your sexual partner well.
    d. Consider the benefits of monogamy.

44. There is no cure for:
    a. chlamydia.
    b. gonorrhea.
    c. genital herpes.
    d. syphilis.

45. According to the text, which of the following sexually transmitted diseases is most widespread?
    a. chlamydia
    b. AIDS
    c. gonorrhea
    d. syphilis

| ESSAY QUESTIONS | *Recite and Review:* ☐ |

Essay Question 12.1: *The Changing Sexual Attitudes*

What are the factors that have led to the changes in sexual attitudes recently? How have they changed since the sexual revolution began in the late 1960s?

_____

_____

_____

_____

_____

_____

_____

_____

_____

_____

_____

_____

_____

_____

_____

_____

_____

_____

Essay Question 12.2: *Date Rape*

Discuss the factors that contribute to the existence and prevalence of date rape. Is date rape similar to nondate rape?

_____

_____

_____

_____

_____

_____

_____

_____

_____

_____

_____

_____

_____

_____

_____

_____

_____

_____

_____

• **Recap and Review III**

Looking Back
Key Terms and Concepts

➤ Now that you have surveyed the chapter, read **Looking Ahead**, pages 414–415. *Question:* ☐
Focus on the questions on page 415. *Read:* ☐

CONCEPTS AND LEARNING OBJECTIVES

Survey: ☐

These are the concepts and the learning objects for Chapter 13. Read them carefully as part of your preliminary survey of the chapter.

Concept 1: The fundamental issue for developmental psychology is the interaction between nature and nurture in human development. Psychologists are interested in finding ways to maximize genetic potential through enriching the environment. Development from conception to birth illustrates the nature-nurture interaction.

1. Define developmental psychology and the phenomena that it studies, especially the issues related to the roles of nature and nurture in development. (pp. 414-419)

2. Distinguish the longitudinal, cross-sectional, and cross-sequential research methods. (p. 419)

3. Describe the events that occur from conception to birth. (pp. 419-421)

4. Discuss the genetic abnormalities and environmental influences that affect the newborn infant. (pp. 421-424)

Concept 2: Physical and social development are marked by dramatic changes through childhood, from birth to about 12 years of age. Physical and perceptual skills grow rapidly in the early months and years, and attachment is one of the most important social developments in the first years of life.

5. Describe the progress of physical growth from birth to the end of childhood. (pp. 425-427)

6. Discuss the cognitive and perceptual capacities of the infant and their course of development. (pp. 427-428)

7. Describe the social influences on development. (pp. 428-432)

8. Compare the contributions to social development made by parents, peers, and day care. (pp. 432-435)

9. Outline and describe the psychosocial stages identified by Erik Erikson. (p. 436)

Concept 3: Cognitive development refers to the changes in the understanding of the world, and the period of childhood shows dramatic stages in the process of development.

10. Outline and describe the cognitive developmental stages identified by Jean Piaget. (pp. 437-442)

11. Identify the major views of the information-processing approach to cognitive development. (pp. 442-443)

CHAPTER SUMMARY

There are several ways you can use this summary as part of your systematic study plan. You may read each concept summary and then read the corresponding pages in the text, or you may read the entire summary and then read the entire chapter in the text. As you finish each section, complete the **Recap and Review** questions that are supplied in the text.

CONCEPT 1: Prologue and Looking Ahead

 Nature and Nurture: A Fundamental Developmental Issue

Survey: ☐
Read: ☐

Pages 414-425

The Prologue describes two sets of twins separated at birth. One set, Gerald Levey and Mark Newman, have greatly similar characteristics. The other set, Joan Gardiner and Jean Nelson, have quite different interests. Though there exists quite a bit of evidence supporting the role of genetics in development, the genetic inheritance does not explain everything.

Developmental psychology is the branch of psychology focused on explaining the similarities and differences among people that result from the growth and change of individuals throughout life. Developmental psychologists look to both the genetic background that provides built-in biological programming and the environmental influences.

Developmental psychologists are interested in a fundamental question of distinguishing the causes of behavior that are **environmental** from the causes that result from **heredity**. This question is identified as the **nature-nurture issue**. The issue can be traced back to John Locke's view that the infant is born with a mind that is like a blank sheet (tabula rasa) as opposed to the French philosopher Jean Jacques Rousseau who suggested that people had natural characteristics that governed their behavior. However, both nature and nurture are involved, and it is not a question of nature or nurture. Both **genetic makeup** (the biological inheritance) and the environment have influence, and the debate is over the extent to which each affects behavior. Some theories focus on learning and the role of the environment and other theories focus on the role of growth and **maturation**, or the development of biologically predetermined patterns, in causing developmental change. The theories agree on some points. Genetics provides for some behaviors and sets limits on some traits and behaviors. Heredity sets limits on intelligence and limits on physical abilities. (Table 13-1 lists characteristics with strong genetic components.) Environment plays a role in enabling individuals to reach the potential allowed by their genetic background. Developmental psychologists take an **interactionist** position arguing that behavior and development are determined by genetic and environmental influences. An example of this interactionist position is presented in the Cutting Edge. Jerome Kagan's study of inhibited and uninhibited children suggests that inhibited children have an inborn characteristic of greater physiological reactivity. However, the stress experienced through childhood is a major factor in the appearance of shyness later.

One major difficulty faced by developmental psychologists is that of being able to find ways to separate the influences of genetics and environment in order to study them. One way is to observe animals with similar genetic backgrounds in different environments. The difficulty presented by this approach is generalizing the results to humans. Another approach is the use of **identical twins**. Different behaviors displayed by identical twins must have some environmental component. Many studies seek to find identical twins who were separated at birth by adoption. Nontwin siblings who are raised apart also make contributions to these kinds of studies. The opposite approach takes people of different genetic backgrounds and examines their development and behavior in similar environments. Animals with different genetic backgrounds can be placed in situations where the environments can be experimentally manipulated.

Two categories of research are used by developmental psychologists. **Cross-sectional research** refers to the use of a sample of subjects that is based on a selection of groups that represent different ages at the same point in time. The problem with this approach is that different age groups may have had significantly different environmental influences. **Longitudinal research** refers to the selection of a sample from the population and following the sample's development through an extended period of time. The problem with this approach is that many individuals may drop out or they may become familiar with the tests being used to measure their development. An alternative method is called **cross-sequential research**. It combines the selection of different age groups with the following of the groups through time. However, the amount of time is less than in longitudinal research since different age groups are represented. In this approach age changes can be observed in different age groups without the lengthy longitudinal approach.

Development begins at the point of **conception** when the male's sperm penetrates the female's egg. The fertilized egg is at this point called a **zygote**. The zygote contains twenty-three pairs of **chromosomes**, one-half from the father the other half from the mother. Each chromosome contains thousands of **genes**, the individual units that carry genetic information. Genes are responsible for the development of the systems of the body, heart, circulatory, brain, lungs, and so on. And many genes control specific unique characteristics. Sex is determined by a set of chromosomes that combines an X chromosome from the mother and a Y or an X from the father. Girls have an XX combination and boys have an XY combination. At four weeks, the zygote becomes a structure called the **embryo**. The embryo has a rudimentary heart, brain, intestinal tract, and other organs. By the eighth week, the embryo has arms and legs. Beginning at the eighth week, the embryo faces a **critical period** of development—a period during which specific growth must occur if the individual is to develop normally. Eyes and ears must form, and environmental influences can have significant effects. At the ninth week the individual is called a **fetus**. At sixteen to eighteen weeks the movement of the fetus can be felt by the mother. At the twenty-fourth week, the fetus has the characteristics of a newborn, though it cannot survive outside the mother if born prematurely. At twenty-eight weeks, the fetus can survive if born prematurely, and this is called the **age of viability**. At twenty-eight weeks the fetus will weigh about three pounds.

In 2 to 5 percent of all cases, children have serious birth defects. Common genetic defects include **phenylketonuria (PKU)**, a metabolic disorder that can be treated; **sickle-cell anemia**, a disease afflicting African-Americans, and children with the disease rarely live beyond childhood; **Tay-Sachs disease**, a disease that results in the inability to break down fat, causing death by age 3 or 4; and **Down syndrome**, a problem where an extra chromosome causes an unusual physical appearance and retardation.

Prenatal environmental influences include: the mother's nutritional and emotional state—emotionally anxious mothers tend to have babies that are irritable and who sleep and eat poorly; illness of the mother—diseases like **rubella** (German measles) can cause serious defects in the unborn child and AIDS can be passed from mother to child; the mother's use of drugs can have serious effects on the child, including **fetal alcohol syndrome**, and some babies can be born with their mother's addiction to drugs like cocaine. Sometimes complications of delivery can cause serious problems, like entanglement of the umbilical cord leading to a loss of oxygen.

CONCEPT 2: How We Develop Physically and Socially

At birth, the newborn baby is called a **neonate**. The neonate looks strange because the journey through the birth canal squeezes and shapes the skull. The neonate is covered with **vernix**, a white greasy material that protects the skin prior to birth, and a soft hair called **lanugo**. The neonate is born with a number of **reflexes**, unlearned, involuntary responses. Most are necessary for survival and maturation. The **rooting reflex** causes neonates to turn their head toward anything that touches their cheeks. The **sucking reflex** makes the neonate suck on anything that touches its lips. The **gag reflex** clears the throat, and the **startle reflex** causes a number of movements when a loud noise is sounded. The **Babinski reflex** fans out the toes when the edge of the foot is touched. These reflexes are lost within a few months and replaced by more complex behaviors. Through the first year of life, major changes in physical ability occur, including learning to stand and walk.

In the first year of life, children triple their birth weight and their height increases by 50 percent. From 3 to 13 years of age, the child adds an average of 5 pounds and 3 inches per year. The proportion of body and body parts changes through the time period as well.

At birth the neonate has a limited capacity to focus vision and can focus only on objects within about 8 to 9 inches. They are also able to follow objects moving in their field of vision. Techniques have been developed to determine the perceptual abilities of neonates that depend upon changes in basic responses and reflexes. Heart rate is closely associated with the reaction to an object being perceived. Changes in heart rate signal **habituation**, or the decrease in responding to the same stimulus. A novel stimulus causes an increase in heart rate. Using this technique, developmental psychologists are able to tell when a baby can detect a stimulus. Other methods include the use of a nipple attached to a computer that measures the rate and force of sucking. Changes in stimuli correlate to changes in sucking. The perceptual abilities of infants have been found to be quite sophisticated. They show preference for certain patterns with contours and edges. They have a sense of size constancy. Neonates can discriminate facial expressions, and they respond to the emotion and mood of care givers. At the end of the first month, infants can distinguish some colors. By four and five months they can distinguish two- and three-dimensional objects. At the age of three days, newborns can distinguish their mothers' voices. By six months they can discriminate virtually any sound.

In addition to physical and perceptual growth, infants grow socially as well. **Attachment** refers to the positive emotional bond between a child and a particular individual. Harry Harlow demonstrated the importance of attachment by showing that baby monkeys preferred a terry cloth "mother" to a wire "mother" even though the wire version provided food and the terry cloth one did not. Others have since suggested that attachment develops from the responsiveness of the care giver to the signals given by the infant. Full attachment is achieved through a complex sequence of events described by the Attachment Behavioral System. Infants play an active role in the development of the bond. According to Klaus and Kennell, a critical period just after birth that is based on skin-to-skin contact is crucial to the mother and child bond. There appears to be little support for the hypothesis. Though early contact does make the mothers more responsive to the children, the effect lasts only three days and no long-term consequence has been found.

Attachment has been measured using a procedure developed by Mary Ainsworth, now called the **Ainsworth strange situation**. The measurement involves a series of events during which the mother and child are separated (briefly) in the presence of a stranger. The reactions of the babies are then observed. Ainsworth identified three kinds of attachment: *securely attached* children use the mother as a home base, *avoidant* children do not cry when the mother leaves but they avoid her on her return, and *ambivalent* children are anxious when the mother leaves and then upset when she returns. Securely attached children tend to have fewer psychological difficulties when older than do ambivalent and avoidant children. They are also more competent socially and more cooperative, capable, and playful.

Recently the father's role in children's development has been researched. Fathers spend less time caring for their children, but the attachments can be just as strong. The differences in the attachment result from the fact that the mothers spend more time with care and feeding and the fathers spend more time playing with infants. Fathers play more physical games and mothers play more verbal games. The amount of time spent with children is less important than the quality of that time.

Friendships with peers are crucial for a preschooler's social development. Children become less dependent on their parents from the age of 2 years on. At 2, children pay more attention to toys, and as they get older, they pay more attention to each other. At school age, the interactions become formalized, and children play complex, structured games with rigid rules. Play serves to increase social competence, provide a perspective on the thoughts and feelings of others, and helps to teach children self-control. Day care has become a central part of the lives of children in our society. Children in high-quality day care do as well as children who stay at home. They may actually do better in terms of social competence, intellectual development, and even their relationship to their parents.

Diana Baumrind has proposed that there are three main categories of child-rearing patterns. The **authoritarian parents** are rigid and punitive and expect unquestioning obedience. **Permissive parents** are lax and inconsistent though warm. **Authoritative parents** set limits and are firm, but as their children get older, they reason and explain things to them. Children of authoritarian parents tend to be unsociable, unfriendly, and withdrawn. Children of permissive parents are immature, moody, and dependent with low self-esteem. Children of authoritative parents are likable, self-reliant, independent, and cooperative. Children are born with **temperaments**, or basic, innate dispositions. The temperament can elicit a certain child-rearing style. The child-rearing styles may be applicable to American culture where independence is highly valued. For instance, Japanese parents encourage dependence to promote values of community and cooperation.

Erik Erikson has proposed an eight-stage theory of social development. Each stage of **psychosocial development** involves a basic crisis or conflict. Though each crisis is resolved as we pass through the stages, the basic conflict remains throughout life. First is the **trust-versus-mistrust stage** (birth to 1 year) in which feelings of trust are built on basic physiological and psychological needs, especially attachment. The **autonomy-versus-shame-and-doubt stage** (1 to 3 years) is marked by the development of independence if exploration and freedom are encouraged or shame if they are not. The **initiative-versus-guilt stage** (3 to 6 years) is marked by the conflict between the desire to initiate independent activities and the guilt that arises from the consequences. The last stage of childhood is the **industry-versus-inferiority stage** (6 to 12 years). On the positive side, development proceeds with the increase in competency while the opposite is failure and inadequacy.

CONCEPT 3: Cognitive Development

Survey: ☐
Read: ☐

Pages 437-444

Cognitive development refers to the developmental changes in the understanding of the world. Theories of cognitive development attempt to explain the intellectual changes that occur throughout life. Jean Piaget proposed that children passed through four distinct stages of cognitive development and that these stages differed in both the quantity of information acquired and the quality of knowledge and understanding. Maturation and relevant experiences are needed for children to pass through the stages.

Piaget's first stage is called the **sensorimotor stage** and it is from birth to 2 years. This stage is marked by the child's lack of ability to use images, language, and symbols. Things not immediately present are not within the child's awareness until the development of **object permanence**, the awareness that objects continue to exist when they are out of sight.

The **preoperational stage** is from 2 to 7 years of age. Children gain the ability to represent objects internally and can use symbols for objects. Children's thinking has improved over the sensorimotor stage, but it is still inferior to adult thought. This stage is marked by **egocentric thought** in which the world is viewed from the child's perspective. The **principle of conservation**, which states that quantity is unrelated to appearance, is not understood during this period.

The **concrete operational stage** is from 7 to 12 years of age. Its beginning is marked by the mastery of the principle of conservation. Children develop the ability to think in a logical manner. They learn to understand reversibility, or the capacity of things to be reverted to a previous state. They are, however, bound to the concrete, physical world rather than abstract thoughts.

The **formal operational stage**, from 12 years to adulthood, is marked by the use of abstract, formal, and logical thought. Though it emerges at this time, it is used infrequently. Studies show that only 40 to 60 percent of college students reach this stage and only 25 percent of the general population do so.

Research has shown that Piaget underestimated the abilities of infants and children. Some psychologists suggest that cognitive development is more continuous than Piaget suggested. In this alternative view, the cognitive development is one of quantitative changes. Piaget has had significant influence on educational theory and curricula, even if some of his theory and research has been challenged.

An alternative to Piaget's theory is that of **information processing**, which examines how people take in, use, and store information. According to this theory, development requires the development of mental programs for approaching problems. The changes that occur relate to speed of processing, attention span, and improvement of memory. The size of chunks increases with age. Information processing also points to the changes in metacognition as a sign of development. **Metacognition** refers to the awareness and understanding of one's own cognitive processes.

The Informed Consumer of Psychology suggests that the potential provided by nature can be maximized if one is responsive to children, providing them with opportunities to explore and investigate their environments. Parents should use language that is highly descriptive and accurate, and they should not push children too hard.

▶ Now that you have surveyed, questioned, and read the chapter and completed
the **Recap and Review** questions, review **Looking Back**, pages 444–445.   *Review:* ❏

▶ For additional practice through recitation and review, test your knowledge of the chapter material by answering the questions in the *Key Word Drill*, the *Practice Questions*, and the *Essay Questions*.

KEY WORD DRILL

Recite: ❏

The following **Fill in the Blank** and **Matching Questions** test key words from the text. Check your answers with the Answer Key in the back of the *Study Guide*.

FILL IN THE BLANK

1. _____ psychology studies patterns of growth and change occurring throughout life.

2. The debate concerning the degree to which both environment and heredity influence behavior describes the _____-_____.

3. Individuals with identical genetic makeup are most likely _____ _____.

4. The first of several stages of development in which specific kinds of growth must occur to enable further normal development are considered to be _____ _____.

5. The point at which a fetus can survive if born prematurely is known as the _____ of _____.

6. Developmental psychologists refer to the positive emotional bond that develops between a child and a particular individual as _____.

7. The _____ _____ _____ is a sequence of events involving a child and his or her mother that provides a measurement of attachment.

8. _____ development focuses on the changes a child's understanding of the world undergoes as a function of age and experience.

9. The way in which people take in, use, and store information is often called _____.

10. _____ refers to our awareness and understanding of our own cognitive processes.

MATCHING QUESTIONS

_____ 11. conception   a. A zygote that has a heart, a brain, and other organs.

_____ 12. zygote   b. The one-celled product of fertilization.

_____ 13. chromosomes   c. A developing child, from nine weeks after conception until birth.

_____ 14. genes

_____ 15. embryo   d. Structures that contain basic hereditary information.

_____ 16. fetus   e. The parts of a chromosome through which genetic information is transmitted.

                                 f. The process by which an egg cell is fertilized by a sperm.

_____ 17. environment

_____ 18. heredity

_____ 19. genetic makeup

_____ 20. maturation

_____ 21. interactionist

_____ 22. cross-sectional research

_____ 23. longitudinal research

_____ 24. cross-sequential research

a. The unfolding of biologically predetermined behavior patterns.

b. A research method which investigates behavior through time as subjects age.

c. Influences on behavior that occur in the world around us—in family, friends, school, nutrition, and many other factors.

d. A research method which combines cross-sectional and longitudinal research.

e. The inherited biological factors that transmit hereditary information.

f. Influences on behavior that are transmitted biologically from parents to a child.

g. Someone who believes that a combination of genetic predisposition and environmental influences determines the course of development.

h. A research method in which people of different ages are compared at the same point in time.

_____ 25. phenylketonuria (PKU)

_____ 26. sickle-cell anemia

_____ 27. Tay-Sachs disease

_____ 28. Down syndrome

_____ 29. rubella

_____ 30. fetal alcohol syndrome

a. A disease of the blood that affects about 10 percent of America's black population.

b. German measles.

c. A disorder caused by the presence of an extra chromosome, resulting in mental retardation.

d. An inherited disease that prevents its victims from being able to produce an enzyme that resists certain poisons, resulting in profound mental retardation.

e. A genetic defect preventing the body from breaking down fat and typically causing death by the age of 4.

f. An ailment producing mental and physical retardation in a baby as a result of the mother's behavior.

_____ 31. neonate

_____ 32. vernix

_____ 33. lanugo

_____ 34. reflexes

_____ 35. rooting reflex

_____ 36. sucking reflex

_____ 37. gag reflex

_____ 38. startle reflex

_____ 39. Babinski reflex

a. A white lubricant that covers a fetus, protecting it during birth.

b. Unlearned, involuntary responses to certain stimuli.

c. The reflex in response to a sudden noise where the infant flings its arms, arches its back, and spreads its fingers.

d. The reflex where an infant's toes fan out in response to a stroke on the outside of its foot.

e. A newborn child.

f. A reflex that prompts an infant to suck at things that touch its lips.

g. A neonate's tendency to turn its head toward things that touch its cheek.

h. A soft fuzz covering the body of a newborn.

i. An infant's reflex to clear its throat.

_____ 40. habituation

_____ 41. authoritarian parents

_____ 42. permissive parents

_____ 43. authoritative parents

_____ 44. temperament

_____ 45. psychosocial development

a. A decrease in responding to repeated presentations of the same stimulus.

b. Development of individuals' interactions and understanding of one another and their knowledge and understanding of themselves as members of society.

c. Basic, innate disposition.

d. Parents who are rigid and punitive and who value unquestioning obedience from their children.

e. Parents who are firm, set clear limits, and reason with and explain things to their children.

f. Parents who are lax, inconsistent, and undemanding, yet warm toward their children.

_____ 46. trust-versus-mistrust stage	a.	The stage of psychosocial development where children can experience self-doubt if they are restricted and overprotected.
_____ 47. autonomy-versus-shame-and-doubt stage		
	b.	The first stage of psychosocial development, occurring from birth to 18 months of age.
_____ 48. initiative-versus-guilt stage		
_____ 49. industry-versus-inferiority stage	c.	The period during which children may develop positive social interactions with others or may feel inadequate and become less sociable.
	d.	The period during which children experience conflict between independence of action and the sometimes negative results of that action.

_____ 50. sensorimotor stage	a.	Characterized by abstract thought.
_____ 51. object permanence	b.	Little competence in representing the environment.
_____ 52. preoperational stage	c.	Characterized by language development.
_____ 53. principle of conservation	d.	Characterized by logical thought.
_____ 54. concrete operational stage	e.	Quantity is unrelated to physical appearance.
_____ 55. formal operational stage	f.	Objects do not cease to exist when they are out of sight.

PRACTICE QUESTIONS

Recite and Review: ❏

Test your knowledge of the chapter material by answering these **True-False** and **Multiple Choice Questions**. Check your answers with the Answer Key in the back of the *Study Guide*.

TRUE-FALSE QUESTIONS

T F 1. Environmental factors enable people to reach the capabilities provided by their genetic background.

T F 2. Characteristics such as memory and height are entirely determined by heredity.

T F 3. The developing embryo is most vulnerable to drugs, toxic chemicals, and X-rays a few weeks before critical periods of development.

T F 4. Birth defects can result from the mother having an inadequate diet during pregnancy.

T   F   5.   The Babinski reflex is an involuntary response enabling an infant to clear his or her throat.

T   F   6.   The amount of time an adult spends with a child is less important than how the adult and child spend the time.

T   F   7.   Infants play just as critical and active roles as care givers in establishing an attachment bond.

T   F   8.   Children who spend their days in day care are more likely to be socially cooperative.

T   F   9.   The type of child-rearing style a parent uses is sometimes dependent on the temperament of the baby.

T   F   10.   Children should be discouraged from attempting tasks which may be difficult because they are more likely to make mistakes on a difficult task.

MULTIPLE CHOICE QUESTIONS

1. When theories stress the role of heredity in their explanations of change in individual development, the focus of their accounts would be on:
   a. maturation.
   b. nurture.
   c. environmental factors.
   d. social growth.

2. The philosophical view that infants are born with a blank slate favors which of the following as a dominant influence upon development?
   a. interactionism
   b. nature
   c. nurture
   d. dualism

3. The view of developmental psychologists today is that:
   a. environmental stimulation is necessary to achieve full genetic potential.
   b. genetic factors are most important in individual development.
   c. environmental influences are most important in individual development.
   d. different factors are important for different individuals.

4. The belief that a combination of genetic and environmental factors determines the course of development is the central point of view for:
   a. all psychologists.
   b. neuropsychologists.
   c. interactionists.
   d. social psychologists.

5. Identical twins who exhibit dissimilar behaviors as adults support:
   a. an environmental explanation for developmental differences.
   b. the notion that developmental differences occur by chance.
   c. a genetic interpretation of developmental differences.
   d. the psychosexual theory of development.

6. Which set of subjects would provide the least information for a study regarding the nature-nurture question in humans?
   a. identical twins reared apart
   b. children adopted from different families reared together
   c. siblings reared apart
   d. siblings reared together

7. A study in which particular individuals are followed as they age is called:
   a. cross-sectional.
   b. maturational.
   c. longitudinal.
   d. cross-sequential.

8. A study in which several different ages groups are examined over different points in time is called:
   a. cross-sectional.
   b. maturational.
   c. longitudinal.
   d. cross-sequential.

9. The units that produce particular characteristics in an individual are called:
   a. chromosomes.
   b. genes.
   c. spores.
   d. somes.

10. Which chromosome combination will result in a male child?
    a. XX
    b. YY
    c. XY
    d. XXX

11. At conception a zygote is formed. What is the next stage the organism progresses through after the zygote has developed?
    a. embryo
    b. neonate
    c. fetus
    d. fertilization

12. Certain events must take place in a specific time frame; otherwise, the entire sequence of fetal growth is thrown off and the result will be either no development or abnormal development. This time frame is called:
    a. longitudinal development.
    b. cross-section maturation.
    c. the resolution phase.
    d. the critical period.

13. Of the organs listed below, which is **not** yet formed at the embryonic stage?
    a. heart
    b. brain
    c. intestinal tract
    d. eyes

14. During what prenatal stage are a lifetime's worth of brain neurons produced?
    a. fetal
    b. embryo
    c. neonatal
    d. conception

15. In prenatal development, the age of viability is a developmental stage in which:
    a. the eyes and other sense organs are functional.
    b. the fetus can survive if born prematurely.
    c. development has advanced sufficiently that the fetus is capable of learning from environmental cues.
    d. the sexual organs of the fetus are differentiated.

16. The unborn fetus has many of the features and characteristics of a newborn as early as:
    a. 8 weeks.
    b. 12 weeks.
    c. 16 weeks.
    d. 24 weeks.

17. One-tenth of the black population in the United States has the possibility of passing on _____, which leaves the newborn with a variety of health problems and very short life expectancy.
    a. hypertension
    b. sickle-cell anemia
    c. phenylketonuria
    d. Tay-Sachs disease

18. A genetic defect that leads to a very short life due to a breakdown in strategic metabolic processes and occurs most frequently among Jews of Eastern European descent is called:
    a. Tay-Sachs disease.
    b. Down syndrome.
    c. meningitis.
    d. phenylketonuria.

19. Which of the following is caused by genetic birth defects?
    a. phenylketonuria (PKU)
    b. AIDS
    c. diethylstilbestrol (DES)
    d. fetal alcohol syndrome

20. Which developmental disorder below results from the presence of an extra chromosome?
    a. Down syndrome
    b. sickle-cell anemia
    c. Tay-Sachs disease
    d. phenylketonuria (PKU)

21. Which developmental influence below does not belong with the others?
    a. mother's nutrition and stress-level
    b. hereditary defects
    c. mother's drug and medication intake
    d. birth complications

22. Which of the following is a difficulty **not** caused by prenatal environmental influences?
    a. birth complications
    b. amount of drugs or alcohol ingested by the mother
    c. infection of the mother with rubella
    d. development of sickle-cell anemia in the mother

23. Rubella is also known as:
    a. Down syndrome.
    b. German measles.
    c. phenylketonuria.
    d. sickle-cell anemia.

24. According to the text, which of the following constitutes the **weakest** environmental factor that can affect a developing fetus?
    a. maternal smoking
    b. maternal ingestion of drugs
    c. maternal age
    d. maternal exercise

25. At birth, the neonate is covered with a white, greasy substance which protects the skin prior to birth, called:
    a. veridical.
    b. vernix.
    c. fornix.
    d. lanugo.

26. A neonate is:
    a. a prenatal infant in its thirtieth to thirty-eighth week of development.
    b. a newborn infant.
    c. an infant born with deformities because of chromosomal abnormalities.
    d. a premature baby, up to the time at which the normal due date passes.

27. Which reflex below helps the newborn infant position its mouth onto its mother's breast when it feeds?
    a. rooting reflex
    b. startle reflex
    c. gag reflex
    d. surprise reflex

28. The most dramatic changes that occur during the first year after birth have to do with:
    a. speech development.
    b. overall growth.
    c. increase in head size relative to the rest of the body.
    d. the disappearance of reflexes.

29. The phenomenon in which an infant attends less and less to a repeatedly given stimulus is known as:
    a. disinhibition.
    b. habituation.
    c. depth perception.
    d. stimulation.

30. According to research findings reported in the text, what is the earliest stage at which a child can imitate adult facial expressions?
    a. neonates
    b. infants
    c. toddlers
    d. preschoolers

31. Which statement below about the sensory and perceptual capabilities of infants is **not** true?
    a. At 4 days of age, they can distinguish between closely related sounds such as "ba" and "pa."
    b. At 60 days of age, they can recognize their mother's voice.
    c. After 6 months of age, they are capable of discriminating virtually any difference in sounds that is relevant to the production of language.
    d. They prefer sweetened liquids to unsweetened liquids.

32. What changes in perception do **not** take place in the first six months after birth in human infants?
    a. They develop discrimination of tastes and smells.
    b. They can recognize two- and three-dimensional objects.
    c. They can discriminate all sounds important for language production.
    d. They understand their native language.

33. Why are there generally differences in the form of attachment between the baby and its mother and father?
    a. Mothers spend more time directly nurturing their children, whereas fathers spend more time playing with them.
    b. Mother spend more time playing with their children, whereas fathers spend more time nurturing them.
    c. Mothers generally are identified as primary caregivers so the attachment is stronger.
    d. Fathers spend more time doing things with their children than mothers.

34. According to the text, which statement best represents the father's typical attachment to his children?
    a. It is superior to the mother's attachment in most situations.
    b. It is aloof and detached.
    c. It is generous with affection, especially during verbal interaction.
    d. It is qualitatively different, but comparable to the mother's attachment.

35. Play in young children has many consequences. Which alternative below is **not** one of them?
    a. They become more competent in their social interactions with other children.
    b. They learn to take the perspective of other people and to infer others' thoughts and feelings.
    c. They learn to control emotional displays and facial expressions in situations where this is appropriate.
    d. They become more independent of other children from ages 2-6.

36. Which type of parents would be most likely to explain things to children and try reasoning with them when conflicts or problems arise?
    a. permissive parents
    b. authoritative parents
    c. caretaking parents
    d. authoritarian parents

37. From Diana Baumrind's categories of parental styles, _____ parents are those who are firm and set limits and goals, reasoning with their children and encouraging their independence.
    a. temperative
    b. permissive
    c. authoritative
    d. authoritarian

38. Attending day care improves intellectual performance in children from _____, but does not significantly influence children from _____.
    a. middle-class families; poor and upper-class homes
    b. poor and middle-class homes; upper-class families
    c. poor families; middle- and upper-class homes
    d. upper-class families; middle-class and poor families

39. Erikson's theory of development:
    a. was based on experiences of psychotic women.
    b. covers an entire lifetime.
    c. takes a behaviorist approach.
    d. was derived from Piaget's cognitive approach to development.

40. According to Erikson, inconsistent care can lead a youngster to find it difficult to:
    a. trust another person.
    b. have feelings of accomplishment.
    c. compete in the real world.
    d. choose appropriate role models.

41. In order to proceed from one of Piaget's stages of cognitive development to another, it is necessary for children to achieve:
    a. a certain level of perceptual and cognitive development.
    b. a certain level of maturation and experience.
    c. a certain level of memory capacity and physical development.
    d. a certain level of social and cognitive development.

42. Piaget's theory is one of:
    a. psychosocial development.
    b. sensorimotor development.
    c. maturation.
    d. cognitive development.

43. A developmental psychologist is evaluating a young child's cognitive development. The psychologist shows the child two separate arrangements of red disks. Eight disks are laid in a straight line in one arrangement. Another eight disks are arranged in a random "scatter" pattern in the other. The psychologist asks, "Is the amount of disks in each arrangement the same?" The psychologist is testing the child's understanding of:
    a. spatial reversibility.
    b. conservation.
    c. spatial inertia.
    d. reorganization.

44. Jess and Luisa were playing with two balls of clay. Luisa was molding a cake and Jess was making a bowl. Jess then suggested they get new balls of clay so that they could make something different. Luisa informed him that no new clay was necessary; the clay could be remolded to make different objects. What principle was Luisa teaching to Jess?
    a. the principle of conservation
    b. the principle of reversibility
    c. the principle of egocentric thought
    d. the principle of logic

45. According to Piaget, _____ is mastered early in the _____ for most children.
    a. reversibility; sensorimotor stage
    b. conservation; concrete operational stage
    c. object permanence; formal operational stage
    d. abstraction; preoperational stage

46. According to Piaget, a child who exhibits logical and abstract thought has achieved the:
    a. sensorimotor stage.
    b. preoperational stage.
    c. concrete operational stage.
    d. formal operational stage.

47. Which of the following is a reason why an individual **might** never achieve the formal operational stage?
    a. He is not intelligent enough.
    b. She comes from a country not as technologically sophisticated as western countries.
    c. He is incapable of abstract and logical reasoning.
    d. She is too old for that specific stage of development.

48. The last time Sara used her personal computer she observed that several files were not copied onto the floppy disk as she had expected. She carefully checked her sequence of operations and considered the characteristics of the software. After evaluating alternative explanations for what had happened, she correctly deduced why the files were not copied. Sara is in Piaget's:
    a. concrete operational stage of cognitive development.
    b. preoperational stage of cognitive development.
    c. sensorimotor stage of cognitive development.
    d. formal operational stage of cognitive development.

49. Metacognition is:
    a. a flaw in one's perception of one's own knowledge.
    b. a phase of thinking that occurs in the preoperational stage of cognitive development.
    c. an alteration in thinking that results from brain damage.
    d. an awareness and a knowledge of one's own cognitive processes.

| **ESSAY QUESTIONS** | *Recite and Review:* ☐ |

Essay Question 13.1: *Nature-Nurture and Child-rearing Practices*

Considering the discussion of the nature-nurture issue at the beginning of the chapter, what is your assessment of the role of child-rearing practices in the development of the person as a unique individual? Are certain styles more likely to help individuals reach their potential?

_____

_____

_____

_____

_____

_____

_____

_____

_____

_____

_____

_____

_____

_____

_____

_____

Essay Question 13.2: *Stimulation of Children*

One of the main points of the chapter is that developmental psychologists are interested in finding ways that the individual potential can be maximized. Children can be stimulated through contact with parents, through play, while at day care, and they can be encouraged to explore by having the appropriate attachments. What would the world of a perfectly "enriched" child look like? Is it possible to overstimulate?

_____

_____

_____

_____

_____

_____

_____

_____

_____

_____

_____

_____

_____

_____

_____

_____

ACTIVITIES AND PROJECTS

1. Make a two column list of genetic and environmental factors that might influence the course of physical, social, and intellectual development. Do any of these factors interact, that is, do genetic factors have environmental influences?

    Genetic Factors   *Environmental Factors*

2. If you have the opportunity, observe a child under one year of age on several occasions for at least five minutes. Prior to the observation, list the activities and abilities you expect to be demonstrated. Include smile, vocalizations, ability to hold and grasp, interaction with others, etc. After making this list, create a tally of the behaviors you actually see in the observation (your list should include a number of specific actions). When your observation is complete, reflect on the types of actions that occurred but which you had not expected. What do your observations suggest concerning the theories described in the chapter?

DEVELOPMENT: ADOLESCENCE
TO THE END OF LIFE

| DETAILED OUTLINE | *Survey:* ☐
| --- |

This detailed outline contains all the headings in Chapter 14: Development: Adolescence to the End of Life. If you are using the SQ3R method, then an examination of the outline is the best way to begin your survey of the chapter.

➤ Now that you have surveyed the chapter, read **Looking Ahead**, page 448. Focus on the questions on page 448.

Question: ☐
Read: ☐

CONCEPTS AND LEARNING OBJECTIVES

Survey: ☐

These are the concepts and the learning objects for Chapter 14. Read them carefully as part of your preliminary survey of the chapter.

Concept 1: Adolescence begins with the growth spurt and puberty, and it continues until the end of the teenage years. Social and moral development occur, with the adolescent focusing on problems of identity.

1. Define adolescence and the physical changes that mark its beginning. (pp. 448-450)

2. Describe the moral and cognitive developments that occur during adolescence. (pp. 450-454)

3. List and describe Erikson's psychosocial stages relevant to adolescence and adulthood. (pp. 545-455)

4. Identify the major problems of adolescence and how they tend to be resolved, and discuss the problem of teenage suicide. (pp. 455-459)

Concept 2: Early and middle adulthood are marked by the formation of a family, the establishment and success (or failure) in work, and the gradual progress toward old age. Some people experience a mid-life crisis, but most pass through middle age easily.

5. Define adulthood and describe the physical changes that accompany it. (pp. 459-460)

6. Discuss the concerns of adulthood that result from demands of society and the pressures of work. (pp. 461-463)

7. Describe the roles of males and females in marriage and the family as they relate to the course of adult development. (pp. 463-466)

Concept 3: Old age does not conform to our myths about it, and the elderly often lead active, happy lives. One of the more difficult transitions is that of facing the prospects of death.

8. Define old age, the physical changes that accompany it, and the theories that attempt to account for it. (pp. 467-469)

9. Identify the changes that occur in cognitive ability, intelligence, and memory during old age. (pp. 469-472)

10. Describe the challenges and changes that the elderly face in their social worlds as they age. (pp. 472-473)

11. List and define the five stages of Kübler-Ross's adjustment to death and the four stages of mourning. (pp. 473-475)

CHAPTER SUMMARY

There are several ways you can use this summary as part of your systematic study plan. You may read each concept summary and then read the corresponding pages in the text, or you may read the entire summary and then read the entire chapter in the text. As you finish each section, complete the **Recap and Review** questions that are supplied in the text.

CONCEPT 1: Prologue and Looking Ahead *Survey:* ☐
          Adolescence: Becoming and Adult *Read:* ☐

Pages 448-459

Development continues throughout life, from adolescence to adulthood and old age. Western society has few rituals that help define the end of childhood, as do the Awa tribe of New Guinea and other tribal societies. The major biological changes that begin with the attainment of physical and sexual maturity and the changes in social, emotional, and cognitive function that lead to adulthood mark the period called **adolescence**.

The dramatic physical changes of adolescence include a growth in height, the development of breasts in females, the deepening of the male voice, the development of body hair, and intense sexual feelings. The growth spurt begins around age 10 for girls and age 12 for boys. The development of the sexual organs begins about a year later. There are wide individual variations, however. Better nutrition and medical care in western cultures is probably the cause of the decreasing age of onset of puberty. Early-maturing boys have an advantage over later-maturing boys, doing better in athletics and being more popular, though they do have more difficulties in school. Early-maturing girls are more popular and have higher self-concepts than those who mature late, but the obvious changes in breasts can cause separation from peers and ridicule. Late-maturers suffer because of the delay, with boys being ridiculed for their lack of coordination and girls holding lower social status in junior and high school.

Lawrence Kohlberg has identified a series of stages that people pass through in their moral development. Preadolescent children make moral judgments based on concrete, inflexible rules. Adolescents are able to reason more abstractly and comprehend moral principles. Kohlberg argues that everyone passes through a fixed series of six stages (though not all reach the final stages) that are divided into three levels. Kohlberg's ideas are considered to be generally valid, with some criticisms that suggest there is a difference between judgments and actual behavior.

Carol Gilligan has argued that Kohlberg's system is flawed in its application to the moral judgment of women. Different socialization experiences bring about a difference between the moral views of men and women. Men view morality in terms of justice and fairness, and women view morality in terms of responsibility toward individuals. Compassion is a more important factor for women. Since Kohlberg's views are based on justice, his system cannot adequately describe the moral development of women. Gilligan defines three stages for the moral development of women: The first stage is termed "orientation toward individual survival." The second is "goodness as self-sacrifice." The third is "morality of nonviolence." Some have argued that she rejected Kohlberg's views too completely.

Erikson's theory of psychosocial development (introduced on Chapter 13) identifies the beginning of adolescence with his fifth stage, called the **identity-versus-role confusion stage**. During this stage individuals seek to discover their abilities, skills, limits, and **identity**. If one resolves this stage with confusion, then a stable identity will not be formed and the individual may become a social deviant or have trouble with close personal relationships later. The stage is marked by a shift from dependence on adults for information and the turn toward the peer group for support. During college, the **intimacy-versus-isolation stage** describes the basic conflict. This stage focuses on developing relationships with others. Middle adulthood finds people in the **generativity-versus-stagnation stage**. The contribution to family, community, work, and society comprise generativity, and feelings of triviality about one's activities indicate the difficulties of the stage and lead to stagnation. The final stage is the **ego-integrity-versus-despair stage**, and it is marked by a sense of accomplishment if successful in life or a sense of despair if one regrets what might have been.

It was once thought that adolescence was a period of stress and unhappiness, but most adolescents pass through the period without much turmoil. There does exist tension in their lives, and attempts at independence can lead to testing a range of behaviors that parents and society find objectionable. Adolescents that experimented with drugs have been found to be better-adjusted than those who do not experiment or those who abuse drugs. One source of the problems that adolescents have is that in western society they are staying at home much longer than at prior times in history. A large portion of men and women who are unmarried continue to live with their parents into their thirties. There are also many stresses outside the home, including coping with school and dealing with relationships and part-time jobs.

Teenage suicide is the third leading cause of death among adolescents in the United States. The major factors underlying suicide are depression and hopelessness. Some suicide cases involve perfectionists who are prone to extreme anxiety when faced with a challenge. Suicide is also related to long-standing problems between parents and children, the existence of behavior problems, and the abuse of drugs and alcohol. The warning signs include school problems, running away, self-destructive behavior, loss of appetite, withdrawal, sleep problems, depression, preoccupation with death, putting affairs in order, and explicit statements about suicide.

CONCEPT 2: Early and Middle Adulthood: The Middle Years of Life

Survey: ☐
Read: ☐

Pages 459-467

Early adulthood is generally considered to begin at about 20 years of age and last until about 40 to 45 years, and middle adulthood lasts to 40 to 45 to about 65 years of age. These ages have been studied less than any other. Fewer significant physical changes occur, and the social changes are diverse.

The peak of physical health is reached in early adulthood, and quantitative changes begin at about 25 years as the body becomes less efficient and more prone to disease through time. The major physical development is the female experience of **menopause**, the cessation of menstruation and the end of fertility. The loss of estrogen may lead to hot flashes, a condition which is successfully treated with artificial estrogen. Problems that were once blamed on menopause are now seen as resulting from the perceptions of coming old age and society's view of it. Though men remain fertile, the gradual decline of physical abilities has similar effects of menopause, causing the man to focus on the social expectations of youthfulness.

Daniel Levinson's model of adult development identifies six stages from beginning adulthood through the end of middle adulthood. At the beginning, the individual formulates a "dream" that guides career choices and the vision the person has of the future. At about 40 or 45, people enter a period called the **midlife transition** during which past accomplishments are assessed, and in some cases, the assessment leads to a **midlife crisis** in which the signs of physical aging and a sense that the career will not progress combine to force a reevaluation of and an effort to remedy their dissatisfaction. Most people go through the midlife transition without any difficulties. During the fifties, people become more accepting of others and their own lives. They realize that death is inevitable and seek to understand their accomplishment in terms of how they understand life. Since Levinson's research was based on males, the difference in roles and socialization has raised questions about whether women go through the same stages.

The most likely pattern today is that a man and woman will first live together, then marry and have children, and then get a divorce. The average age of marriage is higher than at any time since the turn of the century, and about 60 percent of marriages end in divorce. The number of single-parent households has doubled in two decades, with 28 percent of all households having only one parent. Children experience a process of conflict, tension, and breakup, followed by obstacles to establishing relationships with one of the parents. Evidence suggests that children of single-parent households are just as well-adjusted as other children. Close to 95 percent of the population eventually gets married, and people who get divorced tend to get married several more times.

The roles of men and women are changing in marriage, and wives are taking on more responsibilities. Three-quarters of married women with school-aged children work outside the home. The distribution of household chores has not changed substantially. Women still see themselves as responsible for cooking and cleaning, and men see themselves as responsible for fixing things. Working women put in tremendous amounts of time at work and doing household chores. Benefits of working appear to outweigh the disadvantages because of the multiple roles that give women a greater sense of mastery, pride, and competence. Success in work increases happiness, the sense of control, and self-esteem in both men and women. Failure can lead to depression, impotence, and other psychological symptoms.

CONCEPT 3: The Later Years of Life: Growing Old

Survey: ☐
Read: ☐

Pages 467-476

Gerontologists study development and the aging process from the age of about 65. Gerontologists are reexamining our understanding of aging, suggesting that the stereotype of aging is inaccurate. Napping, eating, walking, and conversing are the typical activities of both the elderly and college students. The obvious physical changes that appear in old age include thinning and graying hair, wrinkling and folding skin, and a loss of height. Vision and hearing become less sharp, smell and taste are less sensitive, reaction time slows, and oxygen intake and heart-pumping abilities decrease. Two types of theories have been offered to account for these changes. One group includes the **genetic preprogramming theories of aging** which suggest that here are preset time limits on the reproduction of human cells governed by genetics. The other group includes the **wear-and-tear theories of aging** which suggest that the body simply stops working efficiently. By-products of energy production accumulate, and cells make mistakes in their reproduction. Old age is not a disease, but is instead a natural biological process. Many functions, like sexual behavior, remain pleasurable long into old age. Neither of these theories explains why women live longer than men. At birth there are more males than females; by 65 years of age, 84 percent of women are still alive and 70 percent of men. A consequence of increased health awareness is that the gap is not increasing.

The view that the elderly are forgetful and confused is no longer considered an accurate assessment. IQ tests usually include a physical performance component that measures the reaction time of the elderly even though the reaction time has nothing to do with intelligence. Elderly are often in ill health, and the comparison of healthy young adults with groups of less healthy elderly people. When healthy elderly are used for comparison, differences are less significant. Also, since more young people attend college, the elderly groups are often less educated. Tests show declines in **fluid intelligence** in old age but **crystallized intelligence** actually increases. Fluid intelligence may be more sensitive to changes in the nervous system than crystallized intelligence. Recent studies suggest that cognitive declines may be remedied by increasing the blood flow to the brain. The drug Nimodipine was given to elderly rabbits who could then be classically conditioned faster than rabbits not on the drug. When elderly were given special spatial training sessions, their performance on spatial skills tasks was better than for elderly who were not given the special training.

One assumption about the elderly is that they are more forgetful. Evidence suggests that forgetfulness is not inevitable. Memory declines tend to be in long-term memory and, specifically, with episodic memories. Life changes may cause a decline in motivation rather than actual memory impairment. Impairments can be compensated by mnemonic strategies. The decline in cognitive function associated with old age is called senility, but this is now viewed as a symptom caused by other factors, like **Alzheimer's disease**, anxiety, depression, or even overmedication.

Loneliness is a problem for only a small portion of the elderly, though social patterns do change in old age. Two theories account for how people approach old age. The **disengagement theory of aging** views aging as a gradual withdrawal from the world on physical, psychological, and social levels. Energy is lower and interaction lessens. This view sees aging as an automatic process. The **activity theory of aging** suggests that people are happiest who remain active and that people should attempt to maintain the activities and interests they develop during middle age. The nature of the activity is the most important factor, and not the quantity.

Death requires major adjustments, as the death of those near you causes changes in life and makes you consider the possibility of your own death. Elisabeth Kübler-Ross outlined five stages of the death process. The first is denial of the fact that one is dying. The second is anger at death. The third is bargaining with death, looking for ways to postpone it. The fourth is depression when the bargaining does not work. The fifth and final stage is acceptance.

The process of mourning involves four stages of grief. The first stage is shock and denial, which usually last a few days, followed by depression and anger at being left alone. The second stage involves people in putting their lives back in order. The third involves freeing oneself from the bonds of the lost loved one. The fourth stage involves the construction of a new identity. Sudden deaths, especially those of a child, are very difficult to deal with, and mourning can be extended for extremely long periods of time and can be accompanied by physical illness or long-lasting changes in personality.

▶ Now that you have surveyed, questioned, and read the chapter and completed

the **Recap and Review** questions, review **Looking Back**, pages 476–477.   *Review:* ☐

▶ For additional practice through recitation and review, test your knowledge of the chapter material by answering the questions in the *Key Word Drill*, the *Practice Questions*, and the *Essay Questions*.

| KEY WORD DRILL | *Recite:* ☐ |

The following **Fill in the Blank** and **Matching Questions** test key words from the text. Check your answers with the Answer Key in the back of the *Study Guide*.

FILL IN THE BLANK

1. The developmental stage called _____ marks the transition from childhood to adulthood.

2. The period during which maturation of the sexual organs occurs is known as _____.

3. The distinguishing character of each individual is called _____, comprised of our roles and capabilities as well as our sense of self.

4. The point at which women stop menstruating is called _____.

5. Beginning around the age of 40 _____ _____ can occur, and during this period we come to the realization that life is not indefinite.

6. Sometimes middle-aged individuals will experience _____,

   _____ a realization—accompanied by negative feelings—that important goals have not been accomplished in life.

7. The term _____ refers to specialists who study aging.

8. _____ disease is a progressive brain disease leading to an irreversible decline in mental and physical abilities.

9. The ability to deal with new problems and situations is called _____ intelligence and the intelligence based on the store of specific information, skills, and strategies that

   people have acquired through experience is called _____ intelligence.

10. In the _____ stage of moral development, an individual applies moral principles that are considered broader than the concerns of a particular society, to specific problems.

MATCHING QUESTIONS

_____ 11. identity-versus-role-confusion stage

a. A period from late adulthood until death during which we review life's accomplishments and failures.

_____ 12. intimacy-versus-isolation stage

b. A period in middle adulthood during which we take stock of our contributions to family and society.

_____ 13. generativity-versus-stagnation stage

c. A period during early adulthood that focuses on developing close relationships with others.

_____ 14. ego-integrity-versus-despair stage

d. A time in adolescence of testing to determine one's own unique qualities.

_____ 15. genetic preprogramming theories of aging

a. Theories that suggest that the body's mechanical functions cease efficient activity and, in effect, wear out.

_____ 16. wear-and-tear theories of aging

b. A theory that suggests that the elderly who age most successfully are those who maintain the interests and activities they had during middle age.

_____ 17. disengagement theory of aging

c. Theories that suggest a built-in time limit to the reproduction of human cells.

_____ 18. activity theory of aging

d. A theory that suggests that aging is a gradual withdrawal from the world on physical, psychological, and social levels.

_____ 19. adolescence

a. The point at which women stop menstruating, generally at around age 45.

_____ 20. puberty

b. The stage between childhood and adulthood.

_____ 21. identity

c. The negative feelings that accompany the realization that we have not accomplished in life all that we had hoped.

_____ 22. menopause

_____ 23. midlife transition

d. The distinguishing character of the individual: who each of us is, what our roles are, and what we are capable of.

_____ 24. midlife crisis

e. Beginning around the age of 40, a period during which we come to the realization that life is finite.

f. The period during which maturation of the sexual organs occurs.

_____ 25. Erik Erikson	a.	Moral development.
_____ 26. Lawrence Kohlberg	b.	Death and dying.
_____ 27. Sigmund Freud	c.	Psychosocial development.
_____ 28. Jean Piaget	d.	Psychosocial development.
_____ 29. Elisabeth Kübler-Ross	e.	Cognitive development.
_____ 30. Daniel Levinson	f.	Adult social development.

PRACTICE QUESTIONS	*Recite and Review:* ☐

Test your knowledge of the chapter material by answering these **True-False** and **Multiple Choice Questions**. Check your answers with the Answer Key in the back of the *Study Guide*.

TRUE-FALSE QUESTIONS

T **F** 1. For a male, undergoing puberty late may have detrimental effects that persist for ten to fifteen years.

T **F** 2. Puberty dramatically changes how adolescents see themselves and how others see them.

T **F** 3. According to Kohlberg, only a small percentage of people reach stage 5 of his model of moral reasoning.

T **F** 4. Some of the turmoil of adolescence results from teenagers longing to be independent of their parents but realizing that they must also be dependent on them.

T **F** 5. There is a great transition for women at age 40, whereas men go through a disruption and reorientation at about age 30.

T **F** 6. Since 1970, society has witnessed a doubling of single-parent households.

T **F** 7. Recent studies show that it is almost always better for a child to live in a two-parent home than a one-parent home.

T **F** 8. The distribution of household tasks between husbands and wives has changed significantly since more women have begun to work full time.

T **F** 9. Typically, when both spouses work, each takes equal responsibility for child rearing.

T   F   10.   Pleasure derived from sex usually decreases with age, as does frequency of sexual activity.

MULTIPLE CHOICE QUESTIONS

1.   The period during development which is marked by dramatic physical and psychological change and attainment of sexual maturity is called:
    a.   adulthood.   c.   puberty.
    b.   adolescence.   d.   childhood.

2.   Physical changes at the start of adolescence are largely a result of:
    a.   secretion of hormones.
    b.   the cessation of the secretion of certain hormones.
    c.   growth of the brain.
    d.   psychological turmoil.

3.   The age at which adolescents reach puberty has been steadily decreasing over the last century. Which of the following is a possible reason for this?
    a.   Children have had better nutrition and medical care.
    b.   Cultural prohibitions about sexuality have weakened.
    c.   There has been a higher incidence of sexual promiscuity among children.
    d.   Puberty rituals have been abandoned in most western societies.

4.   How many stages does Kohlberg's model of moral reasoning have?
    a.   two   c.   six
    b.   four   d.   eight

5.   If a person's behavior reflected the desire to please other members of society, he or she would be considered to be at Kohlberg's:
    a.   preconventional level of moral reasoning.
    b.   conventional level of moral reasoning.
    c.   postconventional level of moral reasoning.
    d.   nonconventional level of moral reasoning.

6.   A child thinks, "If I steal a cookie, I will get spanked." In which level of moral development is this child functioning?
    a.   amorality   c.   conventional morality
    b.   preconventional morality   d.   postconventional morality

7.   Which of the following is **not** one of Kohlberg's stages of moral reasoning?
    a.   preconventional   c.   postconventional
    b.   conventional   d.   nonconventional

8.   Kohlberg believed that a certain level of _____ development was necessary before achieving the highest levels of moral development.
    a.   social   c.   psychosocial
    b.   physical   d.   cognitive

9. For Carol Gilligan, the beginning level of moral reasoning for women is the stage of:
    a. goodness equated with self-sacrifice.
    c. orientation toward individual survival.
    b. self-worth and self-respect.
    d. morality of nonviolence.

10. Mary Margaret leads a group that has as its focus rape prevention and assistance in recovery from rape. The group represents moral development consistent with Gilligan's notion of:
    a. morality of nonviolence.
    c. goodness as self-sacrifice.
    b. orientation toward individual survival.
    d. preconventional morality.

11. According to Erikson, role confusion is most likely to occur during:
    a. early adulthood.
    c. adolescence.
    b. early childhood.
    d. middle adulthood.

12. According to Erikson, college-age people typically contend with the conflicts found in the:
    a. intimacy-versus-isolation stage.
    c. ego-integrity-versus-despair stage.
    b. generativity-versus-stagnation stage.
    d. identity-versus-role-confusion stage.

13. Being active in civic groups, assisting in recreational programs, and having a stable career are indications that one is in the _____ stage of development.
    a. intimacy versus isolation
    c. generativity versus stagnation
    b. identity versus role confusion
    d. ego-integrity versus despair

14. According to the text, the most noteworthy feature of Erikson's theory of psychosocial development is that:
    a. both men and women are included in its descriptions of developmental changes.
    b. it accurately describes developmental changes that people in other cultures also experience.
    c. it has greatly increased understanding of infant development.
    d. it suggests that development is a lifelong process.

15. Which of the following is **not** a factor that contributes to the stresses experienced by adolescents outside the home that may cause stress at home?
    a. the number of school changes made
    b. volatile relationships with friends and other peers
    c. frequent arguments about money with family members
    d. holding a part-time job while maintaining studies

16. Over the last two decades, teenage suicide has:
    a. declined.
    c. doubled.
    b. tripled.
    d. been overreported.

17. Recent studies show that _____ represents a major factor in teen suicide.
    a. a sense of hopelessness
    c. conflict with one's parents
    b. generalized anxiety
    d. a tendency toward aggression

18. There are several warning signs which indicate that a teenager may attempt suicide. Which alternative below is **not** one of them?
    a. loss of appetite or excessive eating
    b. withdrawal from friends or peers
    c. a preoccupation with death, afterlife, or what would happen "if I died"
    d. an increase in praying, going to church, or other religious behavior

19. Frank and his wife, who are both in their early thirties, want many children. Frank does not know when he will be incapable of fathering children, and he is getting worried that there might not be enough time. What would you say to Frank?
    a. Men lose their ability to father children in their late forties, just like women.
    b. Men lose their fertility in their late fifties, so his wife will lose her fertility first.
    c. Both men and women remain fertile into their sixties, so there is plenty of time left for them to have children.
    d. Men don't lose their ability to father children until well into old age.

20. For most people, adulthood marks the peak of:
    a. physical health.   c. maturation.
    b. cognitive development.   d. accomplishment.

21. Which of the following represents a major biological change in the life of a female during middle adulthood.
    a. puberty   c. menarche
    b. menopause   d. tumescence

22. At what stage are individuals considered to be full-fledged adult members of society.
    a. adolescence   c. middle adulthood
    b. early adulthood   d. not until late adulthood

23. According to the text, a major developmental task for people 40 to 50 years old who are experiencing the initial stages of middle adulthood is to:
    a. maintain harmonious relationships with their children.
    b. accept that the die has been cast, and that they must come to terms with their circumstances.
    c. carefully choose goals so that all the major career advances can still be realized before old age.
    d. adjust to changes brought about by menopause and physical deterioration.

24. The primary cause of a midlife crisis tends to be:
    a. an awareness of the detrimental physical changes associated with aging.
    b. a series of disappointments and shortcomings in a person's children.
    c. a recognition that a person's reproductive capabilities are decreasing or will soon end.
    d. a failure to achieve desired career goals and objectives.

25. When a male in his early forties assesses his life and finds this a negative, demoralizing experience, he is going through:
    a. a sense of peace.   c. menopause.
    b. a midlife crisis.   d. menarche.

26. According to Levinson, which stage of development seems to show important differences between men and women?
    a. culmination
    b. challenge
    c. dream
    d. reality

27. According to the text, one way that the developmental stages of adult women differ from those of men is that:
    a. women have more difficulties developing a vision of what their future life will include.
    b. women's midlife crises are more likely to occur later in their lives.
    c. women's midlife crises are usually precipitated by their children leaving home, causing the "empty nest syndrome."
    d. women's developmental stages are more influenced by hormonal and physical changes.

28. Which of the following has doubled since 1970?
    a. the number of married couples who get divorced within the first ten years of marriage
    b. the number of children under the age of 5
    c. the number of single-parent households
    d. the number of women who stay at home to raise children

29. According to U.S. census figures, over the last two decades the percentage of unmarried couples has:
    a. increased.
    b. decreased.
    c. remained the same.
    d. fluctuated greatly.

30. Which statement about one-parent families is correct?
    a. Children of one-parent families are usually just as well-adjusted as children of two-parent families.
    b. About 35 percent of one-parent families are headed by the father.
    c. One-parent families are about as likely in one ethnic (racial) group as another.
    d. The proportion of one-parent families has increased very little in the last twenty years.

31. Divorce produces many changes in the emerging one-parent family. Which alternative below is **not** one of them?
    a. Time is always at a premium.
    b. The painful experience of divorce may hinder the building of close relationships throughout life.
    c. Children in a one-parent family develop interpersonal skills, so they are less likely to divorce.
    d. High levels of parental conflict before the divorce may produce increased anxiety and aggressive behavior in the children.

32. When a child's mother and father work, the mother is generally still viewed as holding the main child-rearing responsibility. Yet, there are also great benefits to working. In what way do the benefits outweigh the disadvantages?
    a. Women who work feel a greater sense of mastery and pride, and generally have higher self-esteem.
    b. Women who work play a greater role in the decisions which affect the lives of their families.
    c. Women who work enjoy more responsibility than those who don't work, yet allow their husbands valuable time alone with their children.
    d. Women who work have better-developed social lives.

33. A gerontologist is a:
    a. person who studies family histories and birth lines.
    b. medical specialist who studies arthritis and other degenerative diseases associated with aging.
    c. specialist who studies aging.
    d. health specialist who specializes in nutritional, medical, and exercise regimens.

34. Which theory suggests that some cells may become harmful to the body after a certain amount of time?
    a. opponent-process   c. wear-and-tear
    b. genetic preprogramming   d. gerontological

35. What do the genetic preprogramming theories suggest about physical decline of aging?
    a. Women live four to ten years longer than men.
    b. The body, like a machine, eventually wears out.
    c. There is a built-in time limit to the ability of human cells to reproduce.
    d. Physical aging is a biological process in which all physical functions decline.

36. The theory of aging that is based on the notion that mechanical functions of the body stop working efficiently is called:
    a. genetic preprogramming.   c. wear-and-tear.
    b. genetic breakdown.   d. failure of function.

37. Doris, who is 75 years old, finds that she has a more difficult time hearing than when she was younger. Which theory best supports the conclusion that Doris' poor hearing is due to the fact that mechanical bodily functions stop working efficiently as an individual ages?
    a. genetic preprogramming theory   c. decreased consumption theory
    b. wear-and-tear theory   d. disengagement theory of aging

38. What natural condition, to date, is explained by neither the genetic preprogramming theory nor the wear-and-tear theory, according to developmental psychologists?
    a. deterioration of the circulatory system   c. women living longer than men
    b. confusion and forgetting   d. reduced visual acuity

39. Which type of intelligence actually increases with age?
    a. fluid intelligence   c. basic intelligence
    b. verbal intelligence   d. crystallized intelligence

40. Dr. Beegood is an authority on Egyptian mummies and has been retired for thirteen years. He was recently asked to speak at a monthly faculty luncheon. If he gives one of his "canned" presentations on mummies to the faculty, he will be drawing heavily from his:
    a. crystallized intelligence.   c. fluid intelligence.
    b. common sense.   d. practical intelligence.

41. Fluid intelligence provides the capabilities for many adaptive and functional human behaviors. Which alternative below correctly describes a person's fluid intelligence capabilities?
    a. Fluid intelligence increases after birth until early adulthood.
    b. Fluid intelligence is high all through a person's lifetime.
    c. Fluid intelligence increases more slowly during late adulthood and old age.
    d. Fluid intelligence remains fairly constant until a person's death.

42. One difference between crystallized and fluid intelligence is that, generally:
    a. fluid intelligence is useful only in certain situations.
    b. fluid intelligence declines with age.
    c. crystallized intelligence declines with age.
    d. crystallized intelligence is better in women.

43. In an experiment done on elderly rabbits, a group was given the drug Nimodipine. The elderly group given Nimodipine was able to learn a classically conditioned response as fast as a group of young rabbits. What is the function and advantage of this drug?
    a. It reverses the aging process.
    b. It causes the older rabbits to respond to stimuli much more quickly.
    c. It increases the amount of blood flow to the brain.
    d. It causes the nerves to reject unnecessary information.

44. A study done at Pennsylvania State University involved a program in which elderly individuals were taught strategies for dealing with problems. The results indicated that:
    a. declines in cognitive functioning in old age can, in part, be avoided.
    b. elderly people can be taught new skills.
    c. senility is usually unavoidable in old age.
    d. when elderly people exercise, it gives them less energy for intellectual performance.

45. A pattern of reduced social and physical activity as well as a shift toward the self rather than a focus on others characterizes the:
    a. deactivation theory of aging.
    b. activity theory of aging.
    c. withdrawal theory of aging.
    d. disengagement theory of aging.

46. Elizabeth Kübler-Ross describes five stages that many terminally ill patients experience. Which of the following is **not** one of these stages?
    a. acceptance
    b. bargaining
    c. denial
    d. ambivalence

47. Which of the following is the correct sequence for Kübler-Ross's five stages of facing death?
    a. bargaining, depression, acceptance, anger, denial
    b. denial, depression, anger, bargaining, acceptance
    c. depression, anger, denial, bargaining, acceptance
    d. denial, anger, bargaining, depression, acceptance

| **ESSAY QUESTIONS** | *Recite and Review:* ☐ |

Essay Question 14.1: *The Stresses of Adolescence*

Describe the factors that contribute to problems between parents and teenagers and suggest ways that these may be overcome. Are the recent changes in childhood and adolescence that result in changes in the family to blame for some of these factors?

_____

_____

_____

_____

_____

_____

_____

_____

_____

_____

_____

_____

_____

_____

_____

_____

_____

_____

Essay Question 14.2: *Aging and Retirement*

Apply the disengagement and the activity theories of aging to the question of mandatory retirement. Should there be a mandatory retirement age and, if either yes or no, what are the exceptions and who shall judge?

_____

_____

_____

_____

_____

_____

_____

_____

_____

_____

_____

_____

_____

_____

_____

_____

_____

ACTIVITIES AND PROJECTS

1. Interview one or more people in the middle years of life and find out their views on life-span development. Do they view themselves as continuing through a developmental process physically, socially, cognitively, or in any other way? What are the major issues to be faced during the middle years and how do these issues differ from earlier years that had to be faced?

DETAILED OUTLINE   *Survey:* ☐

This detailed outline contains all the headings in Chapter 15: Personality. If you are using the SQ3R method, then an examination of the outline is the best way to begin your survey of the chapter.

Prologue: John Gotti
Looking Ahead

Psychoanalytic Theories of Personality
Freud's psychoanalytic theory
    Structuring personality: Id, ego, and superego
    Developing personality: A stage approach
    Defense mechanisms
    Evaluating Freudian theory
The neo-Freudian psychoanalysts
● **Recap and Review I**

Trait, Learning, and Humanistic Approaches: In Search of Personality
Trait theories: Labeling personality
    Allport's trait theory: Identifying the basics
    The theories of Cattell and Eysenck: Factoring out personality
    Evaluating trait theories of personality
    Is personality a myth?: Personality versus situational factors
Learning theories of personality
    Social learning theories of personality
    Evaluating learning theories of personality
Humanistic theories of personality
    Evaluating humanistic theories
Comparing approaches to personality
● **Recap and Review II**

Assessing Personality: Determining What Makes Us Special
Reliability and validity
Psychology at Work "Race Norming": Where Psychology and Politics Meet
Self-report measures of personality
Projective methods
Behavioral assessment
The Informed Consumer of Psychology Assessing Personality Assessments
The Cutting Edge To Tell the Truth: Can Integrity Tests Identify Honest People?
● **Recap and Review III**

Looking Back
Key Terms and Concepts

➤ Now that you have surveyed the chapter, read **Looking Ahead**, pages 480–481.   ***Question:*** ☐
   Focus on the questions on page 481.   ***Read:*** ☐

CONCEPTS AND LEARNING OBJECTIVES   *Survey:* ☐

These are the concepts and the learning objects for Chapter 15. Read them carefully as part of your preliminary survey of the chapter.

Concept 1: Personality is the sum of the characteristics that define individuals and the consistency of behavior across situations and time. Psychoanalysis understands personality in terms of how a person manages the unconscious that seeks to dominate behavior.

   1. Define personality and describe the basic structure of personality according to Sigmund Freud. (pp. 480-483)

   2. Describe the psychosexual stages of development according to Freud. (pp. 483-485)

   3. Define and describe the defense mechanisms and their role in psychoanalytic theory. (pp. 485-487)

   4. Discuss the criticisms of the psychoanalytic theory of personality and the contributions made by the neo-Freudians. (pp. 487-488)

Concept 2: Three alternatives to psychoanalytic personality theory are: trait theory, which focuses on basic traits that describe universal characteristics; learning theory, especially social learning theory, which focuses on personality as a set of learned behaviors; and humanistic theory, which focuses on the uniqueness of the individual and the striving toward self-actualization.

   5. Define trait and discuss how trait theories have been criticized based on the person-situation debate. (pp. 489-495)

   6. Describe the approach to personality taken by the learning theorists. (pp. 495-497)

   7. State and define the basic tenets of humanistic personality theory. (pp. 497-499)

Concept 3: Personality can be measured several ways. Tests must prove reliable and valid, and they must have standardized norms. The most frequently given assessments include the MMPI, the Rorschach test, and the TAT.

   8. Discuss personality assessment and define the concepts of validity, reliability, and norms. (pp. 500-502)

   9. Describe and distinguish tests based on self-report and projective techniques. (pp. 502-505)

10. Describe how behavioral assessment works, and discuss the general criticisms of assessment methods. (pp. 505-507)

CHAPTER SUMMARY

There are several ways you can use this summary as part of your systematic study plan. You may read each concept summary and then read the corresponding pages in the text, or you may read the entire summary and then read the entire chapter in the text. As you finish each section, complete the **Recap and Review** questions that are supplied in the text.

CONCEPT 1: Prologue and Looking Ahead
Psychoanalytic Theories of Personality

Survey: ☐
Read: ☐

Pages 480-489

The Prologue describes John Gotti and illustrates how a person can behave very differently from one situation to another. The field of psychology known as **personality** studies the characteristics that make a person unique and attempts to explain what makes a person act the same in different situations and through time.

Psychoanalysts are concerned with understanding the hidden forces that govern people's behavior and remain outside of awareness. These forces have their roots in childhood experiences. This theory, called **psychoanalytic theory**, was developed by Sigmund Freud. Slips of the tongue are examples of how thoughts and emotions are held in the **unconscious**, the part of the personality that remains beyond the person's awareness. Slips reflect these hidden concerns. The unconscious also contains **instinctual drives**, which include infantile wishes, desires, demands, and needs that remain hidden because of the conflicts they can cause. Freud described conscious experience as the top of an iceberg, suggesting that the larger part of our personality was unconscious. In order to understand personality, these unconscious elements must be illuminated. The contents of the unconscious are disguised, thus requiring that slips of the tongue, fantasies, and dreams be interpreted in order to understand how unconscious processes direct behavior. Though his ideas were originally rejected, today we accept the notion that some part of our personality is beyond our awareness.

Freud described a general model of the personality that contains three interacting structures: the id, ego, and superego. The **id** is the raw, unorganized, inherited part of the personality aimed at reducing the tension caused by basic drives of hunger, sex, aggression, and irrational impulses. The drives are powered by **libido**, or "psychic energy," and the id operates according to the **pleasure principle**, or the desire for immediate gratification of all needs. Reality limits the expression of these id impulses. The **ego** is responsible for constraining the id. It serves as a buffer between reality and the pleasure-seeking demands of the id. The ego operates on the **reality principle**, in which restraint is based on the safety of the individual and an effort to integrate into society. The ego is the seat of the higher cognitive functions. The **superego** represents the rights and wrongs of society as represented by the parents. The superego is composed of two parts, the **conscience** and the **ego-ideal**. The conscience prevents us from behaving immorally and the ego-ideal motivates us to do the morally correct thing. Both the superego and the id make unrealistic demands. The ego must compromise between the moral perfectionist demands of the superego and the pleasure-seeking gratification sought by the id.

Freud proposed a theory of development that accounted for how the adult personality comes into existence. Difficulties and experiences from a childhood stage may predict adult behaviors and each stage focuses on a biological function. The first period of development is the **oral stage** during which the baby's mouth is the focus of pleasure. This suggested to Freud that the mouth is the primary sight of sexual pleasure and if infants are overindulged or frustrated, then they can become fixated. **Fixated** means that an adult shows personality characteristics that are related to the stage. At about 12 to 18 months until the age of 3, the child is in the **anal stage**. The major source of pleasure moves to the anal region, and the child derives pleasure from the retention and expulsion of feces. If toilet training is particularly demanding, fixation can occur. Fixation can lead to unusual rigidity and orderliness or the extreme opposite of disorder or sloppiness. At the age of 3, the phallic stage begins and the source of pleasure moves to the **genitals**. The **Oedipal conflict** develops at this time. The differences between males and females becomes a concern, and the male begins to see his father as a rival for his mother, thus developing fantasies that parallel the Greek tragedy about Oedipus. The fear of retaliation causes the development of a "castration anxiety." In the end, the child represses his desires for his mother and chooses an **identification** with father. For girls , the pattern is different. Girls develop desires for father and develop **penis envy**, a wish that they had the anatomical part, the penis, that is clearly missing. According to Freud, they blame their mothers for their "castration." In the end girls identify with their mothers and repress these feelings. The next period is called the **latency period**, beginning around 5 or 6 and lasting to puberty. Sexual concerns become latent. The final period, the **genital stage**, begins at puberty. Mature adult sexuality emerges during this period.

Anxiety, an intense, negative emotional experience, arises as a signal of danger to the ego. Though anxiety may arise from realistic fears, the **neurotic anxiety** arises because of the irrational impulses from the id that threaten to break into consciousness. The ego has developed unconscious strategies to control the impulses called **defense mechanisms**. The primary defense mechanism is **repression**. In repression, unacceptable or unpleasant id impulses are pushed back into the unconscious. In repression, the anxiety-producing impulse is ignored, but it finds ways to be revealed, either through slips of the tongue or dreams or other symbolic ways. When repression does not work, other mechanisms are used. **Regression** involves using behavior from earlier stages of development to deal with the anxiety. **Displacement** is the process of redirecting the unwanted feeling onto a less threatening person. **Rationalization** occurs when reality is distorted by justifying events with explanations that protect our self-esteem. **Denial** occurs when a person simply refuses to acknowledge the existence of an anxiety-producing piece of information. **Projection** involves protecting oneself by attributing unwanted impulses and feelings to someone else. **Sublimation** is the diversion of unwanted impulses to socially acceptable behaviors. According to Freud, these mechanisms are used to some degree by everyone, though some people devote a large amount of energy to dealing with unacceptable impulses to the extent that daily life becomes hampered. He identified this tendency as neurosis.

Freud's theory is an elaborate and complex set of propositions. However, Freud is criticized for the lack of scientific support for his theory. Freud's theory is employed in after-the-fact explanations rather than predictive statements. Also, his observations were made with a limited population of upper-middle-class Austrian women living in a puritanical era of the early 1900s. Freud's theory has had major impact on psychology and many other fields. Freud's emphasis on the unconscious has been partially supported by current research by cognitive psychologists. Experimental techniques have been developed that allow the study of the unconscious in a more sophisticated manner.

The followers of Freud are known as **neo-Freudian psychoanalysts**. They tend to place greater emphasis on the role of the ego. Carl Jung rejected the primary importance of unconscious sexual urges in favor of viewing the primitive urges of the unconscious more positively. He suggested that people have a **collective unconscious**, a set of influences that are inherited from our ancestors. The collective unconscious is shared by everyone and appears in behavior across cultures. Jung also proposed the idea of **archetypes**, or universal symbolic representations of particular persons, objects, or experiences. Alfred Adler focused on the human motivation for striving for superiority as a quest for self-improvement and perfection. His concept of **inferiority complex** describes situations in which an adult attempts to overcome feelings of inferiority that have persisted since childhood. Other neo-Freudians include Erik Erikson (discussed in Chapters 13 and 14) and Karen Horney. Horney focused on the social and cultural factors in personality, particularly the relationship between parents and the child and how well the child's needs are met.

CONCEPT 2: Trait, Learning, and Humanistic Approaches: In Search of Personality

Survey: ☐
Read: ☐

Pages 489-500

A number of theories take a different approach than that of psychoanalysis. These include **trait theory**, which assumes that individuals respond to different situations in a fairly consistent manner. **Traits** are the enduring dimensions of personality characteristics along which people differ. Trait theories assume that all people have certain traits, and the degree to which a trait applies to a specific person varies. The approach taken has been to determine the basic traits necessary to describe personality.

Gordon Allport identified 18,000 separate terms that could be used to describe personality which he then reduced to 4500 descriptors. In order to make sense of this number, he defined three basic categories of traits. A **cardinal trait** is a single characteristic that directs most of a person's activities. Most people do not have cardinal traits, instead they have five to ten **central traits** that define major characteristics. **Secondary traits** are characteristics that affect fewer situations and are less influential than cardinal or central traits. Preferences would be secondary traits.

The statistical technique called **factor analysis**, in which relationships among a large number of variables are summarized into smaller, more general patterns, has been used to identify fundamental patterns or combinations of traits. Raymond Cattell suggested that there are forty-six **surface traits** or clusters of related behaviors. Cattell then reduced this number to sixteen **source traits** that represent the basic dimensions of personality. He then developed the Sixteen Personality Factor Questionnaire (16 PF). Hans Eysenck used factor analysis to identify two major dimensions. **Introversion-extroversion** is the dimension marked by quiet and restrained individuals on one end and outgoing and sociable on the other. Neuroticism-stability is the dimension marked by moody and sensitive (neurotic) on the one hand and calm, reliable, and even-tempered (stability) on the other. Recent research has suggested that their are five traits: surgency, neuroticism, intellect, agreeableness, and conscientiousness.

Trait theories have an advantage of being straightforward and easy to apply to practical situations. However, a determination of which traits are fundamental is difficult to make. The traits offer little more than a basic description of the person and they do not explain behavior.

Another objection that has arisen from trait theories but applies to all is the question of whether behavior is consistent over different situations. Walter Mischel has argued that the broad traits can explain only a minor portion of behavior. Most behavior can be explained by the situation in which it occurs. This has produced an ongoing controversy about the degree to which behavior is caused by personality factors or by situational factors. According to the traditional views, it is necessary to consider behavior over time to see the extent of consistency. Mischel has responded by arguing that consistency over time is not consistency over situations. One result of this controversy has been the realization that trait raters are more accurate if they do not know the subject, when multiple ratings and raters are used, and when the behavior observed is relevant to the trait being rated. Personality psychologists also look more to the characteristics of the situation that influence behavior of individuals with specific traits. The debate has also increased the focus on searching for the factors that produce specific traits. A study of 350 pairs of twins has determined that some traits are influenced more by heredity than others. Social potency and traditionalism have stronger genetic components, and achievement and social closeness had weaker genetic components. Other studies suggest that altruism, aggression, sexuality, political attitudes, and religious values may be influenced by heredity.

According to Skinner, personality is a collection of learned behavior patterns. Similarities across situations are caused by a similarity of reinforcements. Strict learning theorists are less interested in the consistency issue than they are in finding ways to modify behavior. In their view, humans are quite changeable.

Social learning theory emphasizes the role of a person's cognitions in determining personality. According to Bandura, people are able to foresee the outcomes of behaviors prior to carrying them out by using the mechanism of **observational learning**. We observe a model that displays a behavior and then relate the consequences that result from the behavior to determining whether or not to attempt the behavior. Bandura considers **self-efficacy**, the expectations of success, to be an important factor in determining the behaviors a person will display. Social learning theory places an emphasis on the reciprocity between individuals and the environment, viewing the interaction as one in which a feedback flows both ways. The key to understanding behavior, **reciprocal determinism** refers to the interaction between environment, behavior, and the individual.

Traditional learning theories have been criticized for ignoring internal processes and reducing behavior to stimuli and responses. Traditional theories and social learning theory have been criticized for their highly **deterministic** view that maintains that behavior is controlled by forces outside the control of the person. The positive contribution has been to make the study of personality an objective and scientific venture.

Humanistic theory emphasizes the basic goodness of people and their tendency to grow to higher levels of functioning. Carl Rogers is a major representative of this approach. The positive regard others have for us makes us see and judge ourselves through the eyes of other people. The views others have of us may not match our own self-concept. If the difference is great, we may have problems with daily functioning. The discrepancy is overcome by support from another person in the form of **unconditional positive regard**, defined as an attitude of acceptance and respect no matter what the person says or does. Rogers and Maslow (Chapter 11) view the ultimate goal of personality growth to be **self-actualization**.

The criticisms of humanistic theory are centered on the difficulty of verifying the basic assumptions of the theory. The assumption that all people are basically "good" is unverifiable and injects nonscientific values into scientific theories.

Each theory looks to different aspects of the personality, and personality is most reasonably viewed from several perspectives. Personality theories can be compared on the following major issues: The unconscious versus conscious, nature versus nurture, freedom versus determinism, stability versus modifiability of characteristics, and nomothetic versus ideographic approaches. **Nomothetic approaches to personality** focus on broad uniformities in behavior. **Ideographic approaches to personality** focus on individual uniqueness.

CONCEPT 3: Assessing Personality: Determining What Makes Us Special

Survey: ☐
Read: ☐

Pages 500-508

The intentionally vague statements that introduce the topic of assessment suggest that measuring different aspects of personality may require great care and precision. The assessment of personality requires discriminating the behavior of one person from that of another. **Psychological tests** are standard measures that measure aspects of behavior objectively.

Psychological tests must have **reliability**, that is, they must measure something consistently from time to time. A reliable test will produce similar outcomes in similar conditions. The question of whether or not a test measures the characteristic it is supposed to measure is called **validity**. If a test is reliable, that does not mean that is valid. However, if a test is unreliable, it cannot be valid. All types of tests in psychology, including intelligence tests, assessments of psychological disorders, and the measurement of attitudes must meet tests of validity and reliability. If tests are both valid and reliable, then they can be used to establish norms to allow the results of a test to be interpreted. Norms are the standards of test performance that allow comparison of the scores of one test-taker to others who have taken it. The norm for a test is determined by calculating the average score for a particular group of people for whom the test is designed to be given. Then, the extent to which each person's score differs from the others can be calculated. The selection of the subjects who will be used to establish a norm for a test are critical. A contemporary problem faces test creators in the development of a different set of norms for minorities. Critics of such an approach suggest that this is both unfair and contributes to bigotry. Supporters argue that it is an affirmative-action tool that helps minorities.

Instead of conducting a comprehensive interview to determine aspects of childhood, social relationships, and success and failures, the use of **self-report measures** allows individuals to respond to a small sample questions. The most frequently used self-report measure is the **Minnesota Multiphasic Personality Inventory-2 (MMPI-2)**. Originally developed to distinguish people with psychological disturbances from people without, the MMPI scores have been shown to be good predictors of such things as whether college students will marry within ten years and whether they will get an advanced degree. The test has 567 true-false items covering items like mood, opinions, and physical and psychological health. The interpretation of the responses is important; there are no right or wrong answers. The test is scored on ten scales and includes a lie scale for people trying to falsify their answers. The MMPI has undergone a procedure called **test standardization** by which the test authors have determined which items best differentiate among groups of people, like differentiating those suffering depression, from normal subjects. This procedure has produced a number of subscales helpful in diagnosis. When the MMPI is used for proper reasons, it does a good job. However, some employers have used it as a screening tool and have applied the test improperly. Other tests are more appropriate for screening job applicants.

Projective personality tests require the subject to describe an ambiguous stimulus. The responses are considered to be projections of what the person is like. The best known is the **Rorschach test** which consists of symmetrical stimuli. The **Thematic Apperception Test (TAT)** consists of a series of pictures about which the person is asked to write a story. Inferences about the subject are then based on these stories. These tests are criticized because too much inference depends upon the scorer.

In order to obtain an objective test based on observable behavior, a **behavioral assessment** may be conducted either in a natural setting or in a laboratory under controlled conditions. The behavioral assessment requires quantifying behavior as much as possible. For instance, recording the number of social contacts or the number of aggressive acts would quantify the assessment. Behavioral assessment is appropriate for observing and remedying behavioral difficulties and psychological difficulties.

To find people with the right characteristics for a job, many companies are using personality tests for both hiring and advancement. One concern is for the use of these tests to determine if someone is honest. Career counseling has also utilized personality tests. When personality tests are being used, one must keep in mind the purpose of the test and remember that no decision should be made solely on the basis of the test and that tests are not infallible.

▶ Now that you have surveyed, questioned, and read the chapter and completed
the **Recap and Review** questions, review **Looking Back**, pages 508–509. *Review:* ❑

➤ For additional practice through recitation and review, test your knowledge of the chapter material by answering the questions in the *Key Word Drill*, the *Practice Questions*, and the *Essay Questions*.

KEY WORD DRILL

Recite: ☐

The following **Fill in the Blank** and **Matching Questions** test key words from the text. Check your answers with the Answer Key in the back of the *Study Guide*.

FILL IN THE BLANK

1. _____ is defined as the sum total of characteristics that differentiate people, or the stability in a person's behavior across different situations.

2. Physicians or psychologists with special training in Freudian psychology are called

   _____.

3. A child's _____ _____ with his or her opposite-sex parent is typically resolved through identification with the same-sex parent.

4. Theorists who place greater emphasis than Freud did on the functions of the ego and its influence

   on our daily activities have been given the name _____-_____.

5. _____ are characteristics that differentiate people from one another.

6. _____ _____ is used to combine traits into broader, more general patterns of consistency.

7. _____ suggests that people's behavior is shaped primarily by factors outside their control.

8. _____ approaches study personality by accentuating the uniformities across

   behavior while _____ approaches study personality by emphasizing what makes one person different from others and unique.

9. Consistency in the measurements made by a test is described as _____, and the ability of a test to measure what it is supposed to measure is described as

   _____.

10. The standards of test performance are called _____.

11. _____ _____ refers to the use of direct measures of an individual's behavior used to describe characteristics indicative of personality.

MATCHING QUESTIONS

_____ 12. unconscious

_____ 13. instinctual drives

_____ 14. id

_____ 15. libido

_____ 16. fixation

a. Behavior reflecting an earlier stage of development.

b. Infantile wishes, desires, demands, and needs hidden from conscious awareness.

c. A person is unaware of this determinant of behavior.

d. The raw, unorganized, inherited part of personality created by biological drives and irrational impulses.

e. The sexual energy underlying biological urges.

_____ 17. pleasure principle

_____ 18. ego

_____ 19. reality principle

_____ 20. superego

_____ 21. conscience

_____ 22. ego-ideal

a. Provides a buffer between the id and the outside world.

b. Motivates us to do what is morally proper.

c. Prevents us from doing what is morally wrong.

d. Represents the morality of society as presented by parents, teachers, and others.

e. The principle by which the ego operates.

f. The principle by which the id operates.

_____ 23. oral stage

_____ 24. anal stage

_____ 25. phallic stage

_____ 26. identification

_____ 27. penis envy

_____ 28. latency period

_____ 29. genital stage

a. A child's attempt to be similar to the same-sex parent.

b. An infant's center of pleasure is the mouth.

c. Children's sexual concerns are temporarily put aside.

d. Marked by mature sexual behavior.

e. A child's interest focuses on the genitals.

f. A child's pleasure is centered on the anus.

g. A girl's wish that she had a penis.

_____ 30. anxiety

_____ 31. neurotic anxiety

_____ 32. defense mechanisms

_____ 33. collective unconscious

_____ 34. archetypes

_____ 35. inferiority complex

a. The concept that we inherit certain personality characteristics from our ancestors and the human race as a whole.

b. Anxiety caused when irrational impulses from the id threaten to become uncontrollable.

c. Universal, symbolic representations of a particular person, object, or experience.

d. A feeling of apprehension or tension.

e. A phenomenon whereby adults have continuing feelings of weakness and insecurity.

f. Unconscious strategies used to reduce anxiety by concealing its source from themselves and others.

_____ 36. repression

_____ 37. regression

_____ 38. displacement

_____ 39. rationalization

_____ 40. denial

_____ 41. projection

_____ 42. sublimation

a. An unwanted feeling or thought directed toward a weaker person instead of a more powerful one.

b. Justify a negative situation to protect self-esteem.

c. Unacceptable or unpleasant id impulses are pushed back into the unconscious.

d. Attribute inadequacies or faults to someone else.

e. Behavior reminiscent of an earlier stage of development.

f. The refusal to accept anxiety-producing information.

g. The diversion of unwanted impulses into socially acceptable thoughts, feelings, or behaviors.

_____ 43. observational learning

_____ 44. self-efficacy

_____ 45. reciprocal determinism

_____ 46. self-concept

_____ 47. unconditional positive regard

_____ 48. self-actualization

a. The realization of one's highest potential.

b. The impression one holds of oneself.

c. Learned expectations about success determine behavior.

d. Supportive behavior for another individual.

e. The interaction of environment, behavior, and the individual causes people to behave the way that they do.

f. Learning by viewing the actions of others.

_____ 49. cardinal trait

a. A single trait that directs most of a person's activities.

_____ 50. central traits

b. The dimension encompassing shyness to sociability.

_____ 51. secondary traits

c. Clusters of a person's related behaviors that can be observed in a given situation.

_____ 52. surface traits

d. Traits less important than central and cardinal traits.

_____ 53. source traits

e. Encompasses moodiness to even-temperedness.

_____ 54. introversion-extroversion

f. The sixteen basic dimensions of personality.

_____ 55. neuroticism-stability

g. A set of major characteristics that composes the core of a person's personality.

_____ 56. psychological tests

a. Used to identify people with psychological difficulties.

_____ 57. self-report measures

b. Consists of a series of ambiguous pictures about which a person is asked to write a story.

_____ 58. Minnesota Multiphasic Personality Inventory-2 (MMPI-2)

c. Uses inkblots of indefinite shapes.

d. Gathering data by asking people about their behavior.

_____ 59. test standardization

_____ 60. projective personality test

e. Validates questions in personality tests by studying the responses of people with known diagnoses.

_____ 61. Rorschach test

f. Standard measures devised to objectively assess behavior.

_____ 62. Thematic Apperception Test (TAT)

g. Uses ambiguous stimuli to determine personality.

_____ 63. psychoanalytic theory

a. The theory that suggests that personality develops through observational learning.

_____ 64. trait theory

_____ 65. social learning theory

b. A model that seeks to identify the basic traits necessary to describe personality.

_____ 66. humanistic theory

c. The theory that emphasizes people's basic goodness and their natural tendency to rise to higher levels of functioning.

d. Freud's theory that unconscious forces act as determinants of personality.

| **PRACTICE QUESTIONS** | *Recite and Review:* ☐ |

Test your knowledge of the chapter material by answering these **True-False** and **Multiple Choice Questions**. Check your answers with the Answer Key in the back of the *Study Guide*.

TRUE-FALSE QUESTIONS

T   F   1. Children who are in Freud's latency stage are also typically in Erikson's industry versus inferiority stage.

T   F   2. According to psychoanalytic theory, the phallic stage runs from about ages 3 to 5.

T   F   3. A child who begins to wet the bed at night, when he or she never did so before, is probably displaying repression.

T   F   4. The neo-Freudians, Freud's successors, often disagreed with Freud, especially with his emphasis on sex as an influence and motivator of human behavior.

T   F   5. A shortcoming of the trait approach to personality is that it yields only a description of behavior, rather than an explanation.

T   F   6. Recent studies of personality show that heredity plays a larger role in a person's development and personality traits than was thought previously.

T   F   7. Clinicians use stories based on ambiguous pictures to draw inferences about the writer's personality characteristics.

T   F   8. Behavioral assessment and naturalistic observation provide a means for analyzing the results of projective personality tests.

MULTIPLE CHOICE QUESTIONS

1. According to Sigmund Freud, the _____ harbors repressed emotions and thoughts as well as instinctual drives.
   a. unconscious
   b. collective unconscious
   c. conscience
   d. conscious

2. Which of the following theories suggests that behavior is triggered largely by powerful forces found in the unconscious?
   a. humanistic theory
   b. learning theory
   c. psychoanalytic theory
   d. trait theory

3. According to psychoanalytic theorists, what is the most important factor in determining our everyday behavior?
    a. who we come in contact with
    b. how we have learned to behave in the past
    c. our thinking patterns
    d. the unconscious

4. Freud's structure of personality has three major parts. Which alternative below is **not** one of them?
    a. libido   c. superego
    b. id   d. ego

5. Which of the following is **least** likely to involve making unrealistic demands on the person?
    a. the id   c. the superego
    b. the ego   d. the pleasure principle

6. Which of the following controls thought, solves problems, and makes decisions?
    a. id   c. superego
    b. ego   d. conscience

7. Listed below are four alternatives. Three of the four give pairs of items that are related. Which alternative below contains items that are **not** related?
    a. ego; reality principle   c. superego; "executive" of personality
    b. Sigmund Freud; Viennese physician   d. id; pleasure principle

8. From the psychoanalytic perspective, a rapist would be considered to have:
    a. unconditioned positive regard for his victim.
    b. a well-developed ego-ideal.
    c. a deficient superego.
    d. brain damage.

9. According to the text, Freud's concept of the ego-ideal refers to:
    a. infantile wishes, desires, demands, and needs hidden from conscious awareness.
    b. the part of the superego that motivates us to do what is morally proper.
    c. the part of personality that provides a buffer between the id and the outside world.
    d. the part of the superego that prevents us from doing what is morally wrong.

10. According to Freud's theory of psychosexual development, a child who is constantly putting things in its mouth is most likely at the:
    a. genital stage.   c. phallic stage.
    b. anal stage.   d. oral stage.

11. Of the following, a psychoanalyst most likely would view a thumbsucking 7-year-old as:
    a. a normal youngster.
    b. fixated at the oral stage of development.
    c. having been breastfed as an infant.
    d. ready to enter the phallic stage of development.

12. Tim kept his clothes hung up and neatly pressed, while his roommate Jack rarely laundered or hung up his clothes. Freud might have suggested that both men were fixated at the:
    a. anal stage.
    b. oral stage.
    c. phallic stage.
    d. genital stage.

13. A child who is in the midst of toilet training is probably in the:
    a. genital psychosexual stage.
    b. anal psychosexual stage.
    c. phallic psychosexual stage.
    d. oral psychosexual stage.

14. According to the text, mature sexual relationships begin to occur at which psychosexual stage?
    a. phallic
    b. oral
    c. genital
    d. anal

15. Defense mechanisms are developed to:
    a. help the superego gain control of the id.
    b. advance the collective unconscious.
    c. protect the ego.
    d. reveal latent content from dreams.

16. According to Sigmund Freud, defense mechanisms are:
    a. unconscious.
    b. instinctive.
    c. learned.
    d. reflexive.

17. A female college student accepts a date from a young man she greatly admires. At the time of the date, however, the man doesn't show up. In response she exclaims, "I didn't want to go out with him anyway!" This illustrates:
    a. rationalization.
    b. denial.
    c. regression.
    d. repression.

18. Which of the following defense mechanisms did Freud find most socially acceptable?
    a. repression
    b. sublimation
    c. rationalization
    d. projection

19. Generalizing from the text, what aspect of Freudian theory makes the theory most difficult to validate?
    a. The developmental stages are all sexual.
    b. It is difficult to study children.
    c. The early childhood stages are still apparent in the adult.
    d. The parts of the personality are unobservable.

20. Freud's ideas and theories have created an understanding of many phenomena in psychology and psychiatry. Which of the following is **not** one of them?
    a. defense mechanisms
    b. the unconscious
    c. neural disorders as a cause of behavioral problems
    d. childhood causes of adult psychological difficulties

21. According to the text, which of the following statements would **not** be a valid criticism of psychoanalytic theory?
    a. Freud's theory is built from observations of patients who were a highly select and special group of women in Vienna.
    b. It is difficult to make predictions about personality development and behavior from Freud's theory.
    c. Freud used only that data from his cases that supported the ideas of his theory.
    d. Research data do not strongly support Freud's theory.

22. Listed below are four alternatives. Three of the four list pairs of items that are related. Which alternative below contains items that are **not** related?
    a. Jung; collective unconscious
    b. Horney; women do not have penis envy
    c. Adler; inferiority complex
    d. Cattell; striving for superiority

23. Which of the following statements is most likely to be made by a trait theorist?
    a. He really hurt her feelings, but he's rationalizing it away.
    b. He really could have gone a long way, but his inferiority complex destroyed any confidence.
    c. These are five stages in the process of his development toward fulfilling his highest potential.
    d. He is a sensitive, warm, and considerate person.

24. According to trait theorists:
    a. everyone has the same traits, but in different amounts.
    b. everyone has different traits that do not change with time.
    c. everyone has different traits, and they change with time.
    d. everyone has different traits, but they cannot be measured.

25. For Gordon Allport, _____ traits were so distinct that having only one of these traits will define a person's personality.
    a. general   c. central
    b. secondary   d. cardinal

26. Which of the psychologists listed below is **not** a trait theorist?
    a. Albert Bandura   c. Raymond B. Cattell
    b. Gordon Allport   d. Hans Eysenck

27. What are the three important categories of personality dimensions, according to Gordon Allport?
    a. primary, secondary, and tertiary
    b. factors, traits, and features
    c. source, surface, and circumscript
    d. cardinal, central, and secondary

28. Factor analysis is:
    a. a method of recording data that requires sophisticated equipment.
    b. a method of understanding how the unconscious works.
    c. a statistical method of finding common traits.
    d. a sociometric method of determining personality traits in a group.

29. Which of the following statements about trait theories is true?
    a. They agree on a certain number of basic personality dimensions.
    b. They allow a comparison between individuals on the same scale.
    c. They explain the basis for a behavior as well as provide a label.
    d. They help explain how and why the defense mechanisms work.

30. Learning theorists are most interested in the:
    a. heritability of behavior.   c. randomness of behavior.
    b. stability of behavior.   d. modifiability of behavior.

31. According to Bandura, we can modify our own personalities through the use of:
    a. defense mechanisms.   c. psychoanalysis.
    b. drive reduction.   d. self-reinforcement.

32. Humanistic theories of personality assume that:
    a. man's basic goodness is contrasted with an evil unconscious.
    b. man is self-sufficient and the society corrupts the individual.
    c. man is basically good and desires to improve.
    d. man's fundamental depravity may be offset through education.

33. Which of the following theoretical points of view emphasizes to the **greatest** extent the individual's freedom of choice as a determinant of personality?
    a. psychoanalysis   c. social learning theory
    b. humanistic theory   d. trait theory

34. Three of the four alternatives below list pairs of items that are related. Which one contains items that are **not** related?
    a. Maslow; self-actualization   c. Bandura; observational learning
    b. Rogers; imitation   d. Skinner; learning theory

35. Stephanie loves art and wants to study it in college. Her parents want her to be a nurse and criticize her for her love of art. According to Carl Rogers, this conflict will lead to:
    a. Stephanie learning to love being a nurse.
    b. anxiety on the part of Stephanie.
    c. Stephanie becoming a fully-functioning person.
    d. unconditional positive regard.

36. Various approaches to personality have names and concepts uniquely associated with them. Three of the four alternatives below list pairs of items that are related. Which alternative below contains items that are **not** related?
    a. trait theory; assessment of traits that comprise personality
    b. learning theory; experiences with situations in the environment
    c. learning theory; Skinner
    d. psychoanalytic theory; consistency of behavior across situations

37. Which of the following theories are most closely associated with the nomothetic approaches to understanding personality?
    a. psychoanalytic and trait   c. social learning and strict learning
    b. trait and social learning   d. social learning and humanistic

38. If a test provides a consistent score for a particular individual over repeated administrations, the test is said to be:
    a. accurate.
    b. valid.
    c. reliable.
    d. statistical.

39. Which of the following situations best illustrates reliability as a quality of psychological tests?
    a. A prospective Air Force pilot takes a test, passes it, and becomes an excellent pilot.
    b. A college student studies diligently for an important exam and makes an A on it.
    c. A psychiatric patient takes a psychological test which yields the diagnosis the patient had suspected.
    d. A mentally retarded patient takes an intelligence test on Monday and again on Tuesday, getting the same result on each administration.

40. If an individual's test scores vary greatly from one session to the next, it is likely that the test itself is:
    a. unreliable and invalid.
    b. unreliable only.
    c. nomothetic.
    d. ideographic.

41. The MMPI was originally developed to:
    a. identify personality disorders.
    b. uncover unconscious thoughts.
    c. locate traits.
    d. conduct behavioral assessments.

42. Which one of the following tests is most appropriately used in the employment setting?
    a. TAT
    b. Edwards Personal Preference Schedule
    c. MMPI
    d. Rorschach

43. Which one of the following tests is designed to uncover unconscious content?
    a. MMPI
    b. TAT
    c. California Psychological Inventory
    d. Edwards Personal Preference Schedule

44. Test stimuli are the most ambiguous on the:
    a. TAT.
    b. California Psychological Inventory.
    c. Rorschach.
    d. MMPI.

45. Which of the following tests are considered projective instruments?
    a. MMPI and TAT
    b. TAT and 16 PF
    c. Rorschach and MMPI
    d. Rorschach and TAT

46. When personality assessments are evaluated, it is important to keep in mind that:
    a. tests are infallible.
    b. decisions should not be based solely on the results of any one test.
    c. projective measures are more valid than other measures because they delve beneath the surface.
    d. most people lie on self-report measures.

ESSAY QUESTIONS

Essay Question 15.1: *Freud and Female Psychology*

Given that Freud's theory appears to be primarily focused on male development and thus on a male personality, identify the areas of Freud's theory that are the weakest with regard to female psychological issues. Defend your response with other points of view presented in the text.

_____

_____

_____

_____

_____

_____

_____

_____

_____

_____

_____

_____

_____

_____

_____

_____

Essay Question 15.2: *Personality Placement Tests*

A major issue that will affect virtually everyone is the use of personality tests for job placement and promotion. Discuss the hazards and possible benefits of using tests like the MMPI, the TAT, behavioral assessments, and other tests for employment purposes.

_____

_____

_____

_____

_____

_____

_____

_____

_____

_____

_____

_____

_____

_____

_____

_____

_____

_____

_____

ACTIVITIES AND PROJECTS

1. Write four descriptions of someone's personality, each based on a different theory of personality: (a) trait theory, (b) psychoanalytic theory, (c) learning theory, and (d) humanistic theory. You may choose a friend, a family member, or a fictional character. With friends and family members, it is not a good idea to share the information with the subjects described. In your trait description, make a list of central and secondary traits; include situational variables if you like. In your psychoanalytic description, include hypotheses about unconscious conflicts and motivations and the use of defense mechanisms. With learning theory, include the role of early experiences and reinforcement. Your humanistic description might include the person's strivings, level of self-actualization obtained, and self-concept. Which theoretical framework did you find the most useful to work with? Explain.

16

HEALTH PSYCHOLOGY: STRESS, COPING, AND HEALTH

| DETAILED OUTLINE | *Survey:* ☐ |

This detailed outline contains all the headings in Chapter 16: Health Psychology: Stress, Coping, and Health. If you are using the SQ3R method, then an examination of the outline is the best way to begin your survey of the chapter.

Prologue: War in the Gulf
Looking Ahead

Stress and Coping
    The high cost of stress
    The general adaptation syndrome model: The course of stress
    The nature of stressors: My stress is your pleasure
        Categorizing stressors
Psychology at Work Posttraumatic Stress Disorder: Reliving Catastrophe
    Learned helplessness
    Coping with stress
        Coping style: The hardy personality
        Social support: Turning to others
The Informed Consumer of Psychology Coping Strategies That Work
        Turning threat into challenge
        Making a threatening situation less threatening
        Changing one's goals
        Taking physical action
        Preparing for stress before it happens
• **Recap and Review I**

Psychological Aspects of Major Health Problems
    The A's and B's of coronary heart disease
    Psychological aspects of cancer: Mind over tumor?
The Cutting Edge Can Psychological Therapy Extend the Lives of Cancer Patients?
    Smoking
        Quitting smoking
• **Recap and Review II**

Psychological Factors Related to Physical Illness: Going to the Doctor
    Physician-patient communication
    Complying with physicians' orders

● **Recap and Review III**

Looking Back
Key Terms and Concepts

➤ Now that you have surveyed the chapter, read **Looking Ahead**, pages 512–513.   *Question:* ☐
Focus on the questions on page 513.   *Read:* ☐

CONCEPTS AND LEARNING OBJECTIVES

Survey: ☐

These are the concepts and the learning objects for Chapter 16. Read them carefully as part of your preliminary survey of the chapter.

Concept 1: Health psychology focuses on the prevention, diagnosis, and treatment of medical problems. A key factor that health psychologists must understand is that of stress.

1.   Define health psychology and its centrally important concept of stress. (pp. 512-514)

2.   Describe and illustrate Selye's general adaptation syndrome to stress. (pp. 514-517)

3.   Identify major stressors and their consequences, especially posttraumatic stress disorder. (pp. 517-520)

4.   Discuss the concept of learned helplessness and how it develops. (pp. 520-522)

5.   Describe the coping strategies, including defense mechanisms, types of coping, hardiness, and related strategies. (pp. 522-526)

Concept 2: The link between stress and illness continues to be clarified, and studies examine the role of stress in coronary heart disease, cancer, and smoking.

6.   Distinguish Type A and Type B personalities and the major health risks of Type A behavior, including coronary disease. (pp. 526-530)

7.   Discuss the role health psychology has in the treatment of cancer. (pp. 530-532)

8.   Discuss the problem of smoking, how one becomes addicted, and how one attempts to quit. (pp. 532-534)

Concept 3: A major problem that confronts medical practitioners is the difficulty of communication between the patient and the physician.

9.   Outline and describe the various problems that hinder effective communication between the physician and the patient. (pp. 535-537)

10.   Discuss the problems associated with patient compliance to the physician's orders. (pp. 537-539)

CHAPTER SUMMARY

There are several ways you can use this summary as part of your systematic study plan. You may read each concept summary and then read the corresponding pages in the text, or you may read the entire summary and then read the entire chapter in the text. As you finish each section, complete the **Recap and Review** questions that are supplied in the text.

CONCEPT 1: Prologue and Looking Ahead   *Survey:* ☐
              Stress and Coping   *Read:* ☐

Pages 512-526

Health psychology focuses on the application of psychology to the prevention, diagnosis, and treatment of medical problems. Health psychologists view the mind and the body as closely linked. Good health and the ability to stay healthy are affected by how a person manages stress and the person's health habits. The **immune system** of the body is affected by attitudes and emotional state. Health psychology has changed the view of disease from a purely biological problem, and it has had to help people cope with the problems associated with adjustment to diseases that last for a long time.

The response to events that threaten or challenge a person is called **stress**, and the events themselves are called **stressors**. Stressors can be both pleasant and unpleasant events, though the negative events can be more detrimental. Some view life as a sequence of stresses, with our responses being minor adaptations. Sometimes, though, adaptation requires a major effort and may have responses that result in health problems.

The most immediate reaction to stress is a physiological response, including an increase in adrenal hormones, an increase in heart rate and blood pressure, and changes in how the skin conducts electrical charges. This change initially helps the body respond to the stress. Continued stress can result in a decline of the body's ability to cope biologically. Body tissues can actually deteriorate. Minor problems can be made worse. The class of medical problems called **psychosomatic disorders**, disorders caused by the interaction of psychological, emotional, and physiological problems, are also related to stress. Ulcers, asthma, arthritis, blood pressure, and eczema are common psychosomatic disorders. High levels of stress interfere with people's ability to cope with current and new stressors.

Hans Selye proposed that everyone goes through the same set of physiological responses no matter what the cause is, and he called this the **general adaptation syndrome (GAS)**. The first stage is the **alarm and mobilization stage**, during which the presence of a stressor is detected and the sympathetic nervous system is energized. The second stage is the **resistance stage**, during which the person attempts to cope with the stressor. If coping is inadequate, the person enters the **exhaustion stage**. The person's ability to cope with stress declines and the negative consequences appear. These include illness, psychological symptoms like the inability to concentrate, and possibly disorientation and losing touch with reality. People wear out in this stage. In order to escape the problems of this stage, people must often avoid the stressor—essentially, get some rest from the problem. The GAS has provided a model that explains how stress leads to illness. The primary criticism has focused on the fact that the model suggests that every stress response is physiologically the same. There is little room for psychological factors in the model also.

If people are to consider an event stressful, they must perceive it to be threatening and must lack the ability to cope with it adequately. The same event may not be stressful for everyone. The perception of stress may depend upon how one attributes the causes for events.

There are three classes of events that are considered stressors. The first is **cataclysmic events**, strong stressors that affect many people at the same time. The stress of these events is usually dealt with well because so many people experience the event and share the problem. Some people experience prolonged problems due to catastrophic events, and this is called **posttraumatic stress disorder**. People may experience flashbacks or dreams during which they reexperience the event. The symptoms can include a numbing of emotional experience, sleep difficulties, problems relating to others, and drug problems, among others. The second class of stressor is **personal stressors**, which include life events that are of a personal or individual nature, like the death of a parent or spouse, the loss of a job, or a major illness. Typically, personal stressors cause an immediate major reaction that tapers off. Sometimes, though, the effects can last for a long time, such as the effects of being raped. The third class of stressors is called **background stressors**, and they include standing in long lines, traffic jams, and other **daily hassles**. Daily hassles can add up, causing unpleasant emotions and moods. A critical factor is the degree of control people have over the daily hassles. When they have control, the stress reactions are less. On the other side of daily hassles are **uplifts**, positive events that lead to a pleasant feelings.

In an environment in which control is seen as impossible, one can experience **learned helplessness**. Victims of learned helplessness have decided that there is no link between the responses they make and the outcomes that occur. When elderly people in nursing homes were given control over simple aspects of their lives, they were less likely to experience an early death. Not everyone experiences helplessness. The attributions, or explanations, that people make about the nature of the problem affects their experience. Helplessness is most likely when the person attributes the cause to personal characteristics, when it is enduring, and when it is seen as global.

We cannot escape stress; it is a normal part of living. Our efforts to control, reduce, or learn to tolerate stress are known as **coping**. Many of our responses are habitual. The **defense mechanisms** are reactions that help control stress by distorting or denying the actual nature of the situations. Denying the significance of a nearby geological fault is an example. Emotional insulation is another example in which a person does not feel emotions at all. A more positive means of dealing with stress is the use of one of three types of strategies, (1) problem solving, (2) avoidance, or (3) seeking social support. Problem solving involves setting goals to deal with the situation. Avoidance techniques involve doing something other than dwelling on the stressor. Social support involves seeking help from others or confiding in a relative. Another classification of methods distinguishes **emotion-focused coping**, the conscious regulation of emotions, from **problem-focused coping**, the management of the stressful stimulus. People use both strategies, but they are more likely to use the emotion-focused strategy when they perceive the problem as unchangeable.

People can be described as having coping styles. **Hardiness** refers to the style that is associated with a low rate of stress-induced illness. Hardiness consists of three components: commitment, challenge, and control. Commitment is a tendency to be involved in whatever we are doing with a sense that it is important and meaningful. Challenge refers to the view that change is the standard condition of life. Control refers to the sense of being able to influence events. The hardy person is optimistic and approaches the problem directly.

Relationships with others help people cope with stress. The knowledge of a mutual network of concerned, interested people helping individuals experience lower levels of stress is called **social support**. Social support demonstrates the value of a person to others and provides a network of information and advice. Also, actual goods and services can be provided through social support networks. Even pets can contribute to this support.

Stress can be dealt with through several steps: Turn stress into a challenge, make the threatening situation less threatening by changing attitudes about it, change goals in order to remove oneself from an uncontrollable situation, and take physical action. The most successful approach requires that the person be prepared for stress. One method of preparation is called inoculation. With **inoculation**, stress is dealt with through preparation for both the nature of the possible stressors and developing or learning clear strategies for coping.

CONCEPT 2:   Psychological Aspects of Major Health Problems

Survey: ☐
Read: ☐

Pages 526-535

Today, research into the nature of coronary heart disease includes close examination of the psychological factors that contribute to it. Two characteristic behavior patterns have been identified that are associated with coronary heart disease. **Type A behavior pattern** is seen in individuals who are competitive, have a sense of urgency about time, are aggressive, and are driven about their work. **Type B behavior pattern** is seen in individuals who are essentially opposite Type A. They are less competitive, less time-oriented, and not aggressive, driven or hostile. In an extensive study, people with Type A behavior developed heart disease twice as frequently as Type B individuals. One theory says that Type A individuals become excessively aroused when they are placed in stressful situations and that this arousal increases the hormones epinephrine and norepinephrine, in turn leading to higher blood pressure and heart rate. Long-term damage then results. The evidence supporting the connection between Type A behavior and coronary heart disease is not conclusive. One study showed Type A individuals more likely to survive a second heart attack. The important result is that people who experience strong negative emotions are more likely to have coronary heart disease. Type A behavior does not, however, make heart disease inevitable. The evidence is correlational, so it cannot be said that Type A behavior causes heart disease—there may be other factors. In one study, men who had heart attacks and who were considered Type A were taught strategies to change the way they interpret situations. One strategy was to imagine how a Type B person would react and then react similarly. The Type A persons were directed to look for situations where they could practice this, like waiting in line. Other techniques included learning muscle relaxation procedures in order to regulate their arousal. The study showed a lower incidence in repeat heart attacks for those being trained. Another problem is that Type A behaviors are associated with behaviors that are valued by our society: competitiveness, achievement, and a work ethic.

Cancer is the second leading cause of death after coronary heart disease. Though its causes remain unknown, the progress of cancer is from altered cell to tumor, and the tumor robs nutrients from healthy tissue, eventually impairing normal function. Evidence is growing that the emotional response to cancer influences the progress of the disease. Fighters appear more likely to recover than are pessimists. Survival rates for women with breast cancer were higher among those who fought the disease or even denied it than for those who stoically accepted the illness or who accepted their fate. Evidence suggests that the patient's immune system may be affected by emotional state. Positive emotional responses may help increase the natural "killer" cells. Negative emotions may suppress these kinds of cells. Other studies have found that positive emotional states improve longevity of cancer patients. Social support and cancer have also been linked. People who develop cancer have little contact with their families. *The Cutting Edge* reports a study in which individuals who receive psychotherapy live longer than those who do not. The link between personality and cancer is not yet established, but evidence is increasing for the relationship between stress and the functioning of the immune system.

Though the link between smoking and cancer is well-established, millions of people continue to smoke. Most smokers agree that smoking damages their health, but they continue to smoke. Mostly caused by environmental factors, the habit of smoking moves through four stages that end in the habit. The first stage is preparation, during which a relatively positive attitude about smoking develops. The second stage is initiation, when smoking a cigarette becomes a right of passage and is seen as a sign of growing up. The third stage is becoming a smoker, during which smoking becomes part of the self-concept and the body becomes tolerant of nicotine. The fourth stage is maintaining the smoking habit, the stage in which the aspects of smoking become part of the routine.

Quitting smoking is very difficult. Only about 15 percent of those trying to stop smoking will have long-term success. Behavioral strategies for quitting view smoking as a learned habit that needs to be unlearned. Social norms will also eventually lead to reduced smoking, as smoking is banned in more and more public places and society begins to change its attitude about those who smoke. Still more than a quarter of the people smoke, and those who begin do so at an earlier age.

CONCEPT 3: Psychological Factors Related to Physical Illness: Going to the Doctor

Survey: ❑
Read: ❑

Pages 535-539

How the patient and the physician communicate can influence the effectiveness of the diagnosis and medical treatment. Many patients are reluctant to tell their physicians their symptoms. The prestige and power of the physician intimidates many patients. On the other side, physicians have difficulties getting their patients to provide the proper information. The technical nature of their questions does not mesh with the personal nature of the individual's concerns. The reluctance can prevent the health-care giver from understanding the full nature of the problem, and often the patient sees the physician as all-knowing. Patients who do not understand their treatment cannot ask questions about it. Many patients do not know how long they should take their medication and many do not know the purpose of the drug. The use of professional jargon to communicate technical information does not help the patient understand the treatment. Sometimes medical practitioners use "baby talk" and talk down to the patient. The number of patients seen makes it difficult for many physicians to determine how much each patient can understand. Patients often construct their own theories about their illnesses that have little to do with reality. The problem can be dealt with by training patients to ask more direct questions. Physicians who are taught simple rules of courtesy, like saying hello, addressing the patient by name, and saying goodbye, are better perceived by their patients.

One major consequence of the difficulties in communication between the physician and the patient is the lack of compliance with medical advice. Noncompliance can include failing to meet appointments, not following diets, discontinuing medication, and other behaviors. Compliance is linked to the degree of satisfaction a patient has with the physician. Satisfied patients tend to comply better than dissatisfied patients. Patients with a positive view of the physicians may also have a greater sense of control, and they perceive themselves as in a kind of partnership rather than merely following advice. Physicians may themselves be motivated to keep the patient uninformed. Apparently, physicians avoid telling patients when they are terminally ill. On the other hand, almost every survey shows that people want to be informed about the details of their illnesses. Patients prefer to be well-informed, and their degree of satisfaction is linked to how well the physician is able to convey the nature of the illness. An increase in satisfaction tends to have a positive effect on recuperation.

▶ Now that you have surveyed, questioned, and read the chapter and completed the **Recap. and Review** questions, review **Looking Back**, page 540.

Review: ❑

▶ For additional practice through recitation and review, test your knowledge of the chapter material by answering the questions in the *Key Word Drill*, the *Practice Questions*, and the *Essay Questions*.

| **KEY WORD DRILL** | *Recite:* ☐ |

The following **Fill in the Blank** and **Matching Questions** test key words from the text. Check your answers with the Answer Key in the back of the *Study Guide*.

FILL IN THE BLANK

1. _____ _____ explores the relationship between physical and psychological factors.

2. The _____ _____ is composed of the body's natural defenses that fight disease.

3. _____ refers to our response to events that are threatening or challenging.

4. Medical problems caused by an interaction of psychological, emotional, and physical difficulties are

   usually called _____ _____ .

5. Many war veterans experience _____ _____ disorder, a phenomenon in which the victims of major catastrophes reexperience aspects of the original stress event through dreams and flashbacks.

6. _____ _____ involves the belief that one has no control over the environment.

7. People often use _____ _____ which are unconscious strategies that help to reduce anxiety by concealing its source from themselves and others.

8. In _____-_____ coping, an individual consciously regulates emotion in order to deal with stress.

9. Hans Selye's _____ _____ syndrome suggests that a person's response to stress consists of three stages: alarm and mobilization, resistance, and exhaustion.

10. Type _____ pattern behavior is characterized by competitiveness, impatience, a tendency toward frustration, and hostility.

MATCHING QUESTIONS

_____ 11. immune system

_____ 12. stressors

_____ 13. psychosomatic disorders

_____ 14. alarm and mobilization

_____ 15. resistance

_____ 16. exhaustion

a. Circumstances that produce threats to our well-being.

b. A person's initial awareness of the presence of a stressor.

c. The stage of failure to adapt to a stressor, leading to physical, psychological, and emotional problems.

d. The stage of coping with the stressor.

e. Medical problems caused by an interaction of psychological, emotional, and physical difficulties.

f. The body's natural defenses that fight disease.

_____ 17. cataclysmic events

_____ 18. personal stressors

_____ 19. background stressors

_____ 20. daily hassles

_____ 21. uplifts

a. The same as background stressors.

b. Strong stressors that occur suddenly, affecting many people at once (e.g., natural disasters).

c. Events, such as the death of a family member, that have immediate negative consequences which generally fade with time.

d. Minor positive events that make one feel good.

e. Events such as being stuck in traffic that cause minor irritations but have no long-term ill effects, unless they continue or are compounded by other stressful events.

_____ 22. learned helplessness

_____ 23. coping

_____ 24. defense mechanisms

_____ 25. social support

_____ 26. inoculation

a. Preparation for stress before it is encountered.

b. The efforts to control, reduce, or learn to tolerate the threats that lead to stress.

c. A learned belief that one has no control over the environment.

d. Unconscious strategies people use to reduce anxiety by concealing its source from themselves and others.

e. Knowledge of being part of a mutual network of caring, interested others.

_____ 27. emotion-focused coping

_____ 28. problem-focused coping

_____ 29. hardiness

_____ 30. Type A behavior pattern

_____ 31. Type B behavior pattern

a. The conscious regulation of emotion as a means of dealing with stress.

b. Characterized by noncompetitiveness, nonaggression, and patience in times of potential stress.

c. Characterized by competitiveness, impatience, a tendency toward frustration, and hostility.

d. Characterized by commitment, challenge, and control.

e. The management of a stressful stimulus as a way of dealing with stress.

PRACTICE QUESTIONS

Recite and Review: ☐

Test your knowledge of the chapter material by answering these **True-False** and **Multiple Choice Questions**. Check your answers with the Answer Key in the back of the _Study Guide._

TRUE-FALSE QUESTIONS

T   F   1. Stressors are circumstances that produce threats to our well-being, while stress is our response to stressors.

T   F   2. The resistance stage of Selye's general adaptation syndrome is characterized by the failure to adapt to a stressor that may then lead to serious physical and psychological problems.

T   F   3. Situations that are stressful are very similar for different people.

T   F   4. Even daily hassles usually require a lot of coping energy from people.

T   F   5. Research confirms that learned helplessness has negative consequences primarily for the elderly.

T   F   6. The result of loss of control and the ensuing stress is poorer health.

T   F   7. People who exhibit the personality characteristic of hardiness fail to exhibit a sense of control over their lives.

T   F   8. A person's attitudes can have an effect upon his or her recovery and chances for surviving cancer.

T   F   9. Patient-physician communication is, in many cases, very poor.

T   F   10. Compliance with a physician's advice guarantees that the patient's medical problems will go away.

MULTIPLE CHOICE QUESTIONS

1.   The system of organs and glands that forms the body's natural defense against disease is called:
     a.   the limbic system.   c.   the immune system.
     b.   the endocrine system.   d.   the sympathetic system.

2.   Health psychology has many objectives. Which alternative below is **not** one of them?
     a.   Health psychology is concerned with prevention of problems such as heart disease.
     b.   Health psychology considers how different illnesses are caused or influenced by psychological factors.
     c.   Health psychology considers how treatments for diseases can be based on psychological principles and findings.
     d.   Health psychology identifies new drugs and prescription medications that are better suited for treating health and stress-related disorders.

3.   The branch of psychology devoted to exploring psychological factors and principles in treatment, diagnosis, and prevention of physical illness is called:
     a.   health psychology.   c.   forensic psychology.
     b.   physiological psychology.   d.   organizational psychology.

4.   Which alternative about health psychology below is **not** correct?
     a.   Health psychology uses treatments such as prescription medications, surgery, and radiation therapy when indicated.
     b.   Health psychology is concerned with changing people's habits and lifestyles to help them prevent disease.
     c.   Health psychology recognizes that health is interwoven with psychological factors.
     d.   Health psychology recognizes that psychological factors may affect the immune system and have beneficial or detrimental effects upon health.

5.   A circumstance that produces threats to people's well-being is known as:
     a.   a stressor.   c.   a defense mechanism.
     b.   a mobilization state.   d.   an inoculation.

6.   Which of the following individuals developed the general adaptation syndrome model?
     a.   Martin Seligman   c.   B. F. Skinner
     b.   Hans Selye   d.   Sigmund Freud

7.   Which alternative below is **not** a stage of Selye's general adaptation syndrome?
     a.   resistance   c.   alarm and mobilization
     b.   challenge   d.   exhaustion

8.   Selye's model, the general adaptation syndrome, assumes that _____ occur regardless of the cause of the stress.
     a.   the same physiological reactions   c.   physical and psychological adaptations
     b.   stress-related illnesses   d.   the same psychological reactions

9.   The alarm and mobilization stage of Selye's general adaptation syndrome is characterized by:
     a.   preparing to react to the stressor.   c.   emotional and physical collapse.
     b.   increased resistance to disease.   d.   becoming aware of the presence of a stressor.

10. It was the end of the year, and Max realized that he had failed to reach his sales goals, so he set new goals for the following year. Max's behavior is typical for a person at the _____ stage of the general adaptation syndrome.
    a. resistance
    b. exhaustion
    c. alarm and mobilization
    d. repression

11. According to the general adaptation syndrome, the point at which the greatest negative consequences of stress appear is called the:
    a. resistance stage.
    b. acceptance stage.
    c. alarm and mobilization stage.
    d. exhaustion stage.

12. Which event below is likely to cause the greatest general adaptation syndrome (GAS) changes in most people?
    a. studying for an introductory psychology quiz
    b. meeting the author of your psychology text
    c. having a two-day bout with a common cold
    d. learning and adjusting to the fact that your mother has terminal cancer

13. Which event below is likely to produce the greatest changes in various bodily systems activated by the general adaptation syndrome?
    a. getting a first date with that "awesome" person in your English class
    b. learning you've just tested positive for HIV virus (AIDS)
    c. eating Sunday dinner with seconds for dessert
    d. going to your roommate's home next weekend to visit his or her parents

14. According to the text, events that are strong stressors and that occur suddenly and affect many people simultaneously are called:
    a. cataclysmic stressors.
    b. background stressors.
    c. uplifts.
    d. personal stressors.

15. Upon visiting the doctor's office and going through extensive testing, Michael finds out that he has a lung disease. Which type of stress is Michael likely to experience?
    a. cataclysmic stress
    b. personal stress
    c. posttraumatic stress
    d. background stress

16. Another term used to describe daily hassles such as a traffic jam, long lines, or a broken watch is:
    a. uplift.
    b. personal stressors.
    c. natural stressors.
    d. background stressors.

17. Whereas walking to work may be considered _____, walking in the woods may be considered _____.
    a. controlled activity; uncontrolled activity
    b. healthy; stressful
    c. personal stress; background stress
    d. a hassle; an uplift

18. Background stressors do not require much coping or response, but continued exposure to them may produce:
    a. an inability to use problem-focused techniques.
    b. as great a toll as a single, more stressful incident.
    c. as great a toll as a cataclysmic event.
    d. psychosomatic illness.

19. The textbook defines uplifts to be:
    a. minor irritations of life which are encountered daily.
    b. minor positive events that make a person feel good.
    c. exhilarating experiences which leave a person in a dazed state.
    d. major positive life events.

20. According to Seligman, _____ occurs when one concludes that unpleasant or annoying stimuli cannot be controlled.
    a. learned helplessness
    b. hysteria
    c. cataclysmic stress
    d. posttraumatic stress

21. The ability to tolerate, control, or reduce threatening events is called:
    a. defense.
    b. arousal.
    c. coping.
    d. adaptation.

22. According to the text, what are the two types of strategies people may use when consciously attempting to regulate a stressful situation?
    a. control-oriented or defensive coping strategies
    b. emotion-focused or problem-focused coping strategies
    c. emotional insulation or denial coping strategies
    d. conscious or unconscious coping strategies

23. Someone who is classified as hardy:
    a. is unable to cope with stress at all.
    b. is unlikely to develop stress-related disease.
    c. is unlikely to view stress as a challenge.
    d. is affected mostly by hard emotional choices.

24. Which of the following traits is characteristic of a Type B personality?
    a. relaxed
    b. aggressive
    c. scheduled
    d. competitive

25. Which personality type is best described by the following traits: achievement, competitiveness, and commitment to completing a task?
    a. Type B personality
    b. hardy personality
    c. helpless personality
    d. Type A personality

26. The type of individual who usually engages in polyphasic thinking is:
    a. combination Type A and Type B.
    b. Type A.
    c. Type B.
    d. Hardy personality.

27. Which personality type is most highly associated with heart disease, independent of other single factors?
    a. Type A
    b. Type B
    c. Hardy personality
    d. cataclysmic

28. During a physical at the University Medical Center, your father learns that he exhibits Type A behavior pattern. Which alternative below is correct?
    a. There is nothing that can be done to change your father's Type A behavioral pattern.
    b. Your father should remember that the relationship between the Type A behavior pattern and heart attacks or development of coronary heart disease is correlational.
    c. There is little hope for your father, since the Type A behavior pattern has been found to cause heart attacks or development of heart disease.
    d. Your father is fortunate, since women are at even greater risk with Type A behavior patterns.

29. According to the text, there is some evidence suggesting that, rather than focusing on Type A behavior as the cause of heart disease, a more effective approach should concentrate on:
    a. Type A behaviors that affect the immune system.
    b. Type B behaviors which appear critical in the prevention of heart disease.
    c. Type A behaviors which can be altered instead of eliminated.
    d. Type B behaviors that work with the immune system.

30. In a study that placed patients with advanced breast cancer either in psychotherapy or a control that did not receive psychotherapy, what were the results?
    a. The psychotherapy group felt better, and they lived longer.
    b. The psychotherapy group felt better, but there was no impact on their survival rate.
    c. The psychotherapy group became more depressed because of their increased awareness of the cancer, but they also lived longer.
    d. The study proved that psychotherapy increased the survival rate of cancer patients.

31. At what stage in the establishment of the smoking habit does smoking become part of the self-concept of the smoker?
    a. initiation
    b. becoming a smoker
    c. imitation
    d. preparation

32. According to the text, though about _____ of the smokers agree that smoking is bad for your health, only about _____ are able to achieve long-term successes in their efforts to stop smoking.
    a. 95 percent; 40 percent
    b. 80 percent; 30 percent
    c. 70 percent; 15 percent
    d. 30 percent; 15 percent

33. Rhonda, who is 35 years of age, has been smoking for 15 years. She knows it is extremely unhealthy for her and wants to stop but is having a difficult time doing so. What may prove to be the most effective means to help Rhonda to stop smoking?
    a. the "cold-turkey" method
    b. banning smoking in all public places
    c. behavior strategies which concentrate on changing the smoking response
    d. change societal norms and attitudes about smoking

34. Research indicates that the number of patients who cannot accurately report how long they are to continue taking a medication prescribed for them is:
    a. three-quarters of all patients.   c. about one-quarter of all patients.
    b. two-thirds of all patients.   d. about half of all patients.

35. According to the text, which alternative below is **not** a reason for communication difficulties between doctor and patient?
    a. Physicians may ask patients questions which are of a highly technical nature.
    b. Physicians have difficulty encouraging patients to give helpful information.
    c. Physicians sometimes simplify things too much and talk down to the patient.
    d. Patients have the primary responsibility in discussing their medical problems and they are often unskilled in initiating discussions about their problems.

36. Aunt Eunice, who is 77 years old, is in the hospital for minor surgery. However, since she is older, she realizes that even minor surgery can be risky. Her surgeon, apparently trying to calm her fears, says "We'll just pop right in there and sneak back out." The problem with his comments appears to be quite common in that:
    a. they treat Eunice as if she were either a child or senile.
    b. they don't go far enough in minimizing the risk factors.
    c. when spoken to in this manner, patients get an exaggerated sense of the surgeon's ability.
    d. they reflect techniques taught in medical school.

37. Which of the following might a physician do to enhance a physician-patient relationship?
    a. Be courteous and supportive toward the patient.
    b. Use very simplistic explanations.
    c. Explain diagnosis in professional jargon.
    d. Encourage the patient to construct a personal theory to account for the reported symptoms.

38. According to the text, which of the following is **not** a benefit when a patient has enhanced satisfaction with his or her physician?
    a. increased compliance with procedures and medications
    b. fewer respiratory infections
    c. reductions in anxiety
    d. better postoperative recovery

39. According to the text, the accuracy with which physicians present information about the nature of medical problems is related to:
    a. the degree of patient suffering.   c. the degree of patient discontent.
    b. the degree of patient anxiety.   d. the degree of patient satisfaction.

40. Which of the following is **not** likely to bring you the best possible health care?
    a. Choose physicians who communicate well.
    b. Ask questions until you fully understand your treatment.
    c. Accept some responsibility for your treatment.
    d. Do anything necessary to gain the attention of the health-care providers.

| ESSAY QUESTIONS | *Recite and Review:* ☐ |

Essay Question 16.1: *Stress and Its Effects*

Calculate the degree of stress in your life using Table 16-1. Interpret the results using the scoring information at the bottom of the table. What does this say about the cause of illness and the role of stress in your health?

_____

_____

_____

_____

_____

_____

_____

_____

_____

_____

_____

_____

_____

_____

_____

_____

_____

Essay Question 16.2: *Smoking Bans*

Smoking is a serious habit with both psychological and physiological addictions involved. Should smoking be banned in public places? Discuss the problems posed by such a ban and the benefits that should be expected by enforcing it.

_____

_____

_____

_____

_____

_____

_____

_____

_____

_____

_____

_____

_____

_____

_____

_____

_____

_____

_____

CHAPTER
17
ABNORMAL BEHAVIOR

Somatoform disorders: When the psychological leads to the physical
Dissociative disorders
● **Recap and Review III**

Mood disorders: The feeling is wrong
    Major depression
    Mania and bipolar disorders: Ups and downs
    Causes of mood disorders
Schizophrenia: When reality is lost
    Solving the puzzle of schizophrenia
        Biological components
        Psychological components
    The multiple causes of schizophrenia
Personality disorders: Lacking distress
Beyond the major disorders
Psychology at Work DSM and Culture—and the Culture of *DSM*
The Informed Consumer of Psychology Deciding When You Need Help
● **Recap and Review IV**

Looking Back
Key Terms and Concepts

➤ Now that you have surveyed the chapter, read **Looking Ahead**, page 545.   *Question:* ☐
Focus on the questions on page 545.   *Read:* ☐

CONCEPTS AND LEARNING OBJECTIVES

Survey: ☐

These are the concepts and the learning objects for Chapter 17. Read them carefully as part of your preliminary survey of the chapter.

Concept 1: Abnormality is difficult to define, and it is best to consider behavior as on a continuum from normal to abnormal. Disorders are common in America, with as much as 20 percent of the population suffering some kind of abnormality.

  1. Define abnormal behavior and discuss the prevalence of mental disorders. (pp. 544-549)

Concept 2: The contemporary models that attempt to explain abnormal behavior are the medical model, the psychoanalytic model, the behavioral model, the cognitive model, the humanistic model, and the sociocultural model.

  2. Describe and distinguish the models of abnormality presented in the text, including the medical model, the psychoanalytic model, the behavioral model, the cognitive model, the humanistic model, and the sociocultural model. (pp. 550-555)

  3. Apply the models of abnormal behavior to specific instances. (pp. 555-556)

Concept 3: The *DSM-III-R* is the system used by most professionals to classify mental disorders. Anxiety disorders, somatoform disorders, and conversion disorders are three major classes of disorders.

4. Describe the classification system, the *DSM-III-R*, used in the diagnosis and description of mental disorders. (pp. 557-560)

5. Describe the anxiety disorders and their causes. (pp. 560-564)

6. Describe the somatoform disorders and their causes. (pp. 564-566)

7. Describe the dissociative disorders and their causes. (pp. 566-567)

Concept 4: Mood disorders, schizophrenia, and personality disorders are three major disorders in the *DSM-III-R*.

8. Describe the mood disorders and their causes. (pp. 568-571)

9. Describe the types of schizophrenia, its main symptoms, and the theories that account for its causes. (pp. 571-577)

10. Describe the personality disorders and their causes. (pp. 577-579)

11. Discuss the other forms of abnormal behavior described in the *DSM-III-R* and issues related to seeking help. (pp. 579-581)

CHAPTER SUMMARY

There are several ways you can use this summary as part of your systematic study plan. You may read each concept summary and then read the corresponding pages in the text, or you may read the entire summary and then read the entire chapter in the text. As you finish each section, complete the **Recap and Review** questions that are supplied in the text.

Concept 1: Prologue and Looking Ahead   *Survey:* ☐
           Normal Versus Abnormal: Making the Distinction   *Read:* ☐

Pages 544-550

The Prologue illustrates that the development of mental illness can progress over years. The concerns that psychologists have about people like Judy Smith include concerns about why she would live on the street, whether early intervention would have helped, and others. Her case also shows the difficulty in distinguishing normal from abnormal behavior.

A passage from James Joyce's *Ulysses* suggests that madness cannot be determined by a small sample of a person's behavior. The text examines four approaches to the definition of abnormal behavior. They are: (1) *Deviation from the average*. This definition uses the statistical definition of behavior to define "abnormal" as behavior that is statistically unusual or rare. The problem with this approach is that simply being unusual or rare does not define abnormal: individuals with high IQs are rare, but they are not considered abnormal. (2) *Deviation from the ideal.* This definition classifies behavior as abnormal if it deviates from the ideal or standard behavior. However, society has very few standards on which everyone agrees. (3) *Abnormality as a sense of subjective discomfort.* This approach focuses on the consequences of behavior that make a person experience discomfort. However, some people who engage in what others would consider abnormal do not experience discomfort. (4) *Abnormality as the inability to function effectively.* People who are unable to adjust to the demands of society and unable to function in daily life are considered abnormal in this view. Judy Smith would be classified as abnormal in this view even if the choice to live on the streets was her own.

None of the four approaches is broad enough to include all possibilities of abnormal behavior, and the line between normal and abnormal remains unclear. The best way to solve the problem is to consider normal and abnormal as on a continuum, or scale, of behavior rather than to consider them to be absolute states. The point at which society should intervene is also ambiguous. The criteria for intervention in most states require that a person be: (1) dangerous to self, (2) incapable of providing for basic needs, (3) unable to make reasonable decisions about treatment, (4) in need of treatment. *The Cutting Edge* takes up the issue of homelessness and abnormal behavior, and the complexities of intervention.

Determining the number of people with signs of abnormal behavior is a difficult task. A survey of 18,000 Americans found that 20 percent currently had a mental disorder and a total of one-third had experienced a disorder at some time in their lives. Projecting these figures onto the entire population suggests that 29 million people have one or more mental disorders, with 13 million taking a drug to treat anxiety, 10 million abusing alcohol or some other drug, and 11 million having irrational fears. Only about one in five ask for help. Other surveys suggest that 20 percent of the children have a developmental, emotional, or learning problem.

CONCEPT 2: Models of Abnormality: From Superstition to Science

Survey: ☐
Read: ☐

Pages 550-557

In the past, abnormal behavior has been attributed to the bite of a tarantula, to witchcraft, or to demonic possession. The contemporary approach includes six major perspectives on abnormal behavior:

- The **medical model of abnormality** views the cause of abnormal behavior to have a physical origin such as a hormone or chemical imbalance or a physical injury. Many abnormal behaviors have been linked to physical causes, though this view has been criticized because there are many instances in which no physical cause is known.

- The **psychoanalytic model of abnormality** maintains that abnormal behavior comes from childhood. The conflicts of childhood that remain unresolved can cause abnormal behavior in adulthood. One problem with this approach is the difficulty of linking childhood problems with adult behaviors. On the other hand, this approach does suggest that individuals have a rich inner life and that prior experiences do have a profound effect on the present.

- The **behavioral model of abnormality** views the behavior itself as the problem, understanding that behavior is a response to stimuli that one finds in one's environment. In order to understand the behavior one must examine the circumstances in which it occurs. The strength of this approach is its emphasis on the present and on dealing with the observable problems.

- The **cognitive model of abnormality** assumes that **cognitions** are central to a person's abnormal behavior which can then be changed by learning new cognitions. This model is derived from the behavioral model and sometimes called the **cognitive behavioral approach**.

- The **humanistic model of abnormality** emphasizes the control and responsibility people have for their own behavior. This model considers people to be basically rational, oriented to the social world, and motivated to get along with others. Abnormal behaviors are signs of the person's inability to fulfill basic human needs. This model has been criticized for its reliance on unscientific and unverifiable information.

- The **sociocultural model of abnormality** assumes that behavior is shaped by the family group, society, and culture. The stresses and conflicts people experience promote and maintain abnormal behavior. An extreme position suggests that there is no abnormal behavior and that, instead, society is intolerant of deviant behavior. The evidence for the view comes from the link between sociocultural factors and abnormal behavior.

These models can be applied to the case of Judy Smith. A proponent of the medical model would want to have her examined for physical problems. A psychoanalyst would seek to find out about her past. A behavioral theorist would concentrate on the rewards and punishments she received for behaving as she does. Proponents of the cognitive model would focus on her cognitions about the world and try to understand how she developed her misguided cognitions. The humanistic and sociocultural approaches would concentrate on her view of herself in relation to others. The humanistic theorist would suggest that she has made a series of choices about how to live, and the sociocultural theorist would focus on how society has contributed to her problems. Any single approach may be inadequate in dealing with her problems.

One phenomenon that may afflict psychology students is the **medical student's disease**. Often, as medical students learn about a disease or symptom, they begin to believe that they are experiencing the symptom. Psychology students are also likely to interpret their behaviors as reflecting one of the abnormal conditions.

CONCEPT 3: Classifying Abnormal Behavior: The ABCs of DSM The Major Disorders

Survey: ☐
Read: ☐

Pages 557-568

One standard classification system has been accepted by most professionals for classifying mental disorders. Devised by the American Psychiatric Association, the system is known as the ***Diagnostic and Statistical Manual of Mental Disorders***, **Third Edition—Revised (*DSM-III-R*)**. The manual has more than 230 diagnostic categories. It evaluates behavior according to five dimensions called axes. The first three axes address the maladaptive behaviors exhibited, the nature of any personality disorders or developmental problems, and any physical disorders. The fourth and fifth axes address the severity of stressors and the general level of functioning. The *DSM-III-R* attempts to be descriptive and to avoid suggestions of cause. The objective is to provide precise description and classification. The manual is also revised periodically, and the *DSM-IV* is expected in the mid-1990s. Criticisms include the fact that it reflects categories that assume a physiological view of causes (arising from the fact that it was developed by physicians) and that the categories are inflexible. In other views, the labeling of an individual as deviant is seen as a lifelong, dehumanizing stigma. Often, the diagnosis is seen as the explanation of the problem. A classic study by Rosenhan illustrated how the stigma of being labeled mentally ill can linger. Eight people, including Rosenhan, presented themselves to mental hospitals complaining of only one symptom, hearing voices.

Though they did not complain of the symptom again, they stayed for an average of nineteen days and were released with labels like "schizophrenia in remission." None of the impostors was detected by the staff. Despite its drawbacks, the *DSM-III-R* does provide a reliable and valid way to classify psychological disorders.

Everyone experiences **anxiety**, a feeling of apprehension or tension, at some time. When anxiety occurs without external reason and interferes with daily functioning, the problem is known as **anxiety disorder**. The types of anxiety disorder are:

- **Generalized anxiety disorder** refers to the disorder in which an individual experiences long-term consistent anxiety without knowing why. The anxiety makes the person unable to concentrate, and life becomes centered on the anxiety.
- **Panic disorder** is distinguished by panic attacks that may last a few seconds or several hours. In a panic attack, the individual feels anxiety rise to a peak and gets a sense of impending doom. Physical symptoms of increased heart rate, shortness of breath, sweating, faintness, and dizziness may be experienced.
- **Phobic disorder** has as its primary symptom a **phobia**, an irrational fear of specific objects or situations. Exposure to the stimulus may cause a full-blown panic attack. (A list of common phobias is given in Table 17-2.) Phobias may be minor, or they may cause extreme suffering.
- **Obsessive-compulsive disorder** is characterized by unwanted thoughts and the impulse to carry out a certain action. **Obsessions** are thoughts or ideas that keep recurring. Though everyone has some obsessions, when they continue for days and months and include bizarre images, they make it difficult for the individual to function. **Compulsions** are urges to repeat behaviors that seem strange and unreasonable even to the person who feels compelled to act. If they cannot carry out the action, extreme anxiety can be experienced. The cleaning ritual described in the text is a good example of a compulsion. Carrying out the action usually does not reduce the anxiety.

The causes of anxiety disorders are not fully understood. A tendency for both identical twins to have an anxiety disorder if one of them has the disorder suggests that there may be a biological cause. Some chemical deficiencies in the brain have also been linked to the disorder. The behavioral approach suggests that anxiety is a learned response to stress and that the anxiety is reinforced by subsequent encounters with the stressor. The cognitive approach suggests that anxiety grows out of inappropriate and inaccurate cognitions.

Hypochondriasis involves a constant fear of illness, and physical sensations are misinterpreted as disease symptoms. The symptoms are not faked, hypochondriacs actually experience the symptoms. Hypochondriasis belongs to a class of disease known as **somatoform disorders**, which are psychological difficulties that take physical form. There are no underlying physical problems to account for the symptoms, or if there does exist a physical problem, the person's reaction exaggerates it. A major somatoform disorder is **conversion disorder**, a disorder in which actual physical symptoms are caused by psychological problems. Conversion disorders usually have a rapid onset; a person may awaken one morning totally blind or with a numb hand (called "glove anesthesia"). One characteristic is that individuals with conversion disorders seem relatively unconcerned with the symptoms. Conversion disorders have occurred on a large scale. One example is the inexplicable symptoms experienced by student aviators who, rather than quit, developed problems that would otherwise require them to quit, thus allowing a face-saving way to leave the program. Generally, conversion disorders occur when an emotional stress can be reduced by having a physical symptom.

Dissociative disorders have been the most dramatized, including the multiple personality stories of *The Three Faces of Eve* and *Sybil*. The central factor is the dissociation, or splitting apart, of critical parts of the personality. The three major dissociative disorders are:

- **Multiple personality** occurs when two or more distinct personalities are present in the same individual. Each personality is a separate person with desires and reactions to situations. Even vision can change when the personality changes. Since they reside in only one body, they must take turns, causing what appears to be quite inconsistent behavior.
- **Psychogenic amnesia** is a failure or inability to remember past experiences. In psychogenic amnesia, information has not been forgotten; it simply cannot be recalled. In some cases memory loss can be quite total, as illustrated in the case of Jane Doe, who had to go on television to have her identity discovered.
- **Psychogenic fugue** is a state in which people take an impulsive, sudden trip and assume a new identity. After a period of time, they realize that they are in a strange place. They often do not recall what they did while wandering.

CONCEPT 4: The Major Disorders (Continued)

Survey: ☐
Read: ☐

Pages 568-581

Changes in mood are a part of everyday life. However, mood changes can be extreme enough to cause life-threatening problems and to cause an individual to lose touch with reality. These situations result from **mood disorders**, disturbances in mood severe enough to interfere with daily life. **Major depression** is one of the more common mood disorders. As many as 14 million people are experiencing major depression at any time. Twice as many women as men experience major depression, and one in four females will encounter it at some time. Depression is not merely sadness, but involves feelings of uselessness, worthlessness, loneliness, and despair. Major depression is distinguished by the severity of the symptoms.

Mania refers to an extended state of intense euphoria and elation. Also, people experience a sense of happiness, power, invulnerability, and energy. They may be involved with wild schemes. When mania is paired with bouts of depression, it is called a **bipolar disorder**. The swings between highs and lows can occur every several days or can be over a period of years. Typically, the depression lasts longer than the mania.

The psychoanalytic view holds that depression is anger at oneself. Major depression and bipolar disorder may have a biological cause, and heredity may play a role in bipolar disorder. The cognitive approach draws on the experience of **learned helplessness**, a state in which people perceive that they cannot escape from or cope with stress. According to this view, depression is a response brought on by helplessness. Aaron Beck has suggested that depression involves faulty cognitions held by the sufferers about themselves. Theories about the cause of depression have not explained why twice as many women get it as men. One theory suggests that the stress for women is higher at certain times of life. Women are also more subject to physical and sexual abuse, earn less money than men, and report greater unhappiness with marriage.

Schizophrenia refers to the class of disorders in which severe distortion of reality occurs. Thinking, perception, and emotion deteriorate; there is a withdrawal from social interaction; and there may be bizarre behavior. (Classes of schizophrenia are listed in Table 17-4.) The characteristics of schizophrenia include:

- A decline from a previous level of functioning.
- Disturbances of thought and language in which logic is peculiar, thoughts do not make sense, and linguistic rules are not followed.

- **Delusions** are unshakable beliefs that have no basis in reality, involving thoughts of control by others, persecution, or the belief that thoughts are being broadcast to others.
- Perceptual disorders occur in which schizophrenics do not perceive the world as everyone else does, and they may have **hallucinations**, the experience of perceiving things that do not actually exist.
- Emotional disturbances include a lack of emotion or highly inappropriate emotional responses.
- Schizophrenics tend to withdraw from contact with others.

The symptoms follow two courses: **process schizophrenia** develops symptoms early in life, with a gradual withdrawal from the world; and **reactive schizophrenia**, which has a sudden and conspicuous onset of symptoms. Reactive schizophrenia responds well to treatment; process schizophrenia is more difficult to treat. Another distinction has been drawn between positive-symptom and negative-symptom schizophrenia. Negative symptom refers to symptoms like withdrawal or loss of ability to function, and positive symptom refers to disordered behavior like hallucinations, delusions, and extremes of emotionality.

Schizophrenia is recognized to have both biological and psychological components at its root. The biological components are suggested by the fact that schizophrenia is more common in some families than others. This suggests a genetic link to the disease. Another biological explanation suggests the presence of a chemical imbalance or a structural defect. The **dopamine hypothesis** suggests that schizophrenia occurs when there is an excess activity in the areas of the brain that use dopamine to transmit signals across nerve cells. Drugs that block dopamine action are effective in reducing symptoms. These drugs take effect immediately, but the symptoms linger for several weeks, suggesting that there must be other factors at work. Structural differences in the brains of schizophrenics have also been found.

Psychological factors include the immediate environment of the schizophrenic person. Psychoanalysis suggests that schizophrenia is a form of regression to earlier stages. The families of schizophrenics display abnormal communication patterns. The faulty communication patterns support the behavioral view of the **learned-inattention theory of schizophrenia**. According to this view, schizophrenia is a learned set of responses to social stimuli. Schizophrenics have learned to ignore the appropriate stimuli. Others then respond to them in a negative way, reinforcing the behavior until the person tunes out completely.

The predominant approach to explaining schizophrenia that combines both biological and psychological factors is the **predisposition model of schizophrenia**. This model says that individuals inherit a predisposition to schizophrenia that makes them vulnerable to stress, and the effect of the stressors occurs when they are coupled with the genetic predisposition.

Personality disorders are characterized by inflexible, maladaptive personality traits. People with personality disorders tend not to be distressed by them. The best known personality disorder is the **antisocial or sociopathic personality disorder**. People with this disorder have no regard for moral or ethical rules or for the rights of others. The characteristics of the disorder include: a lack of conscience, guilt, or anxiety over transgressions, impulsive behavior and inability to withstand frustration, and manipulation of others. Explanations include a neglecting or rejecting family, coming from a social group where the societal rules have broken down, and severe socioeconomic deprivation. The **narcissistic personality disorder** is characterized by an exaggerated sense of self-importance in which the person with the disorder expects special treatment and disregards the feelings of others.

Other forms of abnormal behavior described by the *DSM-III-R* include **psychoactive substance-use disorder**, **sexual disorders**, and **organic mental disorders**. The *Psychology at Work* section discusses the differences between cultures in the nature of abnormal behavior.

The decision concerning if and when to seek help for psychological disorders is difficult, but several guidelines should help. If the following signals are present, help should be considered: long-term feelings of distress that interfere with functioning, occasions when stress is overwhelming, prolonged depression, withdrawal from others, chronic physical problems, a fear or phobia that prevents normal functioning, feelings that other people are talking about the person or are out to get the person, or the inability to interact effectively with others.

➤ Now that you have surveyed, questioned, and read the chapter and completed the **Recap and Review** questions, review **Looking Back**, pages 582–583.   *Review:* ☐

➤ For additional practice through recitation and review, test your knowledge of the chapter material by answering the questions in the ***Key Word Drill***, the ***Practice Questions***, and the ***Essay Questions***.

KEY WORD DRILL   *Recite:* ☐

The following **Fill in the Blank** and **Matching Questions** test key words from the text. Check your answers with the Answer Key in the back of the *Study Guide*.

FILL IN THE BLANK

1. The approach that focuses on unlearning faulty cognitions about the world is called the

    _____-_____ approach.

2. The feeling that symptoms and illnesses one studies are characteristic of oneself has been named the

    _____ _____ disease.

3. The abbreviation ____ ____ ____-____-____ refers to the manual that presents comprehensive diagnostic categories for identifying problems and behaviors.

4. _____ disorder refers to the occurrence of feelings of apprehension and fear without obvious external cause that may hinder normal function.

5. _____ are thoughts or ideas that keep recurring, and the term

    _____ refers to the urge to carry out an act repeatedly that even the sufferer realizes is unreasonable.

6. Intense, irrational fears of specific objects or situations are called _____.

7. People who suffer from _____ experience severe distortions of reality that may lead to antisocial behavior, silly or obscene behavior, hallucinations, and disturbances in movement.

8. _____ are firmly held beliefs with no basis in reality.

9. _____ are perceptions of things that do not actually exist.

10. The severe form of depression that interferes with concentration, decision making, and sociability is

    called _____ depression.

MATCHING QUESTIONS

_____ 11. medical model

_____ 12. psychoanalytic model

_____ 13. behavioral model

_____ 14. cognitive model

_____ 15. humanistic model

_____ 16. sociocultural model

a. Suggests that abnormality stems from childhood conflicts over opposing desires regarding sex and aggression.

b. Suggests that people's behavior, both normal and abnormal, is shaped by family, society, and cultural influences.

c. Suggests that people's thoughts and beliefs are a central component to abnormal behavior.

d. Suggests that when an individual displays symptoms of abnormal behavior, the cause is physiological.

e. Suggests that abnormal behavior itself is the problem to be treated, rather than viewing behavior as a symptom of some underlying medical or psychological problem.

f. Suggests that abnormal behavior results from an inability to fulfill human needs and capabilities.

_____ 17. generalized anxiety disorder

_____ 18. panic disorder

_____ 19. panic attack

_____ 20. phobic disorder

_____ 21. dissociative disorder

a. Characterized by the splitting apart of critical personality facets that are normally integrated.

b. Sudden anxiety characterized by heart palpitations, shortness of breath, sweating, faintness, and great fear.

c. The experience of long-term anxiety with no explanation.

d. Characterized by unrealistic fears that may keep people from carrying out routine daily behaviors.

e. Anxiety that manifests itself in the form of panic attacks.

_____ 22. hypochondriasis

_____ 23. somatoform disorder

_____ 24. conversion disorder

_____ 25. multiple personality

_____ 26. psychogenic amnesia

_____ 27. psychogenic fugue

a. Characterized by actual physical disturbances.

b. A condition in which people take sudden, impulsive trips, sometimes assuming a new identity.

c. Characteristics of two or more distinct personalities.

d. A misinterpretation of normal aches and pains.

e. Psychological difficulties that take on physical form.

f. A failure to remember past experience.

_____ 28. anxiety

_____ 29. mood disorder

_____ 30. mania

_____ 31. bipolar disorder

_____ 32. learned helplessness

a. A disorder in which a person alternates between euphoric feelings of mania and bouts of depression.

b. Affective disturbance severe enough to interfere with normal living.

c. A state in which people give up fighting stress, believing it to be inescapable, leading to depression.

d. An extended state of intense euphoria and elation.

e. A feeling of apprehension or tension.

_____ 33. process schizophrenia

_____ 34. reactive schizophrenia

_____ 35. dopamine hypothesis

_____ 36. learned-inattention theory of schizophrenia

_____ 37. predisposition model of schizophrenia

a. Suggests that individuals may inherit tendencies that make them particularly vulnerable to stressful factors in the environment.

b. Suggests that schizophrenia is a learned behavior consisting of a set of inappropriate responses to social stimuli.

c. Onset of symptoms is sudden and conspicuous.

d. Symptoms begin early in life and develop slowly.

e. Suggests that schizophrenia occurs when there is excess activity in certain areas of the brain.

_____ 38. personality disorder

_____ 39. antisocial or sociopathic personality disorder

_____ 40. narcissistic personality disorder

_____ 41. psychoactive substance-use disorder

_____ 42. sexual disorders

_____ 43. organic mental disorders

a. Characterized by a set of inflexible, maladaptive traits that keep a person from functioning properly in society.

b. A form of abnormal behavior in which one's sexual activity is unsatisfactory.

c. Disordered behavior involving drug abuse.

d. Problems having a purely biological basis.

e. Characterized by an exaggerated sense of self and an inability to experience empathy for others.

f. Individuals display no regard for moral and ethical rules or for the rights of others.

| PRACTICE QUESTIONS | *Recite and Review:* ☐ |

Test your knowledge of the chapter material by answering these **True-False** and **Multiple Choice Questions**. Check your answers with the Answer Key in the back of the *Study Guide*.

TRUE-FALSE QUESTIONS

T   F   1. Many behaviors discouraged by religious groups, like premarital sex, are considered abnormal because they deviate from an average.

T   F   2. Normal and abnormal behavior are best thought of conceptually as being on the separate ends of a continuum, rather than in distinct categories.

T   F   3. Abnormal behavior is a definite symptom of an underlying problem, according to the behavioral model of abnormality.

T   F   4. The psychoanalytic theory of abnormality has difficulty proving that a person's childhood experiences are related to his or her subsequent abnormal behavior.

T   F   5. *The Diagnostic and Statistical Manual of Mental Disorders*, 3rd Edition, Revised (*DSM-III-R*) was written by clinical psychologists.

T   F   6. The *DSM-III-R* is used primarily as a guide to treat mental disorders.

T   F   7. What all dissociative disorders have in common is that they allow people to escape from some anxiety-producing situation.

T   F   8. Today cases of multiple personality are about as common as cases of bipolar disorder.

T   F   9. Major depression is more common in men than in women.

T   F   10. The classification of undifferentiated schizophrenia is given to patients who cannot be typed into any of the other categories.

MULTIPLE CHOICE QUESTIONS

1. The prologue about Judy Smith in the chapter on abnormal psychology illustrates that:
   a. new programs are helping rehabilitate "street people" who have mental disorders.
   b. women living in the street are subjected to many more hardships than male "street people."
   c. individuals with a behavioral disorder are not always aware of their own abnormal behavior.
   d. when people are denied medication for their mental disorders, they are likely to have serious relapses.

2. Which of the following is **not** an approach to defining abnormality?
   a. the sense of subjective discomfort
   b. behavior that deviates from religious values
   c. inability to function effectively
   d. behavior that deviates from an ideal standard

3. In most states, which one of the following is **not** a criterion for abnormality?
   a. The person requires treatment.
   b. The person is dangerous to himself.
   c. The person suffers subjective discomfort.
   d. The person is not capable of providing for basic physical needs.

4. All of the following are required in order for society to intervene legally and provide mental health treatment **except**:
   a. The person must be dangerous to himself or herself.
   b. The person must be chemically dependent.
   c. The person must be incapable of providing for basic needs.
   d. The person must require treatment.

5. According to community surveys, approximately what percentage of American adults suffer from a mental disorder?
   a. 5   c. 20
   b. 10   d. 30

6. If someone's abnormal behavior is related to an endocrine system malfunction, their problem best fits the:
   a. medical model of abnormality.   c. behavioral model of abnormality.
   b. psychoanalytic model of abnormality. d. sociocultural model of abnormality.

7. Which of the following models of abnormality is likely to hold most strongly to the concept that the patient has little control over his or her actions?
   a. the medical model   c. the behavioral model
   b. the sociocultural model   d. the humanistic model

8. The _____ model of abnormality suggests that when an individual displays the symptoms of abnormal behavior, the diagnosed causes are physiological.
   a. humanistic   c. psychoanalytic
   b. medical   d. sociocultural

9. The psychoanalytic model of abnormality suggests that abnormal behavior derives from:
   a. failure to develop logical thought processes.
   b. physiological malfunctions.
   c. unresolved childhood conflicts.
   d. confusion in the collective unconscious.

10. Which of the following models of abnormality most emphasizes factors such as sex and aggression as being causes of abnormal behavior?
    a. the medical model   c. the behavioral model
    b. the psychoanalytic model   d. the humanistic model

11. According to the text, which of the following models of abnormality has recently been broadened to include cognitive learning factors?
    a. the medical model
    b. the psychoanalytic model
    c. the behavioral model
    d. the humanistic model

12. Which of the following models of abnormality is most likely to emphasize the patient's responsibility and participation in the treatment?
    a. the medical model
    b. the psychoanalytic model
    c. the behavioral model
    d. the humanistic model

13. Which of the following models of abnormality is least likely to see the therapist as the expert who cures the patient?
    a. the behavioral model
    b. the humanistic model
    c. the medical model
    d. the psychoanalytic model

14. Which statement below is **not** consistent with the sociocultural model of abnormality?
    a. Behavior is shaped by our family, by society, and by the culture in which we live.
    b. There is something wrong with a society that is unwilling to tolerate deviant behavior.
    c. Competing psychic forces within the troubled individual erode personal standards and values.
    d. Abnormal behaviors are more prevalent among some social classes than others.

15. "The kinds of stresses and conflicts that people experience in their daily interactions with others can promote and maintain abnormal behavior." This statement is consistent with the _____ model of abnormality.
    a. sociocultural
    b. behavioral
    c. humanistic
    d. psychoanalytic

16. According to the text, proponents of which model are most likely to take the position that there is no such thing as abnormal behavior?
    a. the sociocultural model
    b. the psychoanalytic model
    c. the behavioral model
    d. the medical model

17. Many people with psychological disorders come from broken homes and low-income backgrounds. To understand the effects of these and similar conditions on abnormal behavior, a comprehensive diagnosis must include insights from the:
    a. behavioral model.
    b. psychoanalytic model.
    c. humanistic model.
    d. sociocultural model.

18. Deciding that you suffer from the same sorts of problems you read about is called the:
    a. medical student's disease.
    b. halo effect.
    c. self-fulfilling prophecy.
    d. self-delusional approach.

19. The purpose of the *DSM-III-R* is to:
    a. diagnose physical disorders.
    b. provide a description of an individual's disorder.
    c. define the treatments for particular types of disorders.
    d. reveal the cause of behavior disorders.

20. In the *DSM-III-R* there are approximately _____ different diagnostic categories.
    a. 50   c. 200
    b. 100   d. 500

21. Which of the following pieces of information is **not** included in the *DSM-III-R*?
    a. classification   c. prognosis
    b. description   d. cause

22. Which classification would be found in the *DSM-III-R*?
    a. neurosis   c. psychosis
    b. mood disorders   d. insanity

23. According to the text, which of the following is **not** a reasonable criticism of the *DSM-III-R*?
    a. Mental disorders are classified into a "category" rather than along a continuum.
    b. The *DSM-III-R* materials usually do not reflect changing views in society about mental disorders, since the manual is updated only every fifteen years.
    c. The *DSM-III-R*'s system of classification may be too heavily influenced by the medical model.
    d. A diagnosis may become an explanation for a problem.

24. The term used to describe nervousness and fear that has no apparent justification and impairs normal daily functioning is:
    a. psychosomatic disorder.   c. anxiety disorder.
    b. personality disorder.   d. neurotic disorder.

25. When someone experiences long-term chronic worry without knowing why, the diagnosis is usually:
    a. generalized anxiety disorder.   c. panic attack.
    b. insomnia.   d. microphobia.

26. Feelings of impending doom or even death paired with sudden and overwhelming bodily reactions are typical symptoms of:
    a. obsessive-compulsive disorder. c. personality disorder.
    b. panic attack.   d. generalized anxiety disorder.

27. Sue was having a disagreement with her fiance when she suddenly became extremely anxious and felt a sense of impending, unavoidable doom. Her heart beat rapidly, she was short of breath, became faint and dizzy, and felt as if she might die. Sue was experiencing:
    a. phobic disorder.   c. generalized anxiety disorder.
    b. panic disorder.   d. obsessive-compulsive disorder.

28. The psychiatrist listened patiently as his client revealed a series of episodes involving irrational fears of water. The psychiatrist probably labeled the client's symptoms as:
    a. schizophrenic reactions.   c. organic reactions.
    b. phobic reactions.   d. obsessive-compulsive reactions.

29. Sarah is terrified to ride in an elevator in any building. She is especially bothered by the small, confined space and the fact that she is "trapped" until the elevator doors open. Usually, she avoids this unpleasantness by refusing to ride in elevators. Sarah is experiencing:
    a. phobic disorder.   c. obsessive-compulsive disorder.
    b. panic disorder.   d. tension disorder.

30. Sandra has been having a difficult time at college, since she has been very tense and anxious during her professors' lectures. She has been much better lately because she distracts herself by counting the number of times her professors say "the" during their lectures. Sandra's "counting" suggests she is experiencing:
    a. panic disorder
    b. phobic disorder.
    c. obsessive-compulsive disorder.
    d. generalized anxiety disorder.

31. Psychological difficulties that take on a physical form but have no actual physical or physiological abnormality are called:
    a. somatoform disorders.
    b. psychological disorders.
    c. psychophysical disorders.
    d. freeform disorders.

32. The lead singer for a heavy metal group finds that, two or three hours before an important concert, he cannot talk or sing. The group's doctor cannot find any medical reason for the singer's problem. The doctor is also surprised that the singer seems unconcerned. If the singer's symptoms are the result of a psychological disorder, it would most likely be diagnosed as:
    a. somatoform disorder.
    b. conversion disorder.
    c. panic disorder.
    d. obsessive-compulsive disorder.

33. A woman seeks treatment for her behavioral disorder. A clinical psychologist evaluates her and tells her that she has multiple personalities. This woman is experiencing:
    a. schizophrenic disorder.
    b. conversion disorder.
    c. dissociative disorder.
    d. somatoform disorder.

34. The main character in the book *Sybil* suffered from:
    a. schizophrenia.
    b. psychogenic personality.
    c. disordered personality.
    d. multiple personality.

35. Together, multiple personality, amnesia, and psychogenic fugue are called:
    a. depressive disorders.
    b. schizophrenic disorders.
    c. somatoform disorders.
    d. dissociative disorders.

36. Unable to account for the past three weeks, Portland native Tony X could recall memories prior to his amnesia, but could not relate how he arrived in Tucson. The above description exemplifies:
    a. multiple personality.
    b. psychogenic fugue.
    c. hypochondriasis.
    d. panic attack.

37. What is one difference between psychogenic fugue and psychogenic amnesia?
    a. In fugue, memory can be restored with drugs.
    b. In amnesia, the memory loss is temporary.
    c. In fugue, past memory is eventually regained.
    d. In amnesia, the memories are physically lost.

38. The most common problem experienced in outpatient clinics is:
    a. depression.
    b. anxiety disorders.
    c. personality disorders.
    d. dissociative disorders.

39. A bipolar disorder is one in which an individual has:
    a. opposing phobias.
    b. alternation of mania and depression.
    c. a split personality.
    d. alternation of phobia and panic.

40. According to the text, which mental disorder below is generally the most severe and debilitating to the afflicted person?
    a. panic disorder
    b. hypochondriasis
    c. schizophrenic disorder
    d. obsessive-compulsive disorder

41. According to the text, the most overwhelming characteristic of schizophrenia is:
    a. loss of touch with reality.
    b. split personality.
    c. severe mood swings.
    d. repetitive ritualistic behavior.

42. When minor symptoms of schizophrenia follow a severe case or episode, the disorder is called:
    a. disorganized schizophrenia.
    b. catatonic schizophrenia.
    c. paranoid schizophrenia.
    d. residual schizophrenia.

43. Which mental disturbance below is most likely to result in the afflicted person's using language in ways that do **not** follow conventional linguistic rules?
    a. schizophrenia
    b. multiple personality
    c. psychogenic fugue
    d. depressive disorder

44. According to your text, process schizophrenia is different from reactive schizophrenia, because with reactive schizophrenia, the patient:
    a. experiences a sudden and conspicuous onset of symptoms.
    b. is less withdrawn.
    c. may be dangerously aggressive and abusive to others.
    d. is less likely to have a hereditary basis for the disorder.

45. _____ schizophrenia is characterized by gradual onset, general withdrawal from the world, blunted emotions, and poor prognosis.
    a. Paranoid
    b. Catatonic
    c. Process
    d. Reactive

46. Schizophrenia produces many dramatic and debilitating changes in a person affected with this disorder. Which alternative below is **not** one of them?
    a. delusions
    b. multiple personality
    c. decline from an earlier level of functioning
    d. withdrawal

47. Which of the following accounts of schizophrenia assumes that inappropriate behavior is learned by attending to stimuli that are not related to normal social interaction?
    a. learned helplessness hypothesis
    b. dopamine hypothesis
    c. predisposition model
    d. learned-inattention theory

48. According to the text, personality disorder is best characterized by:
    a. firmly held beliefs with little basis in reality.
    b. a mixture of symptoms of schizophrenia.
    c. a set of inflexible, maladaptive traits.
    d. an extended sense of euphoria and elation.

ESSAY QUESTIONS

Essay Question 17.1: *Defining Mental Illness*

Discuss the implications of Rosenhan's study in which he and seven other individuals faked mental illness in order to test the ability of mental hospitals to distinguish abnormal behavior from normal and the effects of labeling. What are the scientific issues related to his study? Are there any ethical issues?

_____

_____

_____

_____

_____

_____

_____

_____

_____

_____

_____

_____

_____

_____

_____

_____

Essay Question 17.2: *Schizophrenia*

Describe the types of schizophrenia, its symptoms, and its causes. Compare the differing theories concerning the cause of schizophrenia.

_____

_____

_____

_____

_____

_____

_____

_____

_____

_____

_____

_____

_____

_____

_____

_____

_____

_____

_____

ACTIVITIES AND PROJECTS

1. Review the models of abnormality described in the text: medical, psychoanalytic, behavioral, cognitive, humanistic, and sociocultural. Which of these models appeals to you the most? Which the least? Next, find the key issues in Chapter 1. Does the way these models answer these key issues affect their appeal or lack of appeal to you? What measure would you use to test the usefulness or value of each of these models? Can your measure be supported?

18

TREATMENT OF ABNORMAL BEHAVIOR

| **DETAILED OUTLINE** | *Survey:* ☐ |

This detailed outline contains all the headings in Chapter 18: The Treatment of Abnormal Behavior. If you are using the SQ3R method, then an examination of the outline is the best way to begin your survey of the chapter.

Antidepressant drugs (continued)
Antianxiety drugs
Electroconvulsive therapy (ECT)
Psychosurgery
Biological treatment in perspective: Can abnormal behavior be cured?
Community psychology: Focus on prevention
The Informed Consumer of Psychology Choosing the Right Therapist
● **Recap and Review III**

Looking Back
Key Terms and Concepts

➤ Now that you have surveyed the chapter, read **Looking Ahead**, pages 587–588. *Question:* ☐
Focus on the questions on page 588. *Read:* ☐

| **CONCEPTS AND LEARNING OBJECTIVES** | *Survey:* ☐ |

These are the concepts and the learning objects for Chapter 18. Read them carefully as part of your preliminary survey of the chapter.

Concept 1: Psychotherapy seeks to remedy psychological difficulties. Psychodynamic approaches attempt to resolve unconscious conflicts and behavioral approaches apply learning theory to therapy.

1. Define psychotherapy and distinguish its main types. (pp. 586-588)

2. Describe how psychodynamic therapy approaches treatment of abnormal behavior, and discuss the major techniques and concepts employed by psychodynamic therapists. (pp. 589-591)

3. Describe the behavioral approaches to therapy, including aversive conditioning and systematic desensitization, observational learning, and the use of operant conditioning principles. (pp. 591-595)

4. Discuss and distinguish the cognitive behavioral therapy approaches of rational emotive therapy and cognitive therapy. (pp. 595-597)

Concept 2: Humanistic psychotherapy focuses on issues related to the person's taking responsibility for his or her own actions and solving issues regarding the meaning of life. Psychotherapy is considered to be effective, but some therapies are more appropriate for certain disorders than are others.

5. Describe the three kinds of humanistic therapy included in the text: Rogers's client-centered therapy, existential therapy, and gestalt therapy; and describe group therapy. (pp. 598-602)

6. Outline the dimensions used to compare psychotherapy, the methods used to evaluate psychotherapy, and arguments that support the interpretation of the success or failure of psychotherapies. (pp. 602-607)

Concept 3: Drug therapy has made psychotic patients calmer, alleviated depression, and calmed anxiety. Electroconvulsive therapy and psychosurgery are controversial treatments of last resort. The community health movement now must cope with deinstitutionalized patients and has also led to the development of hot lines and campus crisis centers.

7. Name and describe drugs used in the treatment of abnormal behavior and discuss the problems and controversies surrounding their use. (pp. 608-611)

8. Describe the medical techniques of electroconvulsive therapy and psychosurgery, and discuss the effectiveness of drug and medical therapies. (pp. 611-612)

9. Describe possible approaches to the prevention of abnormal behavior through the use of the community approach and deinstitutionalization; also discuss suggestions one may follow in selecting a psychotherapist. (pp. 613-615)

CHAPTER SUMMARY

There are several ways you can use this summary as part of your systematic study plan. You may read each concept summary and then read the corresponding pages in the text, or you may read the entire summary and then read the entire chapter in the text. As you finish each section, complete the **Recap and Review** questions that are supplied in the text.

CONCEPT 1: Prologue and Looking Ahead *Survey:* ☐
  Psychotherapy: Psychological Approaches *Read:* ☐
    to Treatment
Pages 586-597

The Prologue introduces three different approaches to therapy to illustrate that therapy is not a uniform process. There are today over 250 different kinds of treatment. The common goal of therapy is relief of the psychological disorder and enabling individuals to achieve richer, more meaningful lives. Psychologically based therapy is called **psychotherapy**, a process in which a patient (client) and a professional work together to deal with psychological difficulties. **Biologically based therapy** depends on drugs and other medical procedures. Many therapists today draw upon the large number of therapies for the approach most suited to the client, and this is considered an **eclectic approach to therapy**.

Psychodynamic therapy assumes that the primary causes of abnormal behavior are unresolved conflicts from the past and anxiety over unconscious impulses. The **defense mechanisms** that individuals use to guard against anxiety do not bury these anxieties completely, and they emerge in the form of **neurotic symptoms**. Freud said that the way to deal with the unwanted desires and past conflicts was to confront them, to make them conscious. The role of the psychodynamic therapist is then to explore the unconscious conflicts and help the patient understand them.

Freudian therapy is called **psychoanalysis**, and it tends to be lengthy and expensive. Patients meet with their therapists four to six times a week for several years. The technique often used is called **free association**, during which the patient will say anything that comes to mind no matter how insignificant. The ramblings are assumed to be clues from the unconscious, and the therapist look for connections in the patient's words. Another method is **dream interpretation**; again the therapist looks for clues to the unconscious in the dream. People censor thoughts when they dream, so there is a distinction between the

manifest content of dreams, or the description of the dream, and the **latent content of dreams**, or the message of the dreams. Sometimes the patient will unconsciously resist the probing. **Resistance** refers to an inability to discuss or reveal particular memories or thoughts. The patient finds it difficult to talk about these particular issues. **Transference** is a phenomenon in which the relationship between the analyst and the patient becomes emotionally charged, and the analyst symbolically takes on the role of significant others from the patient's past. Transference is used to help the patient re-create the past and work through it more positively.

Today psychodynamic psychotherapy is shorter, and the therapist takes a more active role, controlling the course of therapy and emphasizing the present more than the past. It is still criticized for being time-consuming and expensive, and only certain kinds of patients are well-suited for this kind of therapy. It is difficult to prove that psychodynamic therapies are successful, and some critics challenge the entire theoretical basis for the approach.

The principles of reinforcement are central to **behavioral treatment approaches** which suggest that both abnormal and normal behavior is learned. To modify abnormal behavior, new behaviors must be learned. Behavioral psychologists are not interested in the past history of the individual, focusing instead on the current behavior. Classical conditioning principles are applied to behaviors like alcoholism, smoking, and drug abuse, with a technique known as aversive conditioning. In **aversive conditioning**, the unwanted behavior is linked with a stimulus that produces an unpleasant response, like a drug that produces vomiting when mixed with alcohol. The long-term effectiveness of the approach is questionable. The most successful classical conditioning technique is called **systematic desensitization** in which a person is taught to relax and is then gradually exposed to an anxiety-provoking stimulus. One approach involves the development of a **hierarchy of fears** that the patient can use to become exposed to less threatening stimuli at first. The patient relaxes and then imagines the first stimulus on the list for as long as he or she can remain relaxed. The patient then progresses through the hierarchy, eventually actually being placed in the situation or exposed to the stimuli that causes anxiety. Systematic desensitization has been used successfully with phobias, anxiety disorders, and impotence.

Observational learning is used in therapy by **modeling** appropriate behaviors. People can be taught skills and ways of handling anxiety by observing a model cope with the same situation. The "Fearless Peer" approach helps children overcome their fear of dogs by having another child pet and play with a dog.

Operant conditioning techniques are used in settings where rewards and punishments can be controlled. One example is that of the **token economy** in which individuals are rewarded with tokens that can be exchanged for desired objects or opportunities. **Contingency contracting** is a variant of token economy, and it requires a written agreement between the therapist and the client. The contract sets behavioral goals to be reached and specifies the consequences of reaching the goals. Depending on the problem addressed, behavior therapy claims success rates between 50 and 90 percent.

Cognitive approaches to therapy attempt to change faulty cognitions held by patients about themselves and the world. The therapies are typically based on learning principles and thus are often called **cognitive-behavioral approaches**. **Rational-emotive therapy** is one of the best examples of the cognitive approach. The therapist attempts to restructure the person's belief system into a more realistic, rational, and logical set of views. Therapists take an active and directive role in therapy, directly challenging patterns of thought that appear to be irrational. Another form of therapy is Aaron Beck's **cognitive therapy**. He is less confrontive and more like a teacher. Clients are given assignments to help them uncover information that will lead them to think more appropriately.

CONCEPT 2: Psychotherapy: Psychological Approaches
     to Treatment (Continued)

Survey: ☐
Read: ☐

Pages 598-607

Humanistic psychotherapy depends upon the perspective of self-responsibility as the basis for treatment. The view is that we control our own behavior, make choices about how to live, and it is up to us to solve our problems. Humanistic therapists see themselves as guides or facilitators.

Nondirective counseling refers to approaches that do not offer interpretations or answers to problems. First practiced by Carl Rogers, **client-centered therapy** was founded on the nondirective approach. Rogers attempted to establish a warm and accepting environment in order to enable the client to make realistic and constructive choices about life. The therapist must provide a sense of **unconditional positive regard**, an acceptance of the individual without conditions no matter what attitude is expressed by the client. It is rare to find client-centered therapy practiced in its pure form because therapies usually now include some directive aspects.

Concern with the meaning and uniqueness of life has given rise to **existential therapy**, an approach based on the problem of dealing with personal freedom and the anguish, fear, and concern that accompanies such fear. The goal of existential therapy is to help the client come to grips with freedom, to find his or her place in the world, and to develop a system of values that gives meaning to life. The therapist is more directive, and probes and challenges the client's views.

Gestalt therapy has the goal of integrating the client's thoughts and feelings into a whole, or gestalt. The approach was developed by Fritz Perls. He asked the client to go back and work on unfinished business, playing the part of the angry father and taking other roles of a conflict. This leads the client to increase perspectives on a situation. Humanistic approaches lack specificity, and the form of treatment is most appropriate for the same type of person treated by psychoanalysis. However, the emphasis on human responsibility and uniqueness and on creating an environment that is supportive can help clients find solutions to psychological difficulties.

Group therapy is a form of treatment that has several people meet with a therapist at the same time. Problems, usually one held in common with all group members, are discussed with the group. Members of the group provide social support and share how they may have dealt with similar situations. Groups vary according to therapeutic approach and degree of guidance offered by the therapist. Groups are economical, but critics argue that they do not replace the one-on-one aspect of individual therapy.

Family therapy is a specialized form of group therapy that involves two or more members of a family. Therapists focus on the entire family system rather than only on the family member with the problem, and each family member is expected to contribute to the solution. Family therapists assume that family members engage in set patterns of behavior, and the goal of therapy is to get the family to adopt more constructive behaviors.

Psychotherapy can be classified using several dimensions. They are: directive versus nondirective approaches, inner control of behavior versus external control of behavior, long-term versus short-term therapy, historical versus here-and-now focus, and cognitive change versus behavior change. These dimensions are more on a continuum rather than either/or distinctions.

Deciding which therapy is appropriate for which kind of problem is a difficult task, but a more critical question is whether any psychotherapy is effective. Hans Eysenck published an article in 1952 that challenged whether psychodynamic therapy was effective. He compared a group receiving treatment with one composed of people on a waiting list for treatment. The group that received no therapy had done just as well as the group that received therapy. The symptoms went away due to **spontaneous remission**, or recovery without treatment. Eysenck's study was challenged on the basis of the data he used. One main problem with studies of the effectiveness of psychotherapy is that the data is primarily self-report data from the client and the therapist. Since there is no agreed-upon criteria for mental health, even independent judgment is difficult. Eysenck's early work led to a number of studies, most of which conclude that therapy does work.

The question of which therapy is the best still remains. The methodological issues include questioning the nature of cure. Reducing depression-related anxiety using psychodynamic treatment may not be equivalent to reducing phobia-related anxiety using behavior therapy. One solution is to compare the cure rates for treatment groups and for nontreated control groups. Another treatment can be compared similarly. Then the two treatments can be compared on their cure rates relative to their control groups. In a study based on this method, therapies were 70 to 85 percent more successful than nontreated controls. Other studies have supported this data. The National Institute of Mental Health is currently conducting a large study that compares cognitive therapy, interpersonal therapy, drug therapy, and placebos in depressed patients. In a pilot study, the three therapies had success rates of about 40 percent and the placebo had a success rate of about 20 percent. Evidence suggests that there is only a minor difference between therapies, and that, for most people, therapy is better than no therapy. In a small number of cases, people are actually harmed by therapy. It is also clear that particular kinds of therapy are also more appropriate for some than for others. Psychodynamic and humanistic therapies work well with problems that require insight, behavioral therapy works well with problems that arise because of circumstances like a phobia or lack of specific skills. Some therapies may be more appropriate to specific types of people. Therapists must take into account how the factors of race, ethnicity, cultural heritage, and social class affect the nature of psychological problems and the course of treatment. The number of eclectic approaches to therapy is increasing, and therapists have a number of treatment techniques from which to select. Also, the process of therapy may be as important as the outcome, and people learn to relate therapy to the ongoing changes in their feelings and thoughts about the world.

CONCEPT 3: Biological Treatment Approaches: *Survey:* ☐
The Medical Model at Work *Read:* ☐

Pages 608-615

Biologically based treatments that treat brain chemical imbalances and other neurological factors directly are regularly used for some problems. In **drug therapy**, drugs are given that alleviate symptoms for a number of psychological disturbances. In the mid 1950s, **antipsychotic drugs** were introduced, causing a major change in the treatment of patients in mental hospitals. These drugs alleviate symptoms related to the patient's loss of touch with reality, agitation, and overactivity. Antipsychotic drugs greatly improved the atmosphere in the hospital by calming patients. The drug introduced was **chlorpromazine**, and it proved successful in treating the symptoms of schizophrenia. Drug therapy is now used for more than 90 percent of the hospitalized patients. Antipsychotic drugs work by blocking dopamine production at sites where the electrical impulses travel across nerve receptors. The drugs do not cure, and they have severe side effects, including dryness of mouth, dizziness, and tremors. They also have a numbing effect on the emotional responses of patients. **Antidepressant drugs** are used to improve the moods of severely depressed patients. Antidepressant drugs work by increasing the concentration of certain neurotransmitters. Tricyclic drugs increase the concentration of norepinephrine and serotonin; bupropion drugs increase dopamine. Antidepressant drugs can produce long-term recoveries from depression. One antidepressant, **fluoxetine**—also known as **Prozac**—has been the center of recent controversy. Prozac blocks the reabsorption of the neurotransmitter serotonin. Though it has few side effects, some have claimed that it made them suicidal and a few have claimed that it drove them to homicidal behavior (the "Prozac defense"). One fear is that because of its popularity, people with minor depression will seek prescriptions of the drug rather than seek more suitable treatment. **Lithium**, a form of simple mineral salt, has been used to treat bipolar disorders. It ends manic episodes 70 percent of the time; though its success with depression is not as good. Unlike other treatments, lithium is seen as a *preventive* medication. People who have had manic-depressive episodes in the past take small doses as a means of preventing the return of the symptoms.

Antianxiety drugs—Valium, Miltown, Librium—are the drugs most prescribed by physicians. Antianxiety drugs reduce the anxiety level experienced by reducing excitability and increasing drowsiness. They have side effects that include fatigue and dependence. When combined with alcohol, some are lethal. The drugs also mask the source of the anxiety and allow the person simply to ignore the cause of the problem.

On the mistaken notion that epileptics—who experience convulsions—do not have schizophrenia, physicians in the 1930s found a way to induce convulsions using electric shocks. **Electroconvulsive therapy (ECT)** is administered by passing an electric current of 70 to 150 volts through the head of a patient for about one-twenty-fifth of a second. The patient is usually sedated and given muscle relaxants to prevent violent contractions. ECT is controversial because of its side effects, which include disorientation, confusion, and memory loss. Many patients fear ECT, and some people believe that it may cause permanent neurological damage. It continues to be used because it does help severely depressed patients when other treatments are ineffective.

Psychosurgery is brain surgery used to alleviate psychological symptoms. An early procedure was prefrontal lobotomy in which parts of the frontal lobes are removed or destroyed. The patients are then less subject to emotional impulses. Patients also suffered personality changes, becoming bland and unemotional. Patients can also die from the treatment. Drug therapies ended the frequent use of psychosurgery, and today it is used to alleviate problems like severe and uncontrollable pain. More precise surgical procedures are used with only very small areas of the brain being destroyed.

Psychotherapy and medical therapy are intended to restore the patient to a previous state of health; **community psychology** is intended to help prevent or minimize psychological disorders. In the 1960s, plans were made for a nationwide network of community mental-health centers that could provide inexpensive mental-health services, short-term therapy, and educational programs. Former mental patients were returning to the community in a process known as **deinstitutionalization**. The community centers were expected to ensure that the deinstitutionalized patients continued to get proper treatment and that their civil rights were maintained. The original goals were not met, mental disorders have not declined. Many people who need treatment do not get it. Positive results include the development of "hot lines" where people can call for help and talk to a trained person immediately. The college crisis center also grew out of this movement. The volunteers on hot lines receive careful training for telephone counseling and are prepared to respond to a variety of situations and to make referrals for additional treatment.

Whether one has chosen the right therapist can be determined by considering the following: the relationship between client and therapist should be comfortable, the therapist should have appropriate credentials and training, clients should feel that they are making progress, and clients should be aware that they must contribute effort to the therapy.

▶ Now that you have surveyed, questioned, and read the chapter and completed

the **Recap and Review** questions, review **Looking Back**, page 616.   *Review:* ☐

▶ For additional practice through recitation and review, test your knowledge of the chapter material by answering the questions in the *Key Word Drill*, the *Practice Questions*, and the *Essay Questions*.

KEY WORD DRILL   *Recite:* ☐

The following **Fill in the Blank** and **Matching Questions** test key words from the text. Check your answers with the Answer Key in the back of the *Study Guide*.

FILL IN THE BLANK

1. _____ is the process in which a client and a professional attempt to remedy the client's psychological difficulties.

2. _____ learning occurs by watching others' behavior and the consequences of

    that behavior and then _____, or imitating the behavior.

3. The examination of a patient's dreams to find clues to the unconscious conflicts and problems being

    experienced is called _____ _____.

4. Recovery without treatment is called _____ _____.

5. _____ _____ is a therapeutic technique in which the therapist creates a warm, supportive environment to allow the client to understand and work out problems.

6. In most therapies, the therapist tries to establish a sense of _____ _____ _____, an attitude that is supportive of the client regardless of his or her words or actions.

7. The medical technique of _____ _____ attempts to

    control psychological problems through drugs, and the technique called _____ involves brain surgery.

8. According to Freud, _____ symptoms are abnormal behavior brought about by anxiety associated with unwanted conflicts and impulses.

9. _____ refers to the approach to therapy that uses a variety of treatment methods rather than just one.

10. _____ required the transfer of former mental patients from institutions into the community.

11. Treatment involving the administration of an electric current to a patient's head is known as

    _____ _____.

12. _____ _____ refers to the surgical destruction of a patient's frontal lobes to improve the control of emotionality.

MATCHING QUESTIONS

_____ 13. biologically based therapy

_____ 14. psychodynamic therapy

_____ 15. psychoanalysis

_____ 16. behavioral treatment approaches

_____ 17. cognitive approaches to therapy

_____ 18. rational-emotive therapy

_____ 19. cognitive therapy

a. Basic sources of abnormal behavior are unresolved past conflicts and anxiety.

b. Attempts to restructure one's belief into a more realistic, rational, and logical system.

c. Appropriate treatment consists of learning new behavior or unlearning maladaptive behavior.

d. A form of psychodynamic therapy that often lasts for many years.

e. Uses drugs and other medical procedures to improve psychological functioning.

f. People's faulty cognitions about themselves and the world are changed to more accurate ones.

g. People are taught to change illogical thoughts about themselves and the world.

_____ 20. free association

_____ 21. manifest content

_____ 22. latent content

_____ 23. resistance

_____ 24. transference

a. A patient's transfer of certain strong feelings for others to the analyst.

b. The "true" message hidden within dreams.

c. The patient says everything that comes to mind, providing insights into the patient's unconscious.

d. An inability or unwillingness to discuss or reveal particular memories, thoughts, or motivations.

e. The surface description and interpretation of dreams.

_____ 25. aversive conditioning

_____ 26. systematic desensitization

_____ 27. token system

_____ 28. contingency contracting

a. A person is rewarded for performing desired behaviors.

b. Breaks unwanted habits by associating the habits with very unpleasant stimuli.

c. Requires a written contract between a therapist and a client that sets behavioral goals and rewards.

d. A stimulus that evokes pleasant feelings is repeatedly paired with a stimulus that evokes anxiety.

_____ 29. client-centered therapy

_____ 30. humanistic therapy

_____ 31. existential therapy

_____ 32. gestalt therapy

_____ 33. group therapy

_____ 34. family therapy

_____ 35. community psychology

a. People discuss problems with others who have similar problems.

b. The therapist reflects back the patient's statements in a way that helps the patient to find solutions.

c. People have control of their behavior, can make choices about their lives, and are essentially responsible for solving their own problems.

d. A movement aimed toward preventing psychological disorders.

e. Addresses the meaning of life, allowing a client to devise a system of values that gives purpose to his or her life.

f. Attempts to integrate a client's thoughts, feelings, and behavior into a whole.

g. Family as a unit to which each member contributes.

_____ 36. antipsychotic drugs

_____ 37. antidepressant drugs

_____ 38. antianxiety drugs

_____ 39. chlorpromazine

_____ 40. lithium

_____ 41. fluoxetine

a. Prozac, a widely used antidepressant drug.

b. Used in the treatment of schizophrenia.

c. Improves a patient's mood and feeling of well-being.

d. Used in the treatment of bipolar disorders.

e. Alleviate stress and feelings of apprehension.

f. Temporarily alleviate symptoms such as agitation and overactivity.

PRACTICE QUESTIONS

Recite and Review: ☐

Test your knowledge of the chapter material by answering these **True-False** and **Multiple Choice Questions**. Check your answers with the Answer Key in the back of the *Study Guide*.

TRUE-FALSE QUESTIONS

T   F   1.   If a patient fails to meet an appointment or is reluctant to discuss a particular topic, a psychoanalyst might interpret this as transference.

T   F   2.   A psychoanalyst would be more concerned with your recollection of a dream than the meaning you place on the events of the last week.

T   F   3.   Behaviorists and psychoanalysts alike are concerned with the causes of abnormal behavior.

T   F   4.   Dr. Morgan uses modeling, role play and a token system in order to teach children adaptive social skills. Dr. Morgan is probably a behaviorist.

T   F   5.   Rational-emotive therapy is an example of the cognitive behavioral approach to therapy.

T   F   6.   Humanistic therapists view the doctor as the expert, having primary responsibility for treatment.

T   F   7.   Unconditional positive regard is expressed by the therapist toward the client in the client-centered approach to psychotherapy.

T   F   8.   Eysenck, investigating different psychotherapies in a 1952 study, found that such treatments were approximately 50-70 percent more effective than expected.

T   F   9.   The primary use of antianxiety drugs is to overcome depression.

T   F   10.   More than half of all Americans have a family member who has taken an antianxiety drug at one time or another.

MULTIPLE CHOICE QUESTIONS

1.   According to the text, what is the common goal of all types of therapy?
    a.   integrating the individual into society
    b.   relieving psychological disorders
    c.   relieving fears and anxiety
    d.   reassembling the parts of the personality

2.   According to the text, there are over _____ different kinds of treatment.
    a.   50   c.   175
    b.   100   d.   250

3.   According to the text, the category of therapy in which change is brought about through discussions and interactions between client and professional is called:
    a.   eclectic therapy.   c.   psychotherapy.
    b.   semantic therapy   d.   interpersonal therapy.

4.   An eclectic approach to therapy is one that:
    a.   uses a combination of different methods.
    b.   uses an unorthodox method.
    c.   uses techniques based on hidden motives.
    d.   uses institutionalization along with therapy.

5. Clients requiring some form of medical treatment are typically treated by a:
   a. psychiatric nurse.
   b. counseling psychologist.
   c. psychiatrist.
   d. clinical psychologist.

6. Based on the descriptions in the text, if you were having trouble adjusting to the death of a friend, who would you be most likely to see?
   a. psychiatrist
   b. psychoanalyst
   c. psychiatric social worker
   d. counseling psychologist

7. Charles is the director of guidance at a student mental health clinic. He holds a degree appropriate to his position, so he must hold a doctorate or master's degree in:
   a. psychiatric social work.
   b. counseling psychology.
   c. clinical psychology.
   d. educational psychology.

8. The basic premise of psychodynamic therapy is the notion that abnormal behavior is:
   a. repressing normal behaviors that need to be uncovered.
   b. the result of the ego repressing the superego.
   c. rooted in unresolved past conflicts, buried in the unconscious.
   d. the result of the ego failing to gain access to consciousness.

9. According to Freud, in order to protect our egos from the unwanted entry of unacceptable unconscious thoughts and desires, we all use:
   a. transference.
   b. aversive conditioning.
   c. systematic desensitization.
   d. defense mechanisms.

10. According to Freud, neurotic symptoms are caused by:
    a. defense mechanisms.
    b. anxiety.
    c. inappropriate choices.
    d. contingency contracting.

11. Listed below are terms associated with psychodynamic therapy. Which alternative below does **not** belong?
    a. hierarchy of fears
    b. neurotic symptoms
    c. defense mechanisms
    d. transference

12. What technique is used in psychoanalysis to help the patient remember the experiences of a past relationship?
    a. transcendence
    b. transference
    c. translation
    d. transrotation

13. According to the text, most psychodynamic psychotherapists prefer:
    a. minority patients.
    b. white patients.
    c. YAVIS patients.
    d. schizophrenic patients.

14. Which of the following approaches to therapy would be **least** concerned with the underlying causes of abnormal behavior?
    a. psychoanalytic
    b. behavioral
    c. eclectic
    d. humanistic

15. Which problem below is least likely to be treated with aversive conditioning?
    a. substance (drug) abuse   c. smoking
    b. depression   d. alcoholism

16. What happens to the reaction to alcohol following aversive conditioning for alcoholism?
    a. The reaction takes on that response associated with the aversion.
    b. There is no longer a craving for the alcohol.
    c. There is a fear of the alcohol.
    d. The alcohol becomes a source of anxiety.

17. A technique used to reduce anxiety or eliminate phobias, that is based on classical conditioning, is called:
    a. biofeedback.   c. systematic desensitization.
    b. behavior modification.   d. aversive conditioning.

18. Which of the following is **not** a component of systematic desensitization?
    a. operant conditioning   c. hierarchy of fears
    b. relaxation   d. imagery

19. There is a saying, "Monkey see, monkey do!" This saying illustrates:
    a. observational learning.   c. systematic desensitization.
    b. gestalt therapy.   d. aversive conditioning.

20. The behavioral-treatment approach uses all of the following techniques **except**:
    a. aversive conditioning.   c. modeling.
    b. systematic desensitization.   d. symptom substitution.

21. According to the text, in rational-emotive therapy, the therapist challenges the client's:
    a. defensive views of the world.   c. paranoid views of the world.
    b. self-centered views of the world. d. irrational views of the world.

22. Peggy, a 17-year-old client of Dr. Ertle, explains, "I answered a question wrong in history class and made a perfect fool of myself." In response Dr. Ertle says "Is it important for you to be perfectly competent in every area of your life?" Dr. Ertle is using:
    a. behavioral therapy.   c. humanistic therapy.
    b. rational-emotive therapy.   d. existential therapy.

23. Which therapy assumes people experience unhappiness and psychologically disordered lives because of unrealistic and inappropriate ideas that they hold about themselves and the world?
    a. rational-emotive therapy   c. psychoanalytic therapy
    b. gestalt therapy   d. behavioral therapy

24. Which of the following approaches to treatment takes the view that it is primarily the responsibility of the client to make needed changes?
    a. behavioral therapy   c. humanistic therapy
    b. rational-emotive therapy   d. psychoanalytic therapy

25. The approach that is the best known of the humanistic therapies and assumes at the outset that a person's troubles reflect unfulfilled potential is called:
    a. rational-emotive therapy.
    b. gestalt therapy.
    c. systematic desensitization.
    d. client-centered therapy.

26. In humanistic therapy, unconditional positive regard is provided to the client:
    a. as a reinforcement when goals have been met.
    b. as part of the contingency contract.
    c. no matter what the client says or does.
    d. to help resolve inner conflicts.

27. According to the text, the goal of client-centered therapy is to enable people to reach the potential for:
    a. getting in touch with reality.
    b. understanding the unconscious.
    c. taking control of their thoughts.
    d. self-actualization.

28. According to the text, which of the following therapies is most closely associated with the concepts of freedom, values, and the meaning of human existence?
    a. behavioral therapy
    b. rational-emotive therapy
    c. humanistic therapy
    d. existential therapy

29. If a therapist asks you to act out some past conflict or difficulty in order to complete unfinished business, he or she most likely is using:
    a. behavior therapy.
    b. existential therapy.
    c. rational-emotive therapy.
    d. gestalt therapy.

30. Helen is in therapy with a psychotherapist to work through her feelings about her recent broken engagement. She is telling her therapist that she really didn't love her fiance, and that she realized how different she and her fiance are. Suddenly, her therapist says, "Helen, I heard the words that you just said, but they don't tell the same message that your facial expression and other nonverbal cues do. See if you can sense the differences." Helen's therapist is most likely:
    a. a gestalt therapist.
    b. a psychoanalytic therapist.
    c. a client-centered therapist.
    d. a behavioral therapist.

31. According to the text, which therapies emphasize establishing inner rather than outer control of behavior?
    a. psychodynamic and humanistic
    b. psychodynamic and behavioral
    c. rational-emotive and behavioral
    d. behavioral and humanistic

32. According to the text, psychotherapies are often compared and evaluated in many ways. Which alternative below is **not** one of them?
    a. cognitive change versus behavioral change
    b. long-term therapy versus short-term therapy
    c. personal characteristics versus situational factors
    d. historical focus versus here-and-now focus

33. Which of the following is **not** used to describe the behavioral approach to therapy?
    a. directive
    b. learned behavior
    c. environmentalistic
    d. biological

34. One study showed that cognitive therapy and "interpersonal" therapy were _____ effective in treating depression compared with drug therapy.
    a. much more
    b. more
    c. at least as
    d. less

35. Spontaneous remission refers to:
    a. recovery without treatment.
    b. spontaneous recovery in classical conditioning-based therapies.
    c. return to a state of illness after a period of recovery.
    d. sudden withdrawal from the world into a catatonic state.

36. Generalizing from the discussion in the text, both humanistic and psychoanalytic approaches to therapy are more appropriate for clients who are:
    a. highly verbal.
    b. severely disordered.
    c. experiencing sexually related disorders.
    d. reluctant to converse with someone else.

37. According to the text, chlorpromazine is most commonly used in the treatment of:
    a. mood disorders.
    b. anxiety disorders.
    c. schizophrenia.
    d. bipolar disorder.

38. According to the text, antipsychotic drugs alleviate psychotic symptoms by:
    a. increasing neurotransmitter function.
    b. blocking the production of dopamine.
    c. slowing down the autonomic nervous system.
    d. sedating the patients.

39. Antidepressant drugs modify the concentrations of several neurotransmitters in the brain. According to the text, which brain chemical below is **not** associated with various antidepressant medications for the treatment of depression?
    a. serotonin
    b. dopamine
    c. acetylcholine
    d. norepinephrine

40. According to the text, which drug is used to help prevent future occurrences of the behavioral disorder that it is used to treat?
    a. Valium
    b. Lithium
    c. chlorpromazine
    d. Librium

41. According to the text, which medication would most likely be given to someone experiencing a manic episode?
    a. Lithium
    b. Valium
    c. chlorpromazine
    d. Librium

42. Antidepressant drugs improve the mood of depressed patients by:
    a. increasing the activity of the autonomic nervous system.
    b. suppressing the function of certain neurotransmitters.
    c. increasing the speed of neural transmission.
    d. increasing the concentration of certain neurotransmitters.

43. Which of the following types of treatment appears actually to *cure* the disorder, so that when the treatment is discontinued the symptoms tend not to recur?
   a. antipsychotic drugs
   b. antidepressant drugs
   c. antianxiety drugs
   d. chlorpromazine

44. Which of the following statements about antianxiety drugs is true?
   a. They are relatively free of side effects.
   b. They are used primarily in cases of serious anxiety disorder.
   c. They are the most common drugs prescribed by physicians.
   d. They eliminate the anxiety as well as its source.

45. Today, electroconvulsive shock treatment (ECT) is usually reserved for severe cases of:
   a. mania.
   b. schizophrenia.
   c. depression.
   d. panic attack.

46. According to the text, which of the following types of treatment is rarely if ever still used?
   a. electroconvulsive shock therapy
   b. antipsychotic drugs
   c. psychotherapy
   d. psychosurgery

47. A procedure by which areas of the brain are removed or destroyed in order to control severe abnormal behaviors is called:
   a. psychosurgery.
   b. shock therapy.
   c. electroconvulsive therapy.
   d. personality therapy.

48. According to the text, which of the following would suggest that you had chosen a good therapist or style of therapy?
   a. You feel somewhat afraid of the therapist.
   b. You don't need to put effort into the therapy.
   c. You feel no particular sense of progress.
   d. You are involved in the therapy.

ESSAY QUESTIONS

Recite and Review: ☐

Essay Question 18.1: *The Effectiveness of Psychotherapy*

Describe the reasons why you think that psychotherapy works. Draw upon the principles of psychology that have been discussed in previous chapters, such as learning principles, theories of development, and theories of personality, to explain why you think it is effective.

_____

_____

_____

_____

_____

_____

_____

_____

_____

_____

_____

_____

_____

_____

_____

_____

_____

Essay Question 18.2: *Should Electroconvulsive Therapy Be Banned?*

Describe the advantages and disadvantages of electroconvulsive therapy. Do you think that it should be banned from use? Explain your answer.

_____

_____

_____

_____

_____

_____

_____

_____

_____

_____

_____

_____

_____

_____

_____

_____

_____

_____

19

SOCIAL PSYCHOLOGY: ATTITUDES AND SOCIAL COGNITION

| DETAILED OUTLINE | *Survey:* ☐ |

This detailed outline contains all the headings in Chapter 19: Social Psychology: Attitudes and Social Cognition. If you are using the SQ3R method, then an examination of the outline is the best way to begin your survey of the chapter.

The Informed Consumer of Psychology Forming More Accurate Impressions and Reducing Stereotyping and Prejudice
Psychology at Work Fighting Prejudice on Campus
● **Recap and Review III**

Looking Back
Key Terms and Concepts

➤ Now that you have surveyed the chapter, read **Looking Ahead**, pages 620–621.   *Question:* ☐
Focus on the questions on page 621.   *Read:* ☐

CONCEPTS AND LEARNING OBJECTIVES

Survey: ☐

These are the concepts and the learning objects for Chapter 19. Read them carefully as part of your preliminary survey of the chapter.

Concept 1: Attitudes are composed of affective, behavioral, and cognitive components. People attempt to maintain a consistency between their attitudes and behavior.

1. Define and distinguish the components of attitude; and discuss the relationship of attitude and behavior. (pp. 620-621)

2. Describe the roles of classical and operant conditioning in the formation and maintenance of attitudes. (pp. 621-623)

3. Discuss the means by which attitudes can be changed. (pp. 623-625)

4. Describe cognitive dissonance theory and self-perception theory and how each accounts for the relationship between attitudes and behavior. (pp. 625-629)

Concept 2: We form schemas to help us categorize people and events in the world around us and to help predict the actions of others. Schemas help us form impressions about people. These schemas can lead to stereotypes, which can also be detrimental in the form of prejudice and discrimination.

5. Define social cognition, schemas, and impression formation. (pp. 629-632)

6. Describe how stereotypes are formed and the aspects of stereotypes that lead to discrimination. (pp. 632-635)

Concept 3: Attributions are the efforts to assign causes and otherwise explain behavior. Basic errors or biases in attributions can lead to negative perceptions and other errors that have detrimental consequences. These consequences can be avoided with more accurate information.

7. Outline the basic premises of attribution theory and the biases that arise due to attributions. (pp. 635-638)

8. Discuss self-perception theory and its role in regulating our behavior. (pp. 639-640)

9. Discuss the positive role of stereotypes and the ways available to people to reduce stereotyping and prejudice. (pp. 640-642)

CHAPTER SUMMARY

There are several ways you can use this summary as part of your systematic study plan. You may read each concept summary and then read the corresponding pages in the text, or you may read the entire summary and then read the entire chapter in the text. As you finish each section, complete the **Recap and Review** questions that are supplied in the text.

CONCEPT 1: Prologue and Looking Ahead
            Attitudes, Behavior, and Persuasion

Survey: ☐
Read: ☐

Pages 620-629

The Prologue's description of the Rodney King beating places the incident in the context of social psychology. **Social psychology** is the study of how people's thoughts, feelings, and actions are affected by others. Attempts to persuade people to purchase specific products involve principles derived from the study of attitudes. **Attitudes** are learned predispositions to respond in a favorable or unfavorable manner to a particular person or object. According to the **ABC model**, attitudes have three components. The **affective component** includes emotions about something, the **behavior component** consists of a predisposition or intention to act in a certain way, and the **cognitive component** refers to the beliefs and thoughts we have about a person or object.

The formation of attitudes follows classical and operant learning principles. Attitudes can be formed by association, as soldiers who had been stationed in the Persian Gulf may develop negative attitudes about sand. Advertisers link products with a positive feeling or event so that the product will evoke the positive feeling in consumers. Attitudes can be reinforced positively or punished by the responses others may have to them, and a person may develop an attitude through **vicarious learning**. Vicarious learning occurs when a person learns something through observation of others. Children learn prejudices through others by hearing or seeing others express prejudicial attitudes. Television, films, and other media also are means by which we develop attitudes vicariously.

Celebrity endorsements are meant to match the product with a particular type of person, and the celebrity must be believable and trustworthy and must represent qualities that the advertisers want to project. Changing attitudes depends on these factors in persuasion. The source of the message can have major impact when the communicator is attractive and believable, and has the appropriate expertise, and must not appear to have an ulterior motive. The character of the message is also important, and when an unpopular message is presented, it will be more effective if both sides are presented. Fear-producing messages are also effective unless the fear is too strong and the message is ignored as a defense mechanism.

Another important component consists of the characteristics of the recipient. The intelligence of the recipient influences the ability to remember and recall the message, yet intelligent people are more certain of their opinions. Highly intelligent people tend to be more difficult to persuade. A small difference in persuadability exists between men and women, with women being slightly easier to persuade. The means by which the information is processed also has influence on the persuasion. **Central route processing** occurs when the recipient considers the arguments involved. **Peripheral route processing** occurs when the recipient uses information that requires less thought. Central route processing produces more long-lasting change. In some cases, a celebrity may detract from a central route message by causing the recipient to focus on information other than the message.

Attitudes influence behavior, but the strength of the relationship varies. People do try to keep behavior and attitudes consistent. Sometimes, in order to maintain the consistency, behavior can influence attitudes. **Cognitive dissonance** occurs when a person holds two **cognitions** (attitudes or thoughts) that are contradictory. The individual is motivated to reduce the dissonance by (1) modifying one or both of the cognitions, (2) changing the perceived importance of one cognition, (3) adding cognitions, or (4) denying that the two cognitions are related. In cases where dissonance is aroused, the prediction is that behavior or attitudes will change in order to reduce the dissonance. In a classic experiment, subjects were offered $1 to convince others that a boring task was interesting. Others were paid $20. Those paid a small amount actually changed their attitudes about the task because the small amount caused dissonance where the large amount did not. After collecting information about a decision, people often engage in **selective exposure** to reduce the dissonance caused by making a choice. In this process, people select only information that supports their choice. One alternative to dissonance theory is Darryl Bem's **self-perception theory**. Bem suggests that people form their attitudes by observing their behavior, and sometimes attitudes are not clear until behavior makes them so.

CONCEPT 2: Social Cognition: Understanding Others

Survey: ☐
Read: ☐

Pages 629-635

The area of social psychology called **social cognition** is focused on understanding how we develop our understanding of others and how we explain the behavior of others. Social cognition refers to the processes that underlie our understanding of the world. Individuals have highly developed schemas, or sets of cognitions, about people and experiences. Schemas are important because they organize how we recall, recognize, and categorize information about others. They also help us make predictions about others.

Impression formation refers to the process by which an individual organizes information about another person, forming an overall impression of that person. Information given to people prior to meeting them can have dramatic effects on how the person is perceived. Research has focused on how people pay attention to unusually important traits called **central traits** as they form impressions of others. Information-processing approaches have been used to develop mathematical models of how personality traits are combined to form impressions. Research suggests that we form a psychological average of the individual traits. As we experience people, our impressions become more complex. Schemas are susceptible to a variety of factors—like mood—that can influence the accuracy of our impressions.

The negative side of schemas is the development of stereotypes. **Stereotypes** are the beliefs and expectations about members of groups held simply because of membership in the group. Common stereotypes are maintained concerning racial, religious, and ethnic categories. Though people are unwilling to express the prejudices they feel because these views violate social norms, a recent study has demonstrated that these attitudes persist. Stereotypes apply to more than race, religion, and ethnicity. Any group is subject to stereotyping, a bias known as the **ingroup-outgroup bias**. Less favorable views are held of groups of which we are not members, called **outgroups**, and more favorable opinions about members of groups to which we belong, or **ingroups**. When negative stereotypes lead to negative action against a group or members of a group, the behavior is called **discrimination**. Stereotypes can actually cause members of stereotyped groups to behave according to the stereotype, a phenomenon known as **self-fulfilling prophecy**. Expectations about a future event increase the likelihood that the event will occur. People are also primed to interpret behaviors according to stereotypes. If you are striving to make a positive impression, you may behave according to the stereotyped expectations people have of you.

A phenomenon called **reverse discrimination** occurs when members of a stereotyped group are treated more favorably to compensate for prejudice. In the research example given, teachers used different strategies for grading and were more lenient when they thought a set of papers was written by African-American students. This kind of discrimination can be as damaging as negative discrimination, creating tokenism and other detrimental effects. Schemas can also lead to oversimplification, making the complex too simple.

CONCEPT 3: Attribution Processes: Understanding the Causes of Behavior

Survey: ☐
Read: ☐

Pages 635-643

Attribution theory attempts to explain how we take specific instances of behavior and decide the specific causes of a person's behavior. The first determination is whether the cause is situational or dispositional. **Situational causes** result from the environment. A **dispositional cause** is the person's internal traits or personality characteristics. People use three types of information to determine if a behavior is caused by situational or dispositional factors. First is **consensus information**, or the degree to which other people behave similarly in the same situation. The second is **consistency information**, or the degree to which the individual would behave similarly in a similar situation. The third is **distinctiveness information**, or the degree to which a behavior occurs across situations. Information that is high in all three types of information would lead to attributions that the behavior is situational. When consensus and distinctiveness are low and consistency is high, dispositional attributions are made.

Since people do not always possess knowledge sufficient to make logical attributions, there are several biases in the way they are made. People tend to attribute other people's behavior to dispositional causes and their own behavior to situational causes. This bias is known as the **fundamental attribution bias**. This bias is common because people tend to focus on the behaving person rather than the more stable situation, and when they consider their own behavior, the changes in the environment are more noticeable. The **halo effect** refers to our tendency to assume that if a person has some positive characteristics, then other positive traits are present, and if there are negative traits, other negative traits are present. The halo effect reflects **implicit personality theories**, theories that indicate how we think traits are grouped together in individuals. The **Pollyanna effect** is the tendency to rate others in a generally positive manner. The **assumed-similarity bias** is the assumption that other people think just like you.

People make attributions of others, and they can act as observers of their own behavior. Bem's theory of self-perception suggests that people monitor their own behavior and make judgments about themselves based on what they see. According to the theory, you use your own behavior to understand underlying motivation, acting like an outside observer of your behavior. Racial, ethnic, and social class factors influence attributions. For instance, African-Americans are less likely to attribute success to internal factors. In contrast, white children are more likely to attribute success to ability and effort. When attributions are based on internal factors, the perception is that increased effort will result in success. Japanese and Chinese students attribute their success to internal effort, which may explain the high achievement of Asian students.

There are psychological benefits of inaccurate attributions. Contrary to the notion of accurate perceptions being necessary for mental health, three examples of illusionary perceptions that are healthy that have been supported by research are: unrealistic positive self-evaluation, an exaggerated perception of control, and being unrealistically optimistic.

Everyone forms impressions of others that can be faulty, and the major difficulty is that we then act on those impressions, with undesirable consequences resulting from our schemas and stereotypes. Social psychologists have developed a number of techniques for reducing the negative effects of stereotyping. These include:

- Increasing contact between the target of stereotyping and the holder of the stereotype. The evidence shows that when people come into contact they develop more accurate schemas. The contact must be intimate, individuals must be on an equal status, or there must be mutual dependence.
- Making positive values more conspicuous involves showing people the inconsistencies between the values they hold and the negative stereotypes. Values of equality and freedom are inconsistent with negative perceptions of minority group members.
- Providing information about the targets of stereotyping through education can increase the positive perceptions of people and explain puzzling behavior that may lead to stereotypes.

These strategies have been applied to college campus situations of racial prejudice and have resulted in changes in attitudes. Public denunciation of racism makes the **norms**, or public standards, against racism more visible.

➤ Now that you have surveyed, questioned, and read the chapter and completed

the **Recap and Review** questions, review **Looking Back**, pages 643–644.　　　*Review:* ☐

➤ For additional practice through recitation and review, test your knowledge of the chapter material by answering the questions in the *Key Word Drill*, the *Practice Questions*, and the *Essay Questions*.

KEY WORD DRILL　　　　　　　　　　　　　　　　　　*Recite:* ☐

The following **Fill in the Blank** and **Matching Questions** test key words from the text. Check your answers with the Answer Key in the back of the *Study Guide*.

FILL IN THE BLANK

1. _____ psychology is concerned with how people's thoughts, feelings, and actions are affected by others.

2. The ABC model suggests that an attitude has three components: _____,

   _____, and _____.

3. _____ learning occurs by observing others.

4. The processes that underlie our understanding of the social world are generally considered

   _____ _____.

5. Sets of cognitions about people and social experiences are called _____.

6. When we have certain expectations about the occurrence of an event or behavior, these expectations can become _____-_____ _____ and actually increase the likelihood that the event or behavior will happen.

7. When people who are prejudiced against a group compensate for their prejudice by treating the group's members more favorably than others, they are engaging in _____ discrimination.

8. The theory that seeks to explain how we decide, on the basis of samples of an individual's behavior, what the specific causes of that behavior are is called _____ theory.

9. The causes of behavior that are based on environmental factors are called _____ causes, and the causes of behavior that are based on internal traits or personality factors are called _____ causes.

10. Social psychologists call the theories reflecting our naive notions of what traits are found together in individuals _____ _____ theories.

MATCHING QUESTIONS

_____ 11. attitudes

_____ 12. affect component

_____ 13. behavior component

_____ 14. cognition component

a. A predisposition to act in a way that is relevant to one's attitude.

b. Learned predispositions to respond in a favorable or unfavorable manner to a particular object.

c. That part of an attitude encompassing how one feels about the object of one's attitude.

d. The beliefs and thoughts held about the object of one's attitude.

_____ 15. central route processing

_____ 16. peripheral route processing

_____ 17. cognitive dissonance

_____ 18. selective exposure

_____ 19. self-perception theory

a. Characterized by thoughtful consideration of the issues.

b. An attempt to minimize dissonance by exposing oneself only to information that supports one's choice.

c. Characterized by consideration of the source and related general information rather than of the message itself.

d. Attitudes are formed by observing one's own behavior.

e. The conflict resulting from contrasting cognitions.

_____ 20. impression formation

a. Negative behavior toward members of a particular group.

_____ 21. central traits

b. Major traits considered in forming impressions of others.

_____ 22. stereotype

c. Organizing information about another individual to form an overall impression of that person.

_____ 23. ingroup-outgroup bias

_____ 24. discrimination

d. Beliefs and expectations about members of a group are held simply on the basis of membership in that group.

e. The tendency to hold less favorable opinions about groups to which we do not belong, while holding more favorable opinions about groups to which we do belong.

_____

_____ 25. outgroups

a. The degree to which people behave similarly in the same situation.

_____ 26. ingroups

b. Groups to which an individual belongs.

_____ 27. consensus information

c. The degree to which an individual behaves similarly in similar situations.

_____ 28. consistency information

_____ 29. distinctiveness information

d. The extent to which a given behavior occurs across different situations.

e. Groups to which an individual does not belong.

_____

_____ 30. fundamental attribution bias

a. Tendency to think of people as being similar to oneself.

_____ 31. halo effect

b. A tendency to attribute others' behavior to dispositional causes but to attribute one's own behavior to situational causes.

_____ 32. Pollyanna effect

c. Tendency to rate others in a generally positive manner.

_____ 33. assumed-similarity bias

d. Public attitudes reflecting what is considered to be appropriate social behavior.

_____ 34. norms

e. An initial understanding that a person has positive traits is used to infer other uniformly positive characteristics.

| PRACTICE QUESTIONS | *Recite and Review:* ☐ |

Test your knowledge of the chapter material by answering these **True-False** and **Multiple Choice Questions**. Check your answers with the Answer Key in the back of the *Study Guide*.

TRUE-FALSE QUESTIONS

T   F   1. Classical conditioning has rarely been effective when used in advertising.

T   F   2. Persuasive communications that produce fear are generally effective because they mobilize people to act.

T   F   3. Presenting a viewpoint that is counter to that held by a group of intelligent people is unlikely to be effective in persuading them to change their view.

T   F   4. The intelligence of a target audience has little to do with its persuadability.

T   F   5. People generally strive for consistency between their attitudes and their behavior.

T   F   6. A person usually observes many of another person's traits before fitting the other person into a particular schema.

T   F   7. Stereotyping is applied only to racial, ethnic, and gender groups.

T   F   8. When we view a person in either a negative or positive manner at first impression, the halo effect may lead us to infer the existence of additional, similar traits which we have not observed.

T   F   9. According to the text, the halo effect seriously limits the validity of job interviews.

T   F   10. College instructors who grade students higher than they deserve illustrate the Pollyanna effect.

MULTIPLE CHOICE QUESTIONS

1. Social psychologists study learned predispositions to respond in a favorable or unfavorable way to a particular person or object. These learned predispositions are called:
   a. impressions.
   b. values.
   c. attitudes.
   d. opinions.

2. Our negative and positive feelings about other people, objects, and concepts reveal which component of our attitude?
   a. cognitive
   b. intentional
   c. affective
   d. behavioral

3. Which of the following statements represents a positive cognitive component of an attitude about green beans?
    a. I like green beans better than any other vegetable.
    b. Green beans are a tasty source of vitamins.
    c. Green beans grow on vines.
    d. I eat green beans regularly.

4. The component of an attitude which refers to the beliefs and thoughts we hold about a particular object is called:
    a. affect component.   c. behavioral component.
    b. manner component.   d. cognitive component.

5. One of the basic processes that underlies the formation and development of attitudes relates to learning principles. Which of the following learning methods best explains how attitudes are acquired?
    a. peripheral route processing   c. central route processing
    b. classical and operant conditioning   d. punishment

6. Many corporations link their products with beautiful women or strong, handsome men. Which of the following suggests that classical conditioning is being used to sell the product?
    a. They feel that the product will "sell itself" with this method.
    b. Companies believe that individuals will buy their product since only beautiful people will buy such good quality.
    c. The positive feelings associated with good-looking people will be paired with their products.
    d. They feel that beautiful men and women usually make the best salespeople.

7. Advertisers often try to link a product they want consumers to buy to a:
    a. positive feeling or event.   c. peripheral route.
    b. cognition.   d. dissonant stimulus.

8. A 5-year-old boy who overhears his father tell his mother that "Southerners are ignorant" may grow up to believe this opinion and adopt it as an attitude as a result of the process of:
    a. direct reinforcement.   c. cognitive dissonance.
    b. vicarious learning.   d. persuasive communication.

9. The advertising industry draws upon findings from _____ regarding persuasion.
    a. experimental psychology   c. abnormal psychology
    b. psychometrics   d. social psychology

10. According to the text, a message that presents only the communicator's side of an issue is called:
    a. a two-sided argument.   c. a one-sided argument.
    b. a fear-producing message.   d. a message source.

11. For a message that presents an unpopular viewpoint, if it presents both the communicator's point of view and an opponent's point of view, it is most likely to be:
    a. dangerous because it may cause people to disagree with the communicator.
    b. a one-sided message, because the communicator cannot possibly be fair.
    c. difficult for most audiences to grasp due to the need to present simple messages.
    d. more effective for the communicator because it appears to be more precise and thoughtful.

12. According to the text, if a target audience pays more attention to the celebrity doing the commercial than to the advertisement message, which processing route is being used the most by the audience?
    a. central route processing
    b. circumference route processing
    c. peripheral route processing
    d. the message is not being processed

13. Many variables influence the effectiveness of a communication to create attitude change. In which of the following situations will the impact be the greatest?
    a. The recipient appraises the message with central route processing.
    b. The recipient of the message is male.
    c. The recipient appraises the message with peripheral route processing.
    d. The recipient is very intelligent.

14. An individual who holds two contradictory attitudes or thoughts is likely to experience a kind of psychological tension known as:
    a. attribution theory.
    b. reverse bias.
    c. stereotypes.
    d. cognitive dissonance.

15. According to Festinger's theory of cognitive dissonance, if a smoker holds the cognitions "I smoke" and "Smoking causes cancer," he or she should be motivated to do all of the following *except*:
    a. modify one or both cognitions.
    b. enter a stop-smoking program.
    c. make the attitudes consistent.
    d. change the importance of one cognition.

16. Of the following, the best example of cognitive dissonance is:
    a. stating that women should earn less money than men for doing the same job.
    b. exaggerating the merits of a product in order to promote sales.
    c. knowing that cigarette smoking is harmful, but doing it anyway.
    d. believing that handicapped people cannot hold good jobs and therefore not recommending them.

17. An attempt to minimize dissonance by exposing oneself only to information that supports one's choice is known as:
    a. dissonance reduction.
    b. cognitive reduction.
    c. cognitive dissonance.
    d. selective exposure.

18. The processes that underlie our understanding of the social world are called:
    a. social cognitions.
    b. schemas.
    c. central traits.
    d. stereotypes.

19. Sets of cognitions about people and social experiences are known as:
    a. impression formations.
    b. biases.
    c. prophecies.
    d. schemas.

20. Impression formation is the process by which:
    a. an individual exaggerates the good personality traits of a stranger.
    b. drastic differences in people are determined by contrasting certain important traits.
    c. experiences create an overall picture of an individual and place him or her in a stereotypical ingroup.
    d. an individual organizes information about another individual to form an overall impression of that person.

21. According to the text, when forming an impression of another person, people rely heavily on:
    a. central tendencies.
    b. central traits.
    c. primary traits.
    d. schematic tendencies.

22. Warm and cold are considered:
    a. attributions that have little impact on first impressions.
    b. central traits.
    c. stereotyped descriptions of men and women.
    d. the basis for ingroup-outgroup bias.

23. According to the text, which of the following approaches to impression formation has led to a mathematically oriented model of how personality traits are combined to create overall impressions?
    a. social cognition
    b. consensus information
    c. information-processing
    d. central route processing

24. An individual is most likely to view groups to which he or she belongs as:
    a. outgroups.
    b. subgroups.
    c. ingroups.
    d. central groups.

25. When it was discovered that the new couple who moved into the neighborhood were Jews, conversations among the neighbors revealed the typical _____ picturing Jews as shrewd and self-centered people.
    a. cognition
    b. stereotype
    c. central trait
    d. stigma

26. According to the text, which of the following situations leads people to behave in ways that actually fulfill a stereotype?
    a. when they want to please someone who holds the stereotype
    b. when they want to prevent reverse discrimination
    c. when they think that someone has a self-fulfilling prophecy
    d. when they belong to an outgroup

27. As if to prove that he was not prejudiced against blacks, the manager of a large office promoted a black to a supervisory level usually occupied by a person with twice as much experience as the promoted individual. This illustrates:
    a. prejudice.
    b. reciprocity.
    c. reverse discrimination.
    d. stereotyping.

28. When prejudice toward a group is compensated for by treating members of that group more favorably than if they had not been members of that group, we call this:
    a. reversal shift.
    b. reverse discrimination.
    c. reciprocity.
    d. the ingroup-outgroup bias.

29. The extent to which a given behavior occurs across different situations is known as:
    a. distinctiveness information.
    b. consistency information.
    c. consensus information.
    d. attributional information.

30. Causes of behavior that are based on environmental factors are known as:
    a. attributional causes of behavior.
    c. consensual causes of behavior.
    b. dispositional causes of behavior.
    d. situational causes of behavior.

31. The theory that seeks to explain, on the basis of samples of an individual's behavior, what the specific causes of that behavior are is known as:
    a. situation theory.
    c. attribution theory.
    b. consensus theory.
    d. disposition theory.

32. The task of _____ is to explain how people understand the causes of behavior.
    a. discrimination theory
    c. attribution theory
    b. social cognition
    d. directive-behavior theory

33. Which one of the following statements is the best example of dispositional attribution bias?
    a. John is being good because the teacher is watching.
    b. Even though I am not feeling sociable, I will go to the party if you do.
    c. I become very anxious when criticized.
    d. Sue is staying up all night to study because she is a conscientious student.

34. Which of the following situations best describes a situational cause for the described behavior?
    a. Barbara straightens the guest room, which is normally a messy sewing room, because relatives will be staying at her house for a week.
    b. Chris helps an old lady across the street because he is always thoughtful.
    c. John, who is normally grumpy, frowns about an exam as he walks down the hall.
    d. Mindy is a punctual person who is on time for school every morning.

35. According to the text, information that is high in consensus, low in consistency, and low in distinctiveness leads to attributions which are:
    a. dispositional.
    c. situational.
    b. fundamental.
    d. mixed.

36. The tendency for people to attribute others' behavior to dispositional causes and their own behavior to situational causes is known as:
    a. ingroup versus outgroup bias.
    c. dispositional attribution bias.
    b. fundamental attribution bias.
    d. stereotypic attribution bias.

37. According to the text, the tendency to attribute others' behavior to dispositional causes but one's own behavior to situational causes is best illustrated by which of the following?
    a. The tendency toward this bias is infrequently expressed.
    b. This tendency is often reflected in newspaper columns such as "Dear Abby" and "Ann Landers."
    c. The tendency is rarely found in psychiatric patients who have been diagnosed with schizophrenia.
    d. This tendency applies to close friends, not to casual acquaintances.

38. An important concept that the fundamental-attribution bias illustrates about attributional processes is that:
    a. people make explanations about others that tend to be less flattering than the explanations they make about themselves.
    b. people sometimes observe their own behavior and make judgments about others on the basis of their own behavior.
    c. people tend to overrate the effect of situation on others.
    d. people tend to underrate the effect of situation on themselves.

39. The movie star Mae West reportedly said, "I never met a man I didn't like!" Which of the following concepts best explains her comment?
    a. halo effect.
    c. fundamental-attribution error.
    b. Tinsel-Town effect.
    d. Pollyanna effect.

40. The tendency to rate others in a generally positive manner is called the:
    a. impression formation effect.
    c. assumed-similarity bias.
    b. Pollyanna effect.
    d. fundamental-attribution bias.

41. I put off visiting my aunt for such a long time that I decided I probably did not want to see her. Coming to this conclusion is an example of:
    a. self-perception theory.
    c. dispositional attribution bias.
    b. cognitive dissonance theory.
    d. fundamental attribution bias.

42. Two social psychologists, Timothy Wilson and Patricia Linville, devised a program to change the attribution held by freshmen college students. They did this by telling them that, statistically, grades improve as people continue college and by showing them videotapes of junior and senior students who reported that their grades had improved since they started college. If the results of this program followed the expectations of self-perception theory, then the freshmen who were exposed to this information should have:
    a. showed an improvement in their grades and a lower dropout rate.
    b. made more negative attributions about their fellow students.
    c. formed more friends at a faster rate due to greater pressure to study hard.
    d. considerably increased or decreased their study time.

43. According to methods of reducing stereotypes presented in the text, which alternative below will probably **not** help promote accurate perceptions between two or more people?
    a. providing information about the objects of stereotyping
    b. increasing contact between the target of stereotyping and the holder of the stereotype
    c. emphasizing information that justifies perceived stereotypes
    d. making positive values more conspicuous rather than just relying upon contact to change schemas

ESSAY QUESTIONS

Recite and Review: ☐

Essay Question 19.1: *The Consistency between Attitudes and Behavior*

Much has been made of attitudes and behavior and how they may or may not be consistent. Describe a situation in which your attitudes and behavior may not have been consistent, and then compare the cognitive dissonance explanation and the self-perception explanation of the situation

---

Essay Question 19.2: *Is Prejudice Inevitable?*

Consider the concepts of stereotyping, ingroup and outgroup distinctions, the processes involved in changing attitudes, and attribution biases, and then answer the question: Is prejudice inevitable?

_____

_____

_____

_____

_____

_____

_____

_____

_____

_____

_____

_____

_____

_____

_____

_____

_____

_____

20

SOCIAL INFLUENCE
AND INTERACTION

DETAILED OUTLINE	*Survey:* ☐

This detailed outline contains all the headings in Chapter 20: Social Influence and Interaction. If you are using the SQ3R method, then an examination of the outline is the best way to begin your survey of the chapter.

Prologue: Gertrude Lewis and the Central Park Jogger
Looking Ahead

Social Influence
    Conformity: Following what others do
        Gender differences in conformity: Fact or fiction?
    Compliance: Submitting to direct social pressure
        The foot in the door: When a small request leads to a larger one
        The door-in-the-face technique: Where a large request leads to a smaller one
Psychology at Work The Price Is Right?: The Practice of Social Influence
    Obedience: Obeying direct orders
The Informed Consumer of Psychology Strategies for Maintaining Your Own Position
● **Recap and Review I**

Liking and Loving: Interpersonal Attraction and the Development of Relationships
    How do I like thee? Let me count the ways
The Cutting Edge Is Beauty in the Eye of the Baby?
    How do I love thee? Let me count the ways
    Tracing the course of relationships: The rise and fall of liking and loving
    The decline of a relationship
● **Recap and Review II**

Aggression and Prosocial Behavior: Hurting and Helping Others
    Hurting others: Aggression
        Instinct approaches: Aggression as a release
        Frustration-aggression approaches: Aggression as a reaction to frustration
        Observational learning approaches: Learning to hurt others
        Media aggression: Does it hurt to watch TV?
        The link between aggressive pornography and violence toward women
    Reducing and preventing aggression
    Helping Others: The brighter side of human nature

● **Recap and Review III**

Looking Back
Key Terms and Concepts

➤ Now that you have surveyed the chapter, read **Looking Ahead**, pages 648–649.   *Question:* ☐
Focus on the questions on page 649.   *Read:* ☐

| **CONCEPTS AND LEARNING OBJECTIVES** |

Survey: ☐

These are the concepts and the learning objects for Chapter 20. Read them carefully as part of your preliminary survey of the chapter.

Concept 1: Social influence includes behaviors that result from the actions of others, as found in conformity, compliance, and obedience.

  1. Define social influence and conformity and describe the factors that influence conformity. (pp. 648-651)

  2. Define compliance and describe how the foot-in-the-door and the door-in-the-face techniques lead to compliance. (pp. 651-653)

  3. Describe the factors that influence the extent of obedience and the strategies that one can use to hold a position. (pp. 652-655)

Concept 2: The study of liking has revealed a number of factors that influence the degree of friendship between people. Loving is more than intense liking, being qualitatively different. Sternberg has identified companionship, passion, and commitment as three components of love.

  4. Define interpersonal attraction and describe the factors that contribute to friendship and liking. (pp. 656-660)

  5. Describe the efforts that have been made to understand love, and outline the components of Sternberg's theory of love. (pp. 660-662)

  6. Outline the course of relationships from beginning to end. (pp. 663-666)

Concept 3: Aggression involves the intention to hurt another. Observational learning theory suggests that violence depends in part on seeing others commit and be rewarded for violent acts. Prosocial behavior involves helping others.

  7. Define aggression and compare the instinctual, frustration-aggression, and observational learning theories of aggression. (pp. 666-671)

  8. Discuss the relationship of the media to aggression and pornography. (pp. 671-672)

9. Define prosocial behavior, altruism, and empathy, and discuss their role in leading individuals to help other. (pp. 673-675)

CHAPTER SUMMARY

There are several ways you can use this summary as part of your systematic study plan. You may read each concept summary and then read the corresponding pages in the text, or you may read the entire summary and then read the entire chapter in the text. As you finish each section, complete the **Recap and Review** questions that are supplied in the text.

CONCEPT 1: Prologue and Looking Ahead	*Survey:* ☐
Social Influence	*Read:* ☐

Pages 647-656

The Prologue uses two contrasting stories, one of Gertrude Lewis who has adopted a small child with AIDS and the other of the central park jogger who was a victim of a wilding incident. The first illustrates prosocial behavior and the other an extreme expression of aggression and violence. Both are concerns of social psychologists. The area called **social influence** is concerned with how the actions of an individual affect the behavior of others.

In uncertain situations, we tend to look to the behavior of others to guide our own behavior. **Conformity** is the change in behavior or attitudes that results from a desire to follow the beliefs or standards of other people. An experiment by Solomon Asch demonstrated the power of the judgments of others on the perceptual judgments of an individual subject. The subject would hear the judgments about which one of three lines was identical to a fourth "standard" line, and even though the judgments were quite visibly wrong, the subject would conform to the judgments of the group (which were always uniformly the same). About 75 percent of the subjects conformed to the group judgment at least once. Research since the time of Asch's experiment has found several variables that produce conformity:

- The characteristics of the group influence the judgment more if the group is attractive to the group members. Individuals that have a low social rank—**status**—in the group are more likely to conform to the group.
- The individual's response conforms more when it must be made publicly.
- The nature of the task influences conformity. The more ambiguous the task, the higher the conformity. If the individual is less competent, conformity is also higher.
- If the group is unanimous, pressures to conform are greatest. If people with dissenting views have a supporter, called a **social supporter**, then conformity is reduced.

For a long time the prevalent view was that women are more easily influenced than men. Research in the 1970s showed that the tasks and topics used in earlier research were more familiar to men, thus biasing the outcomes. However, more recent research has now reconfirmed the view that women are more likely to conform, possibly because of the tendency to want to get along with others.

The behavior that occurs in response to direct, explicit pressure to endorse a particular view or to behave in a certain way is called **compliance**. Several techniques are used by salespersons to get customers to comply with purchase requests. One technique is called the **foot-in-the-door technique** in which a person agrees to a small request and is then asked to comply with bigger request. Compliance increases when the person first agrees to the smaller request. The technique works because compliance to the small request increases interest. Another explanation suggests that self-perceptions are formed based on compliance to the initial request, and compliance to the larger request is a result of a desire to be consistent.

The **door-in-the-face technique** is the opposite of the foot-in-the-door technique. The door-in-the-face technique follows a large request with a smaller one, making the second request appear more reasonable. In a study, half the subjects were willing to take on small obligation after being asked to make a major commitment where only 17 percent of the control group agreed. One reason why the technique works is because of **reciprocal concessions**, a process in which the requesters are seen to make a compromise and a second refusal would make the person being asked appear unreasonable. Another reason is that people desire to present themselves well to others. Other techniques include **low-balling** where an agreement is reached and then additional costs are revealed, and we tend to stick to the original virtues of the decision. The *that's-not-all technique* presents a deal at an inflated price; then a number of incentives are added. The *not-so-free sample* is another method that creates a psychic cost by giving "free" samples. These samples instigate a norm of reciprocity, leading people to buy as a matter of reciprocation.

Compliance follows a request, but obedience follows direct orders. **Obedience** is defined as a change in behavior due to the commands of others. Obedience occurs in situations involving a boss, teacher, parent, or someone who has power over us. The classic study by Stanley Milgram involved subjects administering shocks to people they thought to be other subjects, supposedly testing to see if shocks would improve memory. The other subjects were actually confederates of the experimenter. Psychiatrists predicted that no more than 2 percent of the subjects would administer the strongest shocks, but almost two-thirds of the subjects gave the highest level of shock. Subjects reported their reasons for giving the level of shock to be their belief that the experimenter was responsible for the ill effects of the shocks. The experiment has been criticized for establishing extreme conditions and for methodological reasons.

There are several strategies available that will help a person avoid the pressures of compliance and obedience. One method is called **inoculation** in which individuals become resistant to persuasion by being exposed to information that refutes opposing arguments. When people learned that a persuasive message was about to be given, a process called **forewarning**, then they were less likely to be persuaded. With an awareness of the forthcoming argument counter to their own beliefs, individuals tend to prepare arguments that support their own position. **Consistency** is not only effective at reducing persuadability but can also change the attitude of the persuader. Apparently the unyielding repetition of one's own position can cause others to rethink their position. Another strategy requires that individuals initially go along with the group, establish their competence, and then behave more independently.

CONCEPT 2: Liking and Loving: Interpersonal Attraction and the Development of Relationships

Survey: ☐
Read: ☐

Pages 656-666

Another area of social influence is called **interpersonal attraction** which encompasses the factors that lead to positive feelings about others. Research on liking has identified the following factors as important in the development of attraction between people:

- **Proximity** refers to the physical nearness or geographical closeness as a factor in development of friendship. Proximity leads to liking.
- Mere exposure also leads to liking. The more often one is exposed to any stimulus, the more the stimulus is liked. Familiarity with a stimulus can evoke positive feelings.

- Similarity influences attraction because we assume that people with similar backgrounds will evaluate us positively. This is called the **reciprocity-of-liking effect**. We also assume that when we like someone, that person likes us in return.

- Need complimentarity refers to attraction that is based on the needs that the partner can fulfill. We may then be attracted to the person that fulfills the greatest number of needs. The **need-complimentarity hypothesis** was first proposed in the 1950s, and the evidence in support of it has been inconsistent. It does appear that people with complimentary abilities are attracted to one another.

- Physical attractiveness is a key factor if all other factors are equal. More attractive people tend to be more popular. Physical attractiveness may be the single most important factor in college dating. There is also a great deal of consensus about what constitutes attractiveness, including the dimensions of facial configurations that make faces attractive. Emphasis on facial dimensions discounts the effects of personality. Attractiveness has an influence on the levels of attention in infants, and leads them to be more socially responsive; infants played longer with a doll with an attractive face. The downside to physical attractiveness in areas like work, where attractive women are hampered by stereotypes, which view women as having risen to a position as a consequence of attractiveness rather than skill. Physical attractiveness is also an asset in social situations.

For a long time social psychologists considered research into love too difficult to conduct scientifically. Love is not merely a more intense liking, but differs from liking on qualitative grounds. An early effort by Rick Zubin involved a scale that was able to distinguish those who scored high on love from those who did not. High scorers were found to gaze at each other more and to have intact relationships six months after the test. Physiological arousal was hypothesized to characterize loving, and arousal for whatever reason was found to be attributed as a feeling of love for a person present at the time of arousal. This theory does explain that when someone is rejected or hurt by another, they may still feel themselves in love as a consequence of arousal. Several kinds of love have been hypothesized, one being **passionate (or romantic) love**, which is an intense state of absorption in another person. Another is **companionate love**, which is strong affection that we have for someone with whom our lives are deeply involved. Robert Sternberg has proposed that love is made of three components. The **intimacy component** includes feelings of closeness and connectedness; the **passion component** is made of the motivational drives related to sex, physical closeness, and romance; and the **decision/commitment component** encompasses the initial cognition that one loves someone and the long-term feelings of commitment to maintain love.

More than one out of two marriages ends in divorce. The behavior of couples in developing relationships changes in predictable ways. The pattern, in order, is: people interact more often, they seek each other's company, they open up more to each other, they begin to understand each other's points of view, they make investments in the relationship, they begin to feel a psychological well-being associated with the relationship, and then they start behaving like a couple. As the relationship develops, the individuals themselves may experience growth and change. Goals for the relationship may differ. Even if both want marriage, they may want different kinds of mates. Preferences differ according to both culture and sex. Successful relationships can be distinguished by the rate at which the individual components evolve. In strong loving relationships, commitment peaks and then remains stable while intimacy grows over the course of the relationship. Passion shows a marked decline through time.

Relationships deteriorate for a number of reasons. One factor is the change in the judgments about the partner's behavior. Forgetfulness that is initially charming may become "boorish indifference." Communication may become disrupted. Decline follows a common pattern. The first phase occurs when a person decides that the relationship cannot be tolerated. In the second phase, the person confronts the partner and tries to determine if repair is possible. The next phase is marked by a public acknowledgment that the relationship is being dissolved and an accounting is made to others. The fourth and last phase is "grave dressing," which is the major activity of ending the physical and psychological relationship. The degree of distress experienced depends upon what the relationship was like prior to the breakup. The number of activities that were mutually shared and the expectation of the difficulty entering a new relationship influence the amount of distress experienced.

CONCEPT 3: Aggression and Prosocial Behavior: Hurting and Helping Others

Survey: ☐
Read: ☐

Pages 666-675

The Kitty Genovese story (Chapter 2) initiated the study of aggression and prosocial behavior. These kinds of incidents give a negative and pessimistic impression of human behavior. The helping behavior of many, however, counteracts the impression. Social psychology seeks to explain these extremes.

Aggression occurs at societal and individual levels, and the basic questions concern whether aggression is inevitable or whether it results from particular circumstances. **Aggression** is defined as the intentional injury of or harm to another person. Instinct theories explain aggression as the result of innate urges. Konrad Lorenz suggested that aggressive energy is built up through the instinct of aggression and that its release is necessary. The discharge of this energy is called **catharsis**. Lorenz suggested that society should provide an acceptable means of achieving catharsis, like sports. There is no way to test this theory experimentally.

The frustration-aggression theory says that the frustration of a goal *always* leads to aggression. **Frustration** is defined as the thwarting of a goal-directed behavior. More recently the theory has been modified to suggest that frustration creates a *readiness* to act aggressively. Actual aggression depends upon the presence of **aggressive cues**, stimuli that have been associated in the past with aggression. In one experiment, the presence of a rifle and a revolver increased the amount of aggression. Subjects who had viewed a violent movie were also more aggressive.

The observational learning view suggests that we learn to act aggressively by observing others. Aggression is not inevitable and can be seen in terms of the rewards and punishments it involves. In the example of a girl hitting a younger brother for damaging her toy, the instinct theory would suggest that the act results from pent-up aggression, the frustration-aggression theory would say that the frustration of not being able to play with the toy led to aggression, and the observational theory would say that aggression had been previously reinforced. Observational learning theory also suggests that the rewards and punishments received by a model are important in the learning of aggression. This formulation has wide support.

Observational theory suggests that if children observe violence that is in some way rewarded, they will be more likely to act violently. Studies have shown that children who watched a lot of television as third-graders became more aggressive adults than those who did not watch as much television. Watching media violence can lead to an increased readiness to act violently and an insensitivity to the suffering of victims. Violence seems to lower inhibitions against aggression, and viewing violence may cause us to interpret even nonaggressive acts as aggressive. Also, continued exposure may desensitize us to violence.

Recent evidence suggests that there may be a link between certain kinds of erotic material and aggression. In an experiment, angered males who viewed an erotic movie that contained violence later showed more aggression toward a female than subjects who had not viewed the film. Viewing violence toward women desensitizes emotional and physiological reactions about violence directed at women. The issue is made more complicated by the First Amendment rights to free speech. Actually, hard-core pornography contains less violence toward women than do R-rated movies.

Prosocial behavior refers to helping behavior. The prosocial behavior studied most by psychologists is bystander intervention. When more than one person witnesses an emergency, **diffusion of responsibility**, the tendency for people to feel that responsibility is shared among those present, increases. Latané and Darley developed a four-step model describing the process of helping others: The first step is the awareness that someone requires help. In the second step, the individual may look to the behavior of others and interpret their inaction as an indication that help is not needed. The third step involves assuming responsibility for taking action. If people with life-saving training are present, then those that have no training are less likely to help because they do not have expertise. The fourth step is deciding and implementing some form of help. Helping may be indirect, in the form of calling the police, or direct in the form of giving first aid or driving the person to the hospital. A **rewards-cost approach** helps predict the nature of help given. The rewards of helping must outweigh the costs. Once the decision to help has been made, one actual step remains, that of giving help. In some cases people act altruistically. **Altruism** is helping behavior that is beneficial to others but may require self-sacrifice. Some people who intervene in situations and offer help may have personality characteristics that differentiate them from others. People high in **empathy** may be more likely to respond than others. Situational factors and mood may also affect helping behavior. Both good and bad moods appear to increase helping behavior.

➤ Now that you have surveyed, questioned, and read the chapter and completed the **Recap and Review** questions, review **Looking Back**, page 676. *Review:* ☐

➤ For additional practice through recitation and review, test your knowledge of the chapter material by answering the questions in the **Key Word Drill**, the **Practice Questions**, and the **Essay Questions**.

KEY WORD DRILL *Recite:* ☐

The following **Fill in the Blank** and **Matching Questions** test key words from the text. Check your answers with the Answer Key in the back of the *Study Guide*.

FILL IN THE BLANK

1. The study of _____ _____ is concerned with situations in which the actions of an individual or group affect the behavior of others.

2. When a person changes behavior or an attitude as a result of a desire to follow the beliefs or standards of other people, that person is involved in _____.

3. An individual's social rank is called _____.

4. The person who shares an unpopular opinion or attitude of another group member, thereby encouraging nonconformity, is called a _____ _____.

5. _____ occurs in response to direct, explicit pressure to endorse a particular point of view or to behave in a certain way.

6. _____ is expressed when a person intentionally seeks to injure or to harm another person.

7. _____ depends upon the notion that aggression is built up and must be discharged through violent acts.

8. The state produced by the thwarting or blocking of some ongoing, goal-directed behavior is

   referred to as _____.

9. Stimuli that have been associated with aggression in the past are considered to be

   _____ _____.

10. The general term that describes the positive feelings for others, including both liking and loving, is

   _____ _____.

MATCHING QUESTIONS

_____ 11. foot-in-the-door technique

_____ 12. door-in-the-face technique

_____ 13. reciprocal concessions

_____ 14. low-balling

a. After an agreement is reached, the seller reveals additional costs and the buyer complies.

b. Compliance with an important request is more likely if it follows compliance with a smaller previous request.

c. Requesters appear to compromise their initial request, thereby inviting a compromise in return.

d. A large request, refusal of which is expected, is followed by a smaller request.

_____ 15. obedience

_____ 16. inoculation

_____ 17. forewarning

_____ 18. consistency

a. Exposure to arguments opposing one's beliefs, making the subject more resistant to later attempts to change those beliefs.

b. A subject is told in advance that a persuasive message is coming in order to reduce the effect of social influence.

c. A change in behavior due to the commands of others.

d. The persistence of those holding an unpopular view that eventually brings about a change in the majority.

_____ 19. passionate (or romantic) love

a. The motivational drives relating to sex, physical closeness, and romance.

_____ 20. companionate love

b. Feelings of closeness and connectedness.

_____ 21. intimacy component

c. The initial cognition that one loves someone, and the longer-term feelings of commitment.

_____ 22. passion component

_____ 23. decision/commitment component

d. The strong affection we have for those with whom our lives are deeply involved.

e. A state of intense absorption in someone that is characterized by physiological arousal, psychological interest, and caring for another's needs.

_____ 24. proximity

a. Helping behavior that is beneficial to others while requiring sacrifice on the part of the helper.

_____ 25. reciprocity-of-liking effect

_____ 26. need-complementarity hypothesis

b. The hypothesis that people are attracted to others who fulfill their needs.

_____ 27. prosocial behavior

c. One person's experiencing of another's emotions, in turn increasing the likelihood of responding to the other's needs.

_____ 28. diffusion of responsibility

_____ 29. rewards-costs approach

d. The tendency to like those who like us.

_____ 30. altruism

e. The tendency for people to feel that responsibility for helping is shared among those present.

_____ 31. empathy

f. Any helping behavior.

g. Nearness to another, one cause for liking.

h. The notion that, in a situation requiring help, a bystander's perceived rewards must outweigh the costs if helping is to occur.

| **PRACTICE QUESTIONS** | *Recite and Review:* ❏ |

Test your knowledge of the chapter material by answering these **True-False** and **Multiple Choice Questions**. Check your answers with the Answer Key in the back of the *Study Guide*.

TRUE-FALSE QUESTIONS

T   F   1.   Conformity is a social pressure which is not in the form of a direct order.

T   F   2. Compliance to a request will often increase if the requester makes what appears to be a compromise after the first refusal, thus inviting the refuser to offer a compromise in return.

T   F   3. In finding a suitable mate, individuals always look for someone much like themselves.

T   F   4. Unless the initial interactions are negative, repeated exposure to any stimulus makes people enjoy it more.

T   F   5. Love and liking are generally viewed as qualitatively different states, according to latest research.

T   F   6. In Robert Sternberg's conceptualization, passionate love is a kind of love resulting from a combination of components that are the basic elements of love.

T   F   7. The concept of catharsis has been difficult to substantiate since there is little evidence of a pent-up reservoir of aggression that needs to be discharged through catharsis.

T   F   8: Because the proportion of sexual behavior is higher in X-rated movies than in R-rated movies, the effect X-rated movies has on violence toward women is higher.

T   F   9. If your car stops on the highway on a dark evening, you are more likely to be assisted by another motorist if the highway is heavily traveled.

T   F   10. Altruism is aggressive injurious behavior that is enacted without remorse.

MULTIPLE CHOICE QUESTIONS

1. According to the text, the "wilding" that left a female jogger brutalized and near death is an example of violence that is most likely to be studied by:
    a. anthropologists.
    b. physiological psychologists.
    c. instinct theorists.
    d. social psychologists.

2. Conformity is a change in behavior or attitude brought about by:
    a. an increase of knowledge.
    b. a desire to follow the beliefs or standards of others.
    c. intense pressure to be a distinct individual.
    d. an insecure self-image.

3. The classic demonstration of pressure to conform comes from a series of studies carried out in the 1950s by:
    a. B. F. Skinner.
    b. Solomon Asch.
    c. Philip Zimbardo.
    d. Stanley Milgram.

4. Considering that Asch's experiment involved a perceptual judgment that was fairly obvious, what variable related to conformity does the experiment appear to contradict?
   a. The task variable—if an individual feels competent in a task, conformity is less likely.
   b. The characteristics of the group—the group members were completely unknown to the subjects because the experiment was done blindly.
   c. The nature of the response—since the subjects were allowed to write down an answer, there should have been little pressure.
   d. The nature of the group—since the group could not agree, the subject should have be freer to respond without pressure.

5. Considering the discussion of gender differences in conformity, which of these individuals would be most likely to conform?
   a. a man
   b. a woman
   c. an individual who is familiar with the task at hand
   d. an individual who is unfamiliar with the task at hand

6. When you are expected to work out a solution to a problem with which you have not previously had experience, studies in social influence suggest that you may:
   a. simply quit and leave the solution to someone else.
   b. be more susceptible to suggestions of others offering solutions.
   c. attempt to resist suggestions for a solution from others.
   d. be encouraged to rely on your own past experiences.

7. What measure may be most effective for reducing the tendency of people to conform in a group situation?
   a. Make sure all members value the group highly.
   b. Include lots of members in the group.
   c. Use a show of hands when voting.
   d. Use a secret ballot when voting.

8. According to the text, which of the following has been shown to affect the amount of conformity displayed by members of a group?
   a. obedience of each member of the group to the legal authority
   b. the kind of task the group is assigned
   c. the amount of individuality expressed by each person in the group, as measured by how they are dressed
   d. the consistency of the group's leader

9. People working on tasks and questions that are ambiguous are more susceptible to:
   a. inoculation.
   c. forewarning.
   b. obedience.
   d. social pressure.

10. According to the text, a change in behavior that results from direct, explicit social pressure to behave in a certain way is called:
    a. conformity.
    c. commission.
    b. congruence.
    d. compliance.

11. The sales technique by which someone first asks you to comply with a small request and later makes a larger request is called:
   a. door-in-the-face.
   b. foot-in-the-door.
   c. foot-in-the-mouth.
   d. fly-in-the-face.

12. What is the correct term for the technique in which a large request is asked, followed by expected refusal and later a smaller request?
   a. obedience
   b. social compliance
   c. door-in-the-face technique
   d. foot-in-the-door technique

13. According to the text, the term "reciprocal concessions" refers to:
   a. compliance only when the other person offers to do the same at another time.
   b. the increased donation to a cause when something like cookies or candy is given as "thanks" for the donation.
   c. compliance resulting from the perception that the requester compromised by lowering a price or request.
   d. the desire for the requester to leave with a good impression of the person who has been asked to comply with something.

14. The classic experiment demonstrating the power of authority to produce obedience was performed by:
   a. Albert Bandura.
   b. Solomon Asch.
   c. Stanley Milgram.
   d. B. F. Skinner.

15. The social influence technique of the not-so-free sample given in grocery stores involves:
   a. actually paying for the sample in the price of the groceries.
   b. being told that you are allowed a certain number of free samples before you must make a purchase.
   c. creating psychic costs that bring you around to purchasing a product because you feel you owe it to the store, even though you may not need the product.
   d. a cost of resisting the sample that is higher than giving in and buying the product.

16. The Milgram study on obedience showed that:
   a. very few subjects were willing to "electrocute" the learner.
   b. about one-third of the subjects were willing to "electrocute" the learner.
   c. the majority of the subjects were willing to "electrocute" the learner.
   d. all of the subjects were willing to "electrocute" the learner.

17. In the Milgram study on obedience, those who were willing to "electrocute" the learner did so because:
   a. they thought the learner would not be hurt.
   b. they thought they would not be held responsible for injury.
   c. they thought the learner deserved the shocks.
   d. they thought they would be punished for noncompliance.

18. According to the text, a technique that not only is effective in reducing persuasibility but can also actually change the attitude of the majority is known as:
   a. inoculation.
   b. reciprocal concession.
   c. forewarning.
   d. consistency.

19. The procedure in which subjects are warned in advance that a persuasive message is coming is known as:
    a. consistency.
    b. forewarning.
    c. inoculation.
    d. compliance.

20. The unyielding persistence of a minority group in advocating its platform may reduce persuasibility and even change attitudes of many members of the majority. According to the text, this technique is called:
    a. conformity.
    b. consistency.
    c. compliance.
    d. obedience.

21. All of the following are strong influences on the formation of friendships **except**:
    a. others who are like them.
    b. others who live nearby.
    c. others whom they see frequently.
    d. others who are exceptionally attractive.

22. Proximity is defined as:
    a. nearness to another person.
    b. a tendency to like those who like us.
    c. a tendency of those whom we like to like us.
    d. distance from another.

23. Of the following, which factor is the best predictor of whether two people will be initially attracted to each other?
    a. similarity
    b. mere exposure
    c. proximity
    d. complementarity

24. Physical attractiveness is usually advantageous to a beautiful person. Which vocation below sometimes makes physical attractiveness a personal liability?
    a. a male high school teacher
    b. a female nurse
    c. a male defense attorney
    d. a female manager in a major corporation

25. The results of a study on the attractiveness of faces showed that:
    a. different races have different views on attractiveness.
    b. men with different personality types viewed the face differently.
    c. babies and grown-ups judged the same face to be attractive.
    d. most men showed agreement on which facial features were attractive.

26. According to many social psychologists, love represents:
    a. a greater quantity than liking.
    b. a different physiological state than liking.
    c. an emotion, unlike liking.
    d. essentially the same state as liking.

27. The text describes a popular questionnaire used by some social psychologists which contains items such as "I would do almost anything for (person's name to whom the individual completing the questionnaire is attracted)." "I think that (person's name) is unusually well adjusted." The questionnaire is designed to measure:
    a. proximity.
    b. companionate love.
    c. love and liking.
    d. need complementarity.

28. Which of the following elements does love have which liking does not?
    a. proximity
    c. similarity
    b. complementarity
    d. physical arousal

29. According to Sternberg's theory of love, each of the following is a component of love except:
    a. intimacy.
    c. decision/commitment.
    b. passion.
    d. individuation/separation.

30. According to the text, each of the following is a kind of love studied by Sternberg **except**:
    a. empty love.
    c. fatuous love.
    b. compassionate love.
    d. companionate love.

31. According to Sternberg, different types of love are made up of different quantities of:
    a. liking, loving, and commitment.
    c. emotion, motivation, and attraction.
    b. passion, compassion, and attraction.
    d. intimacy, passion, and commitment.

32. The long-term success of loving relationships appears to be dependent upon the levels of the individual components of love at various times in the relationships. According to the text, which alternative below is **not** one of the trends for a long-term, successful loving relationship?
    a. Commitment peaks early in the relationship and then remains stable.
    b. Friendship shows high levels early in the relationship, and these levels are maintained with time.
    c. Intimacy continues to grow over the course of the relationship.
    d. Passion peaks early in the relationship, then shows a marked decline.

33. Knowledge gained about relationships from empirical studies suggests that:
    a. in strong loving relationships, intimacy continues to increase, while commitment reaches a peak and becomes stable.
    b. the demise of each relationship is unique, since it depends upon the particular characteristics each person brings to the relationship.
    c. liking is a very gentle form of love.
    d. husbands' and wives' views differ dramatically on most-often-cited reasons for success in a marriage.

34. According to Levinger, which of the following events seems to be an important reason for the decline of a relationship?
    a. a change in judgments about the meaning of the partner's behavior
    b. an increase in punishment of the partner
    c. turning to others for the needs that the partner used to fulfill
    d. an increase in discussions that are critical of the partner

35. When a loving relationship deteriorates, there are several indications. Which of the following is **not** mentioned in your text as an indicator?
    a. A partner may begin to invite and agree with criticism of the other partner from people outside the relationship.
    b. Communications may become disrupted in the relationship.
    c. There is an increase in adverse judgments about the partner's behavior.
    d. A partner engages in an extramarital affair.

36. During _____ of a relationship on the decline, one partner would be most likely to say, "How do you think we should reshape our relationship?"
    a. Phase 1
    b. Phase 2
    c. Phase 3
    d. Phase 4

37. During _____ of a relationship on the decline, more and more friends and acquaintances of the affected couple are made aware of the demise of the relationship and the reasons for it.
    a. Phase 1
    b. Phase 2
    c. Phase 3
    d. Phase 4

38. According to Duck, the phase of the decline of a relationship in which a person confronts the partner in order to determine whether the relationship should be terminated or repaired is:
    a. Phase 1.
    b. Phase 2.
    c. Phase 3.
    d. Phase 4.

39. The phase of a relationship on the decline, in which each partner copes with the demise of the relationship so that events associated with it appear reasonable and acceptable, is called:
    a. dyadic.
    b. ambivalent.
    c. grave-dressing.
    d. social.

40. The most recent formulation of the frustration-aggression theory states that frustration:
    a. always leads to aggression.
    b. arouses an innate need for catharsis.
    c. leads to aggression only when others are present.
    d. produces anger, leading to a readiness to act.

41. Frustration is most likely to lead to aggression:
    a. in the presence of aggressive cues.
    b. immediately after being frustrated.
    c. during late adolescence.
    d. several hours after being frustrated.

42. Prosocial is a more formal way of describing behavior that is:
    a. helping.
    b. cathartic.
    c. innate.
    d. aggressive.

43. Diffusion of responsibility can occur when:
    a. aggressive cues are present.
    b. the catharsis hypothesis is in effect.
    c. there is more than one bystander to an incident.
    d. innate behaviors are operative.

| **ESSAY QUESTIONS** | *Recite and Review:* ☐ |

Essay Question 20.1: *Conformity and Violence*

What factors would be at work when prejudices erupt into violence against racial groups? Analyze the factors of conformity, obedience, and stereotyping, including ingroup and outgroup biases (this material from Chapter 19).

_____

_____

_____

_____

_____

_____

_____

_____

_____

_____

_____

_____

_____

_____

_____

_____

_____

Essay Question 20.2: *Should Pornography Be Banned?*

Discuss how the evidence of the relationship between pornography and violence against women should be used. Should pornography be banned? Defend your answer with evidence from the text and with reasoned arguments.

_____

_____

_____

_____

_____

_____

_____

_____

_____

_____

_____

_____

_____

_____

_____

_____

_____

ACTIVITIES AND PROJECTS

1. Think about how you became friends or acquaintances with the people you currently know. What roles were played by the following factors in the formation and maintenance of your relationships: proximity, mere exposure, similarity, physical attraction, the reciprocity-of-liking effect?

2. Watch some prime-time television and keep a log of violent incidents. How many violent incidents can you count in one hour? What is the nature of the violence? Do you believe that television violence leads to real violence? Explain.

21

CONSUMER AND INDUSTRIAL-ORGANIZATIONAL PSYCHOLOGY

DETAILED OUTLINE	*Survey:* ☐

This detailed outline contains all the headings in Chapter 21: Consumer and Industrial-Organizational Psychology. If you are using the SQ3R method, then an examination of the outline is the best way to begin your survey of the chapter.

Prologue: Lee Iacocca
Looking Ahead

Consumer Psychology: Psychology in the Marketplace
    Advertising appeals: Soft sell versus hard sell
    Psychographics: The psychology of the consumer
        Subcultural differences in consumer behavior
The Cutting Edge We Are What We Buy: The Philadelphia Cream Cheese Experiment
    Consumer cognitive processing: Decision making in the marketplace
        Problem recognition
        Information search
        Evaluation of alternatives
        Purchase
        Postpurchase evaluation
The Informed Consumer of Psychology The Informed Consumer of Psychology Meets the Informed Consumer
● **Recap and Review I**

Industrial-Organizational Psychology: Work Motivation and Satisfaction
    The motivation to work
    Job satisfaction
        Supervision and satisfaction: It is better to give than to receive
        Back to the future?: Electronic supervision
Psychology at Work Importing Japan to America
        Satisfaction and the nature of the job
        Role conflict

Increasing employee satisfaction: Fitting the person to the job or the job to the person
    Changing the job
    Changing the person in the job
    Matching the person to the job
Satisfaction may not equal productivity: A final note
- **Recap and Review II**

Industrial-Organizational Psychology: Making Decisions on the Job
Who makes decisions: One or many?
Groupthink
- **Recap and Review III**

Looking Back
Key Terms and Concepts

➤ Now that you have surveyed the chapter, read **Looking Ahead**, page 680.   *Question:* ☐
Focus on the questions on page 680.   *Read:* ☐

CONCEPTS AND LEARNING OBJECTIVES

Survey: ☐

These are the concepts and the learning objects for Chapter 21. Read them carefully as part of your preliminary survey of the chapter.

Concept 1: Consumer psychology has evolved effective strategies for analyzing the marketplace, including psychographic analysis and micromarketing, as well as careful analysis of the process involved in making a decision to purchase a product.

1. Define consumer psychology and industrial-organizational psychology. (pp. 680-681)

2. Distinguish hard-sell and soft-sell advertising techniques, and discuss how they influence the consumer. (pp. 681-683)

3. Define psychographics, describe how the technique divides people into lifestyle groups, and describe the groups themselves. (pp. 683-687)

4. Discuss the various ways consumers have of making decisions regarding the selection and purchase of goods and services. (pp. 687-691)

Concept 2: Industrial-organizational psychology focuses on the motivation and satisfaction of the worker with the objective of improving satisfaction and productivity.

5. Describe and distinguish the need theories, cognitive theories, and reinforcement theories of work motivation. (pp. 691-694)

6. Describe the effects of different types of decision making and the types of supervision on job satisfaction. (pp. 694-696)

7. Describe the Japanese management and organizational style. (p. 697)

8. List, define, and discuss the factors that contribute to job satisfaction. (pp. 696, 698-700)

Concept 3: Decisions can be made by one person in a centralized fashion or through group processes in a decentralized decision-making process. One major problem for groups is the phenomenon of groupthink that may cause groups to overlook alternatives and make poor decisions.

9. Compare group and individual decision making. (pp. 701-703)

10. Define groupthink and discuss the hazards that accompany it. (pp. 703-704)

CHAPTER SUMMARY

There are several ways you can use this summary as part of your systematic study plan. You may read each concept summary and then read the corresponding pages in the text, or you may read the entire summary and then read the entire chapter in the text. As you finish each section, complete the **Recap and Review** questions that are supplied in the text.

**CONCEPT 1: Prologue and Looking Ahead
Consumer Psychology: Psychology
in the Marketplace**

Survey: ☐
Read: ☐

Pages 680-691

The Prologue describes the success of Lee Iacocca in the areas of the marketplace and the workplace, areas reflected in consumer and industrial-organizational psychology. **Consumer psychology** specializes in understanding buying habits and the effects of advertising on buying behavior. Its object is to understand how those who make and sell products influence potential purchasers. **Industrial-organizational psychology** is concerned with issues such as worker motivation, satisfaction, and productivity. It also focuses on the operation and design of the workplace.

Consumer psychologists attempt to understand why particular advertising strategies work. There are two major strategies in advertising. One is the **soft sell**, through which the advertiser seeks to associate a product with an image related to the product's use. Potential buyers will in turn obtain a desirable image by using the product. The **hard-sell** approach focuses on the qualities of the product itself. Factors such as how well it works, how it tastes, or how it will improve the quality of the customers' lives when used are qualities of the product. Sometimes hard-sell and soft-sell approaches are combined. The example given is that of the BMW automobile that appeals to both image and quality requirements. Which of the approaches is most persuasive depends on the personality characteristics of the consumer. **Self-monitoring** is the tendency to change behavior in order to present ourselves favorably in particular social situations. High self-monitors adjust their behavior according to the situation, and low self-monitors tend to be insensitive to situations and reflect their own attitudes, values, and beliefs in their behavior. High self-monitors are more sensitive to soft-sell advertising that emphasizes a positive image, and low self-monitors are more sensitive to the qualities of the product. Research has demonstrated that high self-monitors rate a product higher when it is associated with an image-oriented advertisement, and low self-monitors rated a product higher when it was associated with a quality-oriented advertisement. One approach will not be universally effective.

In order to make marketing of products more effective, a technique called **psychographics** has evolved. Psychographics attempts to divide people into groups according to their lifestyle profiles as they are related to purchasing patterns. Profiles take into account marital status, race and ethnic background, educational level, and even activities. One of the more specific profiles is the values and lifestyles system, or VALS. The VALS approach distinguishes four major categories: need-driven consumers who make purchases to satisfy a basic need, outer-directed consumers who are motivated by the desire to impress others, inner-directed consumers who make purchases to increase their own self-awareness, and combined outer- and inner-directed consumers who mesh social and self-needs (Table 21-1, on page 685 in the text, describes specific subcategories). The categories are further divided. Need-driven individuals are either Survivors or Sustainers. The outer-directed category contains Belongers, who are blue-collar workers, and the Emulators and Achievers. Achievers comprise about 20 percent of the population and are successful managers and professionals. The inner-directed category includes the I-Am-Me's, the Experientials, and the Societally Conscious. The highest group, the Integrateds, combines the best of the inner- and outer-directed groups.

Other differences can be identified, such as the differences between racial and ethnic groups. For instance, African-Americans are more loyal to national brands than are whites and they spend less money on food, housing, and transportation, among other characteristics. Hispanics purchase 50 percent more beer than other groups and more juice, spaghetti, and shampoo. Different purchasing patterns reflect different values and interests. Advertisers must be aware of the cultural implications of their advertising. For example, the RJ Reynolds effort to market a brand of cigarettes called "Uptown" led to problems regarding the ethics of targeting a minority population with a potentially life-threatening product. The technique called **micromarketing** targets products at specific groups rather than at geographic regions. Computers enable store managers to determine which products are being sold, when they are being bought, and who is buying them. Shelf space can be allotted according to these buying patterns and specific characteristics of individual shoppers can be examined.

Marketing experts are also interested in how a person decides when and what to purchase. The model employed by most sellers involves five steps. The first step is the problem recognition, that is, recognizing that a need exists. In some cases advertising is intended to create the impression of a need where no need may have existed before. Once the problem is recognized, the consumer begins an information search. This means that greater attention will be given to information about the needed product. The sources of information include: personal sources, commercial sources, public sources like newspaper and magazine articles, and experiential sources that include trying various samples of the product. Commercial sources are the least influential because the source is perceived as self-interested. In the next step, the consumer evaluates alternatives. Judgments include the consideration of **product attributes**, or characteristics of the product that are relevant to the decision. Consumers make decisions regarding their **brand beliefs**. Prior experiences with particular brands influence their judgment. The next step is the purchase. Two factors can intervene and change the decision reached in the evaluation stage. First are the attitudes of others that may override the decision. Second, situational factors may prevent the consumer from making the purchase. These may include excessive cost or a competing product that may be on sale. Finally, the consumer engages in postpurchase evaluation. After the purchase has been made, **cognitive dissonance** suggests that the selected product will receive an even-higher evaluation as a matter of reinforcing the choice made by the consumer, thus avoiding any contradictory cognitions. We may, for instance, convince ourselves that the purchase was an excellent decision, either by attending to additional supportive information or by asking for reassurance from friends and acquaintances.

The Informed Consumer of Psychology discusses steps that can be taken to ensure that an individual makes a good decision. Needs should be considered objectively. Remember that salespeople have their own self-interest when they make their sales pitches. Use objective research to determine the best brand. Do your own research, be systematic, and keep the phases of purchase in mind.

CONCEPT 2: Industrial-Organizational Psychology: *Survey:* ☐
Work Motivation and Satisfaction *Read:* ☐

Pages 691-701

Industrial-organizational psychologists take the examination of the role of work in people's lives as a major focal point of their research. Three types of explanations have developed regarding worker satisfaction. The **need theories of work motivation** are derived from Maslow's theory. Basic needs must be met, and as the basic needs are met, workers will use work to fulfill their need for social contact. Ultimately, work may become a means of self-actualization. **Cognitive theories of work motivation** focus on cognitions about work. One cognitive explanation focuses on goal setting. Effective goals must be both specific and difficult in order to motivate workers. **Reinforcement theories of work motivation** depend on behavioral principles. Employee motivation can be increased through the use of positive reinforcement. Simple reinforcement pays workers for each item produced, called "piecework." More complex methods may use salary increases, bonuses, or additional vacation time as reinforcements.

One of the strongest influences on worker satisfaction appears to be the decision-making process employed in the workplace. **Decentralized decision making** extends authority throughout the organization. **Centralized decision making** places power and authority with the few people at the top. The decentralized approach tends to have more satisfaction associated with it.

Another factor is the supervisory style of the boss. People who see their boss as considerate of their needs are more satisfied. The supervisor must balance the demands of the need for high productivity with the task of motivating employees. Supervisors tend to be blamed for problems that may not even be within their control. Also, supervisors have higher levels of job satisfaction than nonsupervisors.

Electronic supervision can be used to monitor the performance of individuals like the person described in the text. Her pay is dependent upon how many claims she processes, and her work is constantly monitored by the computer, which informs a supervisor whenever she stops working. Electronic monitoring is an example of the **classical** (or **bureaucratic**) **model of management** which is a system of rules, regulations, and procedures that govern every task. It has been discredited as a means of management because it ignores the social characteristics of the workplace. Workers become alienated and lose their sense of control. The **human relations model of management** places emphasis on the social context of work and people's interactions with each other. Managers facilitate workers' achievement of independence and control. Electronic management is difficult to reconcile with the human relations model. A number of factors differentiate the management methods used by Japanese firms from those used in America. Japanese workers are guaranteed lifetime positions. Quality circles are used to ensure the quality of goods. These involve the workers in decisions about improving the quality of the product. Work is done according to the principle of *kaizen* which refers to the constant search for improvement. Collective responsibility is stressed, and everyone shares in the success.

Job satisfaction also depends upon how clearly an employee understands his or her responsibilities. The degree of explicitness is called **job clarity**. The lack of job clarity is most frequent in managerial positions where there may not be clear goals.

Another problem area is **role conflict**, which arises when the expectations of the job make it impossible to accomplish properly. Sometimes two or more conflicting sets of expectations may cause problems. A supervisor who must both increase productivity and keep the workers happy may have an impossible job. Sometimes the role that a person has outside the corporation may conflict with corporate goals. An ill child and the need to make a business trip will create role conflict for a working woman. In addition to lowered job satisfaction, employees report tension and anxiety in situations of role conflict. These factors lead to turnover and lower productivity.

Employee satisfaction can be increased in one of three ways: change the job, improve the match between employee and job, or change the jobs and the people who fit in them. Changing the job may require clarification of the job responsibilities. Another strategy is called **job enrichment** which includes increasing the skills that a position requires, modifying the job so that a person can complete an entire product, increasing the influence a person has over others, and increasing the precision of feedback. When jobs are redesigned, they become more meaningful to the worker and can improve worker satisfaction, as well as turnover and reduce stress. Changing the person can involve things like sensitivity training to change attitudes and improve mutual understanding of the views of others. Role playing is sometimes used to help employees understand how others perform their jobs. Another method is to match the person and the job more closely. Some people do not handle ambiguity well, and some people thrive in supervisory roles.

Having satisfied workers may not necessarily lead to improved productivity. The relationship between the two factors is small, and so the employer may need to use two different techniques, one for satisfaction and the other for productivity.

CONCEPT 3: Industrial-Organizational Psychology: *Survey:* ☐
Making Decisions on the Job   *Read:* ☐

Pages 701-704

Decision making is an important component of the processes organizations undergo. One style of decision making is called **participatory decision making** in which the people who have to implement the decision are also involved in making it. But whether this is better than nonparticipatory decision making depends on the situation. Research suggests that participatory decision making has as much positive effect as negative effect on productivity, but it also leads to higher levels of satisfaction and morale. Highly structured problems may require a different process than unstructured problems. Participation can take the form of joint decisions, recommendations from an advisory group, or the providing of essential information to the manager who must make a specific recommendation. There is also a question of whether the group or the individual makes a better decision. The group has the advantage of shared information and experience and the disadvantage of making compromises that may lead to poor decisions. Powerful individuals may also influence the group. The guidelines for determining whether the decision is better made by a group or an individual include: groups are better at establishing clear objectives, a set of individuals working alone is better at finding the largest number of possible solutions, group judgments are superior when evaluating alternatives, group decisions about which alternative to select commits more individuals to the decision, and individuals are superior at implementing the choice.

When groups make decisions, a phenomenon called **groupthink** can occur. Groupthink is described as a type of thinking undertaken by group members who share a strong motivation to achieve a consensus and thus lose their ability to evaluate critically the alternatives. The phenomenon of groupthink is likely to occur when there is an illusion that the group is invulnerable and cannot make errors, when contradictory information tends to be ignored, discounted, or minimized, when there are pressures to conform to the majority view, when pressures discourage minority viewpoints, and when there is an illusion of a threat to morality. The consequences of groupthink are almost always negative. They tend to limit the alternatives and then to spend little time on them when the leader leans toward a particular choice.

➤ Now that you have surveyed, questioned, and read the chapter and completed
    the **Recap and Review** questions, review **Looking Back**, pages 704–705.   *Review:* ☐

➤ For additional practice through recitation and review, test your knowledge of the chapter material by answering the questions in the *Key Word Drill*, the *Practice Questions*, and the *Essay Questions*.

| KEY WORD DRILL | *Recite:* ☐ |

The following **Fill in the Blank** and **Matching Questions** test key words from the text. Check your answers with the Answer Key in the back of the *Study Guide*.

FILL IN THE BLANK

1. _____ psychologists specialize in understanding buying habits and the effects of advertising on buyer behavior.

2. _____-_____ psychology is concerned with the workplace.

3. _____-_____ can cause us to change our behavior if we desire to present ourselves well in particular social situations.

4. The technique of _____ divides people into lifestyle profiles that are related to purchasing patterns.

5. Characteristics of a product are called _____ _____.

6. Our assumptions about a product that are based on our knowledge of the manufacturer of the product are called _____ _____.

7. The simultaneous holding of two cognitions that are contradictory can cause

_____ _____.

8. Generally discredited, the _____ model of management sets explicit rules that govern every task and establishes a rigid division of labor.

9. The _____ _____ view of management places greater emphasis on the social context of work than competing views.

10. When group members share such strong motivation to achieve consensus, a phenomenon called

_____ can lead to the group losing the ability to critically evaluate alternative points of view.

MATCHING QUESTIONS

_____ 11. soft sell

_____ 12. hard sell

_____ 13. micromarketing

_____ 14. self-monitoring

_____ 15. psychographics

_____ 16. brand beliefs

a. The tendency to change our behavior in order to present ourselves well in particular social situations.

b. Focuses on the qualities of the product itself.

c. Targeting marketing efforts to particular buyers on a neighborhood or even individual store level.

d. Divides people into lifestyle profiles that are related to purchasing patterns.

e. The assumptions held by consumers of a product, based on their knowledge of the manufacturer.

f. A product is associated with an image related to the product's use.

_____ 17. need theories of work motivation

_____ 18. cognitive theories of work motivation

_____ 19. reinforcement theories of work motivation

_____ 20. decentralized decision making

_____ 21. centralized decision making

_____ 22. participative decision making

a. Focus on people's thoughts about their jobs and the workplace as the motivations for work.

b. The people involved in implementing a decision are also involved in making it.

c. Authority rests in the hands of a few people at the top of the organization.

d. A hierarchy of needs underlies the motivation to work.

e. Authority extends throughout the organization.

f. The motivation to work is based on behavioral principles.

_____ 23. job clarity

_____ 24. role conflict

_____ 25. job enrichment

_____ 26. groupthink

a. Group members lose the ability to critically evaluate alternative points of view.

b. Improving the quality of the activities involved in a job.

c. The degree of explicitness of the rules that determine what is expected of a worker.

d. Occurs when job expectations are defined in a way that makes it impossible to perform the job properly.

PRACTICE QUESTIONS	*Recite and Review:* ☐

Test your knowledge of the chapter material by answering these **True-False** and **Multiple Choice Questions**. Check your answers with the Answer Key in the back of the *Study Guide*.

TRUE-FALSE QUESTIONS

T   F   1. Industrial-organizational psychologists are interested in such areas of research as "how advertisers develop and target advertisements to particular individuals."

T   F   2. Individuals who are high self-monitors are more likely to attend to advertisements that follow the soft-sell approach.

T   F   3. The VALS classification system for consumers is based on Abraham Maslow's hierarchy of needs.

T   F   4. For a special science class, you purchase a multi-function scientific calculator, only to discover that all the computations you will be required to do are to be done in the computer laboratory on a program supplied by the school. This situation is likely to cause cognitive dissonance.

T   F   5. The need theories of motivation focus on people's thoughts about their jobs and the workplace as motivations for work.

T   F   6. According to the text, because employees blame everything on their immediate supervisors—even things far beyond the supervisors' control—the positive aspects of the supervisors' actual realms of control are negated.

T   F   7. In Japanese management systems, employees are encouraged to continue doing things as they have been done since norms were established.

T   F   8. Improved worker job satisfaction does not necessarily mean improved worker productivity.

T   F   9. When choosing an alternative from among several alternatives, the involvement of the group insures greater acceptance of the decision and thus makes the choice more effective.

T   F   10. Groupthink arises when the group sees itself as vulnerable and in need of solidarity.

MULTIPLE CHOICE QUESTIONS

1. According to the text, psychologists who specialize in understanding buying habits and the effects of advertising on behavior are called:
    a. psychographers.
    b. consumer psychologists.
    c. market analysts.
    d. social psychologists.

2. Which of the following would be most interested in determining the impact of unionization on workers, management, and productivity?
    a. clinical psychologists
    b. consumer psychologists
    c. social psychologists
    d. industrial-organizational psychologists

3. Which of the following would be most likely to research the timing of a political advertisement and its effectiveness?
    a. consumer psychologist
    b. cognitive psychologist
    c. perception psychologist
    d. forensic psychologist

4. When a new style of jeans is advertised by showing well-built and good-looking young men wearing only the jeans, the advertiser is anticipating that the audience will:
    a. realize that the jeans are very sturdy and durable.
    b. focus on the jeans, since that is all that is being worn.
    c. associate the jeans with the good feelings of youth and vigor.
    d. ignore the commercials presented by other companies.

5. The approach to selling that focuses on the qualities of the product itself is called:
    a. soft sell.
    b. micromarketing.
    c. hard sell.
    d. psychographics.

6. To counter the effects of a competitor who uses sexual imagery to sell their jeans, a clothing manufacturer shows young men and women playing basketball and a small child at a playground to emphasize the durability of their product. This company is focusing on which of the following approaches to sell their jeans?
    a. soft sell
    b. hard sell
    c. psychographics
    d. peripheral route processing

7. The tendency to alter our behavior in order to have others view us in a particular way in given social situations is called:
    a. psychographics.
    b. central route processing.
    c. I-Am-Me approach.
    d. self-monitoring.

8. Which of the following combinations pairs the self-monitoring style with the advertising approach most effective with it?
    a. high self-monitors and high-image advertisement.
    b. high self-monitors and high-quality advertisement.
    c. low self-monitors and low-image advertisement.
    d. low self-monitors and low-quality advertisement.

9. According to the text, the finding reported in the text concerning self-monitors and the effectiveness of specific advertising approaches suggests that:
    a. advertising should focus on the quality of the product.
    b. advertising should focus on the image of the product.
    c. advertising should focus on the characteristics of the potential buyers.
    d. advertising should focus on both image and quality of a product.

10. Psychographics divides people into categories based on the combination of:
    a. lifestyle and purchasing patterns.
    b. attitudes and socioeconomic status.
    c. cultural background and economic status.
    d. attitudes and cultural background.

11. Which of the following is not one of the four major groups in the VALS system?
    a. Need-driven consumers.
    b. Quality-driven consumers.
    c. Inner-directed consumers.
    d. Outer-directed consumers.

12. In the VALS system, the need-driven consumers:
    a. are motivated by the desire to impress others.
    b. make purchases in order to increase their self-awareness.
    c. integrate their social and self-needs.
    d. make purchases that satisfy their basic requirements.

13. In the VALS system, the outer-directed consumers:
    a. are motivated by the desire to impress others.
    b. make purchases in order to increase their self-awareness.
    c. integrate their social and self-needs.
    d. make purchases that satisfy their basic requirements.

14. According to the VALS system, consumers who are intensely striving people seeking to be like those they considered more successful are called:
    a. Achievers.
    b. Belongers.
    c. Emulators.
    d. Socially Conscious.

15. According to the VALS system, the consumers who are typical of middle-class America, and who are traditional and conservative are called:
    a. Achievers.
    b. I-Am-Me.
    c. Socially Conscious.
    d. Belongers.

16. When a store determines what should go on its shelves by monitoring the success of particular products in the store, the store is engaging in:
    a. psychographics.
    b. micromarketing.
    c. hard sell approaches.
    d. soft sell approaches.

17. In the process of consumer decision making discussed in the text, problem recognition refers to:
    a. understanding that a need exists.
    b. identifying problems with particular products while trying to make a choice.
    c. realizing that some sources of information may be flawed.
    d. the development of cognitive dissonance as a result of a purchase.

18. Which of the following is **not** one of the sources of information sought during the phase of decision making called information search?
    a. personal sources
    b. public sources
    c. archival sources
    d. commercial sources

19. According to the text, the characteristics of a product are called:
    a. brand beliefs.
    b. product beliefs.
    c. brand attributes.
    d. product attributes.

20. According to the text, the assumptions held by consumers of a product, based on their knowledge of the manufacturer, are called:
    a. brand beliefs.
    b. product beliefs.
    c. brand attributes.
    d. product attributes.

21. Which of the following theories of work motivation is most likely to recommend training programs that help workers expand their personal interests?
    a. cognitive theories
    b. need theories
    c. reinforcement theories
    d. classical theories

22. Which of the following theories of worker motivation is most likely to place a great emphasis on setting specific, and somewhat challenging goals?
    a. human relations theories
    b. need theories
    c. reinforcement theories
    d. cognitive theories

23. Which of the following theories of worker motivation is most likely to identify incentives for workers such as bonuses and extra vacation time?
    a. reinforcement theories
    b. need theories
    c. cognitive theories
    d. human relations theories

24. In centralized decision making, having a centralized authority means that:
    a. one or a few people hold the decision making power throughout the organization.
    b. many people have the power to contribute to decisions.
    c. union bosses have more authority than management.
    d. union rank and file have more authority than management.

25. Which of the following statements is most accurate?
    a. Workers and supervisors experience about the same job satisfaction.
    b. Workers have more job satisfaction than supervisors.
    c. Supervisors have more job satisfaction than workers.
    d. The worker versus supervisor role has nothing to do with job satisfaction.

26. Decision making in which authority is controlled by a few people at the top of the organization is known as:
    a. decentralized decision making.
    b. enriched decision making.
    c. centralized decision making.
    d. conflicting decision making.

27. Which of the following is **not** a factor associated with being a supervisor?
    a. high prestige
    b. greater power
    c. psychological benefits
    d. less job-related stress

28. Supervisors report greater job satisfaction than the workers they supervise. According to your text, which of the following is **not** a reason for this?
    a. Bosses have greater power to make decisions and to reward and punish.
    b. Bosses have greater status and prestige.
    c. Bosses have greater responsibility and control over their day-to-day activities.
    d. Bosses are less prone to stress and stress disorders.

29. The classical (or bureaucratic) model is a management theory:
    a. emphasizing the social context of work and people's interactions with one another.
    b. recommending few rules or guidelines to specify what is expected of a worker.
    c. describing how an employee resolves a situation with two or more contradictory sets of demands.
    d. advancing explicit rules, regulations, and procedures governing every task.

30. The view of management that places emphasis on the social context of work and people's interactions with one another is called:
    a. the human relations model of management.
    b. kaisen.
    c. groupthink.
    d. the classical model of management.

31. Techniques for improving the quality of the activities involved in a job are known as:
    a. job enrichment.   c. job clarity.
    b. job satisfaction.   d. job conflict.

32. Role conflict occurs when:
    a. people with two different job titles work together.
    b. clerical and management people work together.
    c. two or more sets of job demands contradict one another.
    d. individuals want to strike but cannot do so.

33. The degree of explicitness of the rules determining what is expected of a worker is known as:
    a. role clarity.   c. role conflict.
    b. job clarity.   d. job conflict.

34. Japanese management philosophy tends to be committed to:
    a. the workplace and its goals.
    b. widespread recruitment.
    c. individual career advancement.
    d. labor unions.

35. Which is **not** a goal of Japanese management systems?
    a. creating information groups within the company to promote concerns and interests of the workers
    b. developing employee capabilities
    c. constantly searching for improvement
    d. encouraging strong socialization of employees into the organization

36. Increasing the variety of skills that must be used on a job is one method of:
    a. job clarity.
    b. decision making.
    c. decentralization.
    d. job enrichment.

37. Most research on participative decision making shows that:
    a. the morale of the individuals involved increases.
    b. the morale of the individuals involved decreases.
    c. the morale of the individuals involved stays the same.
    d. no determinations regarding participative decision making can be made owing to the complexity of the research design.

38. Which of the following is associated with the greatest job satisfaction?
    a. group dynamics
    b. brainstorming
    c. centralized decision making
    d. decentralized decision making

39. Group decisions are more likely to be superior to individual decisions for each of the following **except**:
    a. establishing objectives.
    b. identifying alternative solutions.
    c. evaluating alternatives.
    d. choosing an alternative.

40. For implementing a choice:
    a. formal groups are better than informal groups.
    b. informal groups are better than formal groups.
    c. individuals are better than groups.
    d. individuals and groups are equally good.

41. In the phenomenon of groupthink, group members lose the ability to:
    a. think.
    b. decide.
    c. evaluate.
    d. brainstorm.

| **ESSAY QUESTIONS** | *Recite and Review:* ☐ |

Essay Question 21.1: *Selling Politicians*

To what extent are politicians "sold" using the advertising techniques discussed in the chapter? Identify how the techniques would be applied. Is the presentation of a politician through an image just as legitimate as an approach based on quality (assuming quality is the same as the issue).

_____

_____

_____

_____

_____

_____

_____

_____

_____

_____

_____

_____

_____

_____

_____

_____

_____

_____

Essay Question 21.2: *Why Do People Stick with Bad Decisions?*

Describe the problems that arise in decision making and how one might avoid these problems. On the basis of the psychological principles that have been discussed throughout the text, why do people stick with bad decisions?

_____

_____

_____

_____

_____

_____

_____

_____

_____

_____

_____

_____

_____

_____

_____

_____

_____

_____

ACTIVITIES AND PROJECTS

1. Review the VALS system on page 685 of the text and determine where you think others may classify you at this time. Which of the lifestyles would you imagine yourself being identified with when you have finished college?

2. During your favorite television programs (if you watch television), tally the number of hard-sell versus soft-sell advertisements you see. Have the advertisers loaded your programs with a particular approach? Watch a program that you do not regularly watch and take the same tally. Are there differences in the distribution of the commercials? How can you account for this?

CHAPTER 1: Answer Key

FILL IN THE BLANK	MATCHING				TRUE-FALSE
1. psychology	11. c	16. a	25. b	30. d	1. F obj. 3 p. 6
2. social psychology	12. a	17. d	26. c	31. c	2. F obj. 3 p. 6
3. environmental	13. e	18. c	27. e	32. e	3. F obj. 3 p. 9
4. program evaluation	14. d	19. e	28. a	33. a	4. F obj. 5 p. 13
5. models	15. b	20. b	29. d	34. f	5. T obj. 5 p. 13
6. structuralism				35. b	6. T obj. 6 p. 13
7. introspection		21. d			7. T obj. 5 p. 14
8. functionalism		22. c			8. F obj. 7 p. 16
9. gestalt		23. a			9. T obj. 8 p. 17
10. free will; determinism		24. b			10. T obj. 8 p. 17

MULTIPLE CHOICE			
1. d obj. 1 p. 2	14. d obj. 3 p. 8	27. b obj. 5 p. 15	40. b obj. 9 p. 22
2. a obj. 1 p. 2	15. b obj. 3 p. 8	28. a obj. 5 p. 15	41. a obj. 10 p. 23
3. b obj. 1 p. 3	16. c obj. 3 p. 8	29. d obj. 7 p. 15	
4. b obj. 1 p. 3	17. d obj. 3 p. 8	30. a obj. 5 p. 16	
5. a obj. 2 p. 4	18. d obj. 4 p. 8	31. a obj. 6 p. 16	
6. c obj. 2 p. 5	19. d obj. 4 p. 10	32. c obj. 6 p. 16	
7. c obj. 3 p. 5	20. b obj. 5 p. 11	33. b obj. 6 p. 16	
8. d obj. 2 p. 6	21. d obj. 5 p. 13	34. c obj. 7 p. 16	
9. b obj. 2 p. 6	22. d obj. 5 p. 13	35. a obj. 7 p. 16	
10. d obj. 4 p. 6	23. b obj. 5 p. 14	36. b obj. 8 p. 17	
11. d obj. 4 p. 6	24. c obj. 5 p. 14	37. c obj. 7 p. 18	
12. a obj. 3 p. 7	25. c obj. 5 p. 14	38. c obj. 6 p. 19	
13. b obj. 3 p. 7	26. c obj. 5 p. 14	39. c obj. 9 p. 20	

Essay Question 1.1: Conceptual Models

- Identify the key principle of the model you have chosen. For instance, in the psychodynamic model, one of the key principles is unconscious motivation. For the biological model, the focus is on the physiological and organic basis of behavior.

- Offer a reason, perhaps an example, that illustrates why you like this model. Asserting that you just "liked it" or that "it makes the most sense" is not a sufficient answer.

- Identify one or two models that you clearly reject. Again, your response must be reasoned rather than asserted.

Keep in mind that this was the introductory chapter and that you will learn much more about the unique contributions made by each model throughout the book.

Essay Question 1.2: Key Issues

For this answer, "freedom of choice versus determinism" is used as the example.

- The selection of the freedom of choice side of this answer reflects how most people would choose. However, it suggests that all of our actions are thus our responsibility—even our boredom and our mistakes. We should be unable to attribute any causes for our behavior to others than ourselves.

- Should the issue be resolved in favor of determinism, then we should be able to understand all of human behavior as flowing from some root cause. Many religions have this kind of view, and some theorists and philosophers believe that science should be able to find causes. For psychology, this view is most compatible with behaviorism and psychoanalysis.

CHAPTER 2: Answer Key

FILL IN THE BLANK	MATCHING				TRUE-FALSE
1. replication	11. g	19. d	26. c		1. F obj. 2 p. 33
2. informed consent	12. h	20. c	27. b		2. T obj. 3 p. 36
3. experimental bias	13. d	21. e	28. f		3. T obj. 5 p. 39
4. experimenter expectations	14. b	22. b	29. d		4. F obj. 5 p. 39
5. expectations	15. f	23. g	30. e		5. F obj. 5 p. 40
6. placebo	16. e	24. a	31. a		6. T obj. 5 p. 43
7. double-blind procedure	17. c	25. f			7. F obj. 6 p. 44
8. significant outcome	18. a				8. F obj. 7 p. 46
9. meta-analysis					9. T obj. 8 p. 48
10. scientific method					10. T obj. 9 p. 49

MULTIPLE CHOICE			
1. a obj. 1 p. 30	14. d obj. 3 p. 35	27. a obj. 5 p. 41	40. b obj. 10 p. 51
2. c obj. 1 p. 31	15. b obj. 3 p. 36	28. b obj. 5 p. 41	
3. d obj. 1 p. 31	16. c obj. 3 p. 37	29. d obj. 6 p. 45	
4. a obj. 1 p. 31	17. a obj. 3 p. 37	30. c obj. 7 p. 46	
5. c obj. 1 p. 32	18. d obj. 3 p. 37	31. d obj. 7 p. 46	
6. d obj. 2 p. 33	19. a obj. 4 p. 37	32. d obj. 7 p. 47	
7. a obj. 2 p. 33	20. c obj. 4 p. 37	33. c obj. 8 p. 47	
8. b obj. 2 p. 33	21. d obj. 4 p. 39	34. a obj. 7 p. 48	
9. d obj. 3 p. 34	22. c obj. 4 p. 39	35. b obj. 8 p. 48	
10. b obj. 3 p. 35	23. c obj. 5 p. 39	36. d obj. 8 p. 48	
11. a obj. 3 p. 35	24. c obj. 5 p. 39	37. d obj. 9 p. 48	
12. a obj. 3 p. 35	25. a obj. 5 p. 40	38. b obj. 9 p. 49	
13. b obj. 3 p. 35	26. b obj. 5 p. 41	39. b obj. 9 p. 49	

Essay Question 2.1: Designing Experiments

For illustration, "Geniuses usually have poor social adjustment" has been chosen. The answer should include:

■ A hypothesis must be stated, like: People with IQ scores above 130 have difficulty in new social situations. The hypothesis must establish a testable situation, in this case, a contrived social interaction that can be observed and rated. The control must be non-geniuses placed in the same situation for comparison.

■ The independent variable would be the situation, the dependent variable would be the geniuses' social behaviors (behaviors determined to operationalize social adjustment).

■ A discussion of potential problems must be included. In this case, it may be difficult to find individuals who have a higher than 130 IQ.

Essay Question 2.2: Deceptive Practices

■ Try to imagine yourself in this kind of situation—if you have had a similar experience (where you were deceptively manipulated) an example of your reactions would be appropriate.

■ Psychologists are now expected to avoid harm, which can include undue stress, and to inform subjects to the extent possible. Also, informed consent suggests that a subject may discontinue at any point.

■ In some cases there do exist alternatives, but in others, the only alternative is naturalistic observation, and the desired qualities of experimental research, such as establishing cause and effect relationships, are likely to be lost.

CHAPTER 3: Answer Key

FILL IN THE BLANK	MATCHING				TRUE-FALSE
1. neuroscientists; biopsychologists	11. a	23. b	28. f	36. h	1. T obj. 3 p. 61
2. absolute refractory period	12. e	24. e	29. d	37. e	2. T obj. 5 p. 71
3. action potential	13. c	25. c	30. a	38. a	3. T obj. 5 p. 71
4. opiate receptor	14. b	26. d	31. e	39. f	4. F obj. 6 p. 87
5. paraplegia	15. d	27. a	32. g	40. b	5. T obj. 9 p. 89
6. homeostasis			33. c	41. g	6. F obj. 8 p. 85
7. magnetic resonance imaging (MRI) scan	16. e		34. h	42. c	7. F obj. 8 p. 82
8. electroencephalogram (EEG)	17. a		35. b	43. d	8. T obj. 10 p. 90
9. lateralization	18. d				9. T obj. 6 p. 74
10. brain modules	19. f				10. T obj. 3 p. 62
	20. g				11. F obj. 4 p. 66
	21. b				12. F obj. 1 p. 57
	22. c				

MULTIPLE CHOICE

1. b obj. 1 p. 57	14. b obj. 4 p. 66	27. c obj. 7 p. 77	40. b obj. 9 p. 85
2. d obj. 2 p. 58	15. c obj. 4 p. 67	28. b obj. 7 p. 77	41. d obj. 9 p. 85
3. d obj. 2 p. 58	16. b obj. 4 p. 67	29. a obj. 7 p. 77	42. a obj. 9 p. 86
4. b obj. 2 p. 60	17. b obj. 5 p. 69	30. d obj. 7 p. 77	43. c obj. 9 p. 86
5. d obj. 2 p. 60	18. b obj. 5 p. 69	31. a obj. 8 p. 79	44. c obj. 9 p. 86
6. d obj. 3 p. 61	19. d obj. 5 p. 69	32. a obj. 8 p. 80	45. c obj. 9 p. 86
7. d obj. 3 p. 62	20. a obj. 5 p. 71	33. b obj. 8 p. 83	46. b obj. 9 p. 87
8. c obj. 4 p. 63	21. c obj. 5 p. 71	34. a obj. 8 p. 83	47. b obj. 9 p. 88
9. c obj. 2 p. 61	22. c obj. 5 p. 71	35. d obj. 8 p. 84	48. a obj. 10 p. 90
10. d obj. 3 p. 62	23. a obj. 5 p. 71	36. d obj. 8 p. 84	49. a obj. 11 p. 92
11. d obj. 3 p. 64	24. a obj. 6 p. 75	37. b obj. 8 p. 84	50. a obj. 11 p. 92
12. a obj. 4 p. 64	25. b obj. 7 p. 75	38. c obj. 8 p. 85	
13. b obj. 4 p. 65	26. d obj. 7 p. 77	39. a obj. 8 p. 85	

Essay Question 3.1: The Benefits of Knowledge about the Brain

■ Knowledge of the brain leads to improved medical and psychological therapies of the injured and of stroke sufferers.

■ Knowledge about brain function should provide greater knowledge about behavior.

■ An understanding of neurotransmitter function can be applied to many phenomena, such as pain, drug abuse, healing processes, and thinking processes.

■ Knowledge of male and female differences will help us understand differences and similarities among individuals as well.

Essay Question 3.2: Ethics and Brain Research

■ Split brain research may actually create the phenomena observed, yet many people wish to use it to substantiate strong differences between left- and right-brain dominant individuals. Also, this research depends upon this operation.

■ The danger of transplanting tissue is not that it will create some monster, but that tissue needed may come from sources that raise questions, like fetal tissue.

■ You should identify moral and ethical reason both for and against this research and related procedures.

CHAPTER 4: Answer Key

FILL IN THE BLANK	MATCHING				TRUE-FALSE
1. stimulus	11. c	23. d	33. b	41. d	1. T obj. 1 p. 100
2. psychophysics	12. a	24. e	34. f	42. c	2. F obj. 2 p. 100
3. signal detection	13. d	25. c	35. d	43. g	3. F obj. 2 p. 100
4. visual spectrum	14. e	26. b	36. c	44. b	4. F obj. 4 p. 107
5. accommodation; adaptation	15. b	27. a	37. g	45. f	5. F obj. 4 p. 109
6. peripheral vision			38. h	46. a	6. F obj. 5 p. 110
7. trichromatic	16. d	28. d	39. a	47. e	7. T obj. 5 p. 112
8. opponent-process	17. f	29. a	40. e		8. T obj. 7 p. 117
9. olfactory cells	18. a	30. c			9. T obj. 6 p. 119
10. place; frequency	19. g	31. b			10. F obj. 9 p. 124
	20. b	32. e			
	21. e				
	22. c				

MULTIPLE CHOICE

1. b obj. 1 p. 99	14. c obj. 4 p. 107	27. c obj. 5 p. 112	40. d obj. 8 p. 122
2. b obj. 1 p. 99	15. a obj. 4 p. 107	28. a obj. 6 p. 113	41. c obj. 9 p. 124
3. c obj. 1 p. 100	16. b obj. 4 p. 107	29. a obj. 6 p. 115	42. d obj. 9 p. 124
4. d obj. 2 p. 100	17. c obj. 5 p. 107	30. c obj. 7 p. 118	43. a obj. 9 p. 124
5. c obj. 2 p. 100	18. d obj. 4 p. 108	31. a obj. 7 p. 119	44. b obj. 9 p. 125
6. a obj. 2 p. 100	19. d obj. 4 p. 109	32. d obj. 7 p. 119	45. b obj. 9 p. 126
7. a obj. 2 p. 101	20. b obj. 5 p. 109	33. a obj. 7 p. 119	46. d obj. 9 p. 126
8. b obj. 2 p. 101	21. b obj. 5 p. 109	34. b obj. 7 p. 120	47. b obj. 9 p. 126
9. a obj. 3 p. 103	22. c obj. 5 p. 109	35. b obj. 7 p. 120	48. d obj. 10 p. 128
10. a obj. 3 p. 103	23. b obj. 5 p. 110	36. d obj. 7 p. 120	49. a obj. 10 p. 128
11. a obj. 3 p. 104	24. d obj. 5 p. 110	37. a obj. 7 p. 120	50. c obj. 10 p. 130
12. b obj. 4 p. 107	25. d obj. 5 p. 111	38. a obj. 7 p. 121	51. c obj. 10 p. 130
13. a obj. 4 p. 107	26. c obj. 5 p. 111	39. c obj. 7 p. 122	

Essay Question 4.1: Understanding Color Vision

The major points that should be included in your answer:

- Describe the trichromatic and opponent-process theories of color vision.

- Identify problems that color-blind people have. Include the use of color in traffic signals, the color-coding of many aspects of work and life, and the possible embarrassments of mismatched clothing, as well as other problems.

Essay Question 4.2: The Problem of Extra Senses

The major points that should be included in your answer:

- Discuss the importance of sensory selectivity—of sense organs being sensitive to limited ranges of physical stimuli.

- Though we would probably adjust to the differences, additional information might create duplications.

- Describe the things we would be able to hear, smell, taste, and feel if our sensory ranges were broader.

- Reflect on the possibility that our ability at sensory adaptation might have to increase.

CHAPTER 5: Answer Key

FILL IN THE BLANK	MATCHING				TRUE-FALSE
1. perception	11. c	18. d	24. f		1. F obj. 1 p. 136
2. gestalt laws	12. g	19. a	25. c		2. T obj. 1 p. 138
3. feature analysis	13. e	20. f	26. e		3. T obj. 4 p. 145
4. top-down; bottom-up	14. a	21. e	27. b		4. T obj. 4 p. 145
5. constructive	15. d	22. b	28. d		5. F obj. 4 p. 146
6. ecological	16. f	23. c	29. a		6. F obj. 5 p. 148
7. subliminal perception	17. b				7. T obj. 7 p. 150
8. Poggendorf					8. T obj. 8 p. 156
9. Müller-Lyer					9. F obj. 9 p. 159
10. dyslexia					10. F obj. 9 p. 159
					11. T obj. 9 p. 159

MULTIPLE CHOICE

1. d obj. 1 p. 136	14. d obj. 2 p. 138	27. a obj. 5 p. 149	40. b obj. 8 p. 155
2. b obj. 1 p. 137	15. a obj. 3 p. 141	28. a obj. 5 p. 149	41. a obj. 8 p. 155
3. a obj. 2 p. 137	16. d obj. 3 p. 141	29. d obj. 5 p. 149	42. a obj. 8 p. 158
4. b obj. 2 p. 137	17. b obj. 3 p. 142	30. b obj. 5 p. 149	43. d obj. 9 p. 159
5. a obj. 2 p. 137	18. b obj. 3 p. 142	31. c obj. 6 p. 149	44. c obj. 9 p. 159
6. a obj. 2 p. 137	19. a obj. 3 p. 143	32. a obj. 7 p. 150	
7. b obj. 2 p. 137	20. d obj. 4 p. 144	33. b obj. 7 p. 150	
8. b obj. 2 p. 138	21. b obj. 4 p. 146	34. a obj. 7 p. 150	
9. d obj. 2 p. 138	22. b obj. 4 p. 146	35. d obj. 7 p. 150	
10. c obj. 2 p. 138	23. c obj. 4 p. 146	36. d obj. 7 p. 150	
11. d obj. 2 p. 138	24. c obj. 5 p. 147	37. d obj. 7 p. 151	
12. d obj. 2 p. 138	25. b obj. 5 p. 147	38. d obj. 7 p. 152	
13. b obj. 2 p. 138	26. a obj. 5 p. 149	39. b obj. 8 p. 154	

Essay Question 5.1: The Importance of Perceptual Constancy

The major points that should be included in your answer:

■   A definition of perceptual constancy.

■   Examples of perceptual constancy—perhaps the shrinking of objects as they become more distant, the consistency of shapes in our environment like doors, tables, etc., and the predictability of colors based on color constancy.

■   Perceptual constancy aids distance and form perception, so our abilities at depth, movement, and object perception would be greatly limited.

Essay Question 5.2: Gestalt versus Feature Analysis

The major points that should be included in your answer:

■   The major point is perception of wholes versus perception of parts. Top-down processing and bottom-up processing may also be used to distinguish the two approaches.

■   Phenomena such as perception of objects when parts are hidden from view and the reading of words without having to identify each letter are better explained by the gestalt approach. Identification of unusual objects by identifying and analyzing parts of the object is better accounted for by feature analysis.

CHAPTER 6: Answer Key

FILL IN THE BLANK	MATCHING				TRUE-FALSE
1. consciousness	11. d	21. e	29. e	35. b	1. T obj. 2 p. 167
2. altered states of consciousness	12. c	22. c	30. a	36. h	2. F obj. 2 p. 168
3. circadian rhythms	13. e	23. f	31. c	37. a	3. F obj. 3 p. 169
4. unconscious wish fulfillment	14. a	24. g	32. b	38. d	4. T obj. 2 p. 170
5. hypnosis	15. b	25. a	33. d	39. f	5. F obj. 4 p. 170
6. meditation; mantra		26. h	34. f	40. g	6. T obj. 3 p. 175
7. psychoactive	16. a	27. b		41. e	7. F obj. 3 p. 176
8. addictive	17. e	28. d		42. c	8. T obj. 7 p. 186
9. stimulants; depressants	18. c				9. T obj. 7 p. 190
10. narcotics	19. d				10. T obj. 8 p. 193
	20. b				

MULTIPLE CHOICE

1. d obj. 1 p. 165	14. c obj. 2 p. 171	27. b obj. 4 p. 177	40. b obj. 7 p. 190
2. a obj. 1 p. 166	15. c obj. 3 p. 173	28. b obj. 4 p. 177	41. b obj. 7 p. 190
3. a obj. 2 p. 167	16. c obj. 3 p. 173	29. d obj. 4 p. 177	42. b obj. 7 p. 193
4. a obj. 2 p. 168	17. a obj. 3 p. 173	30. a obj. 4 p. 178	43. d obj. 8 p. 193
5. a obj. 2 p. 168	18. d obj. 3 p. 174	31. d obj. 4 p. 179	44. c obj. 8 p. 193
6. b obj. 2 p. 168	19. b obj. 3 p. 174	32. b obj. 5 p. 181	45. c obj. 8 p. 194
7. d obj. 2 p. 168	20. b obj. 3 p. 175	33. d obj. 6 p. 183	
8. d obj. 2 p. 168	21. b obj. 3 p. 176	34. a obj. 6 p. 183	
9. c obj. 2 p. 169	22. d obj. 3 p. 176	35. a obj. 6 p. 183	
10. d obj. 2 p. 169	23. a obj. 3 p. 176	36. d obj. 7 p. 185	
11. d obj. 2 p. 169	24. a obj. 3 p. 177	37. c obj. 7 p. 185	
12. b obj. 2 p. 170	25. c obj. 4 p. 177	38. b obj. 7 p. 186	
13. d obj. 2 p. 171	26. a obj. 4 p. 177	39. b obj. 7 p. 189	

Essay Question 6.1: Hypnotism

The major points that should be included in your answer:

■ One view argues that the phenomenon is real (that of Hilgard), another that the phenomenon is not distinct enough to be considered a separate state of consciousness, and yet another suggests that people pretend to be hypnotized.

■ Whether the state is real or not (you must select and defend one of the points of view), you should make reference to the positive consequences for pain control, behavior change, and other uses.

Essay Question 6.2: Decriminalizing Psychoactive Drugs

The major points that should be included in your answer:

■ Identify the drugs that have been involved in this issue lately. This would include marijuana, but also, some have argued that drug use should be completely legalized and viewed as a medical or psychological problem.

■ State your view, identifying which drug(s) should be decriminalized and which should not. Many people suggest that the medical benefits of some drugs cannot be explored and used because of their status. Other reasons should be offered as well. For instance, the use of some drugs can be considered victimless, though the drug trade has many victims.

■ If you believe that all drugs should remain illegal, then support your reasoning. Harm to society and to individuals is a common argument. Examples could be given.

CHAPTER 7: Answer Key

FILL IN THE BLANK	MATCHING				TRUE-FALSE
1. learning	11. c	23. a	35. b	42. c	1. T obj. 1 p. 203
2. maturation	12. e	24. f	36. e	43. e	2. F obj. 1 p. 206
3. blocking	13. g	25. b	37. c	44. f	3. T obj. 2 p. 208
4. law of effect	14. f	26. d	38. g	45. d	4. F obj. 2 p. 209
5. superstitious behavior	15. a	27. e	39. a	46. b	5. F obj. 3 p. 212
6. shaping	16. d	28. c	40. f	47. a	6. T obj. 4 p. 215
7. programmed instruction	17. b		41. d		7. T obj. 5 p. 216
8. biological constraints		29. c			8. F obj. 5 p. 217
9. cognitive map	18. b	30. e			9. F obj. 6 p. 220
10. learned helplessness	19. a	31. d			10. T obj. 6 p. 220
	20. e	32. f			
	21. c	33. a			
	22. d	34. b			

MULTIPLE CHOICE			
1. d obj. 1 p. 202	14. b obj. 2 p. 208	27. c obj. 4 p. 214	40. b obj. 6 p. 225
2. a obj. 1 p. 203	15. d obj. 2 p. 208	28. a obj. 5 p. 215	41. d obj. 7 p. 225
3. d obj. 1 p. 203	16. d obj. 2 p. 208	29. c obj. 5 p. 215	42. a obj. 7 p. 226
4. c obj. 1 p. 203	17. b obj. 2 p. 208	30. b obj. 5 p. 215	43. b obj. 7 p. 227
5. c obj. 1 p. 206	18. c obj. 2 p. 209	31. b obj. 5 p. 215	44. d obj. 8 p. 228
6. a obj. 1 p. 206	19. a obj. 2 p. 209	32. c obj. 5 p. 217	45. c obj. 9 p. 230
7. a obj. 1 p. 206	20. a obj. 2 p. 209	33. d obj. 5 p. 218	46. c obj. 9 p. 233
8. a obj. 1 p. 206	21. a obj. 3 p. 210	34. d obj. 6 p. 220	47. b obj. 10 p. 234
9. b obj. 1 p. 206	22. b obj. 3 p. 212	35. d obj. 6 p. 221	
10. a obj. 1 p. 206	23. a obj. 4 p. 213	36. a obj. 6 p. 221	
11. d obj. 2 p. 207	24. d obj. 4 p. 214	37. d obj. 6 p. 221	
12. d obj. 2 p. 207	25. d obj. 4 p. 214	38. a obj. 6 p. 222	
13. d obj. 2 p. 208	26. c obj. 4 p. 214	39. d obj. 6 p. 224	

Essay Question 7.1: Using Physical Punishment

■ Cite examples of the use of physical punishment. Describe alternatives for each use.

■ Identify the conditions under which physical punishment may be necessary. These could include the need for swift and attention-getting action to prevent physical harm. Some parents use corporal punishment when children hit one another; some do so to establish control when alternatives have failed.

■ Indicate your views and explain them.

Essay Question 7.2: Which Approach Is Correct?

■ Describe each of the three approaches in such a way that they are clearly distinguished.

■ Identify points of contradiction among the views. In classical conditioning, the stimuli must precede the responses; in operant conditioning, the reinforcing stimuli comes after the response; in observational learning, the behavior does not need to be practiced. Mental processes are also involved in observational learning.

■ Observational learning may actually be reconciled with the other two once mental processes and reinforcement of the model (rather than the learner) are allowed.

CHAPTER 8: Answer Key

FILL IN THE BLANK	MATCHING				TRUE-FALSE
1. memory	11. d	22. f	29. b	36. c	1. T obj. 3 p. 247
2. chunk	12. f	23. a	30. g	37. g	2. T obj. 4 p. 249
3. mnemonics	13. a	24. e	31. c	38. a	3. F obj. 4 p. 249
4. explicit; implicit	14. c	25. d	32. a	39. d	4. T obj. 6 p. 255
5. levels-of-processing theory	15. e	26. b	33. e	40. b	5. F obj. 7 p. 257
6. tip-of-the-tongue phenomenon	16. b	27. g	34. f	41. e	6. F obj. 7 p. 257
7. constructive processes		28. c	35. d	42. f	7. F obj. 9 p. 263
8. schemas	17. e				8. F obj. 9 p. 263
9. decay	18. d			43. a	9. F obj. 9 p. 263
10. interference	19. b			44. c	10. F obj. 11 p. 267
	20. c			45. e	
	21. a			46. d	
				47. b	

MULTIPLE CHOICE			
1. a obj. 1 p. 243	14. b obj. 4 p. 249	27. c obj. 6 p. 257	40. b obj. 11 p. 267
2. b obj. 1 p. 243	15. c obj. 4 p. 249	28. d obj. 7 p. 257	41. a obj. 11 p. 267
3. b obj. 1 p. 243	16. a obj. 4 p. 249	29. b obj. 6 p. 257	42. d obj. 11 p. 267
4. a obj. 2 p. 244	17. b obj. 4 p. 252	30. b obj. 9 p. 263	43. b obj. 12 p. 268
5. b obj. 2 p. 244	18. a obj. 4 p. 252	31. c obj. 9 p. 264	44. a obj. 12 p. 268
6. b obj. 2 p. 245	19. c obj. 4 p. 252	32. d obj. 9 p. 264	45. a obj. 12 p. 269
7. b obj. 2 p. 245	20. d obj. 4 p. 252	33. b obj. 9 p. 264	
8. a obj. 3 p. 246	21. c obj. 4 p. 252	34. a obj. 9 p. 264	
9. b obj. 3 p. 246	22. d obj. 5 p. 253	35. c obj. 9 p. 265	
10. c obj. 3 p. 246	23. a obj. 5 p. 253	36. b obj. 10 p. 266	
11. b obj. 3 p. 247	24. a obj. 6 p. 255	37. d obj. 11 p. 267	
12. b obj. 3 p. 248	25. d obj. 6 p. 255	38. c obj. 11 p. 267	
13. b obj. 4 p. 249	26. d obj. 6 p. 256	39. b obj. 9 p. 264	

Essay Question 8.1: Writing about Eyewitness Testimony

■ State the evidence supporting the fallibility of witnesses and describe the potential problems that can arise from mistaken witnesses.

■ Some of the problems come from questions that are designed to mislead. Psychologists can support efforts to reform this process and to design techniques that will help witnesses improve their memories.

■ One might argue that psychologists would interfere with and compound the problem further by making contributions that are intended to improve witness memory.

Essay Question 8.2: Comparing the Laboratory and Real Life

■ Give several examples of laboratory research. The advantages include control over the experiment and the ability to document that prior memories do not influence the outcome.

■ Identify experiences that are best examined in an everyday context. Much case study and archival research is based on reports that are made when an event occurs or on reports from several points of view and are thus a form of everyday memory research. Other examples should be given.

■ As stated in the text, both of these techniques are needed to understand memory fully.

CHAPTER 9: Answer Key

FILL IN THE BLANK	MATCHING				TRUE-FALSE
1. cognition	11. e	21. b	27. a	32. b	1. F obj. 3 p. 281
2. thought	12. b	22. a	28. d	33. c	2. T obj. 3 p. 281
3. concepts	13. d	23. e	29. e	34. e	3. T obj. 3 p. 282
4. deductive; inductive	14. a	24. f	30. c	35. d	4. T obj. 4 p. 288
5. well-defined; ill-defined	15. c	25. d	31. b	36. a	5. T obj. 5 p. 290
6. functional fixedness		26. c			6. T obj. 5 p. 290
7. language	16. d			37. d	7. T obj. 6 p. 291
8. learning-theory	17. c			38. b	8. F obj. 6 p. 292
9. linguistic-relativity hypothesis	18. a			39. a	9. F obj. 7 p. 293
10. cognitive complexity	19. e			40. c	10. T obj. 7 p. 294
	20. b				11. F obj. 9 p. 298
					12. F obj. 9 p. 298

MULTIPLE CHOICE			
1. d obj. 1 p. 277	14. d obj. 4 p. 285	27. c obj. 7 p. 293	40. b obj. 9 p. 299
2. b obj. 1 p. 277	15. a obj. 5 p. 286	28. c obj. 8 p. 296	41. c obj. 10 p. 299
3. a obj. 1 p. 277	16. d obj. 4 p. 288	29. b obj. 8 p. 296	42. b obj. 10 p. 299
4. c obj. 1 p. 278	17. d obj. 4 p. 288	30. d obj. 8 p. 297	43. b obj. 10 p. 300
5. c obj. 1 p. 278	18. d obj. 4 p. 288	31. b obj. 9 p. 297	44. a obj. 10 p. 300
6. b obj. 1 p. 278	19. b obj. 5 p. 289	32. b obj. 9 p. 297	45. c obj. 10 p. 301
7. d obj. 2 p. 279	20. a obj. 5 p. 289	33. b obj. 9 p. 298	46. d obj. 10 p. 301
8. c obj. 2 p. 279	21. c obj. 5 p. 289	34. c obj. 9 p. 298	47. d obj. 10 p. 301
9. a obj. 2 p. 281	22. d obj. 6 p. 291	35. c obj. 9 p. 298	
10. d obj. 3 p. 282	23. a obj. 6 p. 291	36. d obj. 9 p. 298	
11. b obj. 3 p. 282	24. a obj. 6 p. 291	37. d obj. 9 p. 299	
12. c obj. 5 p. 284	25. b obj. 7 p. 293	38. b obj. 9 p. 299	
13. b obj. 4 p. 285	26. b obj. 7 p. 293	39. a obj. 9 p. 299	

Essay Question 9.1: Problem Solving

■   Describe your problem or challenge. It would be best to identify both the positive and the negative aspects of the challenge. What is gained and what is given up.

■   Define the problem in terms of the steps that must be taken to achieve the solution.

■   State several possible solution strategies as they apply to your problem.

■   State how you will know when you have effectively solved the problem. Remember, if the problem is long-term, selecting one solution strategy may preclude using another.

Essay Question 9.2: Is Language Uniquely Human?

■   Chimpanzees acquire an ability to speak that is comparable to a two-year old child.

■   The physical ability in humans to produce language has the greatest production capability.

■   You may be familiar with research in dolphin and whale communication or work with other animals. Examples could be used to support your answer.

■   What is meant by "unique" must be defined to complete this answer. Indeed human language is unique, but other animals do communicate.

CHAPTER 10: Answer Key

FILL IN THE BLANK	MATCHING			TRUE-FALSE
1. intelligence	11. c	15. f	22. d	1. T obj. 1 p. 311
2. deviation IQ score	12. b	16. g	23. f	2. T obj. 1 p. 312
3. achievement; aptitude	13. a	17. a	24. b	3. F obj. 2 p. 313
4. g-factor	14. d	18. e	25. e	4. F obj. 2 p. 313
5. triarchic		19. d	26. c	5. F obj. 2 p. 313
6. mental retardation		20. b	27. a	6. T obj. 3 p. 314
7. least-restrictive environment		21. c		7. T obj. 4 p. 316
8. mainstreaming				8. F obj. 3 p. 318
9. culture-fair				9. F obj. 6 p. 323
10. heritability				10. T obj. 8 p. 327

MULTIPLE CHOICE			
1. d obj. 1 p. 308	14. c obj. 2 p. 312	27. c obj. 3 p. 315	40. b obj. 6 p. 323
2. d obj. 1 p. 310	15. c obj. 2 p. 312	28. d obj. 4 p. 316	41. a obj. 6 p. 323
3. c obj. 1 p. 310	16. a obj. 2 p. 312	29. a obj. 4 p. 317	42. a obj. 7 p. 323
4. a obj. 1 p. 310	17. d obj. 2 p. 312	30. b obj. 4 p. 318	43. d obj. 7 p. 323
5. a obj. 2 p. 311	18. c obj. 2 p. 313	31. b obj. 4 p. 318	44. c obj. 8 p. 327
6. c obj. 2 p. 311	19. a obj. 2 p. 313	32. b obj. 6 p. 321	45. d obj. 8 p. 327
7. c obj. 2 p. 311	20. d obj. 2 p. 313	33. c obj. 6 p. 321	46. c obj. 8 p. 328
8. c obj. 2 p. 311	21. a obj. 2 p. 313	34. b obj. 6 p. 321	
9. b obj. 2 p. 311	22. c obj. 3 p. 314	35. d obj. 6 p. 322	
10. a obj. 2 p. 311	23. b obj. 3 p. 314	36. d obj. 6 p. 322	
11. a obj. 2 p. 311	24. d obj. 3 p. 314	37. b obj. 6 p. 322	
12. a obj. 1 p. 312	25. a obj. 3 p. 315	38. d obj. 6 p. 322	
13. a obj. 1 p. 312	26. a obj. 3 p. 315	39. b obj. 6 p. 323	

Essay Question 10.1: Defining Intelligence

■ Describe Binet's conception of intelligence, the g-factor view, Gardner's multiple intelligence, the triarchic theory, and the concepts of practical and emotional intelligence. (A good answer would not have to have all of these approaches.)

■ State which you find most acceptable and for what reason. For instance, the concept of practical intelligence may be appealing because it focuses on something other than educational ability.

■ The most important evidence is evidence that predicts, but if a definition appears to agree with commonly held views, then it too will have some validity because people do act upon these kinds of views.

Essay Question 10.2: The Heredity/Environment Question

■ Note that this returns to one of the major issues introduced in the beginning of the text and that there is no ready answer for the debate.

■ The most fundamental issue is that we have quite a bit of evidence supporting both the role of the environment and the role of genetic factors. Psychologists do not want to select one over the other.

■ Of particular relevance was the discussion of problem solving and creativity.

■ The extent to which intelligence is dependent upon the environment affects the possibility of developing a culture-fair test.

CHAPTER 11: Answer Key

FILL IN THE BLANK	MATCHING				TRUE-FALSE
1. motivation	11. d	19. b	30. f	37. b	1. F obj. 1 p. 334
2. homeostasis	12. e	20. d	31. a	38. d	2. T obj. 2 p. 337
3. incentive	13. a	21. f	32. d	39. a	3. F obj. 2 p. 337
4. obesity; twenty (20)	14. h	22. e	33. g	40. c	4. F obj. 4 p. 342
5. weight set point	15. f	23. c	34. b		5. F obj. 4 p. 342
6. anorexia nervosa; bulimia	16. g	24. a	35. e		6. F obj. 5 p. 351
7. Thematic Apperception Test (TAT)	17. c		36. c		7. T obj. 6 p. 353
8. emotions	18. b	25. e			8. T obj. 7 p. 359
9. polygraph		26. d			9. F obj. 9 p. 367
10. channels		27. c			10. T obj. 11 p. 371
		28. b			
		29. a			

MULTIPLE CHOICE			
1. a obj. 1 p. 334	14. b obj. 3 p. 340	27. d obj. 5 p. 350	40. a obj. 8 p. 362
2. d obj. 1 p. 334	15. d obj. 3 p. 340	28. b obj. 5 p. 350	41. a obj. 8 p. 364
3. c obj. 2 p. 335	16. a obj. 3 p. 340	29. c obj. 5 p. 350	42. c obj. 9 p. 366
4. d obj. 2 p. 336	17. a obj. 4 p. 341	30. d obj. 5 p. 352	43. b obj. 10 p. 368
5. b obj. 2 p. 336	18. d obj. 4 p. 341	31. c obj. 5 p. 353	44. c obj. 10 p. 368
6. b obj. 2 p. 336	19. b obj. 4 p. 341	32. b obj. 6 p. 353	45. b obj. 10 p. 368
7. a obj. 2 p. 336	20. b obj. 4 p. 341	33. a obj. 6 p. 353	46. d obj. 10 p. 369
8. c obj. 2 p. 336	21. c obj. 4 p. 342	34. c obj. 6 p. 353	47. a obj. 11 p. 369
9. a obj. 2 p. 336	22. b obj. 4 p. 342	35. d obj. 6 p. 354	
10. b obj. 2 p. 338	23. c obj. 5 p. 345	36. a obj. 6 p. 356	
11. b obj. 2 p. 338	24. c obj. 5 p. 347	37. c obj. 7 p. 359	
12. a obj. 2 p. 338	25. b obj. 5 p. 348	38. a obj. 7 p. 359	
13. b obj. 3 p. 339	26. c obj. 5 p. 349	39. d obj. 8 p. 362	

Essay Question 11.1: Theories of Motivation

■ Describe each of the main theories: instinct, drive reduction, arousal, incentive, opponent process, cognitive, and need theories.

■ Select an activity—it could be anything from watching television to playing a sport—and describe the behavior involved from the point of view of the motivation theories (no more than one sentence each).

■ Remember, some behaviors, like those satisfying basic needs, will be easier to describe from the points of view of some theories while others will be easier to describe from other theories.

Essay Question 11.2: The Polygraph

■ State the conditions for which you consider polygraph use to be appropriate. Give an example from your own experience if you have one.

■ Indicate the rationale that makes its use fair or appropriate. Are the rights of the test taker protected? Would incrimination lead to damage to the individual?

■ Is it fair to use a technique that has established scientific validity in specific areas in applications that go beyond the established validity?

CHAPTER 12: Answer Key

FILL IN THE BLANK	MATCHING				TRUE-FALSE
1. gender	11. a	22. e	32. d	43. d	1. F obj. 1 p. 378
2. androgens; estrogen	12. c	23. f	33. e	44. a	2. T obj. 2 p. 382
3. socialization	13. e	24. a	34. c	45. c	3. T obj. 3 p. 383
4. erogenous zones; erotic	14. b	25. d	35. b	46. b	4. T obj. 4 p. 387
5. masturbation	15. d	26. c	36. a		5. F obj. 5 p. 390
6. semen; penis		27. b	37. f		6. F obj. 6 p. 392
7. double standard	16. d				7. T obj. 6 p. 393
8. permissiveness with affection	17. f	28. b	38. c		8. T obj. 7 p. 393
9. rape; date rape	18. c	29. c	39. e		9. F obj. 7 p. 397
10. STD	19. b	30. a	40. a		10. T obj. 8 p. 398
	20. e	31. d	41. d		
	21. a		42. b		

MULTIPLE CHOICE

1. d obj. 1 p. 377	14. d obj. 4 p. 385	27. b obj. 6 p. 392	40. d obj. 10 p. 404
2. d obj. 1 p. 377	15. b obj. 4 p. 385	28. d obj. 6 p. 393	41. a obj. 10 p. 404
3. b obj. 1 p. 377	16. c obj. 4 p. 385	29. b obj. 6 p. 393	42. d obj. 10 p. 404
4. a obj. 1 p. 377	17. d obj. 4 p. 385	30. b obj. 6 p. 394	43. a obj. 10 p. 405
5. a obj. 2 p. 377	18. b obj. 4 p. 385	31. d obj. 7 p. 395	44. c obj. 10 p. 406
6. d obj. 1 p. 378	19. b obj. 4 p. 387	32. a obj. 7 p. 396	45. a obj. 10 p. 406
7. a obj. 2 p. 382	20. c obj. 4 p. 387	33. d obj. 7 p. 397	
8. c obj. 3 p. 382	21. c obj. 4 p. 387	34. d obj. 8 p. 398	
9. d obj. 3 p. 382	22. c obj. 5 p. 388	35. d obj. 9 p. 401	
10. a obj. 3 p. 383	23. b obj. 5 p. 389	36. a obj. 9 p. 402	
11. c obj. 3 p. 383	24. c obj. 5 p. 389	37. a obj. 9 p. 402	
12. c obj. 3 p. 384	25. d obj. 5 p. 389	38. a obj. 9 p. 402	
13. b obj. 3 p. 384	26. d obj. 5 p. 390	39. d obj. 10 p. 404	

Essay Question 12.1: The Changing Sexual Attitudes

■ Social acceptance of sexual activity and increased visibility of activity in the media have contributed to the increase in activity.

■ AIDS and campaigns for safer sex have caused some populations to reconsider risky sexual practices.

■ The double standard has changed slightly.

■ The sixties were marked by a sexual freedom that has been affected to some extent by AIDS and by the aging of the population.

Essay Question 12.2: Date Rape

■ Consider whether you believe that the penalty for date rape should be the same as for rape. A different attitude toward the penalty would suggest that the two are considered differently.

■ Factors might include a change in social skills, a change in dating practices, and an increased expectation on the woman's part that her interests be respected.

■ A poor ability to interpret signals related to affection and attraction may also be to blame, and with this, a failure on the male's part to accept being turned down.

CHAPTER 13: Answer Key

FILL IN THE BLANK	MATCHING				TRUE-FALSE
1. developmental psychology	11. f	25. d	40. a	50. b	1. T obj. 2 p. 416
2. nature-nurture issue	12. b	26. a	41. d	51. f	2. F obj. 1 p. 417
3. identical twins	13. d	27. e	42. f	52. c	3. F obj. 3 p. 420
4. critical period	14. e	28. c	43. e	53. e	4. T obj. 4 p. 422
5. age of viability	15. a	29. b	44. c	54. d	5. F obj. 5 p. 425
6. attachment	16. c	30. f	45. b	55. a	6. T obj. 7 p. 429
7. Ainsworth strange situation					7. T obj. 8 p. 429
8. cognitive development	17. c	31. e	46. b		8. T obj. 8 p. 434
9. information processing	18. f	32. a	47. a		9. T obj. 8 p. 435
10. metacognition	19. e	33. h	48. d		10. F obj. 11 p. 443
	20. a	34. b	49. c		
	21. g	35. g			
	22. h	36. f			
	23. b	37. i			
	24. d	38. c			
		39. d			

MULTIPLE CHOICE			
1. a obj. 1 p. 416	14. a obj. 3 p. 421	27. a obj. 5 p. 425	40. a obj. 9 p. 436
2. c obj. 1 p. 416	15. b obj. 3 p. 421	28. b obj. 5 p. 426	41. b obj. 10 p. 438
3. a obj. 1 p. 416	16. d obj. 3 p. 421	29. b obj. 6 p. 427	42. d obj. 10 p. 438
4. c obj. 1 p. 417	17. b obj. 4 p. 421	30. a obj. 5 p. 428	43. b obj. 10 p. 439
5. a obj. 2 p. 418	18. a obj. 4 p. 421	31. b obj. 6 p. 428	44. b obj. 10 p. 440
6. d obj. 2 p. 419	19. a obj. 4 p. 421	32. d obj. 6 p. 428	45. b obj. 10 p. 440
7. c obj. 2 p. 419	20. a obj. 4 p. 422	33. a obj. 7 p. 432	46. d obj. 10 p. 441
8. d obj. 2 p. 419	21. b obj. 4 p. 422	34. d obj. 7 p. 432	47. b obj. 10 p. 441
9. b obj. 3 p. 420	22. d obj. 4 p. 422	35. d obj. 8 p. 432	48. d obj. 10 p. 441
10. c obj. 3 p. 420	23. b obj. 4 p. 422	36. b obj. 8 p. 433	49. d obj. 11 p. 442
11. a obj. 3 p. 420	24. d obj. 4 p. 423	37. c obj. 8 p. 433	
12. d obj. 3 p. 420	25. b obj. 5 p. 425	38. c obj. 7 p. 434	
13. d obj. 3 p. 420	26. b obj. 5 p. 425	39. b obj. 9 p. 436	

Essay Question 13.1: Nature-Nurture and Child-rearing Practices

■ Identify the relative importance of nature and nurture for your views. Do you see them as equal or is one stronger than the other?

■ Each of the styles may imply a view of the nature-nurture debate. The authoritarian style, for instance, may see children as naturally unruly and in need of strict discipline to come under control. The permissive parent may expect the child to find his or her own potential, that such exploration is natural.

■ The view that understands nature and nurture as interacting would suggest that the parenting style is the place that an inherited potential can be realized, so child-rearing practices are crucial.

Essay Question 13.2: Stimulation of Children

■ Describe the factors that you consider important for early exposure. Can a child's later learning be enhanced through early exposure to academic skills like spelling and math? Or should the focus be on processes like imagination and creative work?

■ What criteria would you use to identify overstimulation? Keep in mind that the child must feel safe and have a secure attachment in order to explore the environment freely.

CHAPTER 14: Answer Key

FILL IN THE BLANK	MATCHING				TRUE-FALSE
1. adolescence	11. d	15. c	19. b	25. c	1. T obj. 2 p. 450
2. puberty	12. c	16. a	20. f	26. a	2. T obj. 2 p. 450
3. identity	13. b	17. d	21. d	27. d	3. T obj. 2 p. 453
4. menopause	14. a	18. b	22. a	28. e	4. T obj. 4 p. 456
5. midlife transition			23. e	29. b	5. F obj. 6 p. 461
6. midlife crisis			24. c	30. f	6. T obj. 7 p. 463
7. gerontologists					7. F obj. 7 p. 464
8. Alzheimer's					8. F obj. 7 p. 464
9. fluid; crystallized					9. F obj. 7 p. 465
10. postconventional					10. F obj. 8 p. 467

MULTIPLE CHOICE			
1. b obj. 1 p. 449	14. d obj. 3 p. 455	27. a obj. 6 p. 463	40. a obj. 9 p. 470
2. a obj. 1 p. 449	15. c obj. 4 p. 456	28. c obj. 7 p. 463	41. a obj. 9 p. 470
3. a obj. 1 p. 450	16. b obj. 4 p. 457	29. a obj. 7 p. 463	42. b obj. 9 p. 470
4. c obj. 2 p. 451	17. a obj. 4 p. 457	30. a obj. 7 p. 464	43. c obj. 9 p. 471
5. b obj. 2 p. 452	18. d obj. 4 p. 458	31. c obj. 7 p. 464	44. b obj. 9 p. 471
6. b obj. 2 p. 452	19. d obj. 5 p. 460	32. a obj. 7 p. 466	45. d obj. 10 p. 472
7. d obj. 2 p. 452	20. a obj. 5 p. 460	33. c obj. 8 p. 467	46. d obj. 11 p. 474
8. d obj. 2 p. 453	21. b obj. 5 p. 460	34. b obj. 8 p. 468	47. d obj. 11 p. 474
9. c obj. 2 p. 453	22. b obj. 6 p. 460	35. c obj. 8 p. 468	
10. a obj. 2 p. 454	23. b obj. 6 p. 462	36. c obj. 8 p. 468	
11. c obj. 3 p. 454	24. d obj. 6 p. 462	37. b obj. 8 p. 468	
12. a obj. 3 p. 454	25. b obj. 6 p. 462	38. c obj. 8 p. 468	
13. c obj. 3 p. 454	26. c obj. 6 p. 463	39. d obj. 9 p. 470	

Essay Question 14.1: The Stress of Adolescence

■   Note that the text considers the notion of excessive stress to be unsupported.

■   Describe specific instances where parents and adolescents have conflicts (rules, self-determination, school performance), and describe the nature of the disagreements. Identify things either parents or children can do to solve the problem. Are some of the problems an effort to assert a sense of self and identity?

■   Homelife has changed significantly, and many adolescents are growing up in single-parent homes.

Essay Question 14.2: Aging and Retirement

■   First, describe each of these two theories and offer an example of how they differ.

■   The activity theory suggests that a successful retirement would require a level of activity that would allow continuity.

■   Retirement serves as an important marker of age in the disengagement theory.

■   Describe the benefits (such as making room for people entering the job market) or costs (loss of expertise) of mandatory retirement in order to support your yes or no answer.

CHAPTER 15: Answer Key

FILL IN THE BLANK	MATCHING					TRUE-FALSE
1. personality	12. c	23. b	36. c	49. a	56. f	1. T obj. 2 p. 484
2. psychoanalysts	13. b	24. f	37. e	50. g	57. d	2. T obj. 2 p. 484
3. Oedipal conflict	14. d	25. e	38. a	51. d	58. a	3. F obj. 3 p. 485
4. neo-Freudians	15. e	26. a	39. b	52. c	59. e	4. T obj. 4 p. 487
5. traits	16. a	27. g	40. f	53. f	60. g	5. T obj. 5 p. 492
6. factor analysis		28. c	41. d	54. b	61. c	6. T obj. 5 p. 494
7. determinism	17. f	29. d	42. g	55. e	62. b	7. T obj. 9 p. 505
8. nomothetic; idiographic	18. a					8. F obj. 9 p. 506
9. reliability; validity	19. e	30. d	43. f		63. d	
10. norms	20. d	31. b	44. c		64. b	
11. behavioral assessment	21. c	32. f	45. e		65. a	
	22. b	33. a	46. b		66. c	
		34. c	47. d			
		35. e	48. a			

MULTIPLE CHOICE

1. a obj. 1 p. 481	14. c obj. 2 p. 485	27. d obj. 5 p. 490	40. a obj. 8 p. 501
2. c obj. 1 p. 481	15. c obj. 3 p. 485	28. c obj. 5 p. 490	41. a obj. 9 p. 502
3. d obj. 1 p. 481	16. a obj. 3 p. 485	29. b obj. 5 p. 492	42. b obj. 9 p. 504
4. a obj. 1 p. 482	17. b obj. 3 p. 486	30. d obj. 6 p. 496	43. b obj. 9 p. 505
5. b obj. 1 p. 482	18. b obj. 3 p. 486	31. d obj. 6 p. 496	44. c obj. 9 p. 505
6. b obj. 1 p. 482	19. d obj. 4 p. 486	32. c obj. 7 p. 497	45. d obj. 9 p. 505
7. c obj. 1 p. 483	20. c obj. 4 p. 487	33. b obj. 7 p. 497	46. b obj. 10 p. 507
8. c obj. 1 p. 483	21. c obj. 4 p. 487	34. b obj. 7 p. 498	
9. b obj. 1 p. 483	22. d obj. 4 p. 488	35. b obj. 7 p. 498	
10. d obj. 2 p. 484	23. d obj. 5 p. 489	36. d obj. 6 p. 499	
11. b obj. 2 p. 484	24. a obj. 5 p. 490	37. a obj. 7 p. 499	
12. a obj. 2 p. 484	25. d obj. 5 p. 490	38. c obj. 8 p. 501	
13. b obj. 2 p. 484	26. a obj. 5 p. 490	39. d obj. 8 p. 501	

Essay Question 15.1: Freud and Female Psychology

■ The weakest area is Freud's developmental stages, particularly with the Oedipus complex. Freud's concept of penis envy is not well accepted by many.

■ Just as Gilligan contests Kohlberg's views of moral development, one could argue that Freud's concept of a genital stage rests on masculine norms.

Essay Question 15.2: Personality Placement Tests

■ According to the text, MMPI and the TAT were developed for specific purposes, and the extension of them to job placement depends upon their being validated for the application to placement.

■ One major problem is the use of norms or averages to prepare job "profiles." These are still average and composite pictures of the individual and may unfairly discriminate against those who do not fit the profile.

CHAPTER 16: Answer Key

FILL IN THE BLANK	MATCHING				TRUE-FALSE
1. health psychology	11. f	17. b	22. c	27. a	1. T obj. 1 p. 514
2. immune system	12. a	18. c	23. b	28. e	2. F obj. 2 p. 516
3. stress	13. e	19. e	24. d	29. d	3. F obj. 3 p. 518
4. psychosomatic disorders	14. b	20. a	25. e	30. c	4. F obj. 3 p. 520
5. posttraumatic stress	15. d	21. d	26. a	31. b	5. F obj. 4 p. 520
6. learned helplessness	16. c				6. T obj. 4 p. 522
7. defense mechanisms					7. F obj. 5 p. 523
8. emotion-focused					8. T obj. 7 p. 531
9. general adaptation					9. T obj. 9 p. 536
10. A					10. F obj. 10 p. 538

MULTIPLE CHOICE			
1. c obj. 1 p. 512	11. d obj. 2 p. 516	21. c obj. 5 p. 522	31. b obj. 8 p. 533
2. d obj. 1 p. 512	12. d obj. 2 p. 517	22. b obj. 5 p. 523	32. c obj. 8 p. 534
3. a obj. 1 p. 512	13. b obj. 2 p. 517	23. b obj. 5 p. 523	33. d obj. 8 p. 534
4. a obj. 1 p. 512	14. a obj. 3 p. 518	24. a obj. 6 p. 527	34. d obj. 9 p. 536
5. a obj. 1 p. 514	15. b obj. 3 p. 519	25. d obj. 6 p. 527	35. d obj. 9 p. 536
6. b obj. 2 p. 516	16. d obj. 3 p. 520	26. b obj. 6 p. 527	36. a obj. 9 p. 537
7. b obj. 2 p. 516	17. d obj. 3 p. 520	27. a obj. 6 p. 527	37. a obj. 9 p. 537
8. a obj. 2 p. 516	18. b obj. 3 p. 520	28. b obj. 6 p. 527	38. b obj. 10 p. 539
9. d obj. 2 p. 516	19. b obj. 3 p. 520	29. b obj. 6 p. 528	39. d obj. 10 p. 539
10. c obj. 2 p. 516	20. a obj. 4 p. 520	30. a obj. 7 p. 531	40. d obj. 10 p. 539

Essay Question 16.1: Stress and Its Effects

■ Tabulate the stress score for yourself using Table 16-1.

■ Determine whether you are at risk or normal. Do the events that contribute to your score seem part of the normal course of life, or have you experienced an unusual number of things recently?

■ Identify any recent illnesses that would have been influenced by the stress.

Essay Question 16.2: Smoking Bans

■ Identify whether you believe that public places should ban smoking.

■ Under which conditions should a person be allowed/not allowed to smoke in public.

■ Describe the difficulties and problems that would be involved with enforcing a complete ban.

CHAPTER 17: Answer Key

FILL IN THE BLANK	MATCHING				TRUE-FALSE
1. cognitive-behavioral	11. d	22. d	33. d	38. a	1. F obj. 1 p. 546
2. medical student's	12. a	23. e	34. c	39. f	2. T obj. 1 p. 547
3. DSM-III-R	13. e	24. a	35. e	40. e	3. F obj. 2 p. 552
4. anxiety	14. c	25. c	36. b	41. c	4. T obj. 2 p. 552
5. obsessions; compulsion	15. f	26. f	37. a	42. b	5. F obj. 4 p. 557
6. phobias	16. b	27. b		43. d	6. F obj. 4 p. 557
7. schizophrenia					7. T obj. 7 p. 566
8. delusions	17. c	28. e			8. F obj. 7 p. 566
9. hallucinations	18. e	29. b			9. F obj. 8 p. 569
10. major	19. b	30. d			10. T obj. 9 p. 572
	20. d	31. a			
	21. a	32. c			

MULTIPLE CHOICE			
1. c obj. 1 p. 545	14. c obj. 2 p. 554	27. b obj. 5 p. 561	40. c obj. 9 p. 572
2. b obj. 1 p. 547	15. a obj. 2 p. 554	28. b obj. 5 p. 562	41. a obj. 9 p. 572
3. c obj. 1 p. 547	16. a obj. 2 p. 554	29. a obj. 5 p. 562	42. d obj. 9 p. 572
4. b obj. 1 p. 548	17. d obj. 2 p. 555	30. c obj. 6 p. 563	43. a obj. 9 p. 572
5. c obj. 1 p. 549	18. a obj. 3 p. 556	31. a obj. 6 p. 564	44. a obj. 9 p. 574
6. a obj. 2 p. 551	19. b obj. 4 p. 557	32. b obj. 6 p. 564	45. c obj. 9 p. 574
7. a obj. 2 p. 551	20. c obj. 4 p. 557	33. c obj. 7 p. 566	46. b obj. 9 p. 574
8. b obj. 2 p. 551	21. d obj. 4 p. 558	34. d obj. 7 p. 566	47. d obj. 9 p. 576
9. c obj. 2 p. 552	22. b obj. 4 p. 558	35. d obj. 7 p. 566	48. c obj. 10 p. 578
10. b obj. 2 p. 552	23. b obj. 4 p. 559	36. b obj. 7 p. 567	
11. c obj. 2 p. 553	24. c obj. 5 p. 560	37. c obj. 7 p. 567	
12. d obj. 2 p. 554	25. a obj. 5 p. 560	38. a obj. 8 p. 568	
13. b obj. 2 p. 554	26. b obj. 5 p. 561	39. b obj. 8 p. 570	

Essay Question 17.1: Defining Mental Illness

■ The Rosenhan study suggests that mental health workers label their clients with rather unshakable labels. The labels also lead to interpretations of behavior that continue to confirm the diagnosis (note that some stayed for many weeks even though they only complained of the symptom once on admission to the hospital).

■ The issues of deception and the use of subjects who had not given their consent are major issues.

■ A brief examination of the study does not explain the contexts involved: few people voluntarily walk into a mental hospital and complain of a major symptom. The sudden disappearance of the symptom could be considered abnormal as well.

Essay Question 17.2: Schizophrenia

■ Describe the major symptoms (see pages 572 and 573 in the text).

■ Distinguish process and reactive, and examine the list of types on page 572 of the text.

■ Discuss the biological and psychological components.

CHAPTER 18: Answer Key

FILL IN THE BLANK	MATCHING				TRUE-FALSE
1. psychotherapy	13. e	20. c	29. b	36. f	1. F obj. 2 p. 590
2. observational; modeling	14. a	21. e	30. c	37. c	2. T obj. 2 p. 590
3. dream interpretation	15. d	22. b	31. e	38. e	3. F obj. 3 p. 591
4. spontaneous remission	16. c	23. d	32. f	39. b	4. T obj. 3 p. 594
5. nondirective counseling	17. f	24. a	33. a	40. d	5. T obj. 4 p. 596
6. unconditional positive regard	18. b		34. g	41. a	6. F obj. 5 p. 598
7. drug therapy; psychosurgery	19. g	25. b	35. d		7. T obj. 5 p. 599
8. neurotic		26. d			8. F obj. 6 p. 603
9. eclectic		27. a			9. F obj. 7 p. 610
10. deinstitutionalization		28. c			10. T obj. 8 p. 610
11. electroconvulsive therapy					
12. prefrontal lobotomy					

MULTIPLE CHOICE

1. b obj. 1 p. 587	14. b obj. 3 p. 591	27. d obj. 5 p. 599	40. b obj. 7 p. 609
2. d obj. 1 p. 587	15. b obj. 3 p. 592	28. d obj. 5 p. 599	41. a obj. 7 p. 609
3. c obj. 1 p. 587	16. a obj. 3 p. 592	29. d obj. 5 p. 600	42. d obj. 7 p. 609
4. a obj. 1 p. 588	17. c obj. 3 p. 592	30. a obj. 5 p. 600	43. b obj. 7 p. 609
5. c obj. 1 p. 588	18. a obj. 3 p. 594	31. a obj. 6 p. 602	44. c obj. 7 p. 609
6. d obj. 1 p. 588	19. a obj. 3 p. 594	32. c obj. 6 p. 602	45. c obj. 8 p. 612
7. b obj. 1 p. 588	20. d obj. 3 p. 595	33. d obj. 6 p. 602	46. d obj. 8 p. 612
8. c obj. 2 p. 589	21. d obj. 4 p. 596	34. c obj. 6 p. 603	47. a obj. 8 p. 612
9. d obj. 2 p. 589	22. b obj. 4 p. 596	35. a obj. 6 p. 603	48. d obj. 9 p. 614
10. b obj. 2 p. 589	23. a obj. 4 p. 596	36. a obj. 6 p. 606	
11. a obj. 2 p. 590	24. c obj. 5 p. 598	37. c obj. 7 p. 608	
12. b obj. 2 p. 590	25. d obj. 5 p. 599	38. b obj. 7 p. 608	
13. c obj. 2 p. 591	26. c obj. 5 p. 599	39. c obj. 7 p. 609	

Essay Question 18.1: The Effectiveness of Psychotherapy

■   Identify the reasons you think psychotherapy works. These may include: psychotherapy offers a chance to reflect on life's problems in a safe environment, it offers a sense of control over one's problems, it provides new ways of coping with and understanding stress.

■   Select at least two of the previously discussed concepts and describe their roles in depth.

■   Remember, Esyenck's early study that suggested that psychotherapy was no more effective than being on a waiting list.

Essay Question 18.2: Should Electroconvulsive Therapy Be Banned?

■   Describe your response to the idea of electrical shock being passed through your brain as a means of therapy. Would you want this to be done?

■   What assumptions are made about the harm or benefit of using ECT? Do we assume that it must have some unseen long-term effect?

CHAPTER 19: Answer Key

FILL IN THE BLANK	MATCHING				TRUE-FALSE
1. social	11. b	20. c	25. e	30. b	1. F obj. 2 p. 622
2. affect; behavior; cognition	12. c	21. b	26. b	31. e	2. F obj. 3 p. 624
3. vicarious	13. a	22. d	27. a	32. c	3. T obj. 3 p. 625
4. social cognition	14. d	23. e	28. c	33. a	4. F obj. 3 p. 625
5. schemas		24. a	29. d	34. d	5. T obj. 4 p. 626
6. self-fulfilling prophecies	15. a				6. F obj. 5 p. 630
7. reverse	16. c				7. F obj. 6 p. 632
8. attribution	17. e				8. T obj. 7 p. 638
9. situational; dispositional	18. b				9. T obj. 7 p. 638
10. implicit personality	19. d				10. T obj. 7 p. 638

MULTIPLE CHOICE			
1. c obj. 1 p. 621	14. d obj. 4 p. 626	27. c obj. 6 p. 634	40. b obj. 7 p. 638
2. c obj. 1 p. 621	15. b obj. 4 p. 626	28. b obj. 6 p. 634	41. a obj. 8 p. 639
3. b obj. 1 p. 621	16. c obj. 4 p. 626	29. a obj. 7 p. 636	42. a obj. 8 p. 639
4. d obj. 1 p. 621	17. d obj. 4 p. 627	30. d obj. 7 p. 636	43. c obj. 9 p. 641
5. b obj. 2 p. 622	18. a obj. 5 p. 630	31. c obj. 7 p. 636	
6. c obj. 2 p. 622	19. d obj. 5 p. 630	32. c obj. 7 p. 636	
7. a obj. 2 p. 622	20. d obj. 5 p. 631	33. d obj. 7 p. 636	
8. b obj. 2 p. 623	21. b obj. 5 p. 631	34. a obj. 7 p. 636	
9. d obj. 3 p. 624	22. b obj. 5 p. 631	35. c obj. 7 p. 636	
10. c obj. 3 p. 624	23. c obj. 5 p. 631	36. b obj. 7 p. 637	
11. d obj. 3 p. 624	24. c obj. 6 p. 632	37. b obj. 7 p. 637	
12. c obj. 3 p. 625	25. b obj. 6 p. 632	38. a obj. 7 p. 637	
13. a obj. 3 p. 625	26. a obj. 6 p. 633	39. d obj. 7 p. 638	

Essay Question 19.1: The Consistency Between Attitudes and Behavior

▪ Situations that might be relevant are those in which you did something, like go on a date with someone, that you really were not that interested in doing. The mismatch between the attitude (lack of interest) and behavior (going out), while not that great does illustrate the problem.

▪ Describe how you felt after the specific incident or act and whether you changed your attitudes (She/he is actually pleasant to be with). Or perhaps, you wait until after the behavior to form your attitude (consistent with the self-perception theory).

▪ Be sure to make the difference between the two views clear.

Essay Question 19.2: Is Prejudice Inevitable?

▪ Define prejudice as an attitude and differentiate it from discrimination which refers to actual behavior.

▪ Determine your answer and support it. If yes, for instance, you could argue the necessity of using schemas (that then lead to stereotyping). If no, you could argue that prejudice is learned.

▪ Describe how an attribution bias could lead to a prejudice by identifying others as having consistent behavior patterns (due to attributions) and then leading to a broad attribution of the pattern (as a stereotype).

CHAPTER 20: Answer Key

FILL IN THE BLANK	MATCHING				TRUE-FALSE
1. social influence	11. b	15. c	19. e	24. g	1. T obj. 1 p. 649
2. conformity	12. d	16. a	20. d	25. d	2. T obj. 2 p. 650
3. status	13. c	17. b	21. b	26. b	3. F obj. 4 p. 657
4. social supporter	14. a	18. d	22. a	27. f	4. T obj. 4 p. 657
5. compliance			23. c	28. e	5. T obj. 5 p. 661
6. aggression				29. h	6. F obj. 5 p. 662
7. catharsis				30. a	7. T obj. 7 p. 668
8. frustration				31. c	8. F obj. 8 p. 672
9. aggressive cues					9. F obj. 9 p. 673
10. interpersonal attraction					10. F obj. 9 p. 675

MULTIPLE CHOICE			
1. d obj. 1 p. 648	14. c obj. 3 p. 652	27. c obj. 5 p. 661	40. d obj. 7 p. 669
2. b obj. 1 p. 649	15. c obj. 2 p. 653	28. d obj. 4 p. 662	41. a obj. 7 p. 669
3. b obj. 1 p. 649	16. c obj. 3 p. 654	29. d obj. 5 p. 662	42. a obj. 9 p. 673
4. a obj. 1 p. 650	17. b obj. 3 p. 654	30. b obj. 5 p. 662	43. c obj. 9 p. 673
5. d obj. 1 p. 650	18. d obj. 3 p. 655	31. d obj. 5 p. 662	
6. b obj. 1 p. 650	19. b obj. 3 p. 655	32. b obj. 6 p. 663	
7. d obj. 1 p. 650	20. b obj. 3 p. 655	33. a obj. 5 p. 664	
8. b obj. 1 p. 650	21. d obj. 4 p. 657	34. a obj. 6 p. 664	
9. d obj. 1 p. 650	22. a obj. 4 p. 657	35. d obj. 6 p. 664	
10. d obj. 2 p. 651	23. a obj. 4 p. 658	36. b obj. 6 p. 665	
11. b obj. 2 p. 651	24. d obj. 4 p. 659	37. c obj. 6 p. 665	
12. c obj. 2 p. 652	25. d obj. 4 p. 659	38. b obj. 6 p. 665	
13. c obj. 2 p. 652	26. b obj. 5 p. 661	39. c obj. 6 p. 665	

Essay Question 20.1: Conformity and Violence

■ Provide an example of recent violence against an ethnic group (or even an episode identified with a particular group).

■ Gang violence is a clear application of the ingroup-outgroup bias. The recent riots in Los Angeles suggest that many today have very strong stereotypes about the groups represented in the violence, including African-American, Hispanic, and Asian.

■ Describe how each of the factors—conformity, compliance, and obedience—could work toward increasing prejudice and following group behavior.

Essay Question 20.2: Should Pornography Be Banned?

■ R-rated films have more violence against women, and X-rated movies are more explicitly sexual.

■ The evidence needs to be clear regarding whether the link is with pornography and actual violence or between media violence and actual violence.

■ Distinguish banning pornography for moral reasons and banning it for safety reasons.

CHAPTER 21: Answer Key

FILL IN THE BLANK	MATCHING				TRUE-FALSE
1. consumer	11. f	17. d	23. c		1. F obj. 1 p. 680
2. industrial-organizational	12. b	18. a	24. d		2. T obj. 2 p. 682
3. self-monitoring	13. c	19. f	25. b		3. T obj. 3 p. 684
4. psychographics	14. a	20. e	26. a		4. T obj. 4 p. 689
5. product attributes	15. d	21. c			5. F obj. 5 p. 692
6. brand beliefs	16. e	22. b			6. F obj. 6 p. 695
7. cognitive dissonance					7. F obj. 7 p. 697
8. classical					8. T obj. 8 p. 700
9. human relations					9. T obj. 9 p. 702
10. groupthink					10. F obj. 10 p. 703

MULTIPLE CHOICE			
1. b obj. 1 p. 680	14. c obj. 3 p. 685	27. d obj. 6 p. 695	40. c obj. 9 p. 702
2. d obj. 1 p. 680	15. d obj. 3 p. 685	28. d obj. 6 p. 695	41. c obj. 10 p. 704
3. a obj. 1 p. 681	16. b obj. 3 p. 687	29. d obj. 6 p. 696	
4. c obj. 2 p. 681	17. a obj. 4 p. 688	30. a obj. 6 p. 696	
5. c obj. 2 p. 682	18. c obj. 4 p. 688	31. a obj. 8 p. 696	
6. b obj. 2 p. 682	19. d obj. 4 p. 689	32. c obj. 8 p. 696	
7. d obj. 2 p. 682	20. a obj. 4 p. 689	33. b obj. 8 p. 696	
8. a obj. 2 p. 682	21. b obj. 5 p. 692	34. a obj. 7 p. 697	
9. c obj. 2 p. 683	22. d obj. 5 p. 692	35. a obj. 7 p. 697	
10. a obj. 3 p. 683	23. a obj. 5 p. 693	36. d obj. 8 p. 698	
11. b obj. 3 p. 684	24. a obj. 6 p. 694	37. a obj. 9 p. 702	
12. d obj. 3 p. 684	25. c obj. 6 p. 694	38. d obj. 9 p. 702	
13. a obj. 3 p. 684	26. c obj. 6 p. 694	39. b obj. 9 p. 702	

Essay Question 21.1: Selling Politicians

■ Consider the dilemma of issues not being very appealing and well-designed commercials that make the politician sound and look good.

■ Describe several of the techniques that you remember from the latest campaign. Describe whether they are hard sell or soft sell. Do any use fear? Also, distinguish whether the communication follows central or peripheral route processing.

■ Consider whether it is possible to mix strong statements of issues with the kinds of campaigns that can develop using expert marketing techniques.

Essay Question 21.2: Why Do People Stick with Bad Decisions?

■ Describe a bad decision you made and how long you stayed with it.

■ Analyze the reasons one may give for sticking with the decision: "I had invested a lot of time on the project," "It is what everyone else was doing," "It looked good on the model."

■ Learning and reinforcement may explain the tendency to stick with bad decisions fairly well. Often a situation can be reinforcing for reasons other than its intended outcome. It may be strengthened because of partial reinforcement. Other learning principles also apply.